Evaluating Media Richness in Organizational Learning

Albert Gyamfi
Aalborg University Copenhagen, Denmark

Idongesit Williams
Aalborg University Copenhagen, Denmark

A volume in the Advances in Knowledge Acquisition, Transfer, and Management (AKATM) Book Series

IGI Global
DISSEMINATOR OF KNOWLEDGE

Published in the United States of America by
IGI Global
Information Science Reference (an imprint of IGI Global)
701 E. Chocolate Avenue
Hershey PA, USA 17033
Tel: 717-533-8845
Fax: 717-533-8661
E-mail: cust@igi-global.com
Web site: http://www.igi-global.com

Library of Congress Cataloging-in-Publication Data

Names: Gyamfi, Albert, 1974- editor. | Williams, Idongesit, editor.
Title: Evaluating media richness in organizational learning / Albert Gyamfi and Idongesit Williams, editors.
Description: Hershey, PA : Information Science Reference, [2018]
Identifiers: LCCN 2017012034| ISBN 9781522529569 (hardcover) | ISBN 9781522529576 (ebook)
Subjects: LCSH: Organizational learning. | Knowledge management. | Digital media.
Classification: LCC HD58.82 .E93 2018 | DDC 658.3/124--dc23 LC record available at https://lccn.loc.gov/2017012034

This book is published in the IGI Global book series Advances in Knowledge Acquisition, Transfer, and Management (AKATM) (ISSN: 2326-7607; eISSN: 2326-7615)

British Cataloguing in Publication Data
A Cataloguing in Publication record for this book is available from the British Library.

Advances in Knowledge Acquisition, Transfer, and Management (AKATM) Book Series

ISSN:2326-7607
EISSN:2326-7615

Editor-in-Chief: Murray E. Jennex, San Diego State University, USA

MISSION

Organizations and businesses continue to utilize knowledge management practices in order to streamline processes and procedures. The emergence of web technologies has provided new methods of information usage and knowledge sharing.

The **Advances in Knowledge Acquisition, Transfer, and Management (AKATM) Book Series** brings together research on emerging technologies and their effect on information systems as well as the knowledge society. **AKATM** will provide researchers, students, practitioners, and industry leaders with research highlights surrounding the knowledge management discipline, including technology support issues and knowledge representation.

COVERAGE

- Cognitive Theories
- Cultural Impacts
- Information and Communication Systems
- Knowledge acquisition and transfer processes
- Knowledge management strategy
- Knowledge sharing
- Organizational learning
- Organizational Memory
- Small and Medium Enterprises
- Virtual communities

IGI Global is currently accepting manuscripts for publication within this series. To submit a proposal for a volume in this series, please contact our Acquisition Editors at Acquisitions@igi-global.com or visit: http://www.igi-global.com/publish/.

The Advances in Knowledge Acquisition, Transfer, and Management (AKATM) Book Series (ISSN 2326-7607) is published by IGI Global, 701 E. Chocolate Avenue, Hershey, PA 17033-1240, USA, www.igi-global.com. This series is composed of titles available for purchase individually; each title is edited to be contextually exclusive from any other title within the series. For pricing and ordering information please visit http://www.igi-global.com/book-series/advances-knowledge-acquisition-transfer-management/37159. Postmaster: Send all address changes to above address.

Titles in this Series

For a list of additional titles in this series, please visit:
https://www.igi-global.com/book-series/advances-knowledge-acquisition-transfer-management/37159

Philosophical Perceptions on Logic and Order
Jeremy Horne (International Institute of Informatics and Systemics, USA)
Information Science Reference • ©2018 • 402pp • H/C (ISBN: 9781522524434) • US $225.00

Handbook of Research on Tacit Knowledge Management for Organizational Success
Dhouha Jaziri-Bouagina (University of Sousse, Tunisia) and George Leal Jamil (Informações em Rede Consultoria e Treinamento Ltda, Brazil)
Information Science Reference • ©2017 • 542pp • H/C (ISBN: 9781522523949) • US $275.00

Bio-Inspired Computing for Information Retrieval Applications
D.P. Acharjya (School of Computing Science and Engineering, VIT University, India) and Anirban Mitra (Vignan Institute of Technology and Management, India)
Information Science Reference • ©2017 • 388pp • H/C (ISBN: 9781522523758) • US $205.00

Managing Knowledge Resources and Records in Modern Organizations
Priti Jain (University of Botswana, Botswana) and Nathan Mnjama (University of Botswana, Botswana)
Business Science Reference • ©2017 • 280pp • H/C (ISBN: 9781522519652) • US $185.00

Analyzing the Role of Citizen Science in Modern Research
Luigi Ceccaroni (1000001 Labs, Spain) and Jaume Piera (ICM-CSIC, Spain)
Information Science Reference • ©2017 • 355pp • H/C (ISBN: 9781522509622) • US $185.00

Scholarly Communication and the Publish or Perish Pressures of Academia
Achala Munigal (Osmania University, India)
Information Science Reference • ©2017 • 375pp • H/C (ISBN: 9781522516972) • US $190.00

For an enitre list of titles in this series, please visit:
https://www.igi-global.com/book-series/advances-knowledge-acquisition-transfer-management/37159

IGI Global
DISSEMINATOR OF KNOWLEDGE

701 East Chocolate Avenue, Hershey, PA 17033, USA
Tel: 717-533-8845 x100 • Fax: 717-533-8661
E-Mail: cust@igi-global.com • www.igi-global.com

Dedicated to Patricia Agyeman Duah and Jair, Ursula, Afriyie, and Godslove.

Editorial Advisory Board

Table of Contents

Detailed Table of Contents

Learning (OEL) which makes it distinct from Individual Entrepreneurial Learning. As OEL is related to how an established organization learns about the entrepreneurial opportunity, and because of the main role of the interaction between organizational members in its process, this kind of learning can be considered as the opportunity-oriented Interactive learning in organizational context. Through literature review, three relevant dimensions have been identified for OEL, namely: Cognitive Learning Skills, Behavioral learning skills, and Action learning skills. This Model can be a platform for studying EL in organizational level.

Business accelerators are playing a key role in facilitating the process of new venture creation. Start-ups generally look for the best accelerators to make their long journey short. Media start-ups also look for a supportive mechanism to fasten their start-up experience. In this process, one of the main issues is to shorten their learning curve which is possible by use of start-up accelerators. Therefore, this chapter deals with the idea that which factors are important in this regard. To do so, first, a brief review of the support mechanisms is presented, and it is discussed that how start-up accelerators shorten the learning curve of the start-ups. Then, five media start-ups which were created in accelerators are studied. All of the cases were established after 2014, since the accelerators started working from the same year. According to the findings, there are mainly six reasons for shortening of the learning curve by start-up accelerators, including: (1) Short creation period, (2) Seminars and courses, (3) Co-working space, (4) Divided teams, (5) Cohort peers, and (6) Mentorship.

The Absorptive Capacity Theory was used as the theoretical lens for this study to help analyze how organizations absorb new knowledge using social media tools and applications. A survey of fashion designers and employees numbering 196 was carried out in 55 fashion firms whereas two fashion firms were used in a case study. Data analysis was performed using the Structural Equation Modelling. The findings from the study suggest that Ghanaian fashion designers do not intensively use social media to assimilate knowledge but rather to acquire, transform and exploit knowledge. The popular social media applications include; Facebook, Twitter, and Instagram. Facebook, for instance, is used on a daily basis by most Ghanaian fashion designers. Fashion designers use social media to acquire, transform and exploit knowledge through research, interaction, communication, and marketing with suppliers, customers, and other fashion designers. Future research can extend this work by looking at organizational learning and social media use in a different industry.

In our interconnected world, everyday it becomes more difficult to think of a product or a service that could provide its full value if not combined with other products. In this chapter an overview on platforms is presented, illustrating the different types of platforms that exist, its origins, how the literature on platforms evolved, their role in organizations, why understanding how platforms work is crucial to increase the success rate of their roll-out and how those platforms are shaped through platform governance and architecture, including an overview on platform-centric ecosystems.

The Colibri project partners started out in 2014 to make an Erasmus+ strategic partnership project titled "Collaboration and Innovation for Better, Personalized and IT-Supported Teaching" (Colibri). The overall idea is to implement new and innovative teaching methods with students from different universities for needs and challenges faced in higher education in general and within the combination of the ICT domain and entrepreneurship in particular. Erasmus+ funds the Colibri project. A course is developed between seven universities, based on a variety of rich and digital content: Videos, quizzes, articles to read, assignments, etc. In addition to making it all available on online platforms, we are also experimenting with making it available offline as e-books. This has several advantages, e.g. it can be accessed offline, and it is not depending on platforms that can host it. Another interesting potential of e-books is that they can be generated to suit the needs of the individual learner.

Software programming is a task with high analyzability. However, knowledge sharing is an intricate part of the software programming process. Today, new media platforms have been adopted to enable knowledge sharing between virtual teams. Taking into consideration the high task analyzability and the task characteristics involved in software development, the question is if the media richness of the current media platform is effective in enabling knowledge sharing among these virtual teams? An exploratory research was conducted on a software company in Denmark. The data was gathered was analyzed qualitatively using narrative analysis. This paper concludes, based on the case being investigated, that rich media does not fit the task characteristics of a software programmer. It further concludes that Media richness does affect knowledge sharing in these virtual teams. This is because the current lean media actually enables knowledge sharing as it fits the core characteristics of the software programming process.

Knowledge hiding is one of the major obstacles in the progression of organizations that hinder the use of tacit knowledge of employees. The negative impact of this behavior is more significant in enterprises and small firms, because they are more reliant on knowledge of their employees. For this reason, factors that influence on tendency of employees to expose and use their knowledge would be appreciated by managers of organizations. With the aid of a conceptual framework in a qualitative study, this paper investigates the effect of media richness on knowledge hiding. Thematic analysis is used to analyze transcribed interview data from employees in a software company in Iran. Findings of the analysis show that media richness significantly impacts on organizational learning and influences on knowledge hiding behavior in employees. This article suggests that entrepreneurs and managers of small firms should provide employees' access to rich media content.

We stand at the dawn of the greatest evolutionary disruption in the potential for large-scale human learning and development through the rapid convergence of truly transformational communication, cooperation and collaboration technologies and capabilities. The knowledge force is increasingly made up of very diverse employee profiles with differences in not only age and gender, but changing cultural norms and values, pervasive belief systems and large disparities in educational backgrounds. Highly individualised learning styles and behavioural characteristics and a host of other potential societal learning dividers, also magnify the challenge of building truly reflexive and responsive high-impact learning organisations. This chapter introduces the pressing need for a significant step-change in the way we approach company and community learning on a large scale and attempts to offer research-based insights and empirical evidence into media-enriching solutions such as mobile knowledge mentoring which will change the nature and experience of learning forever.

To increase the incentive for external sources to form interactive relationships, some firms selectively reveal their internally developed knowledge for free. However, 'selective revealing' is in conflict with the firm's interest in control over IP and challenges the governance of knowledge flows in open innovation. Taking a behavioral perspective, this paper proposes a complementary role of 'selective revealing' and 'behavioral control' and its relationship with a firm's source choice. We draw upon a sample of 125 large firms in the United States and Europe to statistically support the proposed complementarity. Results suggest that in value chain-centric and competitor relationships, firms may opt for guided revealing. In contrast, firms primarily engaged with universities are unable to establish guided revealing as a governance mechanism.

Recently, KM has found applications in cyber-security. Though the actionable information gathered is intangible, they are used to improve knowledge sharing in organizations. Key cyber-security objectives are to prevent, detect and respond to threats. Using open-sharing of vulnerabilities and exploits, cyber risks could be mitigated through info-sharing. Cyber-intelligence is perceived as a process and a product, with outcomes being alerts that solicit explicit responses, leading to mitigation of possible threats. Using the Scrum approach, relevant articles and databases were reviewed, towards improving mitigation strategies. A virtual machine experiment utilized various tools to gather intelligence. Results from footprinting were used to design a KM-based Cyber-Intelligence Gathering model that incorporates Lewin's Change Theory. It is intuitive and serves as an effective mitigation strategy for most organizations, especially SMEs. The implication is that knowledge sharing could be harnessed to create a pool of mitigation resources for most enterprises in developing economies.

This chapter indicates the overview of Knowledge Management (KM); KM and innovation; KM and human capital; KM and social capital; KM and Human Resource Management (HRM); the significant perspectives on KM; and the advanced issues of knowledge transfer, knowledge sharing, and knowledge mapping. KM is the advanced method toward better organizational performance through knowledge transfer and knowledge sharing, and involves various organizational factors, such as people, process, technology, and culture. Utilizing KM can enhance the execution of innovation, human capital, social capital, decision making, and HRM in modern organizations. Regarding KM perspectives, creating and distributing new knowledge through effective knowledge transfer and knowledge sharing have the potential to increase organizational performance and gain sustainable competitive advantage in the knowledge era.

Foreword

This is a volume that focuses on knowledge management and organizational learning seen in light of the vast array of new developments in communication technologies. How knowledge can be managed and how organizations learn are important approaches to deepening our understanding of how organizations and institutions develop and potentially could improve their functionality. In this volume, emphasis is on how new communication technologies can help enhance knowledge management and organizational learning and what the challenges and pitfalls are. Part of this issue is what the impacts of media richness are likely to be.

More specifically, the volume addresses issues relating to learning curves of companies, entrepreneurial learning, governance of knowledge flows in open innovation, absorptive capacity, etc. The context is not only individual companies but also broader social institutions. Papers report on research regarding grad courses, media start-up companies, the fashion industry, and even institutions at a national perspective.

The volume is edited by two younger researchers originating from Western Africa. The implication is that there are papers taking a developing country perspective on the issues of knowledge management and organizational learning. This perspective is generally not necessarily different from what can be found in research emanating from economically richer parts of the world, but it provides a possibility for examining cases and contexts which are not traditionally covered in the extant literature in the field.

The volume this presents a refreshing view on the ongoing discussions on knowledge management and organizational learning seen in light of the continuously evolving tools and platforms offered by new communication technologies and in light of cases and developments in not only developed but also developing countries.

Anders Henten
Aalborg University Copenhagen, Denmark

Preface

The capabilities and the richness of media platforms are evolving. At the same time the capacity of the Internet needed to support these rich media platforms are evolving as well. This has presented new opportunities for organizations and entrepreneurs to create, store and transfer knowledge in order to enhance their operations. This knowledge management process has enables organizations to learn from retrospection and to conduct an introspection about the effectiveness or otherwise of their organizational, product or service delivery processes. It also helps them generate knowledge on how to proceed. As a result, organizations could bounce back from a potential downturn in their fortunes. They can arrest a potential problem and they can also become more efficient in their production and or service delivery.

Currently web 2.0 platforms and emerging web 3.0 platforms are being adopted and will be adopted by organizations for organization learning purposes. In some cases there are third party providers that have provided cloud knowledge management services delivered via online media platforms to organizations. The most common example includes SalesForce, Vivantio etc. Although some of these platforms do not serve all aspects of an organization, an organization can subscribe to more than one cloud platform. Here companies can save an aspect of their operational cost in deploying their internal knowledge management systems.

However, it is not every organization on earth that has an organizational learning process. Neither is it every organization on earth that is using media platforms for the purpose of knowledge creation or acquisition, storage or transfer. This is part is because some organizations are too small to afford to adopt organizational learning processes. It is also because some organizations may not be aware that organizational learning process would be of value to them. It could also be that they do not know about the possibilities for organizational learning enabled via rich media platforms. One cannot overlook the fact that the organization may also know about these possibilities but do not have an access to the Internet. There are other instances, where certain organizations do have an organizational learning process. Probably, they are looking for how to get it right.

The technical possibilities and the challenges identified here led to the development of this book. This book provides a balanced approach to media richness and organizational learning. The first approach includes case analysis on which highlights the type of media richness needed for certain task characteristics. Here propositions are provided by the experts on what to consider if you are adopting a media platform for organizational learning purposes. The second approach is a critical analysis of cases where the media platform could not really enhance organizational learning. Here the reader can learn from pitfalls of others and gain insight from the analysis and how to succeed in such a scenario. The third approach highlights why organization learning is important and how organizations can learn from external knowledge sources.

IN THIS BOOK

Chapter 1 provides an outcome on a research on how media richness influences learning in organizations. Researchers in the cocoa industry are used as a case for this study. The SECI model was used to analyze the data. The findings in the investigation prove true for the SECI model regarding the usage of social media in organization learning. The first finding was that the richness of the media does affect the choice of the appropriate media for learning in organizations. The second finding was that the task characteristics was also found to be a key determinant regarding the choice of media for learning. The findings were based on the perception of the cocoa researchers in Ghana.

In Chapter 2, a literature review on three dimensions of Organizational Entrepreneurial Learning is presented. These dimensions are the Cognitive Learning Skills, Behavioral learning skills, and Action learning skills. Based on the literature analysis a model is developed which could be used in studying Entrepreneurial learning in an organizational level.

The research in Chapter 3 reveals ways by which knowledge transfer between business accelerators and start-ups could be enhanced to help fasten the start-up experience. The idea is that this knowledge transfer process will shorten the learning curve of start-ups as partner, collaborate and cooperate with their mentors (the business accelerators). The empirical work is based an investigation into start-ups from a developing country. The chapter concludes that, in reality, such a knowledge transfer procedure will shorten the learning curve for start-ups.

In Chapter 4, how Ghanaian fashion designers absorb and exploit knowledge from social media is analyzed. The analysis was performed using the Structural Equation Modelling. The social media tools identified in the chapter, as used in Ghanaian fashion designers, were Facebook, Twitter, and Instagram. The chapter reveals that although social media is used as a source of knowledge for the fashion designers, most Ghanaian fashion designers could not really exploit knowledge gathered from the social media platforms to help their work. This chapter also presents a deeper dynamic on how these fashion designers acquire internal and external knowledge for their task.

Chapter 5 presents an overview of digital platforms. It presents an overview on the evolution of digital platforms and the knowledge sharing mechanisms that are possible on these platforms.

Chapter 6 is a description on how various digital contents can be embedded in an e-book format. The chapter adopts a more practical approach to the description. This is because it is a result of a research project. This chapter is aimed at provoking the thought of the reader on approaches the transfer of rich media. Although the context of the case description in this chapter is in the education sector in the European Union, the findings of this case also has implications to other industries. Traditionally rich media is transferred over the Internet and accessed using mediums such as laptops, Personal Computers etc. The challenge with this mode of information transfer include insufficient Internet network capacity. These results in the loss of bytes transferred which results in the loss of information. In order to deal with this challenge, embedding rich media into e-book is identified an option for the knowledge transfer process. In this way, the knowledge is stored in a portable device, where the recipient can access it whenever they need it.

In Chapter 7, an attempt to find out if media richness would enable more knowledge sharing within virtual software teams in an organization. The context of the task within this team is software programming or coding. The case for the exploration was a Danish company with virtual software teams. In the case studied, media richness did affect knowledge sharing. The chapter also observes that rich media does not necessary fit the tasks characteristics identified in software programming. But lean media, on the other hand, did fit the task characteristics involved in software programming and it also enabled knowledge sharing.

Chapter 8 attempts to understand if media platforms enable or prevents knowledge hiding in software development firms. The context of the discussion is an Iranian software development firm. The findings in this chapter indicates that in the Iranian context, media platforms can actually indirectly promote knowledge hiding.

Chapter 9 presents an insight into the growing need for knowledge in society and organizations. The society is categorized into clusters. These clusters are contextualized within national economic sectors clusters, demography clusters and occupational clusters. In each of these clusters there are knowledge producers and knowledge receivers. Each of these stakeholders either contribute knowledge or receive knowledge from a common national knowledge pool. These common knowledge pool is identified in the chapter as a knowledge hive. The chapter identifies some members of these clusters as knowledge deficient and in need for knowledge to advance within their clusters. Mentoring is identified as a means of bridging the knowledge gap. How this mentoring should occur is explained in this chapter.

Chapter 10 presents a discussion based on an empirical research on how selective revealing could occur without raising conflict with a firm's intellectual property right and impeding the flow of knowledge via open innovation processes. The coupling of selective revealing and behavioral control are proposed in this chapter as a way of solving the problem. The empirical work backing this chapter is based on a sample size of 125 large firms in the US and Europe. More insights into the theoretical framework developers in this work is explained in this chapter.

Chapter 11 provides an insight into the role of knowledge management in cyber security. As Knowledge Management activities occur online, so are there cyber security issues. However, knowledge sharing within the organization can serve as a means of combating this threat. In this chapter, the result of a simulation exercise to prove this concept is reported. The outcome of the research indicates that knowledge sharing could be used to create a pool of mitigation resources to aid the combat of cyber security threats in an organization.

Chapter 12 provides an overview of how knowledge management occur in organizations. Knowledge management is identified in the chapter as a precursor to innovation; an enabler of human capital and human resource management and an enhancer of social capital. Although Knowledge management is deemed central to organizational learning, there are challenges. There are existing challenges with the transfer, sharing and mapping of knowledge within organizations. The challenge with knowledge transfer is assumed to be due the complexities in the nature of knowledge to be transferred. The challenge with knowledge sharing is viewed as a result of the organizational culture. The chapter concludes that despite these challenges, Knowledge management can enhance organizational performance and enable a company's competitive advantage.

In Chapter 13, a practical interdisciplinary approach is adopted to discuss what form of ICT platform that could be used to solve electoral fraud. The context of the discussion is electoral body in Ghana. The electoral body thrives with knowledge generated internally. However, the internal knowledge on how they could carry out their work is based on knowledge derived in their interaction with the electorate. Currently, the agency could sense voter apathy towards elections. This is as a result of the current challenges facing the Ghanaian electoral system. These challenges include the use of paper based ballot systems, double voter registration, ballot stuffing etc. in recent times, the electoral commission has employed different forms of media to aid them gather election related data from the citizens. These media platforms are often lean media, which cannot be accessed remotely. The adoption of these platforms have failed. In most cases it did not solve the challenges for which it was design to. This chapter identifies the failure to be the result of technology determinism. The chapter proposes that the adoption of a media platform for the Electoral commission's activities with the citizens should be based on a thorough socio-technical analysis. The social dimensions of the analysis will enable the electoral commission to understand the social dynamics that will trust in the media and the eventual adoption of the media platform.

The writing style is mostly academic. But there are few industry-based thoughts and writing style included as well. This provides the book with a balance, where anyone could derive benefit from. We are very grateful to all the authors who sacrificed their time to make this book possible.

Albert Gyamfi
Aalborg University Copenhagen, Denmark

Idongesit Williams
Aalborg University Copenhagen, Denmark

Chapter 1
Media Richness Perspective of Social Media Usage for Learning:
Perception of Cocoa Researchers in Ghana

Albert Gyamfi
Aalborg University, Denmark

ABSTRACT

This chapter examines the effect of media richness of four popular social media (Facebook, YouTube, Skype and Wikipedia) applications on their usage for organizational learning. The study is guided by a research framework based on the amalgamation of the SECI model and the media richness theory (MRT). This framework was used to investigate the Ghana Cocoa Board (COCBOD) to investigate which social media platform used by this organization was effective for organizational learning. Data was gathered and analysed using surveys and hierarchical second-order structural equation modeling (SEM). The data was validated using SmartPLS 3. the study concludes that there is a strong relationship between media richness and social media usage for organizational learning.

DOI: 10.4018/978-1-5225-2956-9.ch001

INTRODUCTION

Organizations are increasingly developing various ways of using social media to enhance learning. These technologies keeps gaining popularity in their usage for learning in organizations due to their interactive capacity and ability to handle different types of knowledge. Nevertheless, not much empirical research has been conducted to examine their capacity to convey the different knowledge forms and information cues (media richness) and its impact on learning in organizations. The focus of this chapter is to examine the effect of media richness of four popular social media (Facebook, YouTube, Skype and Wikipedia) applications on their usage for organizational learning.

Findings from the study, which sought to examine the effects of media richness of four popular social media applications (Facebook, YouTube, Skype and Wikipedia) on their usage for learning in organizations. The research framework used for the study was based on the amalgamation of the SECI model (Nonaka, Toyama, & Konno, 2000) and the media richness theory (MRT) (Richard L. Daft, Lengel, & Trevino, 1987). A real world case of the Ghana Cocoa Board (COCOBOD), the governing board of the Ghanaian cocoa sector was used to answer the research question: What is the effect of social media usage on organizational learning? Data were collected using survey and hierarchical second-order structural equation modeling (SEM) was used and validated with SmartPLS 3. Findings suggest a strong relationship between media richness and social media usage for organizational learning.

CONCEPTS AND PRINCIPLES OF WEB 2.0 TECHNOLOGIES

The term web 2.0 is defined as "the business revolution in the computer industry caused by the move to the Internet as a platform, and an attempt to understand the rules for success on that new platform. Chief among those rules is this: Build applications that harness network effects to get better the more people use them" (Musser & O'Reilly, 2007). Web 2.0, which was originally coined in 2004 by O'Reilly Media, is used to refer to a second-generation approach to the World Wide Web (WWW) with community-driven services such as social networking sites, blogs, wikis, etc. (Paroutis & Saleh, 2009). The capabilities of web 2.0 has shifted the focus of end users from being passive content consumers to active user participation where they are allowed to collaborate, communicate, create, control, and share contents using the web as a medium for communication. Web 2.0 tools come in different forms and classes including blogs, collective intelligence (wikis), digital content management (media sharing), social networks, mash-ups, virtual worlds, RSS (Really Simple Syndication), tagging, peer-to-peer programs and so on.

Different classification models have been created in attempt to clarify the functions, tools and web application of web 2.0 in organizations. These classification models include SLATE, FLATNESSES and 4C models designed by McAfee (2006), Hinchcliffe (2007), and Cook (2008), respectively (Cook, 2008; Hinchcliffe, 2007; McAfee, 2006). SLATES is an acronym used to represent six classes of web 2.0 tools namely: search, links, authoring, tags, extensions and signals. Search technologies involve the tools that enable intranet users to find what they are looking for. Links provide guide to users on what they are searching for and provide structure to the online content (Hinchcliffe, 2007). Authoring technologies allow people to create contents for a broad audience either individually or collaboratively. Tags are tools that are used mainly for content categorization. Extensions take tagging a step further to introduce automation into the categorization process and pattern matching. Signals represent tools used to draw users' attention when updates of their contents of interest appear. Dion Hichcliffe (2007) presented another classification model called FLATNESSES (Freeform, Links, Authorship, Tagging, Network-oriented, Extensions, Search, Social, Emergence, and Signals) to augment the SLATES model, to capture the social, emergent, network-oriented and freeform aspects of Enterprise 2.0.

The 4Cs model categorizes social media tools into communication, cooperation, collaboration, and connection tools. Communication tools are platforms that allow users to converse among themselves via text, image, voice, video, or a combination of these. Cooperation with regards to social software involves division of tasks into subtasks with no pre-defined goals where individuals assigned to the various subtasks retain authority of their contributions and share information as and when needed (Cook, 2008). Examples include media sharing, social bookmarking, and social cataloguing. Collaborative social software refers to the group of software that enables group of individuals to solve specific problems through coordination of efforts with a shared commitment and common goals. Examples of collaborative social software include wikis, blogs and virtual communities of practice. Connection social software relies on networking technologies to allow people to connect to others as well as content. Such tools include social networking, tagging, search, syndication (RSS), and Mashups.

THE SECI PROCESS OF ORGANIZATIONAL KNOWLEDGE CREATION AND LEARNING

The idea behind the SECI model is derived from the ACT model. According to the ACT model knowledge is categorized into declarative knowledge (explicit) and procedural knowledge (tacit). Declarative knowledge refers to knowledge that is expressed through propositions whereas procedural knowledge refers to knowledge, which is applied to activities such as remembering how to ride a bicycle or play the piano (Nonaka, 1994). From the standpoint that knowledge transformation is bidirectional and that declarative knowledge can be converted into procedural knowledge and vice versa four modes of knowledge conversion were proposed as: tacit-to-tacit (socialization), explicit-to-explicit (combination), tacit-to-explicit (externalization) and explicit-to-tacit (internalization) (Nonaka, 1994).

- **Socialization:** Socialization is defined as the "process of sharing experience and thereby creating tacit knowledge such as shared mental models and technical skills" (Nonaka, Takeuchi, & Umemoto, 1996). The aim of socialization is to transfer tacit knowledge among individuals through shared experience in day-to-day social interactions (Nonaka & Krogh, 2009).
- **Externalization:** Externalization is the process of articulating tacit knowledge into explicit concepts through dialogue and reflection. It involves two key factors: articulating tacit knowledge and translating tacit knowledge (Nonaka et al., 2000).
- **Combination:** Is the process of collecting explicit knowledge from inside and outside the organization and then combining, editing, or processing to form a more complex and systematic sets of explicit knowledge.
- **Internalization:** Is the process of embodying explicit knowledge into tacit knowledge. Through the process of internalization, individuals convert the explicit knowledge created and shared throughout the organization into tacit knowledge. The internalization process serves as the stage where knowledge is applied and used in practical situations to become the base for new routines. At this stage explicit knowledge (e.g. product concepts, manufacturing procedures) are actualized through action, practice and reflection until it becomes one's own knowledge.

Through these conversions between explicit and tacit forms of knowledge new knowledge is created from existing knowledge (Nonaka et al., 1996; Alavi & Leidner, 2001;Dinur, 2009). As knowledge moves from the individual to the group and from group to organizational level, it is enriched and amplified through the interactions between the individuals and the organization (Cummings & Teng, 2003;Inkpen & Dinur, 1998; Nonaka, 1994b). Organizations create new knowledge when all the knowledge conversion modes are managed continuously in a cycle. Many scholars have alluded to the fact that there exists a positive relationship between the use of web 2.0 applications and the SECI processes (Chatti, Klamma, Jarke, & Naeve, 2007; Boateng, Malik, & Mbarika, 2009; Haag, 2010; Shang, Li, Wu, & Hou, 2011; Panahi, Watson, & Partridge, 2012; Murphy & Salomone, 2013). However, what remains unanswered in the literature is whether the media richness of these tools have any effect on their usage for the SECI processes.

THE MEDIA RICHNESS THEORY

According to the Media Richness Theory (MRT) (R L Daft & Lengel, 1986; Daft et al. 1987), communication media differ in their ability to process information and facilitate understanding. Based on the capacity to facilitate shared understanding and insight, media channels can be classified as low or high in richness. The richness of media is the capacity of the media to process rich information and depends on a combination of four characteristics (Daft and Lengel, 1984; Daft et al. 1987):

- Ability to receive instant feedback
- Multiple cues related to face-to-face communication, e.g. tone of voice and body language
- Availability of different language types
- Personal focus-Level of conveyance of feelings and emotions

Based on the above media characteristics, face-to-face communication emerges at highest position on the media richness hierarchy followed by telephone, letters or memos, impersonal written documents, and numeric documents in that order (Daft and Lengel, 1986).

Media Richness and Message Ambiguity

According to the MRT, the main causes of information processing are uncertainty and equivocality (Daft et al. 1987; (Koo, Wati, & Jung, 2011). Uncertainty is defined as "the difference between the amount of information required for performing a task and the amount of information already possessed by the organization". Equivocality, on the other hand, refers to "the existence of multiple conflicting interpretation of organizational situation" (J. R. Galbraith, 1973). The major difference between uncertainty and equivocality is related to the approach of information processing used to respond to them. Organizations respond to uncertainty issues by acquiring large amounts of data through conventional information systems. However, when issues related to equivocality arise, managers resort to the sharing of subjective views and brainstorming to define problems and resolve disagreements. In other words, uncertainty issues require the sharing of explicit knowledge for resolution, whereas tacit knowledge sharing could be used to resolve issues of equivocality.

Media Richness and Task Characteristics

According to the MRT the technologies used in organizations represent a key source of uncertainty and equivocality (Daft and Lengel, 1986). Resolving the issues of uncertainty and equivocality relating to the use of technology requires the appropriate fit between media richness and the underlying task characteristics (Daft and Lengel, 1986). Depending on the characteristics of the task, managers may rely on the use of rich or lean media for the reduction of equivocality and uncertainty associated with the task (Koo et al., 2011). According to Perrow (1967), two task characteristics underlying the use of organizational technologies are task analyzability and task variety (Daft and Lengel, 1986). When task is analyzable, individuals rely on objective and computational laid down procedures to resolve them. On the other hand when task is unanalyzable, individuals are unable to develop exact procedures that will enable them to resolve the issue and so they would have to rely on judgments and experiences. Task variety refers to the frequency of unexpected issues that arise in the course of the transfer process. When the transfer process is such that individuals are unable to predict problems in advance, then there is a high task variety. High task variety is associated with large amounts of information in other to deal with exceptions whereas low task variety relates to small amount of information.

RESEARCH MODEL AND HYPOTHESES

The research model was derived from the combination of the MRT and SECI processes. According to the MRT, the choice of media is influenced by the richness of the media and the characteristics of the communication task. It's thus proposed that the choice of media used for the SECI processes towards organizational learning depends on the richness of the media (MR) and task characteristics (TC). The relationships among the SECI processes, MR and TC are represented in Figure 1.

According to the MRT, rich media is used to resolve equivocal issues through tacit knowledge sharing and lean media is applied when dealing with issues of uncertainty through the sharing of explicit knowledge. In other words, equivocal issues are resolved through the sharing of tacit knowledge on a lean media platform, whereas uncertainty situations are resolved by sharing explicit knowledge on a rich media platform. Two modes of knowledge creation are chiefly involved in tacit knowledge sharing: socialization and externalization while combination and internalization involves explicit knowledge sharing.

Consequently, socialization and externalization require the use of rich media while internalization and combination require the use of media with low degree of richness. From the discussions so far following hypotheses are in proposed:

Figure 1. Research model

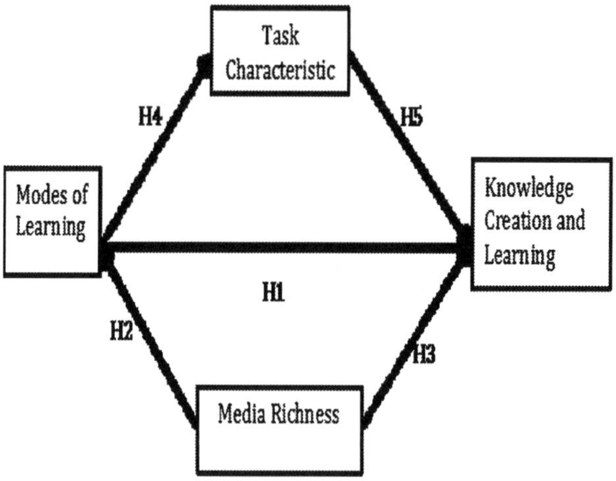

H1: *The use of web 2.0 applications for SECI processes is directly related to organizational knowledge creation and learning.*
H2: *There is a tpositive relationship between media richness of web 2.0 applications and their usage for the modes of organizational learning.*
H3: *There exists a positive relationship between media richness and organizational knowledge creation and learning.*

In a similar vein, socialization and externalization are required when dealing with issues related to unanalyzable tasks while combination and internalization are suitable in resolving analyzable-related issues. On the other hand, dealing with task of high variety requires the adoption of externalization and combination while socialization and internalization are appropriate for low variety task.

It's hypothesized here that:

H4: *There exist a positive relationship between web 2.0 usage for SECI and Task characteristics.*
H5: *There is a positive relationship between task characteristics and organizational knowledge creation and learning.*

Participants and Data Collection

In order to test the research model in figure 1 and validate the proposed hypotheses, a study was conducted to examine the effect of media richness on web 2.0 usage for learning in the Ghanaian cocoa sector. Questionnaires were used for the study and were administered physically by the researcher to the target respondents, all of whom were cocoa researchers stationed at the headquarters of Cocoa Research Institute of Ghana (CRIG) in Akim-Tafo, in the Eastern region of Ghana. All the respondents have been involved in interacting with cocoa farmer and are familiar with the use of web 2.0 applications including Facebook, Wikipedia, YouTube and Skype. The population of the researchers stood at 82. The questionnaire used for the study consisted of four constructs: Media richness, task characteristics, knowledge creation and learning, and modes of knowledge creation (see Table 1).

RESULTS

The Structural Equation Modeling (SEM) approach was used the results of both the validation of the measurement model and the structural model for the testing of the hypotheses were obtained from the use of SmartPLS 2.0 (Hair, Hult, Ringle, & Sarstedt, 2013) and include the test for construct reliability, convergent validity as well as test for discriminant validity. PLS-SEM with SmartPLS was deemed suitable for the study for the reason that all the exogenous constructs (independent variables) are hierarchical in nature-they are comprised of first and second order latent variables-which makes the use of "first generation" techniques limited for such high level analysis. The use of first generation techniques like correlations, regressions or ANOVA and t-tests are more suitable for modeling simple scenarios (Lowry & Gaskin, 2014) and are limited to causal or complex modeling especially with regards to modeling latent variables, interaction effects (mediation and moderation) and assessing the "goodness of fit" of the proposed model (Becker, Klein, & Wetzels, 2012). A two-stage approach is required.

Table 1. Definition of key constructs ad variables

Key Constructs	Indicator Variables	Number of Items	Source of Questions
Media Richness (MR)	Media Richness (MR)	5	Saeed & Sinnappan (2009)
Task Characteristics (TC)	Task analyzability (TA) Task variety (TV)	4	Anothayanon (2007)
Modes of Organizational Learning (MOL)	Socialization (SOC) Externalization (EXT) Combination (COM) Internalization (INT)	20 5 each for SOC, EXT COM and INT	Bercerra-Fernandes and Sabherwal (2001)
Knowledge creation and Learning (KCL)	Knowledge creation and Learning (KCL)	-	-

Table 2. Construct reliability measures

		Cronbach's Alpha	Composite Reliability	AVE
Facebook	COM	0.783	0.859	0.604
	EXT	0.827	0.885	0.660
	INT	0.845	0.895	0.682
	KTC	0.890	0.913	0.572
	MR	0.823	0.884	0.660
	SOC	0.789	0.857	0.549
Skype	COM	0.772	0.854	0.596
	EXT	0.723	0.827	0.547
	INT	0.787	0.864	0.622
	KTC	0.887	0.911	0.563
	MR	0.781	0.859	0.606
	SOC	0.826	0.878	0.591
Wikipedia	COM	0.820	0.881	0.650
	EXT	0.788	0.864	0.615
	INT	0.795	0.815	0.526
	KCL	0.870	0.898	0.525
	MR	0.723	0.827	0.547
	SOC	0.805	0.866	0.571
YouTube	COM	0.781	0.859	0.605
	EXT	0.788	0.863	0.615
	INT	0.723	0.827	0.546
	KTC	0.853	0.887	0.500
	MR	0.820	0.881	0.650
	SOC	0.826	0.878	0.590

First, the indicator approach is used to obtain the latent variable scores for the first-order constructs. These results are then used as manifest variables in the second-order measurement model at the second stage of the analysis.

In doing so, the second-order components become embedded in a nomological net to allow other latent variables to serve as predecessors and explain some of their variances.

Testing the Hypotheses: Measurement of the Structural Model

The study proposed to model the effect of the second-order constructs through the first-order constructs and their measures (Becker et al., 2012). The effect of the antecedent construct on the formative second-order construct could then be measured through the total effect which equals the product of the sum of the effects on the first-order constructs and the effect of the first-order on the second-order construct

Table 3. Discriminants validity of constructs

		SOC	EXT	COM	INT	MR (FB)	KCL
Facebook	SOC	**0.777**					
	EXT	0.657	**0.812**				
	COM	0.673	0.641	**0.826**			
	INT	0.801	0.709	0.700	**0.756**		
	MR	0.624	0.652	0.488	0.618	**0.812**	
	KCL	0.787	0.785	0.618	0.820	0.642	**0.741**
Skype	SOC	**0.772**					
	EXT	0.737	**0.739**				
	COM	0.645	0.630	**0.788**			
	INT	0.758	0.751	0.660	**0.751**		
	MR	0.731	0.732	0.640	0.747	**0.779**	
	KCL	0.689	0.713	0.618	0.769	0.621	**0.769**
Wikipedia	SOC	**0.806**					
	EXT	0.783	**0.784**				
	COM	0.605	0.738	**0.726**			
	INT	0.750	0.752	0.718	**0.724**		
	MR	0.658	0.760	0.714	0.731	**0.739**	
	KCL	0.668	0.730	0.681	0.725	0.687	**0.755**
YouTube	SOC	**0.778**					
	EXT	0.765	**0.784**				
	COM	0.730	0.759	**0.739**			
	INT	0.758	0.795	0.758	**0.707**		
	MR	0.653	0.786	0.662	0.685	**0.806**	
	KCL	0.624	0.727	0.720	0.726	0.730	**0.768**

(Becker et al., 2012). The proposed hypotheses were, thus, tested using the PLS-SEM path modeling by evaluating the proposed structural model on SmartPLS (Ringle et al., 2005). The structural model involving the second-order constructs were tested by first running the PLS-algorithm on the SmartPLS 2.0 to obtain the latent variable scores for the second-order constructs. These latent variable scores of the second-order constructs were then use at the second stage of the test. At this stage, the nonparametric boostraping feature on SmartPLS, which is reported in literature as a standard method for testing the significance of PLS path model, was used (Jörg Henseler, Christian M. Ringle, & Rudolf R. Sinkovics, 2009). The values of the path coefficients and total effects were then examined and reported. The summary of the results from the hypotheses testing is presented in Table 4. The values of the path coefficient provide support for hypotheses H_1, H_2, H_3 and H_4 as the relationships between MR and MOL, MR and KCL, MOL and KCL, MOL and

TC all appear significant regarding the use of all the four web 2.0 applications for learning. Hypothesis H_5 failed to gain support from the analysis of the results, as the t-values are not significant.

DISCUSSION OF FINDINGS

Many insightful results can be summarized from the above findings. The findings indicate that the SECI model holds true for the use of web 2.0 applications (Facebook, YouTube, Wikipedia, and Skype) for knowledge creation and learning. This finding is associated with the third hypothesis regarding the relationship between the use of web 2.0 for SECI processes and knowledge creation and learning. This suggests that media usage has significant impact on knowledge creation and learning in the cocoa sector of Ghana. Both media richness and task characteristics were found to be key determinants regarding the choice and usage of media for the knowledge creation and learning.

First of all, the richness of the media showed a highly significant impact on the use of web 2.0 applications for learning in the cocoa industry through the SECI processes. This suggest that an extended version of the SECI model with the inclusion of media richness (SECI with media richness) could be used to explain the usage of web 2.0 applications (new media) for knowledge creation and learning in the sector, which is in line with previous studies (Gyamfi, 2016).

Second, the use of web 2.0 applications for the modes of knowledge creation had a significant effect on the task characteristics, which is consistent with previous studies conducted by Anothayanon (2006). However, the proposed direct relationship between task characteristics and knowledge creation and learning couldn't be sustained, suggesting that the SECI processes through the use of web 2.0 applications couldn't be adopted to accomplish different task characteristics towards knowledge creation and learning. Possible explanation could be that the individual SECI processes might have been appropriate for specific task characteristics. For example, the use of web 2.0 applications for socialization might be suitable for analyzable tasks, while externalization would have been best used for unanalyzable and vice versa.

IMPLICATIONS AND CONCLUSION

The findings as discussed above have implications for both research and practice. First the study contributes to the field of organizational learning and knowledge management by advancing the significant impact of media richness and task characteristics on the usage of new technologies for learning. The study again has

Table 4. Hypothesis testing results

	Path Coefficient	T Statistics	Significance Level	P-Value
MOL -> KCL	0.3075	2.8309	P<0.05	0.015
MOL -> (TC)	0.6433	7.8391	P<0.001	0.000
MR -> MOL	0.4008	4.2616	P<0.001	0.000
MR -> KCL	0.3493	3.1864	P<0.001	0.000
TC -> KCL	0.0431	0.3408	NS	0.6358

implications for the Ghana Cocoa Board regarding how to incorporate web 2.0 technologies such as Facebook, Wikipedia, YouTube, and Skype into their existing knowledge creation and transfer mechanisms. The importance of media selection for the different stages and modes of knowledge creation and transfer revealed in this study has implications for the training of extension agents and researchers in the cocoa industry in Ghana.

In conclusion, media richness is not new regarding the selection and use of new media technologies. The main objective of the current chapter is to examine the effect of media richness and task characteristics on the use of four popular web 2.0 technologies: Facebook, YouTube, Wikipedia, and Skype for organizational knowledge creation and learning. A theoretical model based on the media richness theory and SECI model was presented and used to examine the impact of media richness on web 2.0 usage for knowledge creation and learning in the Ghanaian cocoa industry. The proposed model was evaluated based on data collected from cocoa researchers in Ghana. Findings suggest that media richness and task characteristics have significant impact on the use of web 2.0 applications for knowledge creation and learning. And that the media richness of the selected web 2.0 applications makes them suitable to be used for the SECI processes towards the attainment of knowledge creation and learning in the cocoa sector of Ghana.

REFERENCES

Alavi, M., & Leidner, D. E. (2001). Review: Knowledge management and knowledge management systems: Conceptual foundations and research issues. *Management Information Systems Quarterly*, *25*(1), 107–136. doi:10.2307/3250961

Anothayanon, W. (2006). *Knowledge management and characteristics* (Ph.D.). Walden University. Retrieved from http://search.proquest.com/docview/304933585/abstract/9056B96088874587PQ/8?accountid=8144

Becker, J.-M., Klein, K., & Wetzels, M. (2012). Hierarchical Latent Variable Models in PLS-SEM: Guidelines for Using Reflective-Formative Type Models. *Long Range Planning*, *45*(5–6), 359–394. doi:10.1016/j.lrp.2012.10.001

Boateng, R., Malik, A., & Mbarika, V. (2009). Web 2.0 and Organizational Learning: Conceptualizing the Link. *AMCIS 2009 Proceedings*. Retrieved from http://aisel.aisnet.org/amcis2009/546

Chatti, M. A., Klamma, R., Jarke, M., & Naeve, A. (2007). The Web 2.0 Driven SECI Model Based Learning Process. In *Seventh IEEE International Conference on Advanced Learning Technologies, 2007. ICALT 2007* (pp. 780–782). https://doi.org/10.1109/ICALT.2007.256

Cook, N. (2008). *Enterprise 2. 0: How Social Software Will Change the Future of Work*. Gower Publishing, Ltd. Retrieved from http://www.google.com/books?hl=en&lr=&id=f4z5yPx8XUsC&oi=fnd&pg=PT8&dq=enterprise+2.0+Cook,+2008&ots=yew0KKSbhC&sig=HbEuDixrkGIGwkZFqIQdhnTfTJ0

Cummings, J. L., & Teng, B.-S. (2003). Transferring R&D knowledge: The key factors affecting knowledge transfer success. *Journal of Engineering and Technology Management*, *20*(1–2), 39–68. doi:10.1016/S0923-4748(03)00004-3

Daft, R. L., & Lengel, R. H. (1986). Organizational Information Requirements, Media Richness and Structural Design. *Management Science*, *32*(5), 554–571. doi:10.1287/mnsc.32.5.554

Daft, R. L., Lengel, R. H., & Trevino, L. K. (1987). Message Equivocality, Media Selection, and Manager Performance: Implications for Information Systems. *Management Information Systems Quarterly*, *11*(3), 355–366. doi:10.2307/248682

Dinur, A. (2009). *Critical context and international intrafirm best-practice transfers*. Academic Press.

Galbraith, C. S. (1990). Transferring Core Manufacturing Technologies in High-Technology Firms. *California Management Review*, *32*(4), 56–70. doi:10.2307/41166628

Galbraith, J. R. (1973). *Designing Complex Organizations* (1st ed.). Boston, MA: Addison-Wesley Longman Publishing Co., Inc.

Gyamfi, A. (2016). The Impact of Media Richness on the Usage of Web 2.0 Services for Knowledge Transfer. *Int. J. E-Services Mob. Appl., 8*(2), 21–37. https://doi.org/10.4018/IJESMA.2016040102

Haag, M. (2010). *Personal knowledge development in online learning environments: A personal value perspective*. Retrieved from http://uobrep.openrepository.com/uobrep/handle/10547/134937

Hair, J. F., Hult, G. T. M., Ringle, C., & Sarstedt, M. (2013). *A Primer on Partial Least Squares Structural Equation Modeling (PLS-SEM)*. SAGE Publications.

Henseler, J., Ringle, C. M., & Sinkovics, R. R. (2009). The use of partial least squares path modeling in international marketing. In New Challenges to International Marketing (Vol. 20, pp. 277–319). Emerald Group Publishing Limited. Retrieved from http://www.emeraldinsight.com/doi/abs/10.1108/S1474-7979%282009%290000020014

Hinchcliffe, D. (2007). *The state of Enterprise 2.0*. Retrieved July 15, 2015, from http://www.zdnet.com/article/the-state-of-enterprise-2-0/

Inkpen, A. C., & Dinur, A. (1998). Knowledge Management Processes and International Joint Ventures. *Organization Science, 9*(4), 454–468. doi:10.1287/orsc.9.4.454

Koo, C., Wati, Y., & Jung, J. J. (2011). Examination of how social aspects moderate the relationship between task characteristics and usage of social communication technologies (SCTs) in organizations. *International Journal of Information Management, 31*(5), 445–459. doi:10.1016/j.ijinfomgt.2011.01.003

Lowry, P. B., & Gaskin, J. (2014). Partial Least Squares (PLS) Structural Equation Modeling (SEM) for Building and Testing Behavioral Causal Theory: When to Choose It and How to Use It. *IEEE Transactions on Professional Communication, 57*(2), 123–146. doi:10.1109/TPC.2014.2312452

McAfee, A. P. (2006). Enterprise 2.0: The dawn of emergent collaboration. *Management of Technology and Innovation, 47*(3). Retrieved from http://www.citeulike.org/group/2518/article/797161

Murphy, G., & Salomone, S. (2013). Using social media to facilitate knowledge transfer in complex engineering environments: A primer for educators. *European Journal of Engineering Education, 38*(1), 70–84. doi:10.1080/03043797.2012.742871

Musser, J., & O'Reilly, T. (2007). *Web 2.0: Principles and Best Practices*. O'Reilly Media.

Nonaka, I. (1994). A dynamic theory of organizational knowledge creation. *Organization Science*, *5*(1), 14–37. doi:10.1287/orsc.5.1.14

Nonaka, I., & Krogh, G. V. (2009). Perspective—Tacit Knowledge and Knowledge Conversion: Controversy and Advancement in Organizational Knowledge Creation Theory. *Organization Science*, *20*(3), 635–652. doi:10.1287/orsc.1080.0412

Nonaka, I., Takeuchi, H., & Umemoto, K. (1996). A theory of organizational knowledge creation. *International Journal of Technology Management*, *11*(7), 833–845.

Nonaka, I., Toyama, R., & Konno, N. (2000). SECI, Ba and Leadership: A Unified Model of Dynamic Knowledge Creation. *Long Range Planning*, *33*(1), 5–34. doi:10.1016/S0024-6301(99)00115-6

Panahi, S., Watson, J., & Partridge, H. (2012). Social Media and Tacit Knowledge Sharing: Developing a Conceptual Model. In *World Academy of Science, Engineering and Technology* (pp. 1095–1102). Paris, France: World Academy of Science, Engineering and Technology (WASET). Retrieved from http://www.waset.org/journals/waset/v64/v64-208.pdf

Paroutis, S., & Saleh, A. A. (2009). Determinants of knowledge sharing using Web 2.0 technologies. *Journal of Knowledge Management*, *13*(4), 52–63. doi:10.1108/13673270910971824

Shang, S. S. C., Li, E. Y., Wu, Y.-L., & Hou, O. C. L. (2011). Understanding Web 2.0 service models: A knowledge-creating perspective. *Information & Management*, *48*(4–5), 178–184. doi:10.1016/j.im.2011.01.005

Chapter 2
The Dimensions of Organizational Entrepreneurial Learning:
A Model of the Opportunity-Oriented Interactive Learning

Leila Fanaee Marhamat
University of Tehran, Iran

Mohammad Reza Zali
University of Tehran, Iran

Mehran Rezvani
University of Tehran, Iran

ABSTRACT

It is more than two decades that the concept of Entrepreneurial Learning (EL) has emerged by combing Entrepreneurship and Business Learning and its researchers have mostly focused on individual entrepreneurs as the unit of analysis. But EL can be observed in many entrepreneurial activities that take place in established organizations. This chapter aimed to clarify the main characteristics of Organizational Entrepreneurial Learning (OEL) which makes it distinct from Individual Entrepreneurial Learning. As OEL is related to how an established organization learns about the entrepreneurial opportunity, and because of the main role of the interaction between organizational members in its process, this kind of learning can be considered as the opportunity-oriented Interactive learning in organizational context. Through literature review, three relevant dimensions have been identified for OEL, namely: Cognitive Learning Skills, Behavioral learning skills, and Action learning skills. This Model can be a platform for studying EL in organizational level.

DOI: 10.4018/978-1-5225-2956-9.ch002

INTRODUCTION

Entrepreneurial learning (EL) has emerged by combing Entrepreneurship and Business Learning and its researchers have mostly focused on individual entrepreneurs as the unit of analysis. (Harrison and Leitch 2005). Developing knowledge about entrepreneurial learning is becoming a feature of study in entrepreneurship (Wang, 2014) and organizational learning in small firms has also been explored (Tan, 2011). Research on learning processes in entrepreneurial ventures is still in an early stage (Minniti & Bygrave, 2001). Past studies of entrepreneurial cognition tended to focus on issues such as risk-taking or opportunity recognition (Ravasi & Turati, 2005). An opportunity is a favorable set of circumstances that creates a solution, a new product, service, business or experience in line with needs. Scholars have classified opportunities into two types, namely incremental opportunities and radical opportunities. Incremental opportunities are situations that emerge from a narrow change in external or internal circumstances, for example, any modest advance in the technology field or variation in customer needs and desires may entail this kind of opportunities for presenting minor developed product or services (Benner & Tushman, 2003). On the other hand, radical opportunities emerge from a broad change in technology or market direction which encompass introducing significantly different product and services (Henderson & Clark, 1996).

More recently, researchers shifted their attention to the learning processes that occur as entrepreneurs or entrepreneurial organizations accumulate and organize knowledge and information within and across developmental efforts (Minniti and Bygrave, 2001). EL research has flourished two decades ago, and existing studies have been originated from different theoretical insights, such as organizational learning (e.g. Argyris and Schön, 1978; Fiol and Lyles, 1985; Pisano, 1994; Senge, 2010), population ecology (Henan and Freeman, 1977), experiential learning (e.g. Cope, 2005; Rae, 2011; (Minniti and Bygrave, 2001). Although numerous studies have addressed issues dealing with EL, there is still scope for a more focused examination of EL in the organizational context. The literature of entrepreneurial learning can be classified into two major areas based unit of analysis of studies: some studies have focused on the individual entrepreneurs as the unit analysis, and others have focused on the established organizations as the context of EL. The first part of studies has investigated personal learning experiences and cognitive processes while learning about opportunities of the 'entrepreneurial individual,' while the latter part has studied entrepreneurial learning in collective activity (Erdélyi, 2010). This chapter focuses on the collective activities related to opportunity exploration and exploitation. EL is often described as a continuous process that facilitates the development of necessary knowledge for being effective in starting up and managing new ventures (Politis, 2005).

The learning process in established organizations has a cyclical nature that means knowledge is processed through transformational stages. In this process members of an organization encode and verbalize their interpretation regarding their experiences and share these experiences which are opportunity oriented with other members. This transformation of knowledge to facilitate experiential learning in the organization and result in creating new knowledge (Kolb, 1984). Organizations must do this selectively: assimilating, organizing, categorizing, and prioritizing information that helps them to make decisions about entrepreneurial opportunities, and selecting one opportunity over others at any specific instance of time. Similar challenges of understanding also arise if the alternate social constructionist view is adopted with regard to how entrepreneurial opportunities are enacted on the basis of the multitude of new data that members accumulate (Dutta & Crossan, 2005). This chapter reviews the conceptual framework of Organizational Entrepreneurial Learning which refers to those EL practices that take place in organizational level and identifies three dimensions of the concept and within the existing literature. The aim of this chapter is to provide a clarified understanding and an updated definition of EL in established organizations. The model of OEL which has been presented here can be applied in Organizations for learning opportunity exploration and also exploitation.

ORGANIZATIONAL ENTREPRENEURIAL LEARNING

OEL as a promising area of research stands at the interface of the domain of Organizational Learning (OL) and Entrepreneurship. OL includes the processes of creating, retaining and transferring valuable knowledge and has implications for the performance and competitiveness of organizations. This knowledge embedded in organizations members, tasks and process and also the networks formed by crossing them (Argote & Hora, 2017). OL was described as transitional processes of organizational knowledge among members in daily interaction, so the interaction plays the main role in this kind of learning (Miller, 1996) which raises performance capacity of the organization and facilitates gaining new abilities (Matlay, 2000) by enabling organization to recognize the inaccuracies between their behavior and market needs and amend them by adapting their actions with the environmental changes (Argyris, and Schön, 1978) so it reinforces organizational ability for recognizing opportunities and advocates in exploiting them (Marquardt, 2002; Lumpkin and Lichtenstein, 2005; Gibb, 2002) by adjusting organizational response to constant environmental changes and taking permanent adapting behaviors.

In this way organizational learning can facilitate the practice of entrepreneurship in established organization. Stevenson defines entrepreneurship as "The process by which individuals – either on their own or inside organizations – pursue opportunities without regard to the resources they currently control" (Stevenson & Jarillo, 1990, p. 23). Many scholars accepted Stevenson's opportunity-based definition as the definition of entrepreneurship(Brown, Davidsson, & Wiklund, 2001). This definition coincides with Austrian economists' views of entrepreneurship as opportunity seeking, recognition and exploitation through novel resource recombination (Schumpeter, 1975; Kirzner, 1973). For connecting OL to entrepreneurship and studying its role we should consider OL in whole process of entrepreneurship which take place in an organization then we can define OEL. As mentioned before the main domain in EL research has been focused on Individual entrepreneurs but some researchers have tried to investigate the nature of EL in collective activities that take place at the organizational level. These authors indicated that over time organizations learn some ways for recognizing new opportunities and exploiting them. So they learn how to create innovative products and services and present them to the market for gaining profit and obtaining competitive advantage (Wang, 2014).

For presenting the model of OEL, three related themes of opportunity-oriented organizational learning have been applied which have been proposed by Lumpkin and Lichtenstein (2005) namely, Behavioral Learning, Cognitive Learning, and Action Learning (Lumpkin & Lichtenstein, 2005). These three themes are used as the dimension of EL in the organizational context. Cognitive Learning is related to the phase of opportunity seeking, recognition while Behavioral Learning and Action Learning are related to opportunity exploitation. Hereafter each dimension and its subcategories have been discussed and explained.

First Dimension: Cognitive Learning Skills

One of the most significant perspectives which have emerged in organizational learning literature is the cognitive approach in studying OL and investigating how changes in the organizational members' cognitive maps are aggregated and translated into changes in an organization's cognitive schema (Weick & Roberts, 1993; Nonaka, 1988; Lumpkin & Lichtenstein, 2005). As Zahra (2005) stated "Organizations have cognitive systems, exhibiting the shared beliefs and information of the members of their dominant coalitions. These cognitive systems relate to organizational identity schematic frameworks, top management beliefs, and dominant logic(Zahra, Korri, & Yu, 2005). The role of OEL in this dimension is changing the cognitive system. In Cognitive Learning, "the focus is on the content of learning rather than on its behavioral outcomes, on processes that improve the creation of knowledge in a firm, and the utilization of knowledge to improve creativity, quality of interaction, and other types of performance" (Lumpkin & Lichtenstein, 2005). In the process of learning about new opportunities, the cognition of learner contains transforming new data into new information, and valuable information into new knowledge, this new knowledge will be integrated by some verbalizing and encoding means and generates Organizational knowledge about specific opportunity, which can increase the strategic resources of the firm if it would be applied efficiently for gaining advantage making more profit. In this way, Cognitive Learning is related to the resource-based view of strategy because it holds that the very process of knowledge creation can generate exclusive organizational capabilities and facilitate accomplishment of competitive advantage (Lumpkin & Lichtenstein, 2005). "Knowledge resources builds capabilities which can be applied in discovery and exploitation of entrepreneurial opportunities (Teece, 1998). As a matter of fact "Organizational knowledge raises the capacity of organization for taking action effectively by providing a forum for a 'spiral of knowledge' creation" (Nonaka, 1994, p. 34When we want to relate The Cognitive Learning Skills to the organizational opportunity-seeking behavior we should consider this matter that this learning is related to the first step of the entrepreneurial process which has three alternatives, named: opportunity recognition, opportunity discovery and opportunity creation. Accordingly, the dimension of The Cognitive Learning Skills has three subcategories, named: Learning Opportunity-Recognition, Learning Opportunity-Discovery, and Learning Opportunity-Creation.

Learning Opportunity-Recognition

Shane and Venkataraman (2000: 218) argued that entrepreneurship research addresses three key questions: (1) Why, when, and how do opportunities for the creation of goods and services come into existence? (2) Why, when, and how do some people and not others discover and exploit these opportunities? and (3) Why, when, and how are different modes of action used to exploit entrepreneurial opportunities? Learning opportunity-recognition relates to the first question. Entrepreneurial opportunity recognition is the ability to identify "situations in which new goods, services, raw materials, markets and organizing methods can be introduced into the formation of new means, ends, or means–ends relationships" (Eckhardt & Shane, 2003 p.336). As many scholars have stated opportunity recognition is underpinned by some distinctive cognitive processes(Sigrist, 1999), in the organization these cognitive processes are under the effect of social networks between members so their interaction plays a key role in acquiring new knowledge about the existence of opportunities. Learning opportunity-recognition manifests in two ways: a) Learning efficient resource allocation by existing knowledge and b) Learning efficient resource allocation by existing knowledge. 1. Opportunity Recognition Opportunity recognition is some kind of incremental development and can not be considered as a fundamental innovation. Therefore, an organization which makes attempt at raising the efficiency of its resource allocation would be able to recognize new opportunities that have the potentiality of incremental development. Finding a new way for allocating resources efficiently can be through reanalyzing of existing knowledge or through acquiring new knowledge from outside of the organization. The allocative view concerns itself with the optimal utilization of scarce resources. In this view, an opportunity is any possibility of putting resources to better use(Sarasvathy, Dew, Velamuri, & Venkataraman, 2003).

Learning Opportunity-Disovery

Through Learning Opportunity-Discovery, the organization is able to identify new areas of value, and consists of a structured process and the methods, facilitate exploring a new or existing but ignored profit potentialities. The Opportunity Discovery is a process of identifing unmet needs and desires in the market which cab be the source of ideas for new business development activities. Kirzner has popularized the notion of opportunity discovery as a means for restoration of markets equilibrium (Kirzner, 1973). Any imbalance between demands and supplies in the market entails new opportunity and profit potentiality for those organizations which focus on learning identification the unmatched spots through deliberate investigation before any other competitors alert. These organization learns about these opportunities by a) defining opportunity originated from market-gaps, b) defining technology-oriented opportunities, and c) defining social-oriented opportunities. As mentioned before in any market gaps there is an unmet demand that needs to be acknowledged and responded by suppliers. On the other hand, any technological change in the industry makes a new platform for supplying new products or services which have not demanded yet, so they need to be effectively commercialized and find their proper market. And finally the market balance can be affected by the social change because the wants and desires of customers are under the effect of social force, so any social change can entail opportunity for more profit.

Learning Opportunity- Creation

As discussed before some opportunities are recognized, some are discovered, and the others are created(Alvarez & Barney, 2007). When considering opportunity creation, where 'rather than searching for a clear opportunity to be exploited, entrepreneurial organizations are creating opportunities through engaging in some learning processes that ultimately could lead to the formation of an opportunity' (Alvarez and Barney, 2007: 11–12). Opportunities are seen as a product of competitive imperfection in the industry or the market (Barney, 1986; Cohen and Winn, 2007). The origin of this imperfection, in the creation theory, is in the transformation of entrepreneurial beliefs into social constructs that guide actions of entrepreneurs and other constituents in the industry or market (Alvarez and Barney, 2007). During the process of discovery and recognition of opportunities, the organization's goal is to find opportunities in the market while one of demand or supply exists. So organizations try to find the right means-ends relationship to capture entrepreneurial profit(Shane, 2003). In this view, opportunities are like mountains that exist somewhere waiting to be recognized or discovered. But in opportunity creation, either entrepreneurial means or the market demand do not exist(Alvarez & Barney, 2007). There is no risk to be measured but there is some kind of uncertainty regarding the result of creating. Learning opportunity-creation is completely related to innovation. Schumpter (1934) divided innovation into five types named: a) launch of new product and service or new types of already known one, b) application of new method of production, c) opening a new market, d) acquiring of a new resource of supply raw material or semi-finished goods, e) new industry structure. Accordingly, in the process of OEL, the organization learns how to create innovative product and services, learns how to create new markets, learns how to new ways of producing existing products and services, learns how to find new raw or semi-finished materials and learns to create new business models.

Second Dimension: Behavioral Learning Skills

In most part of the literature related to Organizational Learning, the most significant assumption is that organization is such a system which is routine-based and goal-oriented. These systems feedbacks to its experience and follows some behavioral patterns that allow it to avoid expected failures and facilitate more success (Lundberg, 1995). Behavioral learning refers to the process of collecting and distribution new knowledge and preserving it in an organization (Huber, 1991; Weick & Roberts, 1993).Based on Literature behavioral learning focuses on some kind of trial-and-error learning and adaptive learning (Van de Ven & Polley, 1991) as mentioned before the prominent nature of this kind of learning is repetition and it focuses on the "antecedents and changes in organizational structures, technologies, routines, and systems as the organization responds to its own experience and that of other organizations" (Lundberg, 1995, p. 7). These theories argue that Organizational Learning is an adaptive process and, thus, is triggered only by performance gaps or other signals of poor market performance (Lumpkin & Lichtenstein, 2005). since trial and error learning reproduces routines in the organization the most of the organizational changes are minor and unless some external events happen in the external environment, it means that behavioral learning has incremental nature (Levinthal, 1991). As mentioned before, Cognitive Learning focuses on external events for acquiring new organizational knowledge but Behavioral learning has a more inward focus. It focuses on the patterns of belief and action of individuals and their interaction in the way of obtaining new capabilities and also managing the uncertainty in the environment which the organization should face with. Behavioral learning skills has two subcategories: a) Learning Dynamic Capabilities and b) Learning Uncertainty managing.

Learning Dynamic Capabilities

Strategic scholars have defined dynamic capabilities as a wide range of resources, processes, and capabilities. Wang and Ahmad (2007) have described dynamic capabilities as "a firm's behavioral orientation constantly to integrate, reconfigure, renew and recreate its resources and capabilities and, most importantly, upgrade and reconstruct its core capabilities in response to the changing environment to attain and sustain competitive advantage" (Wang & Ahmed, 2007 p. 35). They argued that dynamic capabilities are not simply processes, but embedded in organizational processes of managing resources and capabilities. Resources are the basis for firm capabilities. Capabilities are a kind firm's capacity to utilize resources and deploy them in a form of combination though both explicit processes and tacit elements (such as know-how and leadership) embedded in the processes. Hence, capabilities are often firm-specific and are developed over time through complex interactions between the firm's resources (Amit & Schoemaker, 1993). Wang and Ahmed (2007) identify three main component factors of dynamic capabilities, namely adaptive capability, absorptive capability and innovative capability. Adaptive Capability is defined as a firm's ability to identify and capitalize on emerging market opportunities. This capability differs from adaptation (Chakravarthy, 1982).

Adaptation refers to an optimal end state of survival for the organization, while adaptive capability focuses more on effective search and balancing exploration and exploitation opportunities (Wang & Ahmed, 2007). Adaptive capability brings organizational flexibility for capturing the benefit of market change. Through Learning Adaptive Capability, the organization learns to adapt its product–market scope flexibly to respond to entrepreneurial opportunities.

The absorptive capability is described as 'the ability of a firm to recognize the value of new, external information, assimilate it, and apply it to commercial ends (Cohen & Levinthal, 1990). It refers to the ability for evaluating and applying new knowledge. "Firms with higher absorptive capability demonstrate the stronger ability to learn from partners, integrating external information and transforming it into firm-embedded knowledge" (Wang & Ahmed, 2007). Through Learning Absorptive capability, the organizations learn how to evaluate external knowledge, acquire it and utilize it commercially, how to develop the first-hand knowledge by learning from external partners or internal researchers, and how to develop and use complementary technologies. Innovative capability refers to a firm's capability for creating new products and services, or opening new markets, through coordinating entrepreneurial orientation with innovative behaviors and processes (Wang & Ahmed, 2004).Through Learning Innovative Capability, the organizations learn how to develop innovative product and services and find the efficient market for them.

Learning Uncertainity Managing

Uncertainty is one of the most critical problems with which entrepreneurial organizations should face. So managing uncertainty is the fundamental activity for these companies in the way of entrepreneurship. Environmental uncertainty is when conditions are constantly changing within a business environment. As a result, the organization has no influence over external factors and can not control them. Any change in external environment could entail some degree of uncertainty (for example change in economic factors or political factors). These changes require a change in normal business strategies and thus require managing uncertainty. Milliken (1987) defined uncertainty as the organizational inability to predict something accurately(Milliken, 1987). This inability is the result of lacking efficacious information about current situation and future because the discrimination between relevant data and relevant data is too hard. Strategic scholars have suggested differents aspects for uncertainty, some of them focused on organizational inability to assign probabilities as to the likelihood of future event(Pfeffer & Salancik, 1978), the others focused on A lack of information about cause-effect relationship(Duncan, 1972), and some pointed organizational inability to predict accurately what the outcomes of a decision might be(Schmidt & Cummings, 1976). Based on these three aspects, Milliken (1987) proposed three type of uncertainty in organizational environment namely: perceived uncertainty, Effect Uncertainty, and Responsive uncertainty. Accordingly, these three types are used as the subcategories of Learning Uncertainty Managing which are Learning Managing Perceived Uncertainty, Learning Managing Effect Uncertainty, and Learning Managing Responsive Uncertainty.

Learning Managing Perceived Uncertainty

One type of uncertainty with which entrepreneurial organizations may face is the state uncertainty that is related to how the organization perceives the environmental unpredictability.decision makers in the organization might be uncertain about the action of suppliers, competitors, consumers, the government, shareholders, or any other stakeholders. They also might be uncertain about the probability general changes in environmental factors such as economic, social, cultural, legal, political, technological, or ecological trends. Perceived Uncertainty means that organizational decision makers could not understand which environmental factors may change in future, and could not predict their nature. Milliken asserted that this type of uncertainty involves an incomplete understanding of the interrelationships between elements in the environment(Milliken, 1987). During the process of Learning Managing Perceived Uncertainty, the organization tries to acquire new knowledge about the probable changes in the market by reinforcing its analysis of macro and micro environment and tracking the signals of future changes. In this way, the organization expands its perception of uncertainty and fortifies its ability to assign probabilities to the likelihood of future events (Duncan, 1972) and to predict the future consequences of decisions(Milliken, 1987).

Learning Managing Effect Uncertainty

The second type of uncertainty which the organization is forced to deal with is related to its ability to predict the impact of future changes on its profitability.Milliken (1987) has named it Effect Uncertainty and defined it as "an inability to predict what the nature of the impact of a future state of the environment or environmental change will be in the organization" (Milliken, 1987 p.137). Learning Effect Uncertainty involves acquiring new knowledge about whether specific event or change in the environment will have an impact or not. In other words, after finding the point of change, the organization should define how this change can affect the practice of the organization. For learning about these effects, the organization needs to create new knowledge, because there is no knowledge outside the organization about this matter. One way for creating knowledge about Effect uncertainty is developing different scenarios for the event and analyzing the impact by of event on the organization in each scenario.

Learning Managing Responsive Uncertainty.

The last type of uncertaintymanaging is related to identifying and evaluating the alternatives or response options available for the organization as a reaction to the uncertainty. Milliken (1987) has defined Response Uncertainty as "a lack of knowledge of response options and/or an inability to predict the likely consequences of a choice response. Response uncertainty is likely to be salient when there is a perceived need to act because a pending event or change is perceived to pose a threat or to provide some unique opportunity to the organization" (Milliken, 1987 p. 138). In the uncertainty situation, the organization needs to make an immediate decision as a reaction and response. In this way the organization experience response uncertainty either in the course of choosing from a number of possible strategies or in the course of formulating a response to an immediate opportunity or threat in the environment. During learning Managing Responsive Uncertainty, The organization learns how to identify the alternatives response to the uncertainty in entrepreneurial process. It also learns how to evaluate these options to select the approperate one.

Third Dimension: Action Learning Skills

Argyris and Schon (1974) have stated that organizational members apply some mental patterns for planing, implementing and reviewing their actions. They have added that few people are aware that there is difference btween the maps they use to take action and the theories they explicitly espouse. (Argyris & Schön, 1978). They have suggested that there is a theory consistent with what organizational members say and a theory consistent with what they do. Therefore, the distinction is not between "theory and action but between two different "theories of action". Lumpkin and Lichtensein (2005) asserted that In contrast to the other two themes, Action Learning Skills focus on taking effective action in proper time by rectifying incompatibilities between "espoused theory" (what the members of organization believe their behavior is based on) and its "theory-in-use" (what implied by their behaviour, or the maps they use to take action) (Lumpkin & Lichtenstein, 2005). Action learning refers to the patterns of interactions between individuals in the organization which can promote or terminate the process of acquiring new capabilities. Action Learning contains strong commitment made by organizational members and the organization's managers to promote the integrity and coordinating activities within the organization(Torbert, 2000). When organizational members carry out Action Learning, they generate a form of learning practice that can affect the quality of interactions and may result in producing new products or services (Senge, Roberts, Ross, Smith, & Kleiner, 1994). In Action Learning concerns about acting in real time (Lumpkin & Lichtenstein, 2005). Many scholars have argued that the practice of action learning is the distinction between "single-loop" incremental learning and "double-loop" transformative learning (Argyris & Schon, 1978; Bartunek, 1984; Reddick, Chatfield, & Ojo, 2017). "Single loop learning, incremental modifications are made to organizational behaviors that improve the efficiency of organizing and in Double-loop learning, by contrast, challenges the context within which such actions are being done, by continually asking whether the organization and its members are pursuing the right actions that might lead to the appropriate goals" (Lumpkin & Lichtenstein, 2005 p. 445). Through Action Learning, individuals and organizations should be able to break defensive routines that limit organizational potentiality (Argyris & Schon, 1978). In OEL, Action learning skills have two subcategories: a) Learning Opportunity-Exploitation, and b) Learning Organizational Flexibility.

Learning Opportunity-Exploitation

Wiklund has defined Opportunity exploitation as the organizational activities which are opportunity-oriented. The organization conducts these activities to gain economic returns from the recognition, discovery or creation of a potential entrepreneurial opportunity. It involves the decision to act on a perceived opportunity and the associated behaviors aimed at realizing the value of the opportunity (Wiklund, 2003). During opportunity exploitation, the organization acquires and organizes required resources and capabilities to develop a product or service and present it to current market or open new market for it. Not all entrepreneurial opportunities which are perceived by the organization are exploited. It is hard for decision makers to decide about the exploitation because of the cost of resource allocation and also the consequences of attempting to exploit a perceived entrepreneurial opportunity. Therefore, organizations need to learn opportunity exploitation before the closing of opportunity's windows. In this way, organizations should learn first how to evaluate the potential value of the pportunity against the costs of exploiting it, and comparing this to the outcomes of other possible courses of action. There are two organizational modes for exploiting opportunities.The first one is establishing the start-up of a new business Unit and the other one is to exploit opportunities within the framework of an existing organization. the resources needed to pursue the opportunity determine which organizational models should be chosen. If these resources are embedded within the organization, the first mode is more likely, because it can have access to know-how, financial assets, and other resources associated with opportunity exploitation. Meanwhile, if there are no relationships between the resources needed for the new opportunity and the resources of an existing organization, the start-up mode is more likely (Shane S. & Venkataraman S., 2000). During Learning Opportunity-Exploitation, the organization learns how to evaluate and analyze the feasibility of perceived opportunity and how to provide required resources and competencies for taking action in order to gain benefit and make the profit. In this kind of learning, the organization refers to two knowledge sources, knowledge which is embedded within the organization and external knowledge which is outside the boundaries of the organization. Internal Learning for exploitation of opportunities originated from inside of the organization and includes any kind of learning in which existing knowledge of the organization has been applied to create new knowledge, for example, learning from previous failures in one of the past projects can raise the knowledge of the organization regarding the factors of loss and win, and these instructions can be used in similar projects in future. The other one relates to the external environment of an organization. By applying external learning an organization tries to gather new knowledge from external sources such as suppliers, customers, competitors, and strategic partners. Foss et al.(2013) has argued that external knowledge is pivotal source for entrepreneurial opportunities exploitation and some of the external knowledge sources engaged during the opportunity recognition phase may naturally be involved in the exploitation phase and can provide useful contextual information that spurs exploitation and determines its outcomes (Foss, Lyngsie, & Zahra, 2013).

Learning Organizational Flexibility

Environmental complexity and dynamic nature of markets force organizations to be more and more flexible. Organizations need to learn flexibility in order to cope with higher levels of disorder (Hatum & Pettigrew A. M.', 2006). Literature related to flexibility emphasizes mostly on change and initiation or adaptation for obtaining the competitive advantage. However, most definitions of organizational flexibility oppose stability, Volberda (1996) argued that organizational flexibility should refer to both change and stability together. Since without stability, the organization will suffer from overreaction, excessive information search, and wasted resources (Volberda, 1996). the organization could not enjoy and retain a sense of identity and continuity in its practices if there was total flexibility in the organization (Weick, 1982); Volberrda has asserted that flexibility without stability results in chaos (Volberda, 1996). So the main question here is how the organization can deal with these two paradoxical situations in same time. Obviously it should learn. Through learning organizational flexibility, the organization learns how to adapt its internal routines with external changes for providing appropriate circumstances to exploit entrepreneurial opportunities and also it makes some efficient rules to bring sustainability to the system. Keeping the balance between dynamism and sustainability is one of the prominent organizational capabilities that is necessary for responding successfully to of competition and constantly progressing toward competitive advantage. For engendering flexibility, the organization should be able to cope with its inertia. Organizational inertia is the resistance to change or the endurance of stable behaviors in the organization and its members. organizational inertia is the opposite of organizational change. After finding a proper practice for the organization and creating the routines accordingly, it would be so difficult to reorient them again and again so organizational orientation initiates. By definition, when inertia is present the speed of change in the core features of an organization is lower than the rate of environmental change (Hannan & Freeman, 1984). According to Hennan & Freeman (1977), organizations suffer from " strong inertia pressure on structure arising from both internal and external environment" (Hannan & Freeman, 1977). For conducting entrepreneurial practices, the organization should learn how to manage internal factors such as internal policies, suck costs, and the growth of bureaucracy and how to coordinate its operations with external inertia forces such as access to resources, barriers to entry, and competitive pressure. Through learning coping with these inertia forces, the organization is able to provide a proper platform for accomplishing the change (Suddaby, 2017). The other aspect of flexibility refers to strategic flexibility which is related to reallocation and reconfiguration of resources, processes, and strategies to deal with the volatile business environment (Zhou, 2010). Through learning strategic flexibility, organizations learn how to manage their resources dynamically for adapting to high-velocity environments and reducing risks. Learning this kind of flexibility helps organizations to exploit the full potential of their key resource stocks and allows them to respond quickly to unstable environments and act promptly (Kamasak, Yavuz, & Ozturk, 2016). In this way, the organization learns how to reduce the risk by funding prudent solutions for the complexity of competition.

CONCLUSION

EL as a promising area of academic research has mostly focused on individual level of analysis, while it can be manifested on organizational level too. The most important challenge here is that the most model which has been proposed for EL relate to individual entrepreneurs and can not be applied to organizations. In this chapter a model of OEL has been presented which clarify the aspects of EL in established organizations.

Through literature review, three relevant dimensions have been identified for OEL, namely: I) Cognitive Learning Skills (Learning Opportunity-Recognition, Learning Opportunity-Discovery, and Learning Opportunity-Creation), II) Behavioral Learning Skills (Learning Competitive Skills and Learning uncertainty managing), and III) Action Learning Skills (Learning Opportunity-Exploitation and Learning Organizational Flexibility).

Figure 1. The organizational entrepreneurial learning model

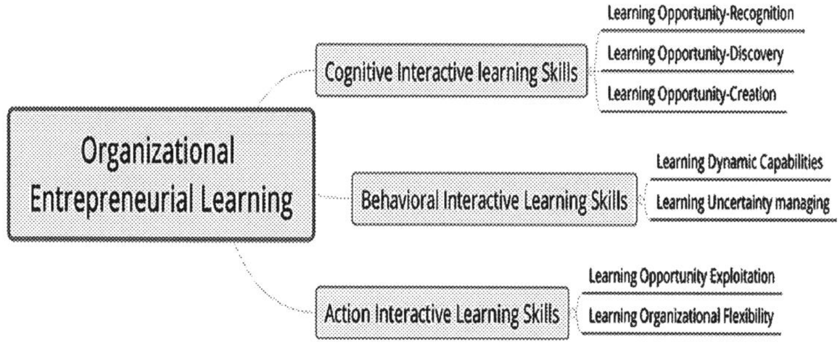

REFERENCES

Alvarez, S. A., & Barney, J. B. (2007). Discovery and creation: Alternative theories of entrepreneurial action. *Entrepreneurship Journal*, *1*(1), 11–26.

Amit, R., & Schoemaker, P. (1993). Strategic assets and organizational rent. *Strategic Management Journal*, *14*(1), 33–46. doi:10.1002/smj.4250140105

Argote, L., & Hora, M. (2017, April). Organizational Learning and Management of Technology. *Special Issue On Management Of Technology*, *26*(4), 579–590.

Argyris, C., & Schön, D. (1978). *Organizational Learning: A Theory of Action Perspective*. Reading, MA: Addison-Wesley.

Bartunek, J. (1984). Changing interpretive schemes and organizational restructuring: The example of a religious order. *Administrative Science Quarterly*, *29*(3), 224–241. doi:10.2307/2393029

Benner, M., & Tushman, M. (2003). Exploitation, exploration, and process management: The productivity dilemma revisited. *Academy of Management Review*, *28*(2), 238–256.

Brown, T., Davidsson, P., & Wiklund, J. (2001). An operationalization of Stevensons conceptualization of entrepreneurship as opportunity-based firm behavior. *Strategic Management Journal*, *22*(10), 953–968. doi:10.1002/smj.190

Chakravarthy, B. S. (1982). Adaptation: A promising metaphor for strategic management. *Academy of Management Review*, *7*(1), 35–44.

Cohen, M. D., & Levinthal, D. A. (1990). Absorptive capacity: A new perspective on learning and innovation. *Administrative Science Quarterly*, *35*(1), 128–152. doi:10.2307/2393553

Cope, J. (2005). Toward a dynamic learning perspective of entrepreneurship. *Entrepreneurship Theory and Practice*, *29*(4), 373–397. doi:10.1111/j.1540-6520.2005.00090.x

D., R., & C., T. (2005). Exploring Entrepreneurial Learning: A Comparative Study of Technology Development and projects. *Journal of Business Venturing*, *20*(1), 137–164.

Duncan, R. B. (1972). Characteristics of organizational environments and perceived environmental uncertainty. *Administrative Science Quarterly*, *17*(3), 313–327. doi:10.2307/2392145

Dutta, K., & Crossan, M. (2005). Entrepreneurial Opportunities: Understanding the Process Using the 4I Organizational Learning Framework. *Entrepreneurship and Practice*, *29*(4), 425–449. doi:10.1111/j.1540-6520.2005.00092.x

Eckhardt, J., & Shane, S. (2003). Opportunities and Entrepreneurship. *Journal of Management*, *29*(3), 333–349. doi:10.1177/014920630302900304

Erdélyi, P. (2010). *The Matter of Entrepreneurial Learning: A Literature Review*. Boston, MA: Northteastern University.

Fiol, M. C., & Lyles, M. A. (1985). Organizational learning. *Academy of Management Review*, *10*, 803–813.

Foss, N. J., Lyngsie, J., & Zahra, S. A. (2013). The Role of External Knowledge Sources and Organizational Design in the Process of Opportunity Exploitation. *Strategic Management Journal*, *34*(12), 1453–1471. doi:10.1002/smj.2135

Gibb, A. A. (2002). In Pursuit of a New Enterprise and Entrepreneurship Paradigm for Learning: Creative Destruction, New Values, New Ways of Doing Things and New Combinations of Knowledge. *International Journal of Management Reviews*, *4*(3), 213–232. doi:10.1111/1468-2370.00086

Hannan, M. T., & Freeman, J. (1977). The population ecology of organizations. *American Journal of Sociology*, 82: Hannan, M. T., & Freeman, J. (1984). Structural inertia and organizational change. *American Sociological Review*, *49*(2), 149–164. doi:10.2307/2095567

Hatum, A., & Pettigrew, A. M. (2006). Determinants of Organizational Flexibility: A Study in an Emerging Economy. *British Journal of Management*, *17*(2), 115–137. doi:10.1111/j.1467-8551.2005.00469.x

Henan, M. T., & Freeman, J. (1977). The Population Ecology of Organizations. *American Journal of Sociology*, *82*(5).

Henderson, R., & Clark, K. (1996). Architectural innovation: The reconfiguration of existing product technologies and the failure of established firms. *Administrative Science Quarterly*, *35*(1), 9–30. doi:10.2307/2393549

Huber, G. P. (1991). A Theory of the Effects of Advanced Information Technologies on Organizational Design, Intelligence, and Decision Making. *Academy of Management Review*, *15*, 47–71.

Kamasak, R., Yavuz, M., & Ozturk, T. Y. (2016). *Reducing Risk Through Strategic Flexibility and Implementation Leadership in High-Velocity Markets Global Business Strategies in Crisis, Contributions to Management Science*. Springer International Publishing AG 2017.

Kirzner, I. M. (1973). *Competition and entrepreneurship*. Chicago, IL: University of Chicago Press.

Kolb, D. (1984). *Experiential Learning: Experience as the Source of Learning and Development*. Prentice Hall inc.

Leroy, F., & Ramanatsoa, B. (1997). The cognitive and Behavioral dimensions of organizational learning in a merger: An empirical stud. *Journal of Management Studies, 34*(4), 871–894. doi:10.1111/1467-6486.00076

Levinthal, D. (1991). Organizational adaptation and environmental selection: Interrelated processes of change. *Organization Science*, *2*(1), 140–144. doi:10.1287/orsc.2.1.140

Lumpkin, G. T., & Lichtenstein, B. B. (2005). The role of entrepreneurial learning in the opportunity-recognition. *Entrepreneurship Theory and Practice*, *29*(4), 451–472. doi:10.1111/j.1540-6520.2005.00093.x

Lundberg, C. (1995). Conceptual issues in organizational learning. *The International Journal of Organizational Analysis*, *3*(1), 7–19. doi:10.1108/eb028821

Marquardt, M. J. (2002). *Building the learning organization: Mastering the 5 elements for corporate learning*. Palo Alto, CA: Davies-Black Publishing, Inc.

Matlay, H. (2000). Organizational learning in small learning organizations Education + Training. London. *EDEXEL*, *42*(4/5), 202–210.

Miller, D. (1996). A preliminary typology of organizational learning: Synthesizing the literature. *Journal of Management*, *22*(3), 485–505. doi:10.1177/014920639602200305

Milliken, F. J. (1987, January). Three Types of Perceived Uncertainty about the Environment: State, Effect, and Response Uncertainty. *Academy of Management Review*, *12*(1), 133–143.

Minniti, M., & Bygrave. (2001). A dynamic model of entrepreneurial learning. *Entrepreneurship Theory and Practice*, *25*(3), 5–16.

Nonaka, I. (1988). Creating organizational order out of chaos: Self-renewal in Japanese firms. *California Management Review*, *30*(Spring), 57–73. doi:10.2307/41166514

Nonaka, I. (1994). A dynamic theory of organizational knowledge creation. Organization Science, 5, 14–37.

Pfeffer, J., & Salancik, G. R. (1978). *The external control of organizations: A resource dependence perspective*. New York: Harper & Row.

Pisano, G. (1994). Knowledge, integration, and the locus of learning: An empirical analysis of process development. *Strategic Management Journal, 15*(S1), 85–100. doi:10.1002/smj.4250150907

Pittaway, L., & Thorpe, R. (2012). A framework for entrepreneurial learning: A tribute to Jason Cope. *Entrepreneurship & Regional Development, 24*(9-10), 837–859. doi:10.1080/08985626.2012.694268

Politis, D. (2005). The process of entrepreneurial learning: A conceptual framework. *Entrepreneurship Theory and Practice, 29*(4), 399–424. doi:10.1111/j.1540-6520.2005.00091.x

Rae, D. (2011). *Entrepreneurial learning: Practice, experience and theory. Paper presented at Entrepreneurial learning and education: From theory to practice.* British Academy of Management.

Rae, D. a. W. (2015). *Entrepreneurial Learning: New Perspectives in Research, Education and Practice*. Routledge Studies in Entrepreneurship.

Ravasi, D., & Turati, C. (2005). Exploring Entrepreneurial Learning: A Comparative Study of Technology Development and projects. *Journal of Business Venturing, 20*(1), 137–164.

Reddick, C. G., Chatfield, A. T., & Ojo, A. (2017). A social media text analytics framework for double-loop learning for citizen-centric public services: A case study of a local government Facebook use. *Government Information Quarterly, 34*(1), 110–125. doi:10.1016/j.giq.2016.11.001

Sarasvathy, S., Dew, N., Velamuri, S., & Venkataraman, S. (2003). Three Views of Entrepreneurial Opportunity. International Handbook Series on Entrepreneurship, 141-160.

Schmidt, S. M., & Cummings, L. L. (1976). Organizational environment, differentiation and perceived environmental uncertainty. *Decision Sciences, 7*(3), 447–467. doi:10.1111/j.1540-5915.1976.tb00692.x

Schumpeter, J. A. (1975). *Capitalism, socialism and democracy*. New York: Harper.

Senge, P., Roberts, C., Ross, R., Smith, B., & Kleiner, A. (1994). *The fifth discipline field book*. New York: Currency/Doubleday.

Senge, P. M. (2010). *The Fifth Discipline: The Art & Practice of the Learning Organization*. Crown Publishing Group.

Shane, S. 2. (2003). A General Theory of Entrepreneurship. Edward Elgar.

Shane, S., & Venkataraman, S. (2000, January). The Promise of Entrepreneurship as a Field of Research. *Academy of Management Review*, *25*(1), 217–226.

Sigrist, B. (1999). Entrepreneurial Opportunity Recognition, Paper presented at the annual UIC/AMA Symposium at the Marketing/Entrepreneurship Interface, Sofia-Antipolis, France.

Stevenson, H. H., & Jarillo, J. C. (1990). A paradigm of entrepreneurship: Entrepreneurial management. *Strategic Management Journal*, *11*, 17–27.

Suddaby, R. F. W., & Foster, W. M. (2017, January). History and Organizational Change. *Journal of Management*, *43*(1), 19–38. doi:10.1177/0149206316675031

Tan. (2011). Research on the relationship between knowledge search and innovation performance—based on the view of organization learning. *Science and Technology Management Research*, *2011*, 166-170.

Teece, D. (1998). Capturing value from knowledge assets: The new economy, markets for know-how, and intangible assets. *California Management Review*, *40*(3), 55–79. doi:10.2307/41165943

Torbert, W. (2000). A developmental approach to social science: A model for analyzing Charles Alexanders scientific contributions. *Journal of Adult Development*, *7*(4), 255–267. doi:10.1023/A:1009515512330

Van de Ven, A., & Polley, D. (1991). Learning while innovating. *Organization Science*, *3*, 91–116.

Volberda, H. W. (1996). Toward the Flexible Form: How to Remain Vital in Hypercompetitive Environments. *Organization Science*, *7*(4), 359–374. doi:10.1287/orsc.7.4.359

Wang, C., & Ahmed, P. (2004). The development and validation of the organizational innovativeness construct using confirmatory factor analysis. *European Journal of Innovation Management*, *7*(4), 303–313. doi:10.1108/14601060410565056

Wang, C., & Ahmed, P. (2007). Dynamic capabilities - A review and research agenda. *International Journal of Management Reviews*, *9*(1), 31–51. doi:10.1111/j.1468-2370.2007.00201.x

Wang, C., & Chugh, H. (2014). Entrepreneurial Learning: Past Research and Future Challenges. *International Journal of Management Reviews*, *16*(1), 24–61. doi:10.1111/ijmr.12007

Wang, C. L., & Chugh, H. (2014). Entrepreneurial Learning: Past Research and Future Challenges. *International Journal of Management Reviews*, *16*(1), 24–61. doi:10.1111/ijmr.12007

Weick, K., & Roberts, K. (1993). Collective mind in organizations: Heedful interrelating on flight decks. *Administrative Science Quarterly*, *38*(3), 357–381. doi:10.2307/2393372

Weick, K. E. (1982). *Management of Organizational Change among Loosely Coupled Element. In Change in Organizations: New Perspectives in Theory, Research, and Practice* (pp. 375–408). San Francisco, CA: Jossey-Bass.

Wiklund, J. D. S. (2003). Aspiring for, and achieving growth: The moderating role of resources and opportunities. *Journal of Management Studies*, *20*, 71–91.

Zahra, S. A., Korri, J. S., & Yu, J. (2005). *Cognition and international entrepreneurship: Implications for research on international opportunity recognition and exploitation*. Management Department Faculty Publications. Paper 113.

Zhou, K. Z. W. F. (2010). Technological capability, strategic flexibility, and product innovation. *Strategic Management Journal*, *31*(5), 547–561.

Chapter 3
Shortening the Learning Curve of Media Start-Ups in Accelerators:
Case of a Developing Country

Aidin Salamzadeh
University of Tehran, Iran

Mirjana Radovic Markovic
Institute of Economic Sciences, Serbia

ABSTRACT

Business accelerators are playing a key role in facilitating the process of new venture creation. Start-ups generally look for the best accelerators to make their long journey short. Media start-ups also look for a supportive mechanism to fasten their start-up experience. In this process, one of the main issues is to shorten their learning curve which is possible by use of start-up accelerators. Therefore, this chapter deals with the idea that which factors are important in this regard. To do so, first, a brief review of the support mechanisms is presented, and it is discussed that how start-up accelerators shorten the learning curve of the start-ups. Then, five media start-ups which were created in accelerators are studied. All of the cases were established after 2014, since the accelerators started working from the same year. According to the findings, there are mainly six reasons for shortening of the learning curve by start-up accelerators, including: (1) Short creation period, (2) Seminars and courses, (3) Co-working space, (4) Divided teams, (5) Cohort peers, and (6) Mentorship.

DOI: 10.4018/978-1-5225-2956-9.ch003

INTRODUCTION

Start-up accelerators are considered as the fourth generation of incubators (Carvalho & Galina, 2015). In the one hand, these entities attempt to shorten the learning curve of start-ups. On the other hand, among different types of start-ups, media start-ups could be considered as one of the main entities which could take advantage of such an acceleration process (Salamzadeh, 2015 a; Salamzadeh & Radovic Markovic, 2016). Nowadays, media start-ups are facing immense competition more than ever. These start-ups, like others, are finding exceptional ways of generating revenue from the very early stages of their establishment (Ferrier, 2013; Salamzadeh & Kirby, 2017). Moreover, they learn so fact, since these start-ups provide people with interactive platforms of communication (Girard & Stark, 2002). Then, learning is an integral part of these entities. It is evident that media start-ups are moving into a new era in which the active players can surpass media rapidly (Sakr, 2016).

In order to understand the different circumstances in which media start-ups are created and operating, one needs to look at the features of media in a specific country (Khajeheian & Tadayoni, 2016). Media entrepreneurship is an emerging field of study around the Globe, and more specifically in Iran, which is attracting the attention of different scholars and practitioners. Therefore, the idea of creating start-ups in this field is also an emerging domain (Ferrier, 2013; Khajeheian, 2013, 2017). Moreover, these start-ups have two choices, that is either to use support measures or not. Based on prior research, rate of failure is higher in not-supported start-ups, while those which used support mechanisms such as incubators, small business development centers (SBDCs), science and technology parks, and accelerators, had higher rates of success (Salamzadeh, 2015 b).

In fact, such support mechanisms facilitate the creation of these start-ups. Among these mechanisms, accelerators are created to shorten the learning curve of start-ups and to accelerate the process. In this chapter, the idea is to present a brief review of the literature on start-up accelerators, and then to investigate how these accelerators shorten the learning curve of media start-ups. To do so, after a theoretical review, five cases are analysed and discussed. Finally the chapter concludes with some remarks and implications for policy makers.

START-UP ACCELERATORS: HOW TO SHORTEN THE LEARNING CURVE?

The existence of a learning curve for [established] organizations has been comprehensively investigated by several scholars. However, there was a problem stating that if start-up founders could learn fast enough during the start-up process to avoid any mistakes or even to fail (Cohen, 2013). Hopefully, this research area has emerged simultaneously by the advent and emergence of start-up accelerators (Davila et al., 2010; Stagars, 2015). As mentioned earlier, there are several support mechanisms which could be used to support media start-ups. Table 1 shows the characteristics of the main mechanisms. According to the table and based on the existing trend, accelerators are more interesting and are highly recommended to media start-ups. This is especially because of their features like short period of acceleration process, useful seminars, co-working space opportunities, and mentorship services. These issues are critical in accelerating the learning curve in start-ups.

First, start-ups are selected competitively and therefore there will be a higher chance of success- to scale up or continue working, or even to fail faster (Nigam, 2014). In fact, having limited time to show your abilities and to learn more and more is a key to success (Ganamotse et al., 2017). Start-up accelerators prepare a fertile ground for founders of start-up companies to show their potentials (Raheem & Akhuemonkhan, 2014). Secondly, start-up accelerators normally offer interesting courses and hold different seminars for start-ups to learn what they need (Rogova, 2014). These courses include topics such as business planning, pitching, negotiating, and the like (Pauwels et al., 2016). Third, co-working space provides start-ups with several opportunities, such as to share both explicit and implicit knowledge. A combination of ideas presented by experts to start-ups and their own

Table 1. Support mechanisms/entities for start-up creation

Science Park	Angel Investor	SBDC	Hatchery	Accelerator	Incubator	
6 months-3yrs	Ongoing	Ongoing	3-6 months	3-6 months	1-5 yrs.	Duration
No	No	No	No	Yes	No	Cohorts
Rent; Non-profit	Investment	Investment	Non-profit	Investment; Non-profit	Rent; Non-profit	Business model
Non-competitive	Competitive, Ongoing	Competitive	Competitive, Cyclical	Competitive, Cyclical	Non-competitive	Selection frequency
Ad hoc	None	If required	Ad hoc, deliverables	Seminar	Ad hoc, hr/legal	Education offered
On-site	Off-site	Usually off-site	On-site	Usually on-site	On-site	Venture location
Minimal-tactical	As needed- by investor	As needed	Intense- peer support	Intense- by self and others	Minimal-tactical	Mentorship
Early or late	Early	Early or late	Early	Early	Early or late	Venture stage

Source: Salamzadeh and Kawamorita (2017).

lived experiences that is all shared among the teams provides them with a unique experience (Bernardez et al., 2007; Kim, 2015). Also, divided teams are located in a same co-working space (Welch, 2012). Then, they try to compete and share what is interesting for both sides, and hide what they believe is their secrets. Some of these start-ups are cohort peers (Lall et al., 2013). In fact, learning process is accelerated by them. Finally, mentorship services are other issues to be considered as accelerating factors in shortening the learning curve of start-ups (Price, 2004).

In sum, start-up accelerators do not have to go through a typical process of trial and error but these entities could shorten the learning curve of start-ups (de Oliveira & Filipe, 2011). Then, start-up accelerators' key function is to assist start-up firms to solve their establishment and scale-up problems; this kind of support will indeed shorten the learning curve of the start-ups and, simultaneously, highly contributes to capabilities creation of start-ups (Ratinho, 2011; Esquivel, 2013). Without paying attention to accelerating the learning curve, these support mechanisms would be less interesting choices for start-ups to reach.

MEDIA START-UPS IN ACCELERATORS: CASES STUDY OF IRANIAN MEDIA START-UPS

Media entrepreneurship is an emerging field of research which deals with entrepreneurial aspects of media firms, and more specifically, how media start-ups face entrepreneurial opportunities (Ferrier, 2013; Khajeheian & Tadayoni, 2016). In other words, it scrutinizes how those start-ups explore, evaluate, and exploit opportunities (Hoag, 2008). In a more comprehensive sense, media entrepreneurship is about applying entrepreneurial theories and practices in media firms. As Ibrus (2015) argues, this approach is becoming prevalent in different countries and even continents. For instance, he investigates the replacement of media policies with media entrepreneurship policies around Europe. However, the topic is not extensively studied in developing/emerging economies (e.g. see Fallah et al., 2012).

Therefore, it is critical and useful to conduct a case study research to know more about the evolution of media start-ups as well as acceleration of their learning curve. In fact, media entrepreneurship in Iran was rarely studied until the last few years. Khajeheian (2013) critically reviewed the concept in Iran and concluded that "*media entrepreneurship in Iranian market is a very potential market*". It did not take so long until the first couple of media start-ups appeared in the country and turned the page. The following tables show the details and main features of these start-up companies and their founders. As it is shown, all of these start-ups are created after year 2014. However, this is also because of the raise of accelerators from 2014 which started working closely with these teams (Salamzadeh & Kawamorita, 2017). As illustrated in Table 2, problem solving approach is followed by start-ups which is because of their attendance in business accelerators.

As mentioned earlier, some of the main roles of accelerators help media start-ups shorten their learning curve. These roles are discussed as follows:

Short Creation Period

Although, some scholars believe that the limited duration of start-up accelerator programs increases the influence of programs, this is not always the case. Since start-ups should strive to succeed in a short period and get ready for the final pitch, the rivalry and competitiveness makes these companies live (Kohler, 2016). Even if they fail, they will notice shortly, and could make a U turn in their business life (Garcia, 2017). As mentioned by founders of media start-ups (case #1, case #3), accelerators helped them analyse their tractions in a very short period, and their success is more probable. As the founder of case #1 argued, this short period made everything quick, even revision of the business plan was so fast and to the point.

Table 2. Characteristic traits and basic profiles of the start-ups

Characteristics of the Start-Up	Case #1	Case #2	Case #3	Case #4	Case #5
Year of establishment	2014	2015	2015	2016	2016
Main activity/ domain	Live mobile broadcasting	Branding via media	Sports broadcasting	Motion graphics	Podcasting and audio books
Legal form	Private Joint Stock	ltd	ltd	ltd	ltd
No. of partners	5	3	4	+10	+10
No. employees	15	9	6	8	6
No. of competitors	+10	+5	+10	+50	+20
Financial sustainability*	95%	70%	30%	20%	20%
Female/male ratio**	20%	33.3%	16.6%	25%	16.6%

Source: Self-elaborated.

* Estimated base on the degree to which their business plans were accomplished (reaching the break-even point);

** Employees

Table 3. Characteristic traits and basic profiles of the start-ups' founding teams

Characteristics of the Founding Teams	Case #1	Case #2	Case #3	Case #4	Case #5
No. of founders	5	3	3	3	4
Age of founders (average)	29	26	24	25	23
Intention/identity	To handle private broadcasting needs	To help small firms make their brands	To create a sports broadcasting platform	To handle multimedia needs of the start-ups	Promote the podcasting culture
Founders' background	Engineering	IT	Software Engineering	Art	IT
Founders' educational level	BSc., MSc.	BSc.	BSc., MSc.	BSc.	BSc.
Female/male ratio*	20%	11.1%	0	0	0

Source: Self-elaborated.
* Founders

Seminars and Courses

Generally speaking, almost any educational program would directly or indirectly shorten the learning curve of the firms. This is more important while dealing with start-ups (Kim & Wagman, 2014). Courses such as business planning, pitching and negotiating are among the most important ones for start-ups which are normally rendered in start-up accelerators (Pauwels et al., 2016). All of the cases experienced the change in their organizations and believed that organizational learning was improved quickly in their teams.

Co-Working Space

Originally, the need for an affordable office space has led to the advent of co-working spaces. Accepting the failures along the way and accelerating the learning curve is inevitable in a co-working space, since there are many positive points in such environments (Fuzi, 2015; Kojo & Nenonen, 2016). As the founder of case #3 mentioned, working in such an environment is a completely different experience for him and his team. They used to get in touch with others while working on their idea.

Divided Teams

As stated earlier, divided teams are located in a same co-working space (Welch, 2012). Then, they try to compete and share what is interesting for both sides, and hide what they believe is their secrets. Divided teams work on different minimum viable products (MVPs), however their market is to a great extent common. Then, by retargeting the customers of the other teams, each team will be able to reach larger market segments (Weiblen & Chesbrough, 2015). However, the teams will be independent and work on a single idea. For instance, case #1 and case #3 used to stay in a shared co-working space and acknowledged that they have learnt a lot from each other.

Cohort Peers

Learning process is accelerated by cohort peers, since their insights and approaches are close to each other and common values could be shared easily among these peers. They teach and learn new things through sharing their experiences and monitoring each other's activities (MacNeil & Schoonmaker, 2017). All of the cases argued that they learnt a lot from the other teams in accelerators.

Mentorship

Mentors work with start-up founders throughout the duration of the acceleration period, give advice, and provide precious feedback based on their own experience as founders, business owners or entrepreneurs. In fact, the accelerators select mentors based on their level of expertise as well as their degree of success in a similar business (Radojevich-Kelley & Hoffman, 2012; Juárez, 2013). Mentors played a significant role in the success of all the cases, as mentioned by them.

Figure 1 shows the six reasons for acceleration of the learning curve by start-up accelerators.

CONCLUSION

Support measures or mechanisms are required to facilitate the process of start-up/ new venture creation, especially for media start-ups. Since media entrepreneurship has become an emerging field, some new windows of opportunity are opened to study

Figure 1. Reasons for shortening the learning curve by start-up accelerators

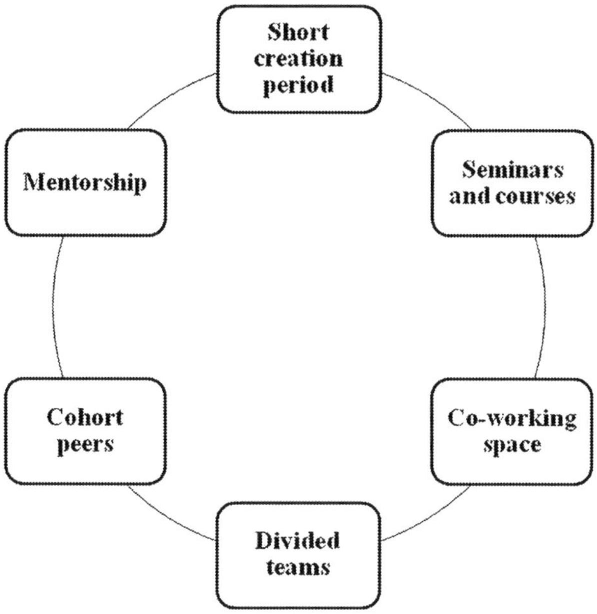

these entities in more detail (Battistella, 2017). Among the existing mechanisms, accelerators are created specifically to shorten the learning curve of start-ups and to accelerate the process of new venture creation (Wang, 2016). Therefore, in the present chapter, a brief review of the literature on start-up accelerators as well as other mechanisms are studied, and then the reasons behind how these accelerators shorten the learning curve of media start-ups are scrutinized. In order to do so, after a theoretical review, five media start-ups are analysed. The cases were selected among the media start-ups created in start-up accelerators of the Iran. According to the findings, there are mainly six reasons for shortening of the learning curve by start-up accelerators, including: (i) Short creation period, (ii) Seminars and courses, (iii) Co-working space, (iv) Divided teams, (v) Cohort peers, and (vi) Mentorship.

It is highly recommended to start-up accelerators to consider these six elements in order to shorten the learning curve of media start-ups. Media start-ups are mostly viral and their reputation might be highlighted in a very short period, since at the center of such start-ups there is content (Heydebrand & Miron, 2002; Mueller, 2012). As it is recommended and accepted by experts, “content is the king”; Then, it is inevitable that media start-ups are shaped based on such a strong basis and policy makers should notice this important issue in the policy makings (Dziadkiewicz, 2015). Start-up accelerators shorten the period media start-ups need to learn; then policy makers might support such mechanisms instead of science parks and traditional incubators which are not so successful in this domain, especially in Iran. Moreover, co-working spaces are required to synergize the learning process through which start-ups help each other. Moreover, providing a fertile ground for media start-ups will be so helpful.

Future researchers might investigate the effect of the six elements on acceleration of the learning curve in media start-ups and measure their impact. However, to do this, a broader sample size is needed. In this chapter, limited access to a large number of media start-ups in Iran is considered as a limitation. Moreover, the mediating effects must be considered along with the contextual factors. Finally, presenting a typology of media start-ups and categorizing the findings would lead to interesting findings regarding this phenomenon.

REFERENCES

Battistella, C., De Toni, A. F., & Pessot, E. (2017). Open accelerators for start-ups success: A case study. *European Journal of Innovation Management*, *20*(1), 80–111. doi:10.1108/EJIM-10-2015-0113

Bernardez, M., Valdez Gomez, J. A., Uribe, A., & Santana, A. (2007). Coaching for new business creation. *International Journal of Coaching in Organizations*, *5*(3), 52–65.

Carvalho, L. M. C., & Galina, S. V. (2015). The role of business incubators for start-ups development in Brazil and Portugal. *World Journal of Entrepreneurship, Management and Sustainable Development*, *11*(4), 256–267.

Cohen, S. L. (2013). *How to accelerate learning: Entrepreneurial ventures participating in accelerator programs*. The University of North Carolina at Chapel Hill.

Davila, A., Foster, G., & Jia, N. (2010). Building sustainable high-growth startup companies: Management systems as an accelerator. *California Management Review*, *52*(3), 79–105. doi:10.1525/cmr.2010.52.3.79

de Oliveira, R. A., & Filipe, T. (2011). *Are they helping? An examination of business incubators' impact on tenant firms*. University of Twente.

Dziadkiewicz, A. (2015). Social media and start-ups. *Zarządzanie Mediami*, *3*(4), 257–267.

Esquivel, R. V. (2013). From a Local Chapter to a Regional Catalyzer (Innovations Case Narrative: New Ventures México). *Innovations*, *8*(3-4), 93-104.

Fallah, A., Sadeghi, M., & Saeedi, K. (2012). Understanding entrepreneurship and media management in Iran. *Advances in Environmental Biology*, 1777-1780.

Ferrier, M. B. (2013). Media entrepreneurship: Curriculum development and faculty perceptions of what students should know. *Journalism & Mass Communication Educator*, *68*(3), 222–241. doi:10.1177/1077695813494833

Fuzi, A. (2015). Co-working spaces for promoting entrepreneurship in sparse regions: The case of South Wales. *Regional Studies. Regional Science*, *2*(1), 462–469.

Ganamotse, G. N., Samuelsson, M., Abankwah, R. M., Anthony, T., & Mphela, T. (2017). The Emerging Properties of Business Accelerators: The Case of Botswana, Namibia and Uganda Global Business Labs. *Journal of Entrepreneurship and Innovation in Emerging Economies*, *3*(1), 16–40. doi:10.1177/2393957516684469

Garcia, D. J. M. (2017). *Do cohorts accelerate? Startups accelerators and unentrepreneurial learning*. Doctoral dissertation.

Girard, M., & Stark, D. (2002). Distributing intelligence and organizing diversity in new media projects. *Sociedade e Estado*, *17*(1), 153–192. doi:10.1590/S0102-69922002000100009

Heydebrand, W., & Miron, A. (2002). Constructing innovativeness in new-media start-up firms. *Environment & Planning A*, *34*(11), 1951–1984. doi:10.1068/a3558

Hoag, A. (2008). Measuring Media Entrepreneurship 1. *The International Journal on Media Management*, *10*(2), 74–80. doi:10.1080/14241270802000496

Ibrus, I. (2015). The replacement of media policies with (media) entrepreneurship policies: A view from Europes periphery. *International Journal of Digital Television*, *6*(3), 311–318. doi:10.1386/jdtv.6.3.311_1

Juárez, B., III. (2013). *Building innovation-based entrepreneurial communities: an assessment of practitioners' interactions with academically driven curriculum* (Doctoral dissertation). Massachusetts Institute of Technology.

Khajeheian, D. (2013). New venture creation in social media platform; towards a framework for media entrepreneurship. In *Handbook of social media management* (pp. 125–142). Springer Berlin Heidelberg. doi:10.1007/978-3-642-28897-5_8

Khajeheian, D. (2017). Media entrepreneurship: A consensual definition. *Administer*, *30*, 91–113.

Khajeheian, D., & Tadayoni, R. (2016). User innovation in public service broadcasts: Creating public value by media entrepreneurship. *International Journal of Technoloy Transfer and Commercialisation, 14*(2), 117–131. doi:10.1504/IJTTC.2016.081635

Kim, J. H., & Wagman, L. (2014). Portfolio size and information disclosure: An analysis of startup accelerators. *Journal of Corporate Finance, 29*, 520–534. doi:10.1016/j.jcorpfin.2014.10.017

Kim, W. (2015). The current transition in management of technology education: The case of Korea. *Technological Forecasting and Social Change, 100*, 5–20. doi:10.1016/j.techfore.2015.03.018

Kohler, T. (2016). Corporate accelerators: Building bridges between corporations and startups. *Business Horizons, 59*(3), 347–357. doi:10.1016/j.bushor.2016.01.008

Kojo, I., & Nenonen, S. (2016). Typologies for co-working spaces in Finland–what and how? *Facilities, 34*(5/6), 302–313. doi:10.1108/F-08-2014-0066

Lall, S., Bowles, L., & Baird, R. (2013). Bridging the "Pioneer Gap": The Role of Accelerators in Launching High-Impact Enterprises. *Innovations, 8*(3-4), 105-137.

MacNeil, H. J., & Schoonmaker, M. G. (2017). Breaking the Entrepreneurial Glass Ceiling: An Examination of Gender Differences in the Early-Stage Accelerator Environment. In *United States Association for Small Business and Entrepreneurship Conference Proceedings* (p. 1222). United States Association for Small Business and Entrepreneurship.

Mueller, S., Volery, T., & von Siemens, B. (2012). What Do Entrepreneurs Actually Do? An Observational Study of Entrepreneurs Everyday Behavior in the Start-Up and Growth Stages. *Entrepreneurship Theory and Practice, 36*(5), 995–1017. doi:10.1111/j.1540-6520.2012.00538.x

Nigam, A. (2014). What Can Design Thinkers Learn from Entrepreneurs?. *Design Management Review, 25*(3), 28–29.

Pauwels, C., Clarysse, B., Wright, M., & Van Hove, J. (2016). Understanding a new generation incubation model: The accelerator. *Technovation, 50*, 13–24. doi:10.1016/j.technovation.2015.09.003

Price, R. (2004). The role of service providers in establishing networked regional business accelerators in Utah. *International Journal of Technology Management, 27*(5), 465–474. doi:10.1504/IJTM.2004.004283

Radojevich-Kelley, N., & Hoffman, D. L. (2012). Analysis of accelerator companies: An exploratory case study of their programs, processes, and early results. *Small Business Institute Journal, 8*(2), 54–70.

Raheem, S., & Akhuemonkhan, I. A. (2014). Enterprise development through incubation management. *Developing Country Studies, 4*(18), 67-82.

Ratinho, T. (2011). The role of Business Incubators in Facilitating Firm Development. In *Are They Helping? An Examination of Business Incubators' Impact on Tenant Firms*. University of Twente.

Rogova, E. (2014). The effectiveness of business incubators as the element of the universities spin-off strategy in Russia. *International Journal of Technology Management & Sustainable Development, 13*(3), 265–281. doi:10.1386/tmsd.13.3.265_1

Sakr, N. (2016). Survival or sustainability? Contributions of innovatively managed news ventures to the future of Egyptian journalism. *Journal of Media Business Studies, 13*(1), 45–59. doi:10.1080/16522354.2015.1125608

Salamzadeh, A. (2015 a). *Innovation Accelerators: Emergence of Startup Companies in Iran. 60th Annual ICSB World Conference*, Dubai, UAE.

Salamzadeh, A. (2015 b). New Venture Creation: Controversial Perspectives and Theories. *Economic Analysis, 48*(3/4), 101–109.

Salamzadeh, A., & Kawamorita, H. (2017). The enterprising communities and startup ecosystem in Iran. *Journal of Enterprising Communities, 11*(4).

Salamzadeh, A., & Kirby, D. A. (2017). Startup Companies: How startups grow?. *AD-minister, 30*(1), 9–29.

Salamzadeh, A., & Radovic Markovic, M. (2016). *Business Accelerators as Champions to achieve Resilient Growth: A Revolutionary Trend in a Developing Country*. International Scientific Conference on Impact of Economic Policies on Attaining Resilient Growth, Belgrade, Serbia.

Stagars, M. (2015). The lean start-up changed everything. In *University Startups and Spin-Offs* (pp. 15–27). Apress.

Wang, F. (2016). *Social Media, Entrepreneurs and Accelerators: Examining the Role of Brands and Networks* (Doctoral dissertation). Rensselaer Polytechnic Institute.

Weiblen, T., & Chesbrough, H. W. (2015). Engaging with startups to enhance corporate innovation. *California Management Review*, *57*(2), 66–90. doi:10.1525/cmr.2015.57.2.66

Welch, J. (2012). The power of collaboration. *Economic Development Journal*, *11*(4), 36–55.

Chapter 4
An Absorptive Capacity Perspective of Organizational Learning Through Social Media:
Evidence From the Ghanaian Fashion Industry

Richard Boateng
University of Ghana, Ghana

Edna Owusu-Bempah
University of Ghana, Ghana

Eric Ansong
University of Ghana, Ghana

ABSTRACT

The Absorptive Capacity Theory was used as the theoretical lens for this study to help analyze how organizations absorb new knowledge using social media tools and applications. A survey of fashion designers and employees numbering 196 was carried out in 55 fashion firms whereas two fashion firms were used in a case study. Data analysis was performed using the Structural Equation Modelling. The findings from the study suggest that Ghanaian fashion designers do not intensively use social media to assimilate knowledge but rather to acquire, transform and exploit knowledge. The popular social media applications include; Facebook, Twitter, and Instagram. Facebook, for instance, is used on a daily basis by most Ghanaian

DOI: 10.4018/978-1-5225-2956-9.ch004

fashion designers. Fashion designers use social media to acquire, transform and exploit knowledge through research, interaction, communication, and marketing with suppliers, customers, and other fashion designers. Future research can extend this work by looking at organizational learning and social media use in a different industry.

INTRODUCTION

Organizational learning is necessary for the successful operation of organizations. Businesses thrive on information and this information accumulates forming a knowledge base. Such knowledge can be acquired both internally and externally and must be managed properly to achieve organizational set goals and objectives (Karkoulian, Messarra & McCarthy, 2013). Therefore, it can be argued that communities that have mechanisms that create and connect relationships between individuals to work collectively for common goals is an organization (Boateng et al., 2009). According to Nonaka, Toyama and Konno (1998), critical among these mechanisms are those that result in sharing information and make the cognitive map of individuals, as employees, accessible for the greater good; thus, creating collective knowledge. Organizations learn and create knowledge through dynamic interactions between employees. Organizations have long recognized knowledge management (KM) as an important business strategy (Hull, Coombs & Peltu, 2000). A 2001 United States Government Accountability Office (GAO) report indicated that a substantial portion of the federal workforce would become eligible to retire or will retire over the next five to 10 years, and hence workforce planning is critical to ensure that agencies have sufficient and appropriate staff to account for these retirements. Usually, when people leave an organization, they take a wealth of knowledge about their jobs with them. Consequently, Lien, Hung, Yang and Li (2006) posits that firms have to pay particular attention to the enhancement of their learning patterns. One of the ways through which organizations can learn is through the use of social media tools or applications to acquire and also disseminate information both internally and externally (O'Reilly, 2005).

Quite a number of organizations have been asking what they can use social media for. Current literature demonstrates a dominance on social media and marketing (Hanna, 2011). On the other hand, in IS literature, social media has been studied from the perspectives of social media and text mining; social media and crisis management; and social media and organizational learning.

One very important area of study regarding social media is social media and text mining. He et al. (2013) carried out an in-depth case study, which applies text mining to analyse unstructured text content on Facebook and Twitter sites of the three largest pizza chains: Pizza Hut, Domino's Pizza and Papa John's Pizza. Results from the text mining and social media competitive analysis show that these pizza chains actively engaged their customers in social media. They suggested future research focus on finding innovative ways to turn businesses' social media fans from "like" to "buy". For example, pizzerias will have to provide consumers easy ways to purchase pizzas using social media from "selecting pizza, adding their selections to shopping carts, and completing purchases through payment with credit cards and points". Rickman and Cosenza (2007) have also examined the theoretical/conceptual development and application of weblog-text mining to fashion forecasting in general and street fashion trending in particular. They postulate that future research should look at semantic and image mining of the web as the next frontiers of data mining and trend spotting. According to Kaiser and Bodendorf (2012), combining text mining and social network analysis enables the study of opinion formation and yields encouraging results. They analysed opinion formation based on consumer dialogs in online forum.

Another area, which has also been studied is social media and organizational learning. A study by Bochenek and Blili (2013) looked at four companies of different sizes, different scopes of operation, and different industries. They found that all the companies learn socially and use social media to strengthen the organization and build business benefits through using social media as a marketing tool and having a strategic framework that makes the company active on social media. Their learning patterns (the learning process and the learning aggregation in social media) are, however, different. It shows that social media is beyond being a tool. They propose that future research should study a larger sample of companies in order to see the learning patterns and profiles of strategic management of social media at the statistically important level. A collaborative setting based on social media principles enables the sharing of different insights on current topic, and therefore adds value to an outcome by enriching information (Vuori & Okkonen, 2012). Chua and Banerjee (2013) analysed the extent to which the use of social media can support customer knowledge management (CKM) in organizations relying on a traditional bricks-and-mortar business model. From their findings, social media is not a tool exclusive to online businesses. It can be a potential game-changer in supporting CKM efforts even for traditional businesses.

Most of these research works on learning processes of organizations were carried out in developed countries (Vuori & Okkonen, 2012; Chua & Banerjee, 2013), little has been carried out in developing countries (Grabski, 2009), specifically Ghana. Moreover, there have been arguably no studies on organizational learning through social media using the Absorptive Capacity Theory as its theoretical lens, ascertaining the need for this study. Also, the most apparent gap in the use of methods was the lack of studies using the mixed-method approach. The qualitative studies tend to dominate this area of study.

Diverse studies have been carried out relating to social media as discussed above. However, this research would do an analysis of how organizations using social media and to understand the knowledge absorption process using the Absorptive Capacity Theory (ACT), which will serve as the theoretical lens for this research. To achieve the research purpose, the following objectives are outlined:

1. To describe the forms of learning for firms in the fashion industry;
2. To describe the sources of learning for firms in the fashion industry; and
3. To explain how social media supports learning in the fashion industry.

The first section is therefore the introduction to this paper. The second section also presents a review of literature pertaining to organizational learning and social media including the research framework that was adopted for this study. The constructs and variables of the framework are explained followed by how they were measured. The third section presents the study setting by providing a brief overview of the Ghanaian fashion industry studying specifically Vlisco and Nallem Clothing. The fifth section describes the research methodology adopted, which includes research design, data collection procedure and development of data collection instruments. The sixth section discusses the data collected from the field and is analysed using Structural Equation Modelling (SEM) and qualitative analysis. The last section presents a summary of the key findings, and contributions made to the study of organizational learning through social media in the Ghanaian fashion industry. Implications for practice and recommendations for future research are also mentioned in this section.

LITERATURE REVIEW

This section comprises of a brief overview of absorption or learning, the social media and learning as well as the research framework for the study which is Absorptive Capacity Theory.

Learning Through Web 2.0

Through knowledge sharing and interaction with people there may be an emerging opportunity for organizations to adapt Web 2.0 for learning. The need to learn and the learning process in organizations are addressed by this opportunity. Web 2.0 can be considered as a learning enabler that allows people to access their knowledge and share with others. Individuals who use Web 2.0 applications are able to create knowledge more efficiently than the conventional methods because of their collaboration properties. It is through this collaboration that knowledge can be shared at the two levels; individual and collective. At the organizational level, knowledge assets must be made accessible by the tools that enable learning (Dixon, 1994; 2000); Web 2.0 facilitates this. The idea is to make internal knowledge visible and to access external sources of new knowledge through 'boundary spanning' (Pawlosky et al., 2001).

For the purpose of this study, social media will include Instant Messaging tools (WhatsApp), Content Management tools (YouTube, Blogger), and social media tools (Facebook, Twitter). Some of these tools are under Web 2.0 technologies.

Absorption/Learning and Social Media

The process of acquiring knowledge is termed learning (Cook & Yanow, 1993). Learning can occur at two levels; the individual and the organizational levels. Employees within an organization can acquire knowledge to facilitate their specific business roles; however, to achieve organizational goals such knowledge must be diffused to other parts of the organization (Hong, 1999). Organizational learning implies knowledge acquisition by members across the organization and the diffusion of lessons learnt by individuals to other parts of the organization to enhance collective understanding, adaptation and easy response to change (Dodgson, 1993).

Arguably, not all learning leads to adaptation. Similarly, not all learning at the individual level generates into learning at the organizational level. Learning occurs in a more limited form and in a less significant way in some organizations. Such learning does not lead to a reassessment of values and adaptation.

There are different types and methods of learning. Argyris and Schön (1978) postulate three types of learning that happen within an organization, namely: single loop-learning; double-loop learning; and deutro-learning. Single-loop learning happens when an organization identifies an error and undertakes corrective measures without questioning or transforming its current policy. Double-loop learning also occurs when the error detected which has to be corrected requires alteration of the organization's underlying policies, norms and objectives. Basic assumptions are re-tested in the quest to understand the problem faced. With deutro-learning, members develop new strategies after they have learnt about previous context of learning and have understood the reasons behind the ability and inability to learn in previous context. According to Dodgson (1993), Organisational learning starts with double-loop learning. Very few organizations are effective with double-loop and deutro-learning; however, most of them tend to do well with single-loop learning.

Social media tends to enhance collaboration within an organization. Social media is certainly in the public eye at the moment. For instance, 2013 statistics from Alexa.com depicts that social media is ranked the 2nd top website out of the top 500 websites worldwide. Today, Facebook is the largest social network in the world with more than 5000 active users of whom 50% log in on a daily basis. It is not surprising therefore, that marketers are devising ways to use Facebook to reach their target audience. In our working lives, an aspect where collaboration plays an important role is the aspect of learning. A greater proportion of what individuals in an organization learn comes through mutual problem-solving and the sharing of experiences. However, Shepherd (2011) is of the view that some people do not benefit from working within the same four walls hence making face-to-face interactions difficult to come by and limiting the opportunities for collaboration in the past. Social media has the potential to maximize collaborative learning, not just now and then but on a continuous basis, and not just when and where it suits others, but at a time and place of your own choice.

There are diverse ways in which social media (Shepherd, 2011) can be used to facilitate workplace learning. Firstly, in order to enrich longer formal programmes, such as professional and postgraduate qualifications and management development programmes, social media can be used as a vehicle for group collaboration that is on-going. Many firms are already reaping benefits from using forums to share ideas and discuss issues, blogs as learning journals, and wikis as a focus for group collaborative projects, not to mention use of podcasts and videos as a means for sharing research. Another example is the use of online communities of practice to share new ideas and debate issues. Those in more of a hurry might now use micro-blogging services such as Twitter and Yammer to quickly update peers on new developments (Pawlosky, 2001). Learning largely takes place on-demand, at the point when it is needed most. Organizations can do their best to satisfy the needs of employees for on-demand information but they will scarcely be able to exhaust it all on a top-down basis. Members of an organization can use social networks to find sources of expertise or offer their own expertise to others; they can also diffuse their own home-made learning content, using whatever medium is best suited to the job and their talents.

Learning at work is as much about ''learning from'' as it is ''learning to''. We learn through our own experiences and the experiences of those around us, but only if we make a deliberate attempt to reflect. Here is where blogging can play a valuable role. This discipline will not be for everybody, but for those that really engage with the medium the opportunities for learning exceed all others. Writing a blog post to capture an idea or review an experience forces you to reflect and clarify your thoughts. It greatly amplifies the possibility that the experience will be a lasting one – in other words, you will have learnt something (Pham, 2011).

Learning and Social Media Models

According to Cook and Yanow (1993) the process of acquiring knowledge is termed as learning. Boateng et al. (2009) used the SECI model to study Web 2.0 and organizational learning. The SECI model (Nonaka & Takeuchi, 1995) looks at knowledge conversion in four modes: socialization, externalization, combination and internalization. The emphasis of this model is knowledge conversion. This study will not lay emphasis on knowledge conversion but the absorptive capacity of firms.

Linke and Zerfass (2012) used the Social Media Governance framework to study online communication management. The emphasis of this framework is social media governance, which involves the formal or informal frameworks, which regulate the actions of the members of an organization within the social web. The framework looks at the following: regulatory frameworks for social media; skills for social media: strategies for social media PR; and activities in social media PR. This is not what this study seeks to do.

Finally, the Theory of Performance Feedback was used by Schwab (2007) to study performance feedback with the goal of identifying principles that will promote a more integrated understanding of learning during the execution of innovative practices and contribute to the development of more fine-grained multilevel models of organizational learning.

Absorptive Capacity Theory (ACT)

Absorptive Capacity Theory inspects the degree to which a firm can perceive the estimation of new outside data, acclimatize it, and apply it toward attaining to organizational objectives (Cohen & Levinthal, 1989; 1990). The theory expects that retaining new learning can help a firm get to be more inventive and adaptable and accomplish larger amounts of execution than it would without engrossing new information. The theory additionally expects that organizations that have higher capacities for retaining new learning will have a game changer over firms with lower capacities. The theory expects that firms oblige an information base to have the capacity to assimilate and utilize new learning. Keeping in mind the end goal to perceive, acclimatize, and utilize new information, firms must have a learning base that is moderately like the new learning that is being transformed. Most hierarchical developments originate from acquiring thoughts from other individuals, as opposed to through imagining them (March & Simon, 1958). There are two components that will influence an association's impetuses to obtain new information: (1) the amount of learning accessible to retain and endeavour; and (2) the trouble and expenses included in engrossing that new learning. An organization's capacity to discover and utilize new information relies on the absorptive limit of its workers. In any case, an association's absorptive limit is not simply the total of its individuals' absorptive limits. Associations rely upon proficient people to survey and assess the potential positives and negatives of new learning. These individuals can serve as "guards" who can avoid or encourage the ingestion of new learning

Zahra and George (2002) re-conceptualized part of the theory. They took the steps of recognizing the value of new knowledge and assimilating and applying it, and created four capabilities or dimensions: (1) acquisition; (2) assimilation; (3) transformation; and (4) exploitation. (They refer to acquisition and assimilation as "potential" absorptive capacity; transformation and exploitation as "realized" absorptive capacity.) Murovec and Prodan (2009) showed that there can be two sorts of absorptive limit: demand-pull and science-push. Demand-pull alludes to new learning obtained from business sources (for instance, clients, rivalry, and suppliers). Science-push alludes to new learning obtained from exploration and exploratory sources (such as books, diaries, meetings, exchange shows, and other scholastic sources).

Justifying the Use of Absorptive Capacity Theory (ACT)

Primarily most of the studies on organizational learning and social media used theoretical frameworks in their studies. For instance, Roblek et al. (2013) used the Social Media Value Added Model to study the role of social media in enhancing organizational change and value creation in knowledge-based industries. However, this research study will use the Absorptive Capacity Theory (ACT) as its theoretical lens.

In addition, the literature reviewed on organizational learning and social media uses several research frameworks, arguably, none of these studies have used the Absorptive Capacity Theory (ACT) as its theoretical lens. Chua and Banerjee (2013) used a Customer Knowledge Management Framework in their study. Vuori (2012) used the Resource-based View (RBV) to study Web 2.0 and social media use. Similarly, Bartlett-Bragg (2009) used the Social Learning Network Approach in studying social learning networks. None of these studies stated used the Absorptive Capacity Theory (ACT). This reinforces the need to use ACT as the theoretical lens to study organizational learning and social media from a different theoretical view.

Lastly, the absorptive capacity theory emphasizes a firm's recognition of new external information, assimilating that information, and applying that information with the aim of attaining organizational goals (Cohen & Levinthal, 1989; 1990). Social media is external to an organization hence using this theory is suitable for this study. Wagner et al. (2014) in their study used the SECI model to study knowledge creation, which can be both internal and external as well as across different sources.

Figure 1. The conceptual framework
Adapted from Zahra and George (2002).

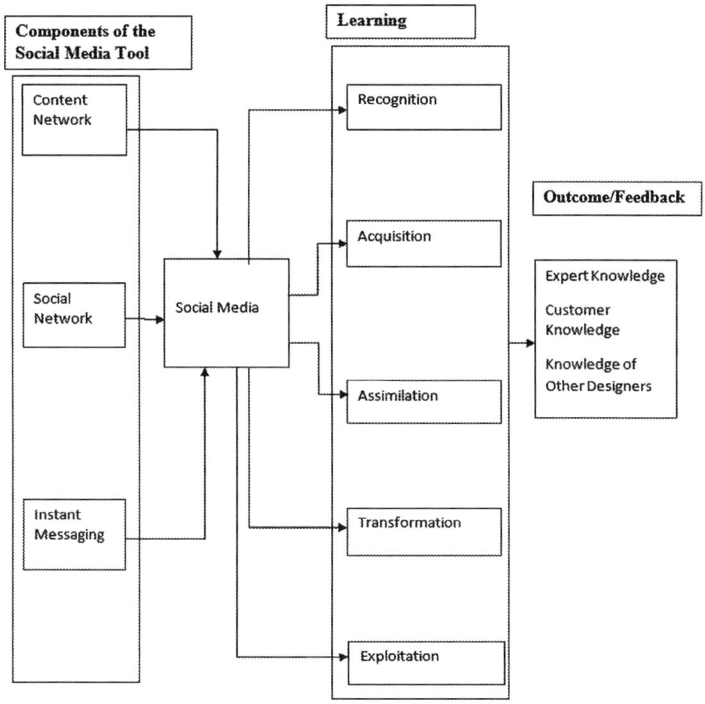

This study however is using social media as its sole external source of knowledge to the industry under study to measure the impact of social media use on organizational learning.

This framework as shown in Figure 1 will help to answer the research question of "what are the sources of knowledge for firms in the Ghanaian fashion industry". According to ACT, the sources of knowledge for an organization are four, which can be categorized into internal and external sources. The internal sources consist of the following;

1. The firm conducts its own research and development (R&D).
2. The firm derives new knowledge from its own current manufacturing operations.
3. The firm borrows new knowledge from other organizations or other sources.
4. The firm purchases new knowledge, such as through buying new equipment, hiring new knowledgeable people, or paying a consultant to train individuals in the use of a new method.

In addition, the framework will help to answer the question: "what are the forms of knowledge for firms in the Ghanaian fashion industry"? According to Murovec and Prodan (2009), there are two kinds of absorptive capacity:

1. Demand-pull; and
2. Science-push.

Demand-pull alludes to new knowledge acquired from market or business sources (for example, customers, competition i.e. from other fashion designers, experts and suppliers). Science-push alludes to new learning derived from exploration and scientific sources (such as books, journals, conferences, trade shows, and other scholarly sources).

Furthermore, the conceptual framework will help to answer the question: "How do social media support organizational learning in fashion firms in Ghana?" And the sub-questions:

1. What are the types of social media often used by firms in the Ghanaian fashion industry?
2. Which of the two types of social media (social network or content network) better enhances PACAP (Potential Absorptive Capacity); and which of the two better enhances RACAP (Realized Absorptive Capacity)?

HYPOTHESIS DEVELOPMENT

Social Media and Absorptive Capacity

The relationship between network structure and absorptive capacity has been addressed by previous studies (Tsai, 2001; Van Gilsing et al., 2008), but without reference to the organization of networking behaviour. In a study by Peltola (2014), social network literature was used to hypothesize on the organization of networking behaviour and its relation with absorption of external knowledge. In a study about networking behaviour of hospitals, Goes and Park (1997) established that the type and degree of ties affect the ability of the firm to integrate and assimilate external knowledge. Frequency of contact, as one of the indicators of strong ties (Granovetter 1982; Krackhardt 1992), is considered an important relational trait, which enables transfer of especially complex knowledge and information entailed in innovation (Krackhardt 1992; Uzzi 1997; Hansen 1999; Reagans & McEvily 2003; Van Gilsing & Nooteboom 2005; Nooteboom et al., 2007). At the same time, a wide network range (Reagans & McEvily 2003) is important to gain new external knowledge.

An individual with a widespread network of connections across multiple pools of knowledge and expertise bridges holes between people and is exposed to more diverse knowledge (Reagans & McEvily, 2003).

Boateng et al. (2009) is of the view that the Internet has introduced the next level of collaboration to the doorsteps of organizations, and it is termed 'Web 2.0' (which includes social media). According to them, arguably little academic research has so far been conducted on the implications of this new approach for the domain of organizational learning.

Social media is a very effective networking structure. For fashion designers, interaction with different types of actors (customers, fashion bloggers, other fashion designers, suppliers etc.) may be important for accumulation of relevant information and knowledge to realize different types of goals and profitability. This is being made possible through the social media. Frequent contact with customers and other actors through social media, for instance Facebook, will enable the dissemination of complex knowledge and information (Nooteboom et al., 2007). Social media tools, applications and web applications are key to enhancing the use of social media to learn.

Reagans and McEvily (2003) conclude that an individual surrounded by a diverse network could transfer knowledge across a structural hole, even when the connection is weak. Apparently, transferring knowledge and maintaining a diverse network are related, as experience with one of the two helps to achieve the other. Debatably, fashion designers engaged in more frequent networking with a wider range of knowledge sources are more likely to experience a rich exchange of knowledge and in this way, are more skilled in recognizing and approaching specific actors for the acquisition of the knowledge that they need. Frequency of interaction and information exchange increases the amount of information the fashion designers accumulate, which contributes to a better ability to identify and understand the pieces of knowledge that are relevant for their own firms and profitability. As the higher level of inter-action increases the likelihood of (tacit and explicit) knowledge recognition, transfer and assimilation (Dhanaraj et al. 2004), it is expected that:

H1: The use of social media by fashion designers has a positive relationship with the recognition capacity of knowledge by these fashion designers.

H2: The use of social media by fashion designers has a positive relationship with the acquisition capacity of knowledge by these fashion designers.

H3: The use of social media by fashion designers has a positive relationship with the assimilation capacity of knowledge by these fashion designers.

Recognition and Acquisition Capacity

The acquisition capacity of fashion designers can be demonstrated in the ability of fashion designers to identify knowledge and the need of that knowledge through frequency of contact with the prevailing social media tools, applications or web applications. According to Zahra and George (2002), the recognition capacity of knowledge implies "recognizing the need for new knowledge". Recognizing the need for new knowledge results in the collection of that knowledge.

H4: The recognition capacity of fashion designers has a positive relationship with their acquisition capacity.

Acquisition and Assimilation Capacity

Acquisition capacity of the fashion designers can be reflected by more skills in collecting knowledge about developments in the sector through discussions with business partners, fashion bloggers and customers through social media: for instance, getting feedback from customers on preferred styles (helping to know fashion trends) and also acquiring information on market competition and using that knowledge to meet customer specifications, make changes to their business (styles, designs and marketing strategies), and detect new possibilities so as to attain the organizational goal of profitability.

Consequently, fashion designers' acquisition capacity is expected to have a positive relationship with their assimilation capacity.

H5: The recognition capacity of fashion designers has a positive relationship with their acquisition capacity.

Assimilation and Transformation Capacity

Fashion designers who are more skilled in the recognition of changes in technical possibilities and who are always among the first to detect changes in fashion trends and changes in market competition are said to have a better ability to analyse, process, interpret and understand external knowledge and information (assimilation capacity). Fashion designers with higher assimilation capacity are also expected to be more skilful in assessing the relevancy of new information and knowledge for their own firms. Greater ability to understand new possibilities and opportunities is expected to result in more skill in recognizing the usefulness of new and external knowledge for profitability of their own firms and a greater capacity to translate new information and knowledge into changes and adaptations. Accordingly, it is hypothesized:

H6: The assimilation capacity of fashion designers has a positive relationship with their transformation capacity.

Transformation and Exploitation Capacity

It is expected that the capacity to transform and apply knowledge to one's own firm has a positive relationship related to exploitation capacity. Skill in assessing the relevancy and usability of new information for profitability on one's own firm, plus the capacity and ability to translate market trends into adaptations in the firm, is expected to result in the ability to make an additional step. The latter is related to exploitation of knowledge. Firms with high transformation capacity are expected to be more skilful in transposing the information into profitable changes and adaptations on the firm. Fashion designers who translate new knowledge into actual adaptations usually also have an idea about how the adaptation will contribute to increased profit. Therefore, it is expected that:

H7: The transformation capacity of fashion designers has a positive relationship with their exploitation capacity.

The hypotheses discussed are captured in the conceptual framework as shown in Figure 2.

METHODOLOGY

This section highlights the methodology adopted for the study. It consists of research paradigm, research design, research approach, sample size, data collection method, data analysis techniques, ethical considerations, research limitations and challenges.

This study was undertaken from the perspective of realism. The realism paradigm provides the information systems researcher with both elements of positivism and constructivism (Healy & Perry, 2000). While positivism concerns a single, concrete reality and constructivism multiple realities, realism enables the IS researcher to acquire multiple perceptions about a single, mind-independent reality (Bisman, 2002). This study in extending the use of realism in IS research, gains the opportunity of obtaining detailed answers to the question of the impact social media has on organizational learning – thus analysing from the perspective of the Absorptive Capacity Theory (ACT). Realism recognizes that perceptions have certain plasticity (Churchland, 1979) and that there are differences between reality and people's perceptions of reality (Bisman, 2002), rather than being supposedly value-free, as in positive research, or value-laden as in interpretive research (Lincoln & Guba,

Figure 2. The conceptual framework and hypothesis
Adapted from Zahra and George (2002).

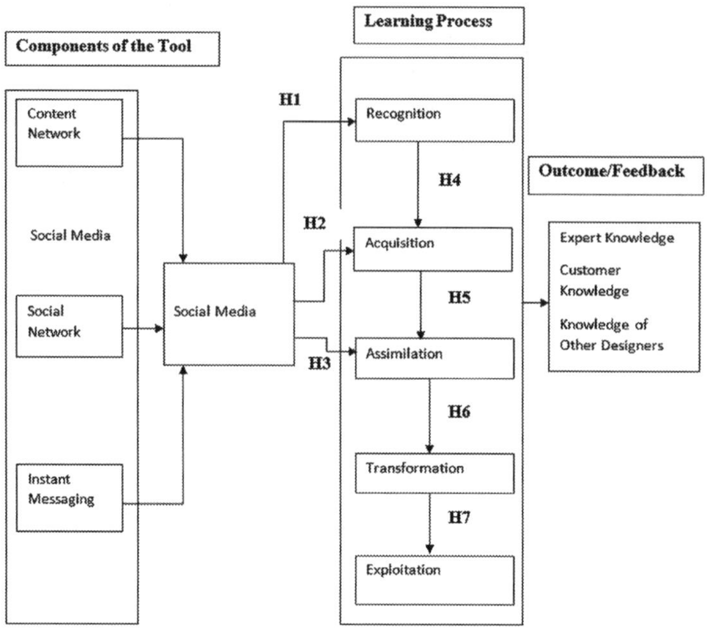

1985). The researcher therefore adopted both quantitative and qualitative methods for this research.

The type of mixed method approach used was the sequential explanatory strategy. The quantitative method was used before the qualitative method. In this approach, quantitative data are collected and analysed first and the results used to inform the subsequent qualitative phase. This explains why this strategy is considered explanatory.

Conducting the Survey

According to Castillo (2009), samples are drawn because it will be impractical to investigate all members of a target population. Sampling is a process of selecting research participants (Creswell, 2009). To arrive at the sample or target population for this study, data collection was therefore scheduled in two stages consisting of a pilot study, which took place from 1st May, 2014 to 5th May, 2014; and a main study which took place from 6th May 2014 to 12th May, 2014. In the pilot study, data (questionnaires) were collected across five different Ghanaian fashion firms. The firms selected were obtained from the internet. The criteria for selection were related to the researcher's theoretical concepts, namely:

- Learning organizations
- Fashion firms which learn though the social media

After the pilot survey, fifty (50) organizations were added to the sample size to continue with the actual data collection.

Questionnaire Development

The questionnaires for the survey were designed to meet the purpose of the research and to answer the research questions. The researcher administered the questionnaires among the 55 fashion firms used for the study. The Table 1 shows how the researcher designed the survey questionnaires.

Data Collection

Data was collected among the 55 fashion houses in Ghana on a purposive as well as snowballing basis. The questionnaires were left with the organizations to complete after which they called the researcher to fetch them. In all, 196 completed questionnaires were returned.

Table 1. Questionnaire development

Hypothesis	Factors	No. of Questions
H1: The use of social media by fashion designers has a positive relationship with their recognition capacity **H4:** The recognition capacity of fashion designers has a positive relationship with their acquisition capacity	Recognition Capacity	2
H2: The use of social media by fashion designers has a positive relationship with their acquisition capacity. **H5:** The acquisition capacity of fashion designers has a positive relationship with their assimilation capacity	Acquisition Capacity	3
H3: The use of social media by fashion designers has a positive relationship with their assimilation capacity.	Assimilation Capacity	3
H6: The assimilation capacity of fashion designers has a positive relationship with their transformation capacity	Transformation Capacity	3
H7: The transformation capacity of fashion designers has a positive relationship with their exploitation capacity	Exploitation Capacity	3

Source: Author's Construct.

Selecting Case Organization

At the end of the survey data collection, only two organizations; Aya Morrison and Inka Accessories gave access to the researchers for a case study and had sufficient experience to enable such a detailed analysis of Organisational Learning through social media. The selected companies had been in operation for over 5 years and were actively involved in using social media for Organisational Learning. Evidence of their use of social media for Organisational Learning was authenticated through documents and interviews with CEOs and the responses of employees to the questionnaires administered to them. The firm also assured its commitment to the case study.

Questions Used and Data Collection

The primary data collection method employed was semi-structured interviews. The researcher interviewed the fashion designers and Chief Executive officers (CEO) of the case firms with regard to the issue being discussed. For Aya Morrison Fashion firm, the CEO was the person the researcher interviewed for the case study. She has a Bachelor of Arts degree. For Inka Accessories, the CEO who holds a Bachelor of Science degree was interviewed. The interview for Aya Morrison Fashion firm was conducted on 12th June, 2014 at the office of the CEO with the aim of determining the impact of social media on the organization's learning ability and the profitability of the organization. The interview for Inka Accessories was carried out on 14th June, 2014 via telephone. The CEOs were interviewed to obtain a wider view of the ideal situation of learning in a typical Ghanaian fashion firm and they were indeed able to account largely for the impact of social media on their learning potential as a business. The interviews were taped and transcribed, with copies of transcribed interviews returned to the interviewees to check and resolve any discrepancies.

Realism encourages the use of multiple data collection methods to enhance triangulation of perspectives and know the single reality and people's perception of the reality. The researcher further observed the CEOs, brand managers and other employees of these firms to find out their perception on the use of social media in organizational learning. Secondary data sources included documentary materials of the organization's history, industry reports and verified online information.

Mode of Analysis

The survey questionnaires were coded and entered into the IBM SPSS Amos software (version 22) in order to run the analysis. The data set was screened and cleaned. This was done to rectify mistakes that occurred during data entering.

Three techniques were used, namely: Confirmatory Factor Analysis to analyse the factors of the Absorptive Capacity Theory (ACT) to understand how social media supports organizational learning; Excel was used to analyse the forms and sources of knowledge and to analyse the tools and applications to verify those which are frequently used by fashion designers, and to discover those applications which have an effect on the Potential Absorptive Capacity (PACAP); and crosstabs were used to test the hypothesis whereas the Structural Equation Modelling was used to confirm the factors of the Absorptive Capacity Theory (ACT) and to as well test the fitness of the model using Pclose.

RESEARCH ANALYSIS AND DISCUSSION

This section presents the results of the study and is organized into two main sections: background of the sample and examination of the hypotheses. To examine the hypotheses, descriptive statistics of cross tabulations were used to test the hypothesized model of social media facilitating organizational learning and identify important relations between the variables (Recognition, Acquisition, Assimilation, Transformation and Exploitation) of interest. PACAP means Potential Absorptive Capacity which encapsulates Recognition, Assimilation and Acquisition of knowledge whereas RACAP implies Realized Absorptive Capacity which captures Transformation and Exploitation Capacity. Confirmatory factor analysis was used to confirm the factors in the hypothesized model. Descriptive statistics were used to explain the forms and sources of knowledge and the tools and applications predominantly used in the Ghanaian fashion industry.

Background of the Study

One hundred and ninety-six (196) respondents participated in this study. The participants' backgrounds, i.e., age, level of completed education and the number of workers in the organization, the number of years the company has been in existence and the company's turnover are shown in Table 2.

Frequency Distribution

The frequency analysis shown below answer the following research questions:

1. What are the forms of learning for firms in the Ghanaian fashion industry?
2. What are the sources of learning for firms in the Ghanaian fashion industry?

Table 2. Frequency table of demographic variables

Category	Variables	*f*	Percent
Age	Less than 18	4	2.0
	18-25	90	45.9
	26-30	88	44.9
	31-35	14	7.1
	Total	196	100
Education	Senior High	67	34.2
	Diploma	16	8.2
	Bachelor's Degree	96	49.0
	Master's Degree	14	7.1
	Professional Certificate	3	1.5
	Total	196	100
Years of company's existence	1-5	81	41.3
	6-10	32	16.3
	11-15	55	28.1
	Over 20 years	28	14.3
	Total	196	100
Turnover	Less than 3,000	20	10.2
	3000- 10,000	114	58.2
	100,000 or more	62	31.6
	Total	196	100

Source: Field survey, 2014.

3. How does social media support organizational learning in fashion firms in Ghana?

Forms of Learning for Firms in the Fashion Industry

Demand-Pull Form of Learning

The respondents were asked to indicate the extent to which they communicate and interact with others (customers, fashion bloggers, other fashion designers) to acquire knowledge through social media. The results of the analysis showed that 11.2% (n= 22) of respondents indicated they have a neutral stance on the usage of social media for communication and interaction with others. Whereas, 32.7% (n= 64) of respondents indicated that they intensively use social media to communicate and interact with others through social media to acquire knowledge. Acquiring knowledge through others demonstrates the form of knowledge termed demand-pull postulated from the Absorptive Capacity Theory (ACT). This answers an aspect of a research question raised for this study: "what are the forms of knowledge which aid learning in fashion firms in Ghana?"

Finding 1: Most fashion firms use social media to communicate with others (who could be customers, suppliers, fashion bloggers, fashion enthusiasts etc.) very intensively to acquire knowledge

In addition, respondents were asked to indicate the extent to which they make use of social media knowledge and information for marketing (communication). The data analysis also showed that, 48.5% (n= 95) of respondents intensively use the social media, knowledge and information for marketing; 32.1% (n=63) of respondents semi-intensively use the social media, knowledge and information for marketing; whereas 19.4% (n=38) of respondents use the knowledge and information for marketing. Knowledge acquired from market sources such as marketing can be classified under the demand-pull form of knowledge. Further answering the research question: "what are the forms of knowledge which aid learning in fashion firms in Ghana?"

Finding 2: Most fashion designers in Ghana intensively use social media to acquire knowledge from market sources through marketing.

Respondents also indicated the extent to which they used of social media knowledge and information for designing (generative purposes). From the analysis, 52.6% (n= 103) of the respondents intensively use social media knowledge and information for designing; 35.2% (n=69) of respondents semi-intensively use social media knowledge and information for designing; whereas 12.2% (n=24) of respondents use the knowledge and information very intensively for designing. Knowledge acquired from market sources such as competition and suppliers as well as customers can be used for designing which falls under the demand-pull form of knowledge, also answering the research question: "what are the forms of knowledge which aid learning in fashion firms in Ghana?"

Finding 3: Most fashion designers in Ghana intensively use knowledge from social media for designing

Science-Push Form of Learning

The respondents indicated the extent to which they prevented all employees voluntarily transmitting useful scientific and technological knowledge acquired to others. The data analysis showed that most fashion firms in Ghana do not prevent their employees from disseminating useful scientific information to other employees or even to customers. This knowledge falls into the category of science-push knowledge as defined by ACT, also answering the research question: "what are the forms of knowledge which aid learning in fashion firms in Ghana?"

Finding 4: Most fashion designers in Ghana do not prevent their employees from transmitting useful scientific and technological knowledge.

Sources of Learning (Knowledge) for Firms in the Fashion Industry

Internal Source of Knowledge

The extent at which the respondents coordinated and integrated all phases of the Research and Development process with its interrelations with the functional tasks of production, marketing and translated external information into adaptations were also analysed. Deductions from the analysis indicated that most fashion firms in Ghana use social media to carry out research intensively and the knowledge (new styles, new designs and new fashion trends) is adapted by these fashion houses into new designs. Knowledge of this form is acquired internally through R&D; answering the research question: "what are the sources of knowledge which aid learning in fashion firms in Ghana?"

Finding 5: Most fashion firms in Ghana use social media to carry out research intensively and the knowledge (new styles, new designs and new fashion trends) is adapted by these fashion houses into new design.

External Source of Knowledge

The analysis of data indicated that 7, 54.6% (n= 107) of respondents "strongly agree" that they translate external information into new business applications; 41.8% (n=82) of respondents "agree" that they translate external information into new business applications; whereas 3.6% (n=7) of respondents have a neutral stance on translating external information into new business applications. External information according to ACT could either be borrowed knowledge or purchased knowledge.

Hence, fashion designers either borrow or purchase external knowledge and translate them into new business applications (new marketing strategies, new designs etc.); also, answering the research question: "what are the sources of knowledge which aid learning in fashion firms in Ghana?"

Finding 6: Fashion designers either borrow or purchase external knowledge and translate them into new business applications (new marketing strategies, new designs etc.).

Both External and Internal Source of Knowledge

Respondents indicated how they make use of social media knowledge and information for interaction. According to ACT, knowledge could be obtained both internally and externally and the analysis showed that fashion firms in Ghana obtain knowledge or disseminate knowledge through interaction with customers or suppliers through social media (for instance; Facebook, Blogger); further answering the research question: "what are the sources of knowledge which aid learning in fashion firms in Ghana?"

Finding 7: Fashion firms in Ghana obtain knowledge or disseminate knowledge through interaction with customers or suppliers through social media (for instance; Facebook, Blogger).

Social Media as Tools and in Usage

Application of Social Media

Respondents indicated the extent to which they normally use social media applications to identify knowledge and the data analysis showed that communicative, interactive and generative social media applications are mostly used by fashion firms in Ghana to recognize new knowledge, and the tools and web applications under these applications can be classified as social networks. Hence, social networks are mostly used for acquiring new knowledge. Recognition capacity forms a part of PACAP, hence it can be concluded that the type of social media that supports PACAP the most are social networks, thus, answering the research question: "How do social media support organizational learning in fashion firms in Ghana?" and the sub-questions:

1. What are the types of social media often used by firms in the fashion industry?
2. Which of the two types of social media (social network and content network) greatly enhance PACAP (Potential Absorptive Capacity) and which of the two greatly enhance RACAP (Realized Absorptive Capacity)?

Finding 8: Social networks are mostly used for acquiring new knowledge. Recognition capacity forms a part of PACAP, hence it can be concluded that the type of social media that supports PACAP the most are social networks.

Social Media as Tools for Assimilation

The analysis of data shows that Facebook, YouTube, Myspace, Twitter, Podcasts and Flickr are the social media tools very intensively used by fashion firms to acquire knowledge. These web applications can be classified under social network type of social media web application. And these web applications are those mostly used to acquire knowledge. Hence, it can be concluded that social networks support PACAP since acquisition capacity is an aspect of PACAP. This further answers the research question: "How do social media support organizational learning in fashion firms in Ghana?"

Finding 9: Social networks support PACAP since acquisition capacity is an aspect of PACAP.

Confirmation of Factors

Discussion of Factors of Absorptive Capacity

This section is in two parts: the measurement model will be completely assessed to find out the factors which are significant from the conceptual model and which fit the measurement model; as well as a summary of the hypotheses which were accepted and rejected respectively.

The factors of ACT according to Zahra and George's (2002) re-conceptualizing of part of the ACT theory, thus including the step of recognizing the value of new knowledge are these four capabilities or dimensions: (1) acquisition; (2) assimilation; (3) transformation; and (4) exploitation. However, based on the critique of Turodan and Dorova (2007), the step of recognizing the value of new knowledge is included in this study. The following are therefore the constructs that measure ACT for the purpose of this study:

1. Recognition Capacity
2. Acquisition Capacity
3. Assimilation Capacity
4. Transformation Capacity
5. Exploitation Capacity

The Figure 3 has factor loadings, which measure the four capabilities of the Absorptive Capacity Theory (ACT). From the measurement, some first order latent variables have factor loading below the recommended threshold of 0.70. Consequently, those variables were dropped resulting in a final measurement model, which shows the factors which truly measure the absorptive capacity of fashion designers in the Ghanaian fashion industry.

Assessment of the Overall Measurement Model

Some first order latent variables that had factor loading below the recommended threshold of 0.70 were deleted at the validation stage of the measurement model. The variables which were dropped include; AC2 (from the Acquisition Capacity Factor), AS1, AS2, AS3 (from the Assimilation Capacity Factor), TR2 (from the Transformation Capacity Factor), and EC2 (from the Exploitation Capacity Factor). The Assimilation Capacity Factor was dropped completely. After the problematic factors were deleted from the initial constructs, there was a regeneration of the measurement model with just eight first order latent variables; and there was much improvement in the results as compared to the initial measurement model. Standardized factor loadings above the threshold were recorded for all the eight first order latent variables. Then, the model was fitted as was done earlier with the first model using the goodness of fit indices of absolute, incremental and parsimonious fit measures. The final measurement model is depicted in Figure 4 with the respective

Figure 3. Initial measurement model
Source: Field Data.

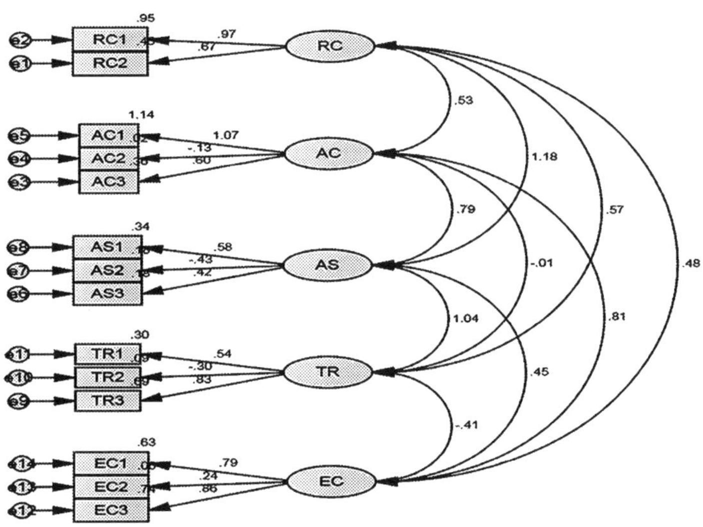

Figure 4. Final measurement model
Source: Field Data.

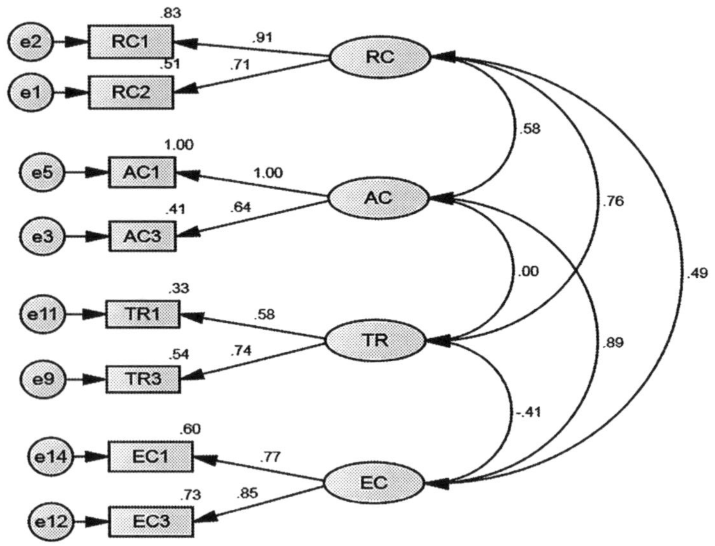

factor loadings while Tables 3 and 4 shows the goodness of fit indices and average variable estimation.

The p-value of the final measurement was not significant therefore showing that there is no statistical difference between the factors of the measurement model, implying that the model best fits this study. In terms of the RMSEA, the final model had a value of 0.076, which is less than 0.08 as recommended, therefore, the model fits the dataset. The incremental fit indices obtained in the final measurement model were greater than 0.90 ranging from 0.97 to 0.99 which shows the model fits the data set. Whereas the parsimonious fit indices also recorded values of 0.315 and 0.318 less than the recommended value of greater than 0.50.

The Figure 3 has factor loadings, which measure the four capabilities of the Absorptive Capacity Theory (ACT). From the measurement, some first order latent variables have factor loading below the recommended threshold of 0.70. Consequently, those variables were dropped resulting in a final measurement model, which shows the factors which truly measure the absorptive capacity of fashion designers in the Ghanaian fashion industry.

Assessment of the Overall Measurement Model

Some first order latent variables that had factor loading below the recommended threshold of 0.70 were deleted at the validation stage of the measurement model.

Table 3. Goodness-of-fit indices for final measurement model

Goodness-of-Fit Indices	Benchmark	Final Model
Absolute Goodness of Fit Measure		
Chi-square (CMIN) ($\chi 2$)	P ≥ 0.05	19.011
Chi-square /degree of freedom	≤ 2	2.112
Absolute Badness of Fit Measure		
Root mean Square Error of Approximation (RMSEA)	≤ 0.08	0.076
Incremental Fit Measure		
Comparative Fit Index (CFI)	≥ 0.90	0.989
Incremental fit index (IFI)	≥ 0.90	0.989
Turker-Lewis Index (TLI)	≥ 0.90	0.965
Parsimony Fit Measure		
Parsimony Comparative of Fit index (PCFI)	≥ 0.50	0.318
Parsimony Normed of Fit index (PNFI)	≥ 0.50	0.315

Source: Field Data.

Table 4. Shared variance

Construct	CR	AVE	MSV	ASV	EC	RC	AC	TR
EC	0.796	0.661	0.797	0.380	0.813			
RC	0.875	0.791	0.726	0.407	0.469	0.890		
AC	0.816	0.698	0.797	0.358	0.893	0.524	0.835	
TR	0.669	0.530	0.726	0.283	-0.348	0.852	0.052	0.728

Source: Analysis output.

The variables which were dropped include; AC2 (from the Acquisition Capacity Factor), AS1, AS2, AS3 (from the Assimilation Capacity Factor), TR2 (from the Transformation Capacity Factor), and EC2 (from the Exploitation Capacity Factor). The Assimilation Capacity Factor was dropped completely. After the problematic factors were deleted from the initial constructs, there was a regeneration of the measurement model with just eight first order latent variables; and there was much improvement in the results as compared to the initial measurement model. Standardized factor loadings above the threshold were recorded for all the eight first order latent variables. Then, the model was fitted as was done earlier with the first model using the goodness of fit indices of absolute, incremental and parsimonious fit measures. The final measurement model is depicted in Figure 4 with the respective factor loadings while Tables 3 and 4 shows the goodness of fit indices and average variable estimation.

The p-value of the final measurement was not significant therefore showing that there is no statistical difference between the factors of the measurement model, implying that the model best fits this study. In terms of the RMSEA, the final model had a value of 0.076, which is less than 0.08 as recommended, therefore, the model fits the dataset. The incremental fit indices obtained in the final measurement model were greater than 0.90 ranging from 0.97 to 0.99 which shows the model fits the data set. Whereas the parsimonious fit indices also recorded values of 0.315 and 0.318 less than the recommended value of greater than 0.50.

To sum it all, eight latent variables fitted the final measurement model instead of the proposed fourteen in the conceptual model. The factors which critically measure the absorptive capacity of knowledge through social media in the Ghanaian fashion industry are Recognition Capacity, Acquisition Capacity, Transformation Capacity and Exploitation Capacity.

Regarding the test of discriminate validity, the Average Variable Estimate (AVE) recorded by the second order latent variables ranges from 0.53 to 0.79, above the validity threshold of 0.50, which shows an acceptable convergent validity of the measuring scales (Hair et al., 2006). The square of the correlation between a construct and any other factor is higher than the AVE for each latent variable, which indicates adequate discriminant validity between the constructs (Chin, 1998). Table 5 also shows an assessment of the normality test for the study.

Summary of Hypotheses Confirmation

The Table 6 shows the confirmation of the hypothesis.

Table 5. Assessment of normality

Variable	Min	Max	Skew	c.r.	Kurtosis	c.r.
Q26	3.000	5.000	-.628	-3.591	-.622	-1.777
Q28	3.000	5.000	-.563	-3.216	-.657	-1.879
Q23	3.000	5.000	-.588	-3.358	-.770	-2.199
Q25	3.000	5.000	-.391	-2.233	-.691	-1.976
Q15	3.000	5.000	-.855	-4.886	-.486	-1.389
Q17	1.000	5.000	-1.580	-9.029	4.729	13.513
Q12	4.000	5.000	-1.063	-6.077	-.870	-2.485
Q13	4.000	5.000	-2.166	-12.380	2.691	7.691
Multivariate					17.105	9.466

Source: Analysis Output .

Table 6. Hypothesis confirmation of cross tabulation

Hypothesis	p-Value	Support for Model
Social Media & Recognition Capacity	0.612	H1: Rejected
Social Media & Acquisition Capacity	0.000	H2: Supported
Social Media & Assimilation Capacity	0.787	H3: Rejected
Social Media & PACAP	0.030	H4: Supported
Recognition Capacity & Acquisition Capacity	0.000	H5: Supported
Acquisition Capacity & Assimilation Capacity	0.000	H6: Supported
Assimilation Capacity & Transformation Capacity	0.000	H7: Supported
Transformation Capacity& Exploitation Capacity	0.000	H8: Supported

Source: Analysis Output.

DISCUSSION OF FINDINGS

Social media is an asset for firms who use it in absorbing knowledge. From the findings, most fashion designers use the documentative Applications to recognize knowledge and those who use the communicative Applications to assimilate knowledge are in the majority. YouTube, for instance, is mostly used by fashion designers to acquire knowledge.

From literature, research has concentrated on communicative applications of Web 2.0 technologies not concentrating on other applications such as the documentative which this study has been able to cover (Vuori & Okkonen, 2012; Chua & Banerjee, 2013). Statistics from Alexa.com depicts that traffic on social media sites especially Facebook is on the rise. Other findings from this study confirm this assertion that social media usage is on the rise. According to the findings of this study, most fashion firms in Ghana use social media intensively on a daily basis to acquire knowledge.

From the analysis of findings, it can be argued that fashion designers do not intensively use social media to assimilate knowledge as proposed by Zahra and George (2007). Thus, assimilation of knowledge when absorbing new knowledge does not play an inevitable role in the fashion firms absorption new external knowledge.

Most fashion firms use social media to communicate with their customers, suppliers, fashion bloggers, and fashion enthusiasts. This they do very intensively to acquire knowledge. The knowledge they acquire through these means may include but not limited to fashion trends, consumer taste and preferences, existing prices, orders from customers, supplier lists, comments and suggestions among others.

There is also a positive relationship between the Transformation Capacity and the Exploitation Capacity of fashion firms in Ghana. Thus, knowledge acquired when transformed is mostly used by these fashion firms to develop new ideas and designs.

The findings further suggest that most Fashion designers in Ghana use social media to research and acquire knowledge which informs future designs. However, they do not prevent their employees from using social media to transmit scientific and technological knowledge.

In addition, the findings suggest that, these fashion designers acquire knowledge from both internal (among employees), for instance through WhatsApp and external sources (from suppliers, customers, fashion enthusiasts and other fashion designers), through for instance, Facebook, Twitter, Instagram, WhatsApp among others. From the case studies, it can also be deduced that ideas for designs can be derived from social media. Another source of ideas for designs could be the designer's own mind as well as inspiration from nature.

Hong et al. (2013) studied blogs as a tool for learning which seems to be unpopular among fashion designers in Ghana. However, some Ghanaian fashion designers use blogs to communicate internally (with employees) as well as externally (with customers and suppliers). Trending ideas are communicated by designers through this social media platform.

Findings from this study also depicts that WhatsApp technology which falls under the instant messaging category of the social media tool is also used mostly by fashion designers for internal communication and sharing of design patents but not through other social media platforms like Facebook to avoid theft of designs. However, social media applications such as Facebook is an ideal application for marketing.

Some popular social media web applications include Facebook and YouTube, which has also been studied by most researchers (Vuori & Okkonen, 2012; He et al., 2013; Bochenek & Blili, 2013; Chua & Banerjee, 2013). Twitter is also popular among Fashion designers. Facebook is popular for marketing and publicity.

From the findings of the study, WhatsApp is the emerging Web 2.0 technology that is gaining popularity and dominance among fashion designers in Ghana today. The assertion is that it is convenient and easily accessible.

Arguably, the findings of the study also suggest that Facebook is popular among Ghanaian fashion designers for the reasons of its wider network coverage, accessibility and convenience of use. This finding is corroborated by Vuori and Okkonen (2012) who carried out a study on social media and discovered Facebook as one of the popular social media applications.

CONCLUSION AND RECOMMENDATIONS

This study examined the use of social media for organizational learning in the Ghanaian fashion industry. To this end, these research questions were formulated:

1. What are the forms of learning for firms in the Ghanaian fashion industry?
2. What are the sources of learning for firms in the Ghanaian fashion industry?
3. How does social media support organizational learning in fashion firms in Ghana?

Absorptive Capacity Theory (ACT) therefore appropriately helped answer these research questions. The constructs of the ACT were ideal for gathering the needed information on fashion designers and their usage of social media to absorb knowledge. Knowledge on recognition, acquisition, assimilation, transformation and exploitation of new external knowledge among Ghanaian fashion designers is thereby attained.

Summary of the Research Findings

The findings of the study are in three divisions: first, the findings on the forms of knowledge that aid learning in the Ghanaian fashion industry; second, the sources of knowledge that aid learning in the Ghanaian fashion industry; and third, how social media supports organizational learning in the Ghanaian fashion industry.

Nature of Absorptive Capacity

It was discovered that most fashion firms in Ghana use social media to communicate with others (who could be customers, suppliers, fashion bloggers, fashion enthusiasts etc.) very intensively to acquire knowledge. They also use social media to market designs as well as to acquire knowledge to create new designs. Acquiring knowledge through others or through market sources demonstrates the form of knowledge termed demand-pull postulated from the Absorptive Capacity Theory (ACT).

Interestingly, most fashion designers in Ghana do not prevent their employees from transmitting useful scientific and technological knowledge, which falls under a form of knowledge termed as science-push. The forms of knowledge for fashion firms in Ghana can therefore be classified as demand-pull and science-push as postulated by ACT.

Another finding was that the sources of knowledge predominantly used by fashion designers were both internal sources and external sources. The internal source predominantly being through research since most fashion firms in Ghana use social media to carry out research intensively and the knowledge (new styles, new designs, and new fashion trends) is adapted by these fashion houses into new designs. The external sources of knowledge on the other hand were customarily borrowed or purchased knowledge. Fashion designers either borrow or purchase external knowledge and translate them into new business applications (new marketing strategies, new designs etc.). This knowledge is disseminated to others (customers, suppliers) both internally and externally by means of social media.

Moreover, it was revealed that social networks are mostly used for acquiring new knowledge. Recognition capacity forms a part of PACAP; hence, it can be concluded that the type of social media that supports PACAP the most are social networks. Facebook, YouTube, Myspace, Twitter, Podcasts and Flickr are social media tools that are used very intensively by fashion firms to acquire knowledge. These web applications can be classified under social network type of social media web applications and these web applications are mostly used to acquire knowledge. Hence, it can be concluded that social networks support PACAP since acquisition capacity is an aspect of PACAP.

From the findings of the study, it can be stated that Ghanaian fashion designers also use social media to recognize, acquire, transform and exploit knowledge intensively. They poorly use social media to assimilate knowledge.

Critical Constructs of Absorptive Capacity Theory (ACT)

In order to see the fitness of the conceptual model derived from ACT, with the objective of determining the factors critical to the absorption of knowledge, the Confirmatory Factor Analysis technique under Structural Equation Modelling was used; and cross tabulation was used to test the stipulated hypothesis.

The first conceptual model was built from ACT with 5 factors and 14 variables. The results of the measurement model validation under CFA indicated that Recognition Capacity (RC1), Acquisition Capacity (AC1, AC3), Transformation Capacity (TR1, TR2) and Exploitation Capacity (EC1, EC2) were the factors critical to the absorption of knowledge through social media in the fashion industry of Ghana. Other variables like AS1, AS2 AS3 (Assimilation Capacity factor), TR3 and EC3 were insignificant to the model; hence, were deleted from the final model.

Cross tabulations were used to test and validate the hypotheses proposed regarding the 5 factors of ACT (14 variables) and two (2) of the hypotheses were rejected whereas the rest (7) were accepted. The seven hypotheses supported were H2, H4, H5, H6, H7, H8 and H9 and two rejected were H1 and H3 with a p-value greater than the threshold of 0.05. Overall, the critical factors for measuring absorption of knowledge through social media in the Ghanaian fashion industry are Recognition, Acquisition, Transformation and Exploitation.

Implications of Research

In terms of research, this study will add up to existing studies on fashion designing, social media as well as adding to studies which use the Absorptive Capacity Theory as its theoretical Lens.

In relation to practice, the findings of this study will inform the decision of other firms or fashion designers who are not currently using social media in absorbing knowledge to decide to do so for the purposes of research and ease of communication, effective marketing and publicity both internally and externally and also reap the benefit of cutting down cost.

Regarding policy, policy makers in the fashion industry of Ghana can embrace the idea of social media adoption and usage by Ghanaian fashion houses, by explicitly stating and communicating its benefits to practice and research.

Limitations and Future Research

The study focused on fashion houses within the Greater Accra Region of Ghana; consequently, not covering fashion firms in other parts of Ghana. Thus, future studies should cover other areas of the country to provide a holistic understanding of the use of social media in organizational learning.

REFERENCES

Argyris, C., & Schön, D.A. (1978). Organizational Learning: A Theory of Action Perspective. *Reis, 77*(78/97), 345-348.

Bartlett-Bragg, A. (2009). Reframing practice: Creating social learning networks. *International Journal of Development and Learning in Organizations, 23*(4), 16–20. doi:10.1108/14777280910970747

Boateng, R., Malik, A., & Mbarika, V. (2009). Web 2.0 and Organizational Learning: Conceptualizing the link, Americas Conference on Information Systems. *Proceedings of the Fifteenth Americas Conference on Information Systems*, 1-2.

Bochenek, L., & Blili, S. (2013). Social Media Champions- Drivers and Sophistication Process of Social Media Strategic Management. *Social Media in Strategic Management*, 143-167.

Chua, A. Y., & Banerjee, S. (2013). Customer knowledge management via social media: The case of Starbucks. *Journal of Knowledge Management, 17*(2), 237–249. doi:10.1108/13673271311315196

Cohen, W. M., & Levinthal, D. A. (1989). Innovation and learning: The two faces of R&D. *The Economic Journal, 99*(397), 569–596. doi:10.2307/2233763

Cohen, W. M., & Levinthal, D. A. (1990). Absorptive capacity: A new perspective on learning and innovation. *Administrative Science Quarterly*, *35*(1), 128–152. doi:10.2307/2393553

Cook, S. D. N., & Yanow, D. (1993). Culture and Organizational Learning. *Journal of Management Inquiry*, *2*(4), 373–390. doi:10.1177/105649269324010

Creswell, J. W. (2009). *Research design: Qualitative Quantitative and Mixed Methods Approaches*. Thousand Oaks, CA: SAGE Publications.

Dixon, N. (1994). *The Organizational Learning Cycle: How We Can Learn Collectively*. London: McGraw-Hill Company.

Dixon, N. (2000). *Common Knowledge: How Companies Thrive by sharing what they know*. Boston: Harvard University Press.

Dodgson, M. (1993). Organizational learning: A review of some literatures. *Organization Studies*, *14*(3), 375–394. doi:10.1177/017084069301400303

Grabski, J. (2009). Making fashion in the city: A case study of tailors and designers in Dakar. *Senegal. Fashion Theory*, *13*(2), 215–242. doi:10.2752/175174109X414268

Hanna, R., Rohm, A., & Crittenden, V. L. (2011). Were all connected: The power of the social media ecosystem. *Business Horizons*, *54*(3), 265–273. doi:10.1016/j.bushor.2011.01.007

Hong, K. S. (2002). Relationships between students and instructional variables with satisfaction and learning from a Web-based course. *The Internet and Higher Education*, *5*(3), 267–281. doi:10.1016/S1096-7516(02)00105-7

Hull, R., Coombs, R., & Peltu, M. (2000). Knowledge management practices for innovation: An audit tool for improvement. *International Journal of Technology Management*, *20*(5-8), 633–656. doi:10.1504/IJTM.2000.002885

Kaiser, C., & Bodendorf, F. (2012). Mining consumer dialog in online forums. *Internet Research*, *22*(3), 275–297. doi:10.1108/10662241211235653

Karkoulian, S., Canaan Messarra, L., & McCarthy, R. (2013). The intriguing art of knowledge management and its relation to learning organizations. *Journal of Knowledge Management*, *17*(4), 511–526. doi:10.1108/JKM-03-2013-0102

Lien, B. Y. H., Hung, R. Y. Y., Yang, B., & Li, M. (2006). Is the learning organization a valid concept in the Taiwanese context? *International Journal of Manpower*, *27*(2), 189–203. doi:10.1108/01437720610666209

March, J. G., & Simon, H. A. (1958). *Organizations*. Hoboken, NJ: Wiley.

Murovec, N., & Prodan, I. (2009). Absorptive capacity, its determinants, and influence on innovation output: Cross-cultural validation of the structural model. *Technovation*, *29*(12), 859–872. doi:10.1016/j.technovation.2009.05.010

Nonaka, I., & Takeuchi, H. (1995). *The Knowledge-creating Company: How Japanese Companies Create the Dynamics of Innovation*. Oxford University Press.

Nonaka, I., Toyama, R., & Konno, N. (1998). Leading Knowledge Creation: A New framework for dynamic Knowledge Management. *Proceedings at the 2nd Annual Knowledge Management Conference.*

Nooteboom, B. (2000). Learning by interaction: absorptive capacity, cognitive distance and governance. *Journal of Management and Governance, 4*(1-2), 69-92.

O'Reilly, T. (2005). *What is Web 2.0?*. O'Reilly Media. Available: http://tinyurl.com/743r5

Pham, M. H. T. (2011). Blog ambition: Fashion, feelings, and the political economy of the digital raced body. *Camera Obscura*, *26*(176), 1–37. doi:10.1215/02705346-2010-013

Rickman, T. A., & Cosenza, R. M. (2007). The changing digital dynamics of multichannel marketing: The feasibility of the weblog: text mining approach for fast fashion trending. *Journal of Fashion Marketing and Management*, *11*(4), 604–621. doi:10.1108/13612020710824634

Shepherd, C. (2011). Does social media have a place in workplace learning?. *Strategic Direction*, *27*(2), 3–4. doi:10.1108/02580541111103882

Vuori, V., & Okkonen, J. (2012). Refining information and knowledge by social media applications: Adding value by insight. *Vine*, *42*(1), 117–128. doi:10.1108/03055721211207798

Zahra, S. A., & George, G. (2002). Absorptive capacity: A review, reconceptualization, and extension. *Academy of Management Review*, *27*(2), 185–203.

Chapter 5
Understanding Digital Platforms:
Types of Platforms and Their Evolution in the Organizational Context

Alexander Chekanov
Esade Business School, Spain

ABSTRACT

In our interconnected world, everyday it becomes more difficult to think of a product or a service that could provide its full value if not combined with other products. In this chapter an overview on platforms is presented, illustrating the different types of platforms that exist, its origins, how the literature on platforms evolved, their role in organizations, why understanding how platforms work is crucial to increase the success rate of their roll-out and how those platforms are shaped through platform governance and architecture, including an overview on platform-centric ecosystems.

INTRODUCTION

Innovations in multimedia have been spreading around organizations in different forms and shapes. Gradually, knowledge management tools became cornerstones within organizations to ensure that professionals can leverage organizational knowledge to its most. Among the emerging multimedia innovations adopted by organizations, the use of digital platforms became one of the most promising ones. Thus, the purpose of this chapter is to provide the reader with an overview of what digital platforms are and how the concept of platform evolved over time. First, in this chapter we provide

DOI: 10.4018/978-1-5225-2956-9.ch005

a literature review that studied platforms over the last decades; second, we elaborate on why it is crucial to understand how platforms function; third, we provide the reader with some real examples of knowledge sharing platforms to illustrate their knowledge management potential; and finally, we provide perspective on promising research streams within this field.

The Origins of Platforms

Digital platforms can be defined as the foundation technology or set of components used beyond a single firm that bring multiple parties together for a common purpose or to solve a common problem (Gawer and Cusumano, 2002). In our interconnected world, it becomes difficult to think of a product or a service that could provide its full value if not combined with other products. For example, to produce the Microsoft XBOX video console Microsoft used components from IBM (CPU processor), Nvidia (GPU processor), Samsung and Qimonda (memory chips), and several other manufacturers among others. Led by Microsoft, this coordination and integration of different elements into one single product involved knowledge sharing among different components' suppliers and their participation in collaborative projects. Once the product was released it had to achieve also a sufficient target audience. That is, attracting new users through its continuous growth and capture and redistribute the monetary value obtained in exchange across different platform participants that contributed with resources. This example just illustrates the increased challenge that represent the wide range of different relationships that platform owners need to coordinate in order to make a platform successful. There are plenty of examples of industries where different products and services complement each other for providing combined a service that otherwise they would not be able to provide on their own. In fact, a group of economists that studied platforms as products (product platforms) (Katz & Shapiro, 1994) pointed that, indeed, certain products and services only become valuable when they are combined with other elements (e.g. other products and services). Such examples range from the combination between smartphones and wireless communication providers for providing mobile communication services; computers and internet for providing a very wide range of other services (e.g. email, news, social networks); or video consoles and video games or other multimedia content providers that together provide entertainment services. As we can observe in all these cases, products and services are strongly complementary to each other and can be considered as the forming systems where the collections of two or more of these components allow them to work together as one single product or service (Katz and Shapiro, 1994).

Over time platforms have emerged at multiple levels within organizations as well. Platforms became part not only of the daily resources that are used to increase productivity and efficiency, but also as tools to drive innovation in a wide range of industries and settings. As we saw, platforms can be found in high-tech industries, telecommunications, entertainment industries or even in finance and banking services sector. As the speed of innovation of firms increase and the dedication of resources grow, the impact of platforms on actors at all levels is becoming extremely high. Therefore, understanding how platforms function is crucial as one of the main challenges that organizations need to face is that technology markets (including digital platforms) tend to be extremely path dependent. Such path dependency implies a significant exposure to random events that might lead to both, success or failure, when an organization opts for certain type of technological platform.

A set of factors can influence and determine the success of the adoption of certain technology or type of digital platform. That is, there is a natural trend in technology markets in adopting a standard or a dominant design (e.g. a product configuration or certain platform architecture). However, the adoption of a dominant design increases the risk of a technological lockout if there's a change in the market to a different standard or a different technology solution. Good examples of such changes could be observed in the battles between VHS and Beta standards, or the Blue-ray and HD DVD standards. In both cases companies whose standards were rejected were still able to rejoin the market, but in some cases firms might end up having a double technological lockout (e.g. when the standard they are trying to rejoin is patent protected). Understanding the dynamics of technological platforms increases the chances of organizations of avoiding the what is called a "technological lockout", a concept that scholars who closely studied this phenomenon (Schilling, 1998) define as "a situation in which a firm finds itself unable to develop or competitively sell products to a particular market because of technology standards." Therefore, understanding the nature of digital platforms becomes especially critical for fast-cycle industries, where product life cycles might be very short and falling behind might drive a firm directly out of business. Nevertheless, when looking back and observing some of the most representative technology disruptions, it is not always that the technically most advanced solutions become the most successful ones. Other factors, such as timing, adoption speed and even a promising future use of a certain technology can become even more important than the technological improvement itself. All these observations apply to knowledge-sharing platforms as well.

Nevertheless, regardless of what technological solution an organization might be willing to adopt as a knowledge sharing or cooperation tool, there's a set of factors that might still lead to a technological lockout. Some of the most cited ones and that managers should be aware of are usually three (Schilling, 1998): First, that an organization might choose a standard that might not meet customer's expectations in terms of quality, features or price; second, that there might be not enough critical installed base for the technology for being massively adopted or there is a lack of complementary goods to enable the technology to form an ecosystem around it; third, an inappropriate market entry timing (e.g. introducing a technology in an emerging market or into an already established market) can also significantly influence the chances of the incumbent platform to succeed. Therefore, in order to understand how to mitigate the risks of a technological lockout there's a need to understand more in detail the reasons why first of all a firm might end up in a technological lockout from a digital platforms' perspective. In this chapter, we review concepts as platform architecture, governance and modularity, as platform design might provide some hints on its future potential. Moreover, certain platform architecture design principles might help to approach some specific issues as how to have more chances in successfully overcoming the starting phase of a platform.

Starting with platform architecture, it can be defined as the conceptual blueprint that describes how a platform or an ecosystem is divided into a relatively stable platform and a set of complementary modules that are encouraged to vary, and the design rules binding on both (Baldwin & Woodard, 2009). The concept of platform architecture has been also the central focus of study of the literature on ecosystem innovation and evolution (Tiwana, 2010; van Schewick, 2010). Understanding the concept of platform architecture is key to understand the concept of platform because the main role of platform architecture is to define and coordinate a set of constrains or design rules to manage the relationship between the different participants of a platform while having at the same time a direct impact on platform evolution (Baldwin & Woodard, 2009). Furthermore, by observing the architecture of a platform it is possible to establish its boundaries and understand possible governing mechanisms between platform participants, allowing to gain a better understanding of what is platform governance and its role within the platform.

Regarding platform governance, it can simply be defined as "who makes what decisions about a platform" (Baldwin & Woodard, 2009) and allows to understand how it can function as a regulation mechanisms for the platform owner to capture economic value (Parker & van Alstyne, 2010; Boudreau & Hagiu, 2009). This nuance is not negligible because, as we saw in the previous sections of this chapter, a platform is a set of components that are coordinated together to pursue one common goal through their interactions with each other. Thus, the platform owner can orchestrate or shape the behavior of the different platform components or participants by distributing decisions rights and obligations over the platform (Baldwin & Woodard, 2009). Therefore, platform governance can also be considered as the element through which the platform owner can exert his influence over the different actors participating in a platform (Schilling, 2005). Katz & Shapiro (1986) illustrated how without the platform undertaking the platform governing role, in a two-sided market context a platform could left ungoverned, involving that building successful platforms require effective management of the interactions between the different platform participants to collaborate and cooperate successfully while pursuing one common goal (Beath & Orlikowski, 1994; Walz et al., 1993). This research stream evolved into studying this relationship between the platform owner and the rest of platform participants as a classical principal-agent relationship that has been further studied in the context of control theory (Kirsch, 1997). Indeed, platform governance has been mainly studied in the context of control theory, leading to scholars to observe that the lack of control over platform's creative output proved to be not necessarily beneficial for the platform's ecosystem (Hagiu, 2010: Boudreau, 2011) and further illustrating platform governance as a paradox of change and a paradox of control (Tilson, 2010), displaying how a set of tensions in technology ecosystems can be managed by platform governance (Wareham et al., 2014). Moreover, existing research on platform governance also illustrated how governing and regulating activities can ensure the appropriate peace and quality of innovation on a platform (Gawer & Cusumano, 2008), showing how governing and regulating activities can, indeed, encourage the adoption of the platform by new users and how can the platform owner attract new components to the platform through network effects (Boudreau, 2012).

Overall, there is a whole stream of academic literature devoted to study the platform phenomenon (Gawer & Cusumano, 2002) to build understanding on different aspects on how platforms function. From a product design perspective, it has been studied how to develop modular components and design patterns that would ensure that a given platform has a set of stable components that support variety and evolvability over time by constraining the linkages among other components (Gawer, 2009, p.13). This led to build a better understanding of the relationships between platforms and the environments in which they are embedded (that could be other platforms), to understand their role in organizations and on an industry level. Referring to the concept of "platform", industrial economists described it as a mediating or transaction point between groups of agents (Rochet & Tirole, 2003). In such context, such market places rely, again, on the generation of network effects as mechanisms that would reinforce their growth, becoming the mechanisms to generate such networking effects a stream of research literature on its own (Rysman, 2009). Finally, in the context of product development, platforms were used to describe a generation or family of products. Actually, the notion of "platform product" was introduced by Wheelwright and Clark (1992a) to describe how this platform products were targeted to meet the needs of a core group of customers while allowing at the same time to introduce modifications and variations that would allow creating derivative products.

As we can see, there is a whole set of different research streams that have been studying platforms from different perspectives. Why this has been so relevant we discuss in the next section of this chapter.

Why Understanding Platforms Is Relevant

In a context where the investments in innovation and R&D are constantly growing, companies face an increasingly complex challenge of how effectively conduct innovation and make the best use of the available knowledge. New technological platforms emerge and provide companies with the opportunity to create value through new forms of collaboration (Swink, 2006), integrating in innovation platforms large communities of users, providers and end-consumers. As companies engage in collaboration in innovation activities they create digital platforms that can be seen as a form of collaboration in innovation.

Existing research has proved that cooperative innovation and knowledge sharing can bring great benefits: reduction of the amount of time and workload, improving the development cycle time from 15 to 25%, reduction of product time-to-market by 15% or reduction of non-value-added work up to 60% (Swink, 2006). Actually, innovation platforms are considered as one of the most well-established forms of open innovation and collaboration networks (Marais & Schutte, 2009). Given that innovation can be seen as a cumulative result of a collaborative innovative process between company and its environment it is key to establish and maintain strategic relationships and alliances with other partners (Ulaga & Eggert, 2005; Westerlund, Rajala, 2010). Thus, companies create collaborative platforms for the communities of users, customers and developers in order to achieve innovativeness improvement and knowledge sharing (Foss et al., 2011; Foss et al., 2013; Colombo et. al, 2013).

Knowledge sharing through digital platforms can be related with the existing research on open innovation that analyzed cooperation in innovation with external sources at the phases of obtaining, integrating and commercializing of innovation, emphasizing its interaction stage (West, Bogers, 2013). This stream of research considers platforms as an enabling or filtering mechanism for innovation obtaining (Piller, Walcher, 2006; West, Bogers, 2013) and feedback, co-creation and communities as elements of the interaction (West, Bogers, 2013). Existing research also investigated the linkage between network structure (Colombo et al., 2011) like the number of networks competing to develop a product and the number of alternative technology platforms (Amaldoss, Rapoport, 2005), network competences and network location (Chiu, 2009). By focusing on networks of heterogeneous actors (Tuomi 2002, Van de Ven 2005) existing research showed that increased network diversity promotes new combinations, fosters learning, and enables faster diffusion (Tuomi 2002; Brown and Duguid 2000, von Hippel, 2005). However, other scholars have also pointed that such networks can also limit their spread because of increasing boundaries (Ferlie, 2005) as collaboration in innovation can be bounded by a set of different factors such as: physical and temporal; organizational and hierarchical; relational barriers; or knowledge barriers (Swink, 2006).

Knowledge platforms do not exist in isolation and there is usually a whole ecosystem formed around them. That is because platform-centric ecosystems and their modules can be embedded in other platforms and ecosystems at different levels. Given that the environments in which platforms are embedded are dynamic and that heterogeneous, actors that usually participate in them (e.g. platform owners, 3rd party developers, customers, etc.) can have different interests it is complex to understand the evolutionary dynamics of such platforms. The architecture design decisions and platform governance mechanisms, that we mentioned earlier in this chapter, provide the platform owner with the possibility to shape the development of the platform on its different stages of evolution. These design decisions can have a direct effect not only on the platform owner, but also on the rest of participants of the platform, its ecosystem and the evolution of the platform itself.

Nevertheless, depending on the development stage of a platform (e.g. incipient or mature), its market position (e.g. dominant, niche, new entrant) or its environmental context (e.g. industry, type of technology, availability of complementary goods) similar architecture design decisions might lead to different outcomes in terms of platform's evolution. The existing literature on the dynamic complexity in the design of Information Infrastructures (IIs) already suggests that evolutionary dynamics of IIs tends to be non-linear, influenced by network effects and as we already mentioned, path dependent. From the design theory of dynamic complexity Hanseth & Lyytinen (2010) provide guidance to understand the tensions between two main design problems: the bootstrap problem understood as the need of the IIs to meet early users' needs in order to be started, and the adaptability problem understood as the need of local designs to recognize II's unbounded scale and functional uncertainty. Scholars presented empirical evidence on how different approaches to open a system through architectural design might influence the rate of innovation (Boudreau, 2010) and provided a conceptual frameworks for understanding how in multi-sided platforms the access and interactions are regulated through legal, technological or price setting mechanisms (Boudreau and Haigu, 2009) contributing to the platform governance literature, while other scholars has focused on a variety of aspects of platforms and platform innovation (Eaton et al., 2011; Gawer, 2009; Gawer and Cusumano, 2012; Ghazawneh and Henfridsson, 2010, 2013; Hanseth and Lyytinen, 2010; Herzhoff, 2011; Herzhoff et al., 2010; Monteiro, 1998; Zittrain, 2006, 2009).

Platforms as Knowledge Sharing Tools and Types of Platforms

As we already mentioned at the beginning of this chapter, beyond the role of product and service platforms, digital platforms have gradually become increasingly relevant inside organizations. Firms seek to capture new ideas and gain efficiency for sharing knowledge, developing new products or services in an environment where the competition is constantly growing (Wheelwright, 1992). This trend led scholars to study platforms in a broader context and beyond the initial definition of product platform, considering them on a more generic level and beyond their traits or technical specifications. This extended context included considering platforms beyond being mere products or services but also understanding them as a mean to connect different departments within the organization (Wheelwright, and Clark, 1992). Actually, scholars studied how information can flow horizontally across the company, reflecting that processes, distribution channels or marketing efforts are being shared and benefit different parties. It also brought focus to study up to what extent platforms could increase efficiency within organizations, not limiting them only to be understood as products that share physical components but also as platform processes (Muffato, 2002). In the remaining part of this chapter we provide some examples of types of digital platforms to illustrate their potential as data, information and knowledge sharing tools.

One of the most widespread understanding of platforms is within the online domain and the domain of software-based platforms that in turn enable the creation of knowledge networks. Among other possibilities, web platforms also enable the presence of a person or a firm on the web or a virtual space where different type of data and information resources can be shared or stored. It is not uncommon to associate websites or any other web presence as synonyms for online platforms. In fact, this association between web based services and online platforms is common because online presence facilitates the exchange of data, information and knowledge between people and business. In the organizational domain, the concept of platform usually refers to a service or an application that might help processing or coordinating workflows and, therefore, facilitating knowledge exchange and increasing productivity in the organizational context.

Thanks to the evolving multimedia capabilities, digital platforms can also be used as private presentation of individuals, in which a person can share such information as his or her personal details, interests, photos, music, or even comments and opinions (that can be triggered by satisfaction or dissatisfaction with a product) among other possibilities. Such type of knowledge-sharing platforms enables companies to understand better their existing customers and even potential customers by allowing them to collect and share more data about their customers. This information allows building a more personalized image of who their customers are, what do they want or even what customers think about and what they complain about. In such context, digital platforms as knowledge-sharing tools can overall help improving companies' services and products and create even more satisfied customers. At the same times, platforms can also be purely informative or data-exchange focused, like information platforms for businesses with which an organization or a company present their qualifications and past activities. Other examples within this domain include sales-related websites of companies whose main area of activity is online trading, such as online auction houses, mail-order houses, online shops or online insurance companies. Such digital platforms provide products and services on the web, to make offers to visitors and to receive or to convey orders. This online presence makes a significant difference in terms of consumer purchasing experience and therefore can lead to improved sales, consumer loyalty and higher consumer satisfaction.

Lastly, phone or mobile applications (apps) are a very interesting type of platforms that facilitate the access to other online platforms. These platforms help companies reach their potential consumers at any given moment and provide consumers with a whole new range of possibilities not only to communicate with each other but to also participate in collaborative and innovative activities. Examples of such mobile platforms could be calendars, online collaboration working tools, and even WhatsApp. These mobile platforms expand the possibilities to communicate and coordinate within and beyond the boundaries of a single organization or firm and increase productivity. Such advanced type of communication can also have a positive side effect on the social interaction with co-workers making the overall working atmosphere friendlier and cozier, therefore indirectly boosting motivation and productivity.

As we can observe, most online platforms are created to share information and facilitate knowledge exchange between different users and communities of users. Many digital platforms are offered for free and accessible for anyone. Hence, their potential to create and share community knowledge should not be overlooked. Companies can make use of platforms like YouTube, Quora, and other similar platforms to import and organize unlimited content for free and use them to inform other firms about their products or services and create knowledge within the consumers' communities. There is a great potential in uncovering the new sources of collective intelligence by adapting or expanding internal organizational knowledge sharing platforms for external use as well. With the reflection of this chapter we do not suggest for each and every organization to create their own Wikipedia, although is probably the best-known knowledge-generating platform for free and accessible in many different languages. However, being knowledge at the core of every organization, we do encourage to explore further the potential benefits that collective intelligence platforms can bring to organizations. To accomplish that successfully, we hope that the provided insights on the evolution of platforms, the notion of platform architecture and platform governance would help scholars and practitioners in such endeavor.

Open Questions Left

In this chapter, we have seen how much research advanced on platforms over the last decades and different types of knowledge-sharing platforms. However, there are still several research directions that are very promising and wait for research and practitioners to find the answer to questions that still remain open in this domain: how knowledge platforms should be created/designed to have greater chances to succeed? What would be an ideal platform architecture? How platform architecture can determine the effectiveness of platform governance? Is always the best solution to be the owner of a platform and develop it in-house or in certain settings it might be more efficient to use 3rd party platforms? While platforms contribute to knowledge, information and data sharing, is there a threshold in terms of network size when coordination costs of the platform do not compensate the value obtained from it? And what would be the future of platforms in organizations once the participants of such networks become not only individuals and organizations but also AI based actors? These are just some of the questions that still don't have a clear answer, but what is clear is that the future of the field looks very promising and invites scholars and practitioners to keep navigating further in this adventure of understanding how the platforms function on all their levels.

REFERENCES

Afuah, A. (2013). Are network effects really all about size? The role of structure and conduct. *Strategic Management Journal*, *34*(3), 257–273. doi:10.1002/smj.2013

Amaldoss, W., & Rapoport, A. (2005). Collaborative Product and Market Development: Theoretical Implications and Experimental Evidence. *Marketing Science*, *24*(3), 396–414. doi:10.1287/mksc.1040.0105

Athaide, G. A., & Klink, R. R. (2009). Managing Seller-Buyer Relationships during New Product Development. *Journal of Product Innovation Management*, *26*(5), 566–577. doi:10.1111/j.1540-5885.2009.00681.x

Atuahene-Gima, K. (2005). Resolving the capability—rigidity paradox in new product innovation. *Journal of Marketing*, *69*(4), 61–83. doi:10.1509/jmkg.2005.69.4.61

Baldwin, C. Y., & Woodard, C. J. 2009. The architecture of platforms: a unified view. In Platforms, Markets and Innovation (pp. 19–44). Cheltenham, UK: Edward Elgar Publishing. doi:10.4337/9781849803311.00008

Becker, W., & Dietz, J. (2004). R&D co-operation and innovation activities of firms: Evidence for the German manufacturing industry. *Research Policy*, *33*(2), 209–223. doi:10.1016/j.respol.2003.07.003

Belderbos, R., Carree, M., & Lokshin, B. (2004). Cooperative R&D and Firm Performance. *Research Policy*, *33*(10), 1477–1492. doi:10.1016/j.respol.2004.07.003

Biyalogorsky, E., Boulding, W., & Staelin, R. (2006). Stuck in the past: Why managers persist with new product failures. *Journal of Marketing*, *70*(2), 108–121. doi:10.1509/jmkg.70.2.108

Boudreau, K. (2010). Open platform strategies and innovation: Granting access vs. devolving control. *Management Science*, *56*(10), 1849–1872. doi:10.1287/mnsc.1100.1215

Boudreau, K. J., & Hagiu, A. (2009). Platform rules: multi-sided platforms as regulators. In Platforms, Markets and Innovation (pp. 163-191). Cheltenham, UK: Edward Elgar Publishing Limited. doi:10.4337/9781849803311.00014

Calia, R. C., Guerrini, F. M., & Moura, G. L. (2007). Innovation networks: From technological development to business model reconfiguration. *Technovation*, *27*(8), 426–432. doi:10.1016/j.technovation.2006.08.003

Chesbrough, H. (2006). Open innovation: A new paradigm for understanding industrial innovation. *Open innovation: Researching a new paradigm*, 1-12.

Chiu, Y. T. H. (2009). How network competence and network location influence innovation performance. *Journal of Business and Industrial Marketing*, *29*(1), 46–55.

Colombo, M. G., Laursen, K., Magnusson, M., & Rossi-Lamastra, C. (2011). Organizing inter-and intra-firm networks: What is the impact on innovation performance?. *Industry and Innovation*, *18*(6), 531–538. doi:10.1080/13662716.2011.601958

Colombo, M. G., Piva, E., & Rossi-Lamastra, C. (2013). Authorising employees to collaborate with communities during working hours: When is it valuable for firms? *Long Range Planning*, *46*(3), 236–257. doi:10.1016/j.lrp.2012.05.004

Corsaro, D., Cantu, C., & Tunisini, A. (2012). Actors heterogeneity in innovation networks. *Industrial Marketing Management*, *41*(5), 780–789. doi:10.1016/j.indmarman.2012.06.005

De Propris, L. (2002). Types of innovation and inter-firm co-operation. *Entrepreneurship & Regional Development*, *14*(4), 337–353. doi:10.1080/08985620210144974

Dosi, G. (1998). Sources, Procedures, and Microeconomic Effects of Innovation. *Journal of Economic Literature*, *26*, 1120–1171.

Eaton, B., Elaluf-Calderwood, S., Sørensen, C., & Yoo, Y. (2011). Dynamic Structures of Control and Generativity in Digital Ecosystem Service Innovation: The Cases of the Apple and Google Mobile App Stores. In *Information Systems and Innovation Group Working Paper Series*. The London School of Economics and Political Science.

Erbes, A., Robert, V., & Yoguel, G. (2010). Capacities, innovation and feedbacks in production networks in Argentina. *Economics of Innovation and New Technology*, *19*(8), 719–741. doi:10.1080/10438590903040807

Faria, P., Lima, F., & Santos, R. (2010). Cooperation in Innovation Activities: The Importance of Partners. *Research Policy*, *39*(8), 1082–1092. doi:10.1016/j.respol.2010.05.003

Ford, D., & Johnsen, T. (2001). Managing networks of supplier and customer relationships for technological innovation: initial case study. *17th IMP Conference Proceedings*.

Foss, N. J., Laursen, K., & Pedersen, T. (2011). Linking Customer Interaction and Innovation: The Mediating Role of New Organizational Practices. *Organization Science*, *22*(4), 980–999. doi:10.1287/orsc.1100.0584

Foss, N. J., Lyngsie, J., & Zahra, S. A. (2013). The role of external knowledge sources and organizational design in the process of opportunity exploitation. *Strategic Management Journal*, *34*(12), 1453–1471. doi:10.1002/smj.2135

Freytag, V. (2002). Innovation in co-operation and co-operation innovation. *18th IMP Conference Proceedings*.

Fritsch, M., & Lukas, R. (2001). Who co-operates on R&D?. *Research Policy*, *30*(2), 297–312. doi:10.1016/S0048-7333(99)00115-8

Gawer, A. (2009). Platform dynamics and strategies: From products to services. *Platforms, Markets and Innovation*, 45-76.

Gawer, A., & Cusumano, M. A. (2002). *Platform Leadership How Intel, Palm, Cisco and Others Drive Industry Innovation*. Cambridge, MA: Harvard Press.

Gawer, A., & Cusumano, M. A. (2012). How companies become platform leaders. MIT. *Sloan Management Review*, 49.

Gemunden, H. G., Ritter, T., & Heydebreck, P. (1996). Network configuration and innovation success: An empirical analysis in German high-tech industries. *International Journal of Research in Marketing*, *13*(5), 449–462. doi:10.1016/S0167-8116(96)00026-2

Ghazawneh, A., & Henfridsson, O. (2013). Balancing Platform Control and External Contribution in Third-Party Development: The Boundary Resources Model. *Information Systems Journal*, (23), 173–192.

Ghazawneh, A., & Henfridsson, O. (2010). Governing third-party development through platform boundary resources. *ICIS 2010 Proceedings*. AIS Electronic Library (AISeL).

Hanseth, O., & Lyytinen, K. (2010). Design theory for dynamic complexity in information infrastructures: The case of building internet. *Journal of Information Technology*, *28*(1), 1–19. doi:10.1057/jit.2009.19

Herzhoff, J. (2011). *Unfolding the Convergence Paradox: The Case of Mobile Voice-Over-IP in the UK* (Unpublished PhD Thesis). London School of Economics and Political Science.

Herzhoff, J., Elaluf-Calderwood, S., & Sørensen, C. (2010). Convergence, Conflicts, and Control Points: A Systems-Theoretical Analysis of Mobile VoIP in the UK. *Proceedings of joint 9th International Conference on Mobile Business (ICMB 2010) and 9th Global Mobility Roundtable (GMR 2010).*

Hwang, J., Kim, E., & Kim, S. (2009). Factors affecting open technological innovation in open source software companies in Korea. *Innovation-Management Policy & Practice*, *11*(3), 279–290. doi:10.5172/impp.11.3.279

Inemek, A., & Matthyssens, P. (2013). The impact of buyer–supplier relationships on supplier innovativeness: An empirical study in cross-border supply networks. *Industrial Marketing Management*, *42*(4), 580–594. doi:10.1016/j.indmarman.2012.10.011

Jorde, T. M., & Teece, D. J. (1990). Innovation and Cooperation: Implications for Competition and Antitrust. *The Journal of Economic Perspectives*, *4*(3), 75–96. doi:10.1257/jep.4.3.75

Katz, M., & Shapiro, C. (1994). Systems competition and network effects. *The Journal of Economic Perspectives*, *8*(2), 93–115. doi:10.1257/jep.8.2.93

Langley, A. (1999). Strategies for theorizing from process data. *Academy of Management Review*, *24*(4), 691–710.

Laursen, K., & Salter, A. (2006). Open for Innovation: The role of openness in explaining innovative performance among UK manufacturing firms. *Strategic Management Journal*, *27*(2), 131–150. doi:10.1002/smj.507

Linton, J. D. (2000). The role of relationships and reciprocity in the implementation of process innovation. *Engineering Management Journal, 12*(3), 34–38. doi:10.1080/10429247.2000.11415080

Mahoney, J. T., & Qian, L. (2013). Market frictions as building blocks of an organizational economics approach to strategic management. *Strategic Management Journal, 34*(9), 1019–1041. doi:10.1002/smj.2056

Marais, S. J., & Schutte, C. S. L. (2009, October). The development of open innovation models to assist the innovation process. *23rd Annual SAIIE Conference, Conference Proceedings*, 96.

Mention, A. L. (2011). Co-operation and co-opetition as open innovation practices in the service sector: Which influence on innovation novelty?. *Technovation, 31*(1), 44–53. doi:10.1016/j.technovation.2010.08.002

Miotti, L., & Sachwald, F. (2003). Co-operative R&D: Why and with whom? An integrated framework of analysis. *Research Policy, 32*(8), 1481–1499. doi:10.1016/S0048-7333(02)00159-2

Monteiro, E. (1998). Scaling information infrastructure: The case of the next generation IP in Internet. *The Information Society, 14*(3), 229–245. doi:10.1080/019722498128845

Narasimhan, O., Rajiv, S., & Dutta, S. (2006). Absorptive capacity in high-technology markets: The competitive advantage of the haves. *Marketing Science, 25*(5), 510–524. doi:10.1287/mksc.1060.0219

Nieto, M. J., & Santamaria, L. (2007). The importance of diverse collaborative networks for the novelty of product innovation. *Technovation, 27*(6-7), 367–377. doi:10.1016/j.technovation.2006.10.001

Okamuro, H. (2007). Determinants of successful R&D cooperation in Japanese small businesses: The impact of organizational and contractual characteristics. *Research Policy, 36*(10), 1529–1544. doi:10.1016/j.respol.2006.12.008

Piller, F. T., & Walcher, D. (2006). Toolkits for idea competitions: A novel method to integrate users in new product development. *R & D Management, 36*(3), 307–318. doi:10.1111/j.1467-9310.2006.00432.x

Powell, W. W. (1990). Neither market no hierarchy: Networks form of organisation. *Research in Organizational Behavior, 12*, 295–336.

Rampersad, G., Quester, P., & Troshani, I. (2010). Managing innovation networks: Exploratory evidence from ICT, biotechnology and nanotechnology networks. *Industrial Marketing Management*, *39*(5), 793–805. doi:10.1016/j.indmarman.2009.07.002

Rese, A., & Baier, D. (2011). Success factors for innovation management in networks of small and medium enterprises. *R & D Management*, *41*(2), 138–155. doi:10.1111/j.1467-9310.2010.00620.x

Romano, N. C., Donovan, C., Chen, H., & Nunamaker, J. F. (2003). A methodology for analyzing web-based qualitative data. *Journal of Management Information Systems*, *19*(4), 213–246. doi:10.1080/07421222.2003.11045741

Rubera, G., & Kirca, A. H. (2012). Firm innovativeness and its performance outcomes: A meta-analytic review and theoretical integration. *Journal of Marketing*, *76*(3), 130–147. doi:10.1509/jm.10.0494

Sanchez, R., & Mahoney, J. (1996). Modularity, flexibility, and knowledge management in product organization and design. *Strategic Management Journal*, *17*(1), 63–76. doi:10.1002/smj.4250171107

Seawright, J., & Gerring, J. (2008). Case Selection Techniques in Case Study Research A Menu of Qualitative and Quantitative Options. *Political Research Quarterly*, *61*(2), 294–308. doi:10.1177/1065912907313077

Shaw, B. (1994). User–supplier links and innovation. In M. Dodgson & R. Rothwell (Eds.), *The Handbook of Industrial Innovation*. Cheltenham, UK: Edward Elgar.

Smirnova, M. M., Podmetina, D., Väätänen, J., & Torkkeli, M. (2012). Collaborative approaches to new product development: The case of Russia. *International Journal of Entrepreneurship and Innovation Management*, *15*(1/2), 91–107. doi:10.1504/IJEIM.2012.044078

Swink, M. (2006). Building collaborative innovation capability. *Research Technology Management*, *49*(2), 37–47.

Teece, D. J. (1992). Competition, cooperation, and innovation: Organizational arrangements for regimes of rapid technological progress. *Journal of Economic Behavior & Organization*, *18*(1), 1–25. doi:10.1016/0167-2681(92)90050-L

Tether, B. (2002). Who co-operates for innovation, and why. An empirical analysis. *Research Policy*, *31*(6), 947–967. doi:10.1016/S0048-7333(01)00172-X

Tidd, J., Bessant, J., & Pavitt, K. (1997). *Managing Innovation: Integrating Technological, Market and Organisational Change*. Chichester, UK: Wiley.

Tilson, D., Lyytinen, K., & Sørensen, C. (2010). Research commentary -- Digital infrastructures: The missing IS research agenda. *Information Systems Research, 21*(4), 748-759.

Tilson, D., Sørensen, C., & Lyytinen, K. (2012). *Change and Control Paradoxes in Mobile Infrastructure Innovation – The Android and iOS Mobile Operating Systems Cases System Science*. HICSS.

Tiwana, A., Konsynski, B., & Bush, A. A. (2010). Platform evolution: Coevolution of platform architecture, governance, and environmental dynamics. *Information Systems Research, 21*(4), 675–687. doi:10.1287/isre.1100.0323

Trossen, D., & Fine, C. (2005). *Value Chain Dynamics in the Communication Industry*. MIT Communications Futures Program. Retrieved from http://cfp.mit.edu/docs/core/edgedec2005.pdf

Tuli, K. R., Kohli, A. K., & Bharadwaj, S. G. (2007). Rethinking customer solutions: From product bundles to relational processes. *Journal of Marketing, 71*(3), 1–17. doi:10.1509/jmkg.71.3.1

Tuusjärvi, E., & Möller, K. (2009). Multiplicity of norms in inter-company cooperation. *Journal of Business and Industrial Marketing, 24*(7), 519–528. doi:10.1108/08858620910986758

Ulaga, W., & Eggert, A. (2005). Relationship value in business markets: The construct and its dimensions. *Journal of Business-To-Business Marketing, 12*(1), 73–99. doi:10.1300/J033v12n01_04

Ulrich, K. (1995). The role of product architecture in the manufacturing firm. *Research Policy, 24*(3), 419–440. doi:10.1016/0048-7333(94)00775-3

Weerawardena, J., & Mavondo, F. T. (2011). Capabilities, innovation and competitive advantage. *Industrial Marketing Management, 40*(8), 1220–1223. doi:10.1016/j.indmarman.2011.10.012

West, J., & Bogers, M. (2013). Leveraging external sources of innovation: A review of research on open innovation. *Journal of Product Innovation Management*.

Westerlund, M., & Rajala, R. (2010). Learning and innovation in inter-organizational network collaboration. *Journal of Business and Industrial Marketing, 25*(6), 435–442. doi:10.1108/08858621011066026

Williamson, O. (1992). Markets, hierarchies, and the modern corporation: An unfolding perspective. . *Journal of Economic Behavior & Organization, 17*(3), 335–352. doi:10.1016/S0167-2681(95)90012-8

Woodard, C. J., Ramasubbu, N., Tschang, F. T., & Sambamurthy, V. (2013). (forthcoming). Design Capital and Design Moves: The Logic of Digital Business Strategy. *MISQ Special Issue: Digital Business Strategy: Toward a Next Generation of Insights*.

Woodard, J. (2008). Architectural Control Points. *Third International Conference on Design Science Research in Information Systems and Technology (DESRIST 2008)*, Atlanta, GA.

Wuyts, S., Dutta, S., & Stremersch, S. (2004). Portfolios of interfirm agreements in technology-intensive markets: Consequences for innovation and profitability. *Journal of Marketing*, *68*(2), 88–100. doi:10.1509/jmkg.68.2.88.27787

Yin, R. K. (2009). *Case study research: Design and methods* (Vol. 5). Sage.

Yoo, Y., Henfridsson, O., & Lyytinen, K. (2010). The new organizing logic of digital innovation: An agenda for information systems research. *Information Systems Research*, *21*(4), 724–735. doi:10.1287/isre.1100.0322

Chapter 6
Dynamic Content in Future Internet Opportunities Grad Course

Jan Frick
University of Stavanger, Norway

Jens Myrup Pedersen
Aalborg University, Denmark

ABSTRACT

The Colibri project partners started out in 2014 to make an Erasmus+ strategic partnership project titled "Collaboration and Innovation for Better, Personalized and IT-Supported Teaching" (Colibri) (http://www.tuhh.de/colibri/home.html). The overall idea is to implement new and innovative teaching methods with students from different universities for needs and challenges faced in higher education in general and within the combination of the ICT domain and entrepreneurship in particular. Erasmus+ funds the Colibri project. A course is developed between seven universities, based on a variety of rich and digital content: Videos, quizzes, articles to read, assignments, etc. In addition to making it all available on online platforms, we are also experimenting with making it available offline as e-books. This has several advantages, e.g. it can be accessed offline, and it is not depending on platforms that can host it. Another interesting potential of e-books is that they can be generated to suit the needs of the individual learner.

DOI: 10.4018/978-1-5225-2956-9.ch006

INTRODUCTION

This chapter describes how various kinds of digital content can be embedded into an e-book. The advantages and challenges are discussed, and finally an example of how it is actually done is provided. The overall idea of the course described is to implement new and innovative teaching methods with students from different universities for needs and challenges faced in higher education in general, and within the combination of the ICT domain and entrepreneurship in particular. (Crittenden, Esper, Karst, & Slegers, 2015; Lopez et al., 2015; Pedersen, Şükrü, Frick, & Mank, 2016).

THE COURSE

The course developed as part of the Colibri project is ideal for exploring the potentials in dynamic content due to the diversity of students, teaching staff and content.

The interdisciplinary joint grad course Future Internet Opportunities started spring 2015 with 30 students and was given by more than 10 different teachers from Alborg University in Denmark, Hamburg University of Technology in Germany, Riga Technical University in Latvia, University of Stavanger in Norway, University of Technology and Life Sciences in Bydgoszcz in Poland, Universitat Politechnika de Catalunya in Spain, and Bogazici University in Turkey. We also include the organisations National Documentation Centre in Greece, atene KOM GmbH in Germany, and Talaia Networks S.L. in Spain. These organisations both provide their own projects/ problems for the groups and they serve as providers of issues from other companies.

The students following the course represent the same universities; Erasmus+ is providing funding for four students per university per year, so a total of 28 students per year. Each year we had 1-2 additional students joining, which were then funded by or through their home universities. The students come with different technical backgrounds, i.e. telecommunications, computer engineering, bio informatics, entrepreneurship and business informatics, and at the same time they also represent different cultural backgrounds and learning traditions. First of all, this makes for very interesting projects and collaborations, but it is also a good living lab for testing the different teaching methods and receive feedback from such a diverse group of students.

The course has different parts (or phases) as seen in Figure 1. Parts 1 and 2 contain modules where the students study content. Parts 3 and 4 are where the students in groups utilise this content in Project Based Learning (PBL) projects with problems from real companies.

The course covers Internet technologies, the usage of Internet technologies, and business applications as entrepreneurship based on the Internet technologies. These topics are divided into 10 modules. In part 2 all students individually follow the introductory level of the 10 modules, then they choose 5 basic level modules, and at last they choose 2 advanced level modules. Then in part 3 and 4 they work in groups on solving a problem based project case (PBL) from a real company. At last the groups present and defend their understanding and proposal for the company case.

During the work with the company case the groups are expected to utilise the content provided in the 10 modules.

The course is based on blended learning in the sense that it consists of a combination of virtual and physical learning spaces: While most of the time is spent on virtual collaboration, there are also two seminars where all students and teachers get together: A 5-day workshop in part 3, where the modules are finalised and the project work started, and a 5-day workshop in part 5, where the projects are finished and presentations given and exams conducted.

As Figure 1 shows, there is not only a mixture of teaching technologies, but also a mixture of pedagogic approaches. As examples of such approaches there are individual online learning, on site lectures, group work, peer learning, and project based learning. The course accepts students from several universities and both

Figure 1. Flowchart of the Future Internet Opportunities grad course
The capital letters refer to the section on "Elements of blended learning in the course" below. "P"= "personalise", "S"= "socialise", "E" = "explore new pedagogical approaches", and "C" = "collaborate".
Frick & Laudal, 2016.

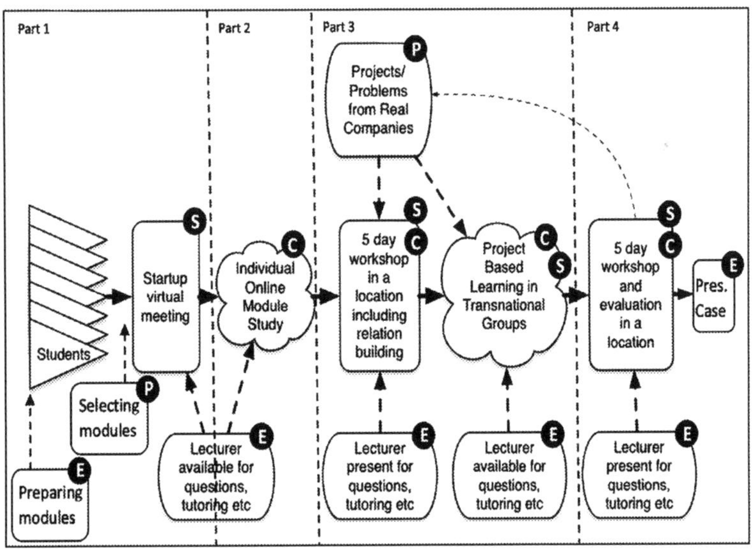

business and engineering backgrounds, and therefore a Personalisation of the content is seen as one of the important tools: In principle, each student will have his own learning path, depending on his background, his personal learning objectives, and possibly also his learning style preferences. This also ensure that the students in each group have the knowledge required to deal with the company cases. In addition, socialise is another method, as to develop a network between the students where they know and trust each other. This is important for the group work and it ensure that they learn as a group which means an Organisational Leaning process (Riis & Frick, 1990). This is emphasised as we encourage Collaboration as an increasing tool through the course. We therefore need content packaging that can be utilised both for the individual learning process and the PBL organisational learning process where the same content shall be utilised in a context depending on the group and the problem to be solved. While keeping this utilisation in mind, the remainder of the chapter will focus on presenting the material developed in part 1-2 as dynamic content in e-books.

HOW CONTENT IS DEVELOPED AND MADE AVAILABLE

The content utilised has different formats: journal papers, videos stored at YouTube, presentations with and without sound, links to webpages, multiple choice quizzes, essays assignments, and peer learning activities such as peer assessments. These 10 modules of content were developed at the 7 participating universities but coordinated through common workshops between the teaching staff. The first version of the content was distributed by the Moodle Learning Management System at Aalborg University, an LMS system enabling tracking of student activities, two-way delivery and access of content, and cooperation between students.

However, better tools for content delivery and use are needed, as well as ways to provide feedback to the students as well as teachers. Moreover, we would like to make the content available offline without losing the interactive/dynamic aspects. Regarding the feedback, we are investigating Learning Analytics tools and methods. (Anderson & Gavan, 2016; ElAtia, Ipperciel, & Zaiane, 2017; Kim, 2014; Larusson & White, 2014; McQuiggan, Kosturko, McQuiggan, & Sabourin, 2015; Means, Bakia, & Murphy, 2014; Reimann, 2016; Wild, 2016) The combination of Learning Analytics and content packaging with multiple content formats demand adaptable content packaging that also supports platform independence and offline access. It is also an important part that the content and as much as possible of the Learning Analytics student feedback can be utilised. We have experimented with the iBook as a tool. (Hagedorn, 2012; Robley, Felsen, & Spatz, 2010; Shapiro, 2013)

The first version of an iBook module was developed with the iBook Author tool. This was our Module 8 “Applications and Services”, and the content was easily transferred from the Moodle LMS to the iBook. This is a more accessible format than the .zip files that were used before, and it provides a relatively easy way to meet the requirements stated above.

In the following we will elaborate more on some of the different forms of content that were used, and discuss the advantages and disadvantages of converting these to e-books format.

Interactive Videos and Quizzes

Videos can be made interactive in different ways. In the first year of Colibri videos of usually 5-10 minutes were created, where each video is finished by a quiz that serves as self-assessment for the students. In this case, the video is not itself interactive, but the combination of videos and quizzes makes the experience interactive. The videos were both integrated with Moodle and made available on YouTube. The videos integrated into Moodle made a more integrated experience for most students - but it was not compatible with all browsers/operating systems, and/or not very viewable on some tablets/phones. YouTube has the advantage that it works well on almost all platforms and devices, and it can also be displayed directly in Moodle. Both platforms require (generally) that the students are online with a decent Internet connection. For this video material, an e-book provides a good alternative, especially if it is made in a format that is viewable on different platforms and devices.

In the third year of Colibri we used the H5P plugin, which allows creation of many different forms of interactive content, integrated with different LMSs including Moodle. Essentially this is a layer “on top of” the YouTube video, which for example makes it possible to stop the video at a specified point a provide a single-page quiz that the students reply to before moving on with the videos. The quiz options are not as many as in Moodle, and it does not give teachers the same kind of feedback, but it has at least two advantages. It allows for a more real and seamless interactive learning experience, because questions can be placed more often, and it also gives the learner a more integrated experience because he does not need to manually open the quiz once the video has played.

We found that the quiz possibilities in Moodle are quite powerful and flexible. There are many different kinds of questions, and it is possible to do grading either automatically or manually. The latter can be useful when the answers are not easily checked automatically, for example in forms of longer pieces of text. Moreover, the results are stored in database, which creates options for the teacher to follow each student, but also for the students to keep track of his own achievements, and/

or see or continue previous quiz attempts even from different devices. However, the drawback of this is that the student needs to be registered and online for this to work.

While e-books are also different, we have not seen platforms that offer the same variety of questions as Moodle does. In general, the content is kept simpler, and the quizzes are not connected to a database: While this gives more flexibility and e.g. allows for offline access, it also limits the ability to access and analyse data from student's results.

If this kind of interactive content is to be provided to students who do not (always) have access to learning platforms, we see the e-books as a very good way of providing the content to students, because it comes in an integrated and seamless fashion, and it is relatively easy to create in a way that looks and feels professional. The alternative of providing quizzes and videos in separate documents, e.g. in a zip-file, is much harder to use for the students. Moreover, creating an e-book can be a good alternative to transferring content from one platform to another, which is often a tedious task.

Assignments and Workshops

Moodle allows for activities of what is called "Assignments" and "Workshops". In Colibri both were used, especially for the advanced modules. They are generally more demanding from the teachers, since manual processing/grading of submissions is needed.

Assignments are essentially spaces where students can upload their work (e.g. mini projects, essays, assignments, problems they are given, etc.). These are then commented and graded by the teachers.

Workshops are similar to assignments, but also contain a peer assessment element. So, after students have submitted their assignment, they are asked to review (comment and/or grade) the work by one or more of their peers. The assignment of tasks can be fully automatized, i.e. assigned when the submission deadline has passed, or it can be handled manually by the teacher. Finally, the teacher has the ability to grade the students work based on both their assignment and the feedback they have provided to their peers.

We found these to be less suitable for e-books, because they are not stand-alone activities but require interaction with other students. That requires also some platform that connects the students to each other, such as Moodle, but maybe such a functionality could be implemented in future e-books - especially were the books are used in a specific context, for example for a course with synchronisation of deadlines for assignments/peer tasks.

Static Content, Such as Papers and PDF-Presentations

When producing interactive content, static content is often used as part of the learning material, either self-contained or as part of an interactive experience. When integrated in a platform like Moodle, while easy to find, open and navigate, they often appear as individual elements, e.g. PDF-files which takes up a full browser window or is opened in a separate viewer application. Here, the e-book can have the advantage of presenting the content in a more integrated fashion, i.e. it is one book.

In conclusion, we see both advantages and disadvantages of providing interactive content in the form of e-books, compared to using a LMS platform such as Moodle. The integrated platforms provide possibilities for creating more complex materials, and a much wider array of e.g. quizzes, assignments, and workshops. On the other hand, the e-book is a simple way of presenting the content in an integrated and portable fashion, which might be especially interesting for students who either are not always online, or who do not have access to such portals.

As we will see in the next section, creating the e-book based on existing content can be a relatively simple process: Thus, it might be possible to create e-book versions of course materials, which can supplement content in an LMS, and also serve as a document the students can keep even after finishing the course.

CREATING THE E-BOOK BASED ON DYNAMIC CONTENT

To develop an e-book there are several possibilities. A very simple way is to save a PDF or other document formats into an ePub format. The result can then be in most e-book readers. This will be convenient as it is easily done, and it will be widely accessible. The downside is that the functionality is quite limited as it does not provide any media access, and it is not possible to add a dynamic user interface.

The more common way is to utilise a development tool such as the iBook Author software (Apple Inc). This tool provides a huge number of templates that gives a possibility to generate a dynamic medium. It has most of the tools as found in usual desktop publishing programs, but since this is supposed to be used on devices like computers, tablets, or phones, it provides many opportunities. Most of the tools we have in the the H5P plugin in Moodle is available as widgets.

The first step utilising such an authoring tool is to select a template. There are many templates available with the tool, and additional templates can be found and downloaded from third parties both as freeware and to be bought. These templates have different structures available and suggestions for pages: The pages can be text only, a mixture of text and multimedia content, or special pages like Glossary, Table of Content etc.

The second step is to determine the structure to be used. You may change this later, but it is easier to have a structure from the start. You may use chapters, parts (of chapters), and single pages. In our case, we used the 3 levels of the module as chapters: Introduction, Basic level, and Advanced level.

The third step is to add the content to chapter introduction and pages.

In our case, we had most of the content in our Moodle LMS system. Titles, graphics, and text could be copied and pasted into the templates (or imported from Pages or Microsoft Word documents). We also had a possibility to import video or PowerPoint presentations that runs as videos with audio explanations. An example of this is shown in Figure 2. However, video and/or audio in PowerPoints increases the size of the iBook, and for this reason we chose to place the videos into a website or YouTube and refer to it from the iBook. The downside of this approach is that it demands connectivity of the user, which was one of the reasons to go for the e-book, so minor sized videos were included in the first version.

Often we want to refer to material written or published by others, which can be a problem with intellectual property rights. However, all material available with open access on the Internet can be linked. And by providing such links in the iBook, we can comment on a published paper or video, give the reader a link to the original, and thus use such content without republishing it. Instead we give the publisher more traffic. The drawback with this approach is again that it requires Internet connectivity.

The fourth step is to add the widgets that creates the dynamic of the document compared to a static PDF document. These can be included into the content pages or added as separate pages. The options are to add Quizzes, Keynotes (Apples version of PowerPoint documents), Multimedia content, Interactive media, 3D animations, Pop-up notes, etc. If the text on a page is too long, and it is not desired to add another page, scrolling can be added. If even more flexibility is needed, there is also an option of adding HTML code.

A specific issue in our case was the quiz/test parts. In the Moodle LMS we utilised the multiple-choice test function. There were no direct import possibilities, but question and answers could be copied into the widget template provided with the iBook Author. Again, there is also the option to make a larger variation of test-tools on a website and link the book into it, but the limitations in terms of Internet access, user access to the LMS system etc. should be taken into account when considering this option.

The fifth step is to do the finishing by adding a cover picture, introduction media, copyright, author presentation etc.

At last the sixth step is to distribute it. From the iBook Author the distribution options is to publish directly to iTunes Store or export as an iBook. You may also export to PDF, but then you lose the dynamic parts.

Feedback from the users was a reason for keeping all into one document, probably because they were used to one source for a course module from Moodle. But the integration between an iBook and the multitude of tools, sources and possibilities on the Internet provides wide possibilities for Blended Learning, and has a large potential that should be explored in the future. However, it takes more effort to make such an integration look seamless for the reader, and. as Internet changes, there is a risk that references might disappear or change away from the intended content.

EVALUATIONS FROM THE STUDENTS

In this section, we will describe how the students have rated the different kinds of content provided. This part is not specifically related to the e-books, since the material was mainly made available in the Moodle portal. The numbers presented are from the second year of Colibri, collected in July 2016.

The data were collected for each module, and each module was designed differently with not everyone using all of the following elements: Videos, quizzes, Q&A forums, self-study activities and peer learning activities. Instead of presenting

Figure 2. Example screen from the Colibri iBook for Module 8 showing a page with an imbedded PowerPoint with audio video

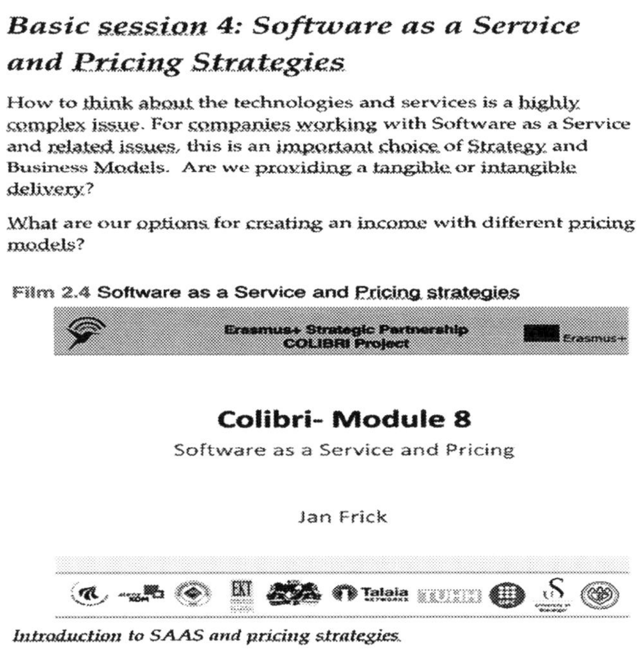

the results for each of the 10 modules, we have here summarised the evaluation of video and quizzes, which was used in similar ways for all the modules. In addition to this statistical evaluation, we have summarised the comments from the students regarding the form of the materials provided, especially focusing on topics relevant for the production of e-books.

The statistics provided below is therefore average numbers over all the modules. The data are collected through electronic evaluation forms for all 29 students who participated in the final seminar (only one student started, but did not participate in the final seminar). They are filled out during the last day of the seminar, after the examinations were finished. Figures 3-4 show how the students rate the efficiency for their learning of videos and quizzes, and both are rated quite high: For each of these elements, around 74% of the students rate them as either efficient or very efficient.

In addition to the numbers, the students provide also comments, both during evaluation meetings in the seminars and in the final electronic evaluation. They are generally very positive to the modules where short videos and quizzes were used as described above, but we also learnt a lot from reading the students comments. In the following we mention these points, and highlight some of the implications for production of e-books.

- Especially when the modules are supposed to be self-contained and possible to complete without interacting with teachers, it is important that it is very

Figure 3. Students evaluation of the efficiency of the videos for their learning (percentage)

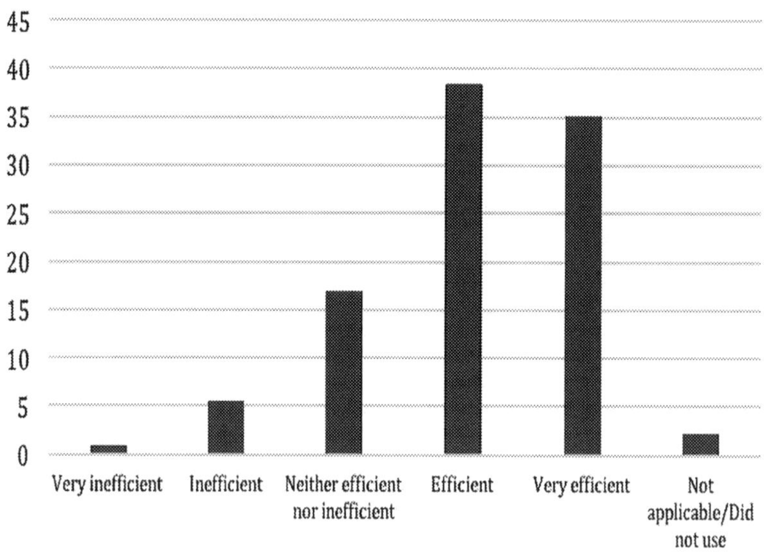

Figure 4. Students evaluation of the efficiency of the questions/quiz material for their learning (percentage)

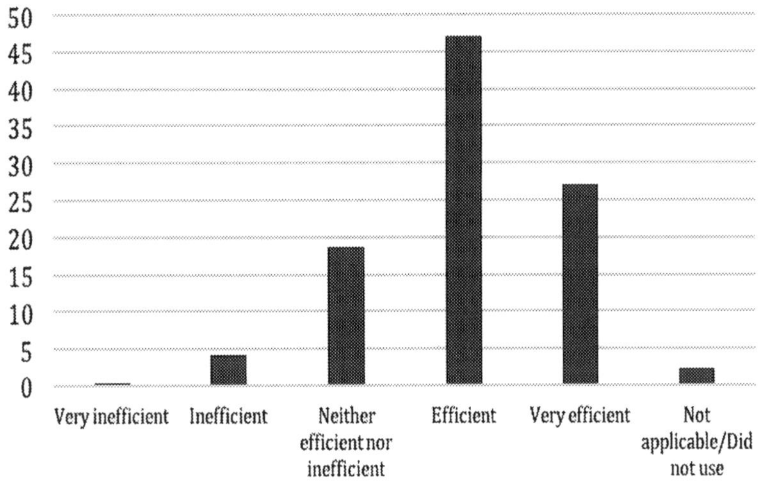

clear what should be done, and in what order. Completion tracking so you can monitor your progress is also crucial. This is important to keep in mind when designing the e-books, which has a clear advantage in that all material/activities can be collected in one place, and presented in the order in which it should be studied. It is also worth keeping in mind when designing individual learning paths, so each student follow different activities - a personalised view, for example an e-book only showing what is relevant for the individual student could be desirable. This is however also a trade-off between making a clear path, and providing optional material for the student that he can choose to study.

- One of the things that some students are missing is the ability to ask questions during a video recorded lecture. Sometimes, a student can get stuck in the middle of a presentation, where the lack of understanding of one part makes it hard to understand subsequent content. When the material is available in a learning portal, there is an option to ask questions to teachers and other students in order to clarify any such questions. When presenting the material in an e-book format the contact with a teacher can be unfeasible (and there might not even be a teacher), and therefore other solutions should be thought. Online forums could be helpful here, but we would also suggest to include a "Frequently Asked Questions" for each video, where students can seek for immediate help to clarify their questions and move on.

- Good audio quality is important. This is an important observation, since often it will be necessary or at least desirable to compress the videos embedded in e-books in order to limit the file size.
- Many of the videos used during the modules contained a large picture of presentation slides, and a smaller image of the lecturer speaking. While this worked well, many students also asked for PDF versions of the presentation slides. This makes it easier for them to browse through, for example for getting an overview or when looking for specific information. It also provides an easy reference when discussing the material with others or asking questions. There are some slight drawbacks when presenting the same information in multiple formats/files, as it increases file sizes and makes it hard to have the simple and integrated view of all the materials. This should be thought carefully through when designing e-book material.

E-BOOKS WITH DYNAMIC CONTENT FOR PROBLEM BASED LEARNING

As part of developing the course, it has also been interesting to explore how the content of modules support the project work. Initially, the idea was that the students should first study the modules, which would enable them to then do the problem based project work. The challenge with this model is that the students when they study the modules do not yet know exactly what knowledge they need to work on the PBL projects. This can affect the student's motivation for studying the modules, and it also creates a time gap between learning skills/methods from the modules and applying them to the problems they work on.

While the students need some background knowledge before starting to work on the projects, the more in-depth learning could be timed better: If the students learn the tools and methods they need just when they realise they need them, and then get to apply the knowledge as soon as they have learned about it, it could create much more efficient learning.

For this reason, the model of Just-in-time resources for PBL was developed, see Figure 5. First the students obtain an overview of the problem domain, for example through studying the modules and other materials. Then, when the students work on the projects and meet a specific challenge/problem this will help them identify relevant tools/methods that they need to learn.

This is a good time to study these tools/methods by the use of what we call just-in-time resources, such as interactive learning materials. Such materials can be supplemented by other materials including literature studies, articles, lectures/

Figure 5. Just-in-time resources for PBL

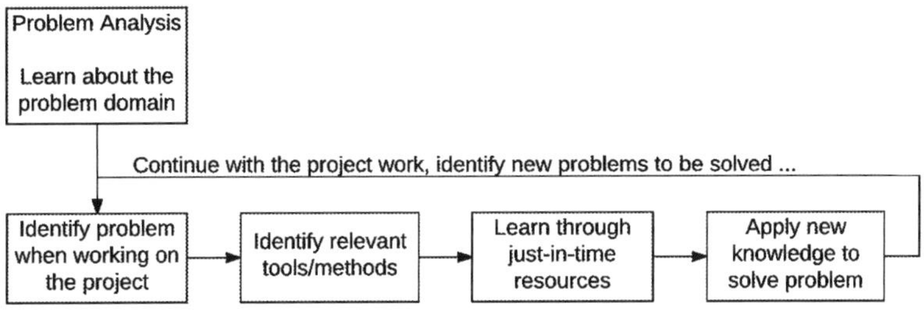

study groups etc. Once they have learned these skills they can apply it to their specific challenge/problem, and continue with the project, where they will meet new challenges that can be tackled in the same way.

The advantage of this model of access to just-in-time resources for PBL is that the students are provided the material when they are most motivated, and that they get to apply the newly gained knowledge straight away. On the other hand, creating a tailor-made learning path specifically reflecting the students demands can be a significant task, also keeping in mind that different student groups often will require different skills, and they will do so at different times.

To tackle this challenge, we suggest to construct smaller "building blocks" of material, which can then be either combined into one just-in-time resource, or the students can choose to compose their own path through the material by choosing the relevant such building blocks. It is the experience of the authors that setting up this in a learning management system can be quite a workload for the teachers as it is not sufficient to construct these once: They should be maintained, sometimes moved between semester, students should be given access to what is relevant for them etc. Hopefully these processes will become smoother as the systems develop, but the e-book seems again to be a handy alternative as once it is made it does not require any maintenance and is easy to distribute to students.

PLAN TO FURTHER DEVELOP THE INITIATIVE

A significant issue related to the virtual learning environment is how the content are made available to the students. The immediate way is to present it through a Learning Management System (LMS), but to have an easier transfer to other courses and possible future use or references by students after the course, we are planning to further experiment with the development and use of e-book as an included and complimentary medium.

In the first place, we will make the books created available for both our own students and the general public. Based on the evaluations and comments received, we will update the content and format for the last year of the Colibri project.

There are also discussions between partners in the Colibri network on how to utilise and continue the experiences gathered in the master course. One such approach is through the ECIU, European Consortium of Innovative Universities, where 3 of the Colibri partners are members. Potentially, the material could be used by other universities, either in the current form or after modifications to fit the needs of particular learners.

More and more university teachers are creating interactive content, to smaller or larger extend, to support their teaching whether it is meant as supplementary material or used for converting the form to e.g. Flipped classroom. If this material can be converted to an e-book format without too much work, we believe this would often be an interesting add-on, and provide the students with an offline version of their materials, which would be available even after the course has finished. Also, it could serve as a reference and support the students during e.g. examination preparation, and it could be used in contexts outside of the traditional classroom.

When e-books are created as an add-on based on existing material in e.g. a Moodle LMS, it is important that the e-book can be created as automatic as possible, so the teacher does not have to go through a work-intensive process of converting and formatting the materials. We have demonstrated that this is not too difficult for traditional context, such as text, videos, images, and sound, but it seems much more challenging for more interactive content such as quizzes and quizzes integrated with videos. Here it would be a big advantage if more quiz formats were supported, and if it was possible to important content directly to the e-book using standard formats. This is of course less of an issue when e-books are created independently of existing materials.

CONCLUSION

In this chapter, we have demonstrated how different forms of digital content can be embedded into an e-book format, and we have discussed advantages and disadvantages compared to using online platforms and learning management systems. We would like to highlight the point that e-books can be seen as more than just an extension of the normal book: It has a good potential in being used for storing course content already published on other platforms, making it available in a relatively simple, offline format. This is especially so if the process of creating the interactive content becomes easier and more automatic.

REFERENCES

Anderson, M., & Gavan, C. (2016). *Developing effective educational experiences through learning analytics*. Hershey, PA: Information Science Reference. doi:10.4018/978-1-4666-9983-0

Crittenden, V. L., Esper, K., Karst, N., & Slegers, R. (2015). *Evolving entrepreneurical education, Innovation in the Babson Classroom*. Emerald Group Publishing Ltd.

ElAtia, S., Ipperciel, D., & Zaiane, O. R. (2017). *Data mining and learning analytics: applications in educational research*. Hoboken, New Jersey: John Wiley & Sons, Inc.

Frick, J., & Laudal, T. (2016). *COLIBRI: Blended Learning In An Innovative Transnational Approach*. Paper presented at the Danning og Utdanning- mellom klassiske idealer og ytre relevans, Stavanger, Norway.

Hagedorn, S. (2012). *How to Create on iBooks*. Author.

Hansen, P. K., Gertsen, F., Larsen, J. H., & Frick, J. (2002). Does Efficiency and Project based Learning comply? Paper presented at the Norddesign 2002, Trondheim, Norway.

Kim, P. (2014). *Massive open online courses: The MOOC revolution*. New York: Routledge.

Kjersdam, F., & Enemark, S. (1997). The Aalborg experiment project innovation in university education (3rd ed.). Faculty of Technology and Science Aalborg University Press.

Kolmos, A., Fink, F. K., & Krogh, L. (2004). *The Aalborg PBL Model: Progress, Diversity and Challenges*. Aalborg, Denmark: Aalborg University Press.

Larusson, J. A., & White, B. (2014). *Learning analytics: from research to practice*. New York: Springer. doi:10.1007/978-1-4614-3305-7

Lopez, J. M., Frick, J., Kirikova, M., Solé-Pareta, J., Pedersen, J. M., & Tran, N. (2015). The Colibri Project: Overcoming diversity in blended e-learning activity preparation *Proceedings of the 43rd SEFI Annual Conference 2014: Diversity in engineering education: an opportunity to face the new trends of engineering*. SEFI: European Association for Engineering Education.

McQuiggan, S., Kosturko, L., McQuiggan, J., & Sabourin, J. (2015). *Mobile learning: a handbook for developers, educators, and learners*. Hoboken, NJ: John Wiley & Sons, Inc. doi:10.1002/9781118938942

Means, B., Bakia, M., & Murphy, R. (2014). *Learning online: what research tells us about whether, when and how*. New York: Routledge.

Pedersen, J. M., Şükrü, M., Frick, J., & Mank, L. (2016). *Colibri: An International Blended Learning Experience based on Real-World Problems*. Paper presented at the PAEE/ALE2016, Minho, Portugal.

Reimann, P. (2016). *Measuring and visualizing learning in the information-rich classroom*. New York, NY: Routledge.

Riis, J. O., & Frick, J. (1990). *Organizational Learning: A Neglected Dimension of Production Management Systems design.* Paper presented at the Advanceds In Production Management Systems, Helsinki, Finland.

Robley, C., Felsen, B., & Spatz, S. (2010). *Making your eBook. The author's guide to eBook publishing, design, distribution, and marketing.* Academic Press.

Shapiro, C. a. R. (2013). *Creating Accessible iBooks Textbooks with iBooks.* Author.

Wild, F. (2016). *Learning analytics in R with SNA, LSA, and MPIA*. New York, NY: Springer Berlin Heidelberg. doi:10.1007/978-3-319-28791-1

Chapter 7
Media Richness, Knowledge Sharing, and Computer Programming by Virtual Software Teams

Idongesit Williams
Aalborg University, Denmark

Albert Gyamfi
Aalborg University, Denmark

ABSTRACT

Software programming is a task with high analyzability. However, knowledge sharing is an intricate part of the software programming process. Today, new media platforms have been adopted to enable knowledge sharing between virtual teams. Taking into consideration the high task analyzability and the task characteristics involved in software development, the question is if the media richness of the current media platform is effective in enabling knowledge sharing among these virtual teams? An exploratory research was conducted on a software company in Denmark. The data was gathered was analyzed qualitatively using narrative analysis. This paper concludes, based on the case being investigated, that rich media does not fit the task characteristics of a software programmer. It further concludes that Media richness does affect knowledge sharing in these virtual teams. This is because the current lean media actually enables knowledge sharing as it fits the core characteristics of the software programming process.

DOI: 10.4018/978-1-5225-2956-9.ch007

INTRODUCTION

This chapter explores how media richness influences knowledge sharing activities in virtual teams involved in software programming. The task of interest is the process of programming or coding of the software. In recent times, large corporations have been involved in the decentralization of the operational aspects of their companies. Such corporations include SAP, IBM and General etc. (Lepsinger, 2015). The facilitation of their virtual operations has been enabled by the opportunities enabled by globalization and the evolution of the Internet. Based on our previous knowledge of the first author in software development and a brief practice in the trade, it was intriguing to learn that software development companies have been embracing virtual teams (Ramesh & Dennis, 2002). These companies have different software developers in different locations collaborating online to implement or programme software. This, of course, was not the intriguing part. That was because software development has always been developed with computers. So having such collaborative development effort with different computers connected to each other over the Internet was not that exciting. What was exciting though was how media richness enabled knowledge sharing within a virtual software development team as they implement or code the software. In a software development team domicile in a particular location, knowledge sharing is not difficult. Knowledge could be shared via face-to-face interaction using a device with rich media; placing comments in a programming code to explain a code in the software, documentation of daily team meetings, one on one tutorials in a company training session and codes and other relevant materials stored in repositories (see examples (Ramesh & Dennis, 2002; Ying, Wright, & Abrams, 205; DeRosa, 2014)). In this way, various members of the team are able to learn something new from one another. The new knowledge will help them implement their codes. If this scenario is transposed online, the need for this kind of knowledge sharing activities will still exist.

But knowledge sharing, as a result of the complexity in communication programming languages outside the software designed for it, might be challenging. This will definitely be the case in a scenario where two remote software developers working on the same project for the same company run into challenges on how to implement the codes. Depending on the level of information richness they need from each other in order to collaborate, different media platforms can be used. However, the more they try to unravel how to solve a programming code, rich media platforms may not be helpful. But lean media platforms might be helpful because they could read each other's codes, ponder on it and possibly verbalize their thoughts. A media platform used for such an activity should be able to enhance knowledge sharing in less ambiguous and equivocal manner. But in a situation where the software developers are discussing the requirement specifications they were given or they are presenting their thoughts in a scrum meeting. The nature of information being transmitted may not necessary be complex. The other team members will not only be interested in hearing what their colleague says, they will want to take not of non-verbal gestures. Here they can sense if they are on the same page or there are minor differences in opinion. In such a situation, rich media will be helpful. Therefore the media needs for the transmission of different forms of information by the team will differ. The fact that knowledge sharing in software teams, and by extension virtual software teams, require different set of media is supported in literature. The literature states that no media tool supports every facet of the operational dynamics in the development of a software (see (Bindrees, Pooley, Ibrahim, & Taylor, 2014)). For example, virtual teams use collaborative platforms such as GitHub to share programming codes and other media platforms such as WebEx, adobe connect or GoToMeeting, to support their daily tasks (DeRosa, 2014). Therefore one cannot dispute the use of multiple media platforms by these virtual software teams. But this raises a question. Does the media richness in the existing media platforms used by virtual software development teams for their core task support knowledge sharing?

In order to gain some insight into this phenomena, an inductive qualitative exploratory study was conducted. A Danish software company with 200 employees was chosen as a source for identifying a case. They are present in about seven countries and they possess virtual software teams. Data was gathered from a software engineer employed in this company. Narrative analysis was used to analyse the data. Inferences were drawn from the narrative analysis to draw conclusions. Based on the inferences drawn, it was clear that knowledge sharing activities via the media platforms used by the virtual teams did occur. However, it did not happen with rich media platforms, rather it occurred with lean media platforms. This was because the lean media platforms were tailored to fit the task characteristics identified in the task of the programmers.

The organization of the chapter are as follows. This section is the introduction of the chapter. This is followed by the background concepts guiding the chapter. These are the concepts of Software development, media richness and knowledge sharing. The purpose for identifying these background concepts is to explain how they relate within the context of this chapter. The next section is the presentation of the context of discussion in the chapter. This is the context of virtual software development teams and the collaborative media platforms they use. This explanation is followed by the research method by which this research was conducted; the findings and the analysis of the findings; and finally by the discussion and conclusion sections. The findings in this chapter are not generalizable. They are meant to inspire more research into the context.

SOFTWARE DEVELOPMENT, MEDIA RICHNESS, AND KNOWLEDGE SHARING

In this section, the concepts used in this paper and how they relate are described. The development of a software has a lot of processes. The process of interest to this chapter involves software engineer from remote locations implementing various code aspects of a particular software. However, before discussing virtual software teams, it was important to provide a background to this chapter. The foundation of this discussion is the interplay between software development, media richness and knowledge sharing. Knowledge in this chapter is defined as "Justified personal belief" (King, 2009). And knowledge sharing here implies "less focused dissemination of knowledge, such as through a repository (ibid). Knowledge sharing in this chapter is examined as a potential effect of the interaction between media platforms and the software development process. These media platforms are believed to enhance knowledge sharing as it becomes richer (See (Andres, 2002)). The implication is that the richness of the platform serves as a motivation to adopt the platform for knowledge sharing. Therefore in this chapter, an overview on the role of media richness in software development and an overview on the implication of the media richness theory on the knowledge sharing process in the development of software are discussed. To aid this discussion, an overview of the Media richness theory is also presented.

The Role of Media in Software Development

There has always been a fundamental interplay between software development and the media. This is because software is now developed on platforms with access to the media, enabled by the Internet. These media platforms enable knowledge sharing. These platforms exist for independent developers. An example is the Sun's online forum support for Java programmers (Rus, Lindvall, & Sinha, 2001). Here java software programmers can use this repository to gain knowledge on how to deal with their daily tasks. It also exists within software companies. The natural tool is the code base. The company's codebase is the collection of source code used to build a particular software (Ying, Wright, & Abrams, 205). Software developers working on that software are able to access that codebase to modify it and improve on it. Within these codes, there are comments explaining the functions of the codes. Here newer developers are able to learn new ways of working with that programming language.

Although this relationship did exist, it existed away from the influence of the mass media. In a way one would say that the advancement in software development did create a rippling effect that ended up affecting the trade as well. This is because advances in software development has resulted in the evolution of the mass media.

The coincidental evolution in Broadband technology has resulted in the convergence between the mass media, telecommunications and the software development industry. Hence using the personal computer, a software developer using the internet can code a software in a remote server in a country he or she has never visited.

But for software programmers, these evolutions has presented an opportunity for enhanced knowledge sharing. This involves knowledge sharing that is transferred offline to the Internet. This is because the Internet has enabled Media platforms that could support the activities of Software developers to be able to deliver rich information.

THEORETICAL BACKGROUND

The underlying theory in this chapter is the Media richness Theory. In this section, an overview of the theory as it relates to knowledge sharing in virtual software teams is explained.

Overview of Media Richness Theory

The concept of information richness can be explained using the Media Richness Theory. The media richness theory was introduced by Daft and Lengel (1986). Their aim was to understand why organization process information (Daft & Lengel, 1986). They identified that information is required to perform the daily tasks within the organization. However for the information to be received successfully, the information should contain a low degree of uncertainty and equivocality. Hence there has to be debates, and clarification in the communication process until the parties concerned can understand each other perfectly. Within this process the information is made rich as the frame of reference is synchronized and ambiguity is reduced (ibid). This they referred to as information richness. However for an information to be rich, the medium of conveying the information should enable immediate feedback and provide an accurate picture of how both parties verbally and non-verbally interpret the information. They identified 5 medium of communication and how they affect information richness. These forms of media include face-to-face communication, telephone, personal documents such as letters or memos, impersonal written documents, and numeric documents (Daft & Lengel, 1986). The level of richness of each media, from the highest to the lowest, ranges as listed from face-to-face communication to impersonal written documents, and numeric documents. The closer the form of media to face-to-face communication, the greater its ability to enable information richness. In this chapter, this scale is used later on to grade the level of media richness of platforms adopted in the software company studied based on the frequency of usage of the platform for the core task.

Media Richness Theory and the Task Characteristics in Software Programming

In order to determine the level of media richness needed for task, an important issue to take into consideration is the task characteristics (Daft & Lengel, 1986). Task characteristics can be classified into extrinsic and intrinsic task characteristics (Kim & Soergel, 2006). The intrinsic task characteristic implies the intrinsic nature of the task (ibid). The extrinsic characteristics *"originate from outside the task"* (ibid). Kim & Soergel (2006) identify the intrinsic and extrinsic task characteristics as seen in Table 1.

From the Media Richness Theory standpoint, the task characteristics of interest to this chapter are the task variety and the task analysability (Daft & Lengel, 1986). These was so to create a delimitation on our scope of investigation. However the task frequency, which is an extrinsic characteristics of the task will be used to simulate the frequency at which knowledge is shared on media platforms.

In the Media Richness Theory, the variety of the task is determined by the "frequency of unexpected and novel events" while the task analysability refers to the way people in organizations respond to problems (Daft & Lengel, 1986). Based on the theory, if a task is unanalysable and its task variety is low, rich media can be used to resolve the unanalysable issues. If the task is unanalysable and possesses a high task variety, rich media is still needed to solve the unanalysable issues. However, if the task analysability is low the task variety is low, lean media is needed because ambiguity and equivocality is reduced due to the standardized nature of the information. But if a task analysability is high and the task variety is high, leam media is still needed. This is because the data or information transferred is rich to enable decisions being taken.

Table 1. Types of task characteristics

	Intrinsic Task Characteristics	Extrinsic Task Characteristics
1	Task Analysability	Task Frequency
2	Task variety	Task imposition
3	Task difficulty	Locus of the task
4	Task Routines	Task autonomy
5	Task complexity	Task significance
6	Task Structuredness	Task urgency
7		Task risk
8		Task reward

Source: Kim & Soergel (2006).

In the programming of a software, each programming language possess standardized syntax and logic which cannot be interpreted otherwise. Therefore there is an objective way of solving challenges within the software coding process. Therefore the task is highly analysable. In the same vain it is a task with a high variety. This is because business in the software industry is created from ideas. The ideas could be internal or external ideas. These ideas have to be converted into a set of requirement specifications and handed over to the software developers to develop the software. The software developer has to engage in a mind mapping process to develop a flowchart and identify the necessary algorithms needed to implement the software. These software programming or coding process begins, once the software developer has an idea of the syntax needed to implement the software. The programmer then has to run the code on a compiler till he has no errors. It is in this process, that the programmer goes in search for knowledge on how to correct the errors. Therefore the programmer encounters a lot of unexpected events in this process until he or she has could get a solution. Hence due to the unexpected events, which sometimes occur in creating novel solutions, software programming has a high task variety.

Therefore, the level of richness of a media platform chosen by the programmers, as proposed in the theory, will depend the task analysability and task variety. These task characteristics are constant and it will be the same if the software programming is conducted by virtual teams or otherwise.

Implication of Media Richness Theory on the Knowledge Transfer Process in Software Development

The media richness theory explains more of a knowledge transfer process and not too much of a knowledge sharing process. This is because when the theory was proposed, the forms of media and their capabilities were limited. But in recent times, it is safe to say that the theory is also valid for knowledge sharing. This is because, although so far no one has perfectly simulated face-to-face interactions, the technologies today possess a greater level of media richness. It is a matter of time before an almost face-to-face interaction is made possible using technology. And current platforms used for knowledge transfer, even in software industries, support knowledge storage. In addition currently there are researches documenting the potential of media richness in various sectors of the economy (see (Baehr, 2012; Gyamfi, 2016)).

However, based on the Media Richness Theory and the concept of Information richness, independent software developers can assess online software development platforms such as Atom, Cloud9ide and Eclipse PHP developer tools etc. These portals are designed to enable the core task analysability and task variety features in the programming of software. The media richness on this portal is not so much about having access to their remote software development editors, debuggers and compilers for the programmers. Rather, it is also about the support provided to the programmers on these platforms to have access to a knowledgebase for knowledge sharing, collaborative work spaces and an interactive dashboard. However, one cannot say that the media richness on these platforms are high based on the media hierarchy created by Daft and Lengel (1986). But the level of richness they possess enables knowledge sharing. Information on these platforms can be stored and accessed later by relevant parties. In software companies, similar portals exist. Although these media platforms have the ability to enhance knowledge sharing, the software developers still have need for additional rich media platforms to share knowledge on issues supporting the core tasks, such as verbal interactions etc. An example of platforms that can aid these supporting tasks are Skype and Adobe connect etc.

In the next section, an overview of virtual software development teams and the collaborative media platforms they used will be explained.

VIRTUAL SOFTWARE DEVELOPMENT TEAMS AND COLLABORATIVE MEDIA PLATFORMS

This section provides an overview on the contexts by which the concepts of media richness, knowledge sharing within software development was investigated. It provides an insight into virtual teams and why they exist. It further provides a brief overview on virtual software development teams, why they exist and their mode of operation and what enables them collaborate remotely. In that discussion, the role of media platforms in the coordination of the virtual team is mentioned. In the last bit of this section, collaborative media platforms used by virtual software development teams are analysed.

Virtual Teams

Virtual teams are knowledge workers that collaborate on varieties of tasks, but members of the team are geographically distributed (Warkentin, Sayeed, & Hightower, 1997). From a general perspective, different academics do have different view of why virtual teams exist. One perspective is that virtual teams are seen as innovations that are suitable in turbulent business environments (Workman, Kahnweiler, & Bommer, 2003). Another perspective is that virtual teams are viewed as a consequence of technological developments and internationalization (Klitmøller & Lauring, 2013). There are still others, who view virtual teams as a means of organizations gaining competitive advantage over their competitors. Here organizations are able to rapidly respond to the needs of remote customers (Bergiel, Bergiel, & Balsmeier, 2008). There will obviously be more reasons why virtual teams exist in a plethora of industries within any sector within the economy of a nation.

Virtual Teams and Software Development

However, if one narrows these reasons down toward software development, the emergence of virtual teams are identified as a result of globalization, competition, evolution of technological possibilities, access to skilled resources, reduction in operational cost (see (Herbsleb & Moitra, 2001)). These reasons are evident in the creation of virtual teams to assist different operations in the development of software. Such operations include communication, project management, process engineering, knowledge transfer and the enhancement of technical abilities (Casey & Richardson, 2006). In each of the aforementioned operations, different forms of Media platforms can be adopted to connect the remote teams. Thereby creating an opportunity for visibility in coordination, communications and cooperation to take place in the software development process (Casey & Richardson, 2006). In this chapter, the focus is on the actual coordination and cooperation in an aspect of process engineering. This aspect is the actual programming, implementation or coding of the software by the software engineers.

Collaborative Media Platforms Used by Virtual Software Development Teams

Currently for software programmers, there are media platforms used by virtual software programming teams. These platforms can be grouped into two categories namely the main task (core task) supporting media platforms and the complimentary task-supporting media platforms.

- **Main Task-Supporting Platforms:** These are media platforms that support the task of programming the software. These platforms could be owned by the software company or it could be a third party platform. Examples of how such platforms work is GitHub, BitBucket, GitLab, CodePlex (owned by Microsoft), BeanStalk etc. Aside Codeplex, these are third party platforms used by software development companies and independent software developers. On these platforms, software programming teams operating virtually can remotely cooperate and coordinate the development of a software or webpage development for their firm. These platforms enables them to develop, store, transmit and reuse programming codes. In this manner, knowledge transfer occurs as the software developers within the team learn from each other as they work together. These collaborative platforms are mostly text based and they do not require instant feedback and gestures. Programming languages are also text based According to the Media Richness Theory, this a lean media.

These platforms are greatly patronized. An example is GitHub. Currently a lot of software development teams globally patronize GitHub. The owners of the platform claim that 22 million developers and 117 thousand companies use the platform to store, share and reuse the programmed codes for developing software (GitHub, 2017). Some of these companies listed on the GitHub portal are known to use virtual teams in their software development process. Such companies include SAP, IBM and Google (ibid). The same platform also hosts 61 million repositories (ibid). Most of these repositories are open source repositories. This implies that aside internal collaborative software development activities, software companies are also beneficiaries of codes provided by independent software developers. The reverse is unfortunately not the case, as most software companies develop proprietary and not open source software.

- **Complementary Task-Supporting Platforms:** These are media platforms that support tasks that does not involve the programming of the software. Such tasks include, the attendance of remote meetings with other software developers in the company and the presentation of reports to the team etc. Media platforms such as Skype, Google hang out, Adobe connect are often adopted for meetings. The platforms used for live meetings possess various media functionality with varied degrees of media richness. If the meeting is less formal, the chat functionalities of the media platform is used. But if the meeting is formal, a media platform that would support at least voice communication is used. Hence a functionality with medium media richness, according to the Media hierarchy proposed by daft & Lengel (1986), is used.

On the other hand email and Google documents are often used for the presentation of reports to the team. These are platforms with low level of media richness and the task is not performed on real time.

Therefore, one would say that software programmers have various media tools at their disposal to perform their tasks. Each of these tools possess different levels of media richness. Apart from the code repositories such as GitHub, which encourages knowledge sharing, do other media platforms with various levels of media richness encourage knowledge sharing? This is the question this chapter hopes to answer based on the case being investigated. In the next section, the methodology and findings from the case study is presented.

Methodology

This is a qualitative study. The exploratory research approach was adopted to investigate the case. The case were the virtual software development teams in a Danish company in about six locations. The unit of analysis was the team involving the respondent. The respondent requested anonymity as he had not requested permission from his bosses to speak. He preferred to be off the record. The respondent was chosen via purposive sampling. The interview was a face-to-face interview and it lasted for one hour. He was asked open-ended questions with respects to the issues bothering on organizational learning, knowledge sharing and media richness. The context of these questions were on the virtual software teams operating in their company. Although there were guiding concepts to the open-ended questions, the idea behind the open-ended question was not to receive immediate answers to questions. It was rather aimed at deriving enough data to aid in understanding the role rich media played in knowledge sharing activities in these teams. The data gathered from the interviews were recorded using a voice recorder. It was transcribed and narrative analysis was used in analysing the data. The choice of narrative analysis was informed by the need to have a full picture on the media platforms used by software developers in the company; how they share knowledge on these platforms and how they share knowledge offline. Based on the narrative outcome, inferences could be drawn on the type of media platform used; the amount of information richness the platform permits; the level of media richness of the medium; the type of task the medium is used for; and the identifiable level of knowledge sharing permitted by the medium. The narrative analysis was supplemented with a thematic approach towards coding the data.

FINDINGS AND ANALYSIS

This section is divided into two. The first section provides the outcome of the narrative analysis. The second section provides an inference derived from the narrative analysis. The inferences are aimed at providing answers to the main question posed by this chapter. That question was aimed at investigating if the media richness of current media platforms used by virtual software developers for their task are effective for knowledge sharing within their context.

Outcome of Narrative Analysis

In this subsection, findings on the profile of the case company and knowledge sharing procedures in the company are outlines. The finding on knowledge sharing are presented under two headings. These are their online knowledge sharing activities and their offline knowledge sharing activities.

Overview of Case

The case studied was a Danish medium sized company involved in software development. It is business to business company that provides a platform for the delivery of business process products online to companies. They serve both Danish and international clients and they have offices in 7 location outside Denmark. About 100 software developers work for this company. These developers are scattered in the 7 locations. The operational process for the development of the software is the same in the 7 locations. Initially, products developed by the company occurred via the collaboration between virtual teams. Now, products developed at each location are owned by the engineers at that location. However, all developers in the company work on the same kind of code base on the same platform. This enables developers working remotely to have access to other codes from other teams. Also in some cases remote developers still work together.

Knowledge Sharing Procedure

Online Knowledge sharing procedure:

1. **Company's Code Base:** For other developers in the remote teams to access the code, you commit your code to the code base. This process is accompanied by a message and time. Other developers will see the code and the message accompanying it
2. **GitHub:** The developer further pushes the code to GitHub. A developer can access the code here, modify the code and others will see the changes.
3. **Ownership of Code Lines:** In order to identify who added which code, a software is used to identify the developer, who modified and recommitted the code to GitHub, as the owner of those lines. Remote developers gain inspiration from each other using this process.

Table 2. Overview of the company

	About the Company
Type of company	Software development
Activity of company	Handle Business processes
Number of software developers	100
Number of remote locations	7 locations

4. **Comments:** Developers leave comments on the codes stored in GitHub. This helps other developers learn and understand the codes.
5. **Use of VoIP:** Skype and google hangout is used to meet with members of remote teams. Sometimes these tools are used to drop messages for the remote team member. An example is informing the remote team member that a task has been performed. But these meeting are not regular.
6. **Wiki-Page:** The Company has an internal Wikipedia page where new developers can learn about the company's software product and how they were developed. But it is only used as a source of reference to understand the original intention of the product developer.

Offline knowledge sharing procedure:

1. **Team Reshuffling:** Although each location owns each product, developers are often shuffled to allow them familiarize themselves with what other teams are working on. This helps the company to quickly replace a team member if one team member is fired or resigns. The downside is the lack of product ownership by a set of engineers. It is impossible to blame a certain engineer if the product fails.
2. **Team Manager Reshuffling:** Each new team manager comes with a new idea from previous teams. The manager comes with knowledge gathered from clients. The downside is the subtle clash of ideas between the team and the new manager.
3. **Team Manager to Development Team:** The team also receives knowledge of the product from the manager based on requirement specifications developed by the manager in daily scrum meetings.
4. **Documentation:** Initially engineers did provide documentation on their codes. This was because the product development turnout was slow and the company was new. As the company expanded and the product turn out increased documentation was encouraged. Documentation was to help the developers' fine tuning the codes to understand the intent of the previous developer. Else, the new developer will have challenges understanding the code.
5. **Mentorship:** New employees are made to undertake a code programming challenge. A mentor is assigned to new employees within this period. The codes are derived from the company's code base. The mentor reviews the codes and shows the new employees how the codes should be handled for the product.
6. **Sprint Meetings:** The developers meet with the scrum master, project manager every day to discuss the previous day's task. Each developer receives feedback from members of the team. They also share the problems they encountered in their task and decide what they will do next. Knowledge is also shared via casual conversations on a project related issue after each meeting.

Inference From Findings

Below is an attempt to make sense of the data extracted from the narrative analysis. The first thing was to identify each media platform, its level of media richness and the task supported by the platform. This is represented in Table 3.

The second thing was to identify the frequency at which knowledge sharing occur on each media platform. Software developers have various ways of communicating, as they commit codes to the pool every day. Here the members of the virtual team will access these codes and also use it to update their work. The software developers, as thy work, insert comments in the codes, drop messages and notes which will alert the other team member on real time on when they commit their codes to the pool. Hence Knowledge sharing occurs frequently during the day. Based on this backdrop, the frequency of knowledge sharing on the codebase and Github are deemed high.

But on a platform where knowledge is shared once a product is developed and delivered to a Knowledge storing device, the frequency of knowledge sharing is deemed medium. Hence Knowledge sharing on Wikipedia for this case is deemed to occur is deemed medium. On a platform where more of information than knowledge on the core task is shared, and knowledge on the core task is shared occasionally, the level of knowledge sharing is deemed low. Based on this criteria, the level of knowledge sharing in each medium is presented in Table 4.

Table 3. Amount of information richness on the media platforms identified in the case

	Platform	Amount of Information Richness It Allows	Level of Media Richness	Type of Task
1	GitHub	low	Low	Main task
2	Codebase	low	Low	Main task
3	Wikipedia	low	low	Complementary task
4	VoIP	High	High	Complementary task

Table 4. Frequency of knowledge sharing on each media platform

	Platform	Frequency of Knowledge Sharing	Type of Task
1	GitHub	High	Main task
2	Codebase	High	Main task
3	Wikipedia	Medium	Complementary task
4	VoIP	low	Complementary task

Inference 1

Based on the findings, the use of lean media made knowledge sharing effective in the context of the case studied. The reason for this was not the media platform in itself. This was because the media platform with lean media such as the company's codebase and GitHub had the following characteristics:

1. **The Task-Fit of the Media Platform:** As programmers and people who implement codes, GitHub and the code base did fit the task of programming. The programmers could fetch new codes or be inspired by the codes in GitHub or codebase. The programmers were also obliged to commit their codes to these platforms. So programmers from every location working on the same software are synchronized.
2. **The Nature of Programming Languages:** Programming languages are text based and highly explicit, making lean media most suitable for knowledge sharing. Therefore, the best media platform that would enable knowledge sharing had a lean media.
3. **The Transposition of Offline Knowledge Sharing Attributes:** The placements of comments in a code is one way software programmers communicate with each other. This makes the task of software programming highly analysable, hence prompting the use of lean media. In addition, platforms such as GitHub and the code base protects the integrity of the codes. Thus preserving the high analysability characteristics of the software codes. This is one of the main reasons lean media fits the task characteristics of the core task in software programming.

Wiki is lean media as well, but it was not used as much as the company's codebase or GitHub. This was because it did not necessary fit into the task characteristics. However, it was utilized more than the VoIP solutions. This was not because of the media richness of wiki. It was rather because, it was a constant reference material, where other developers will find out how each product works. This was valuable in the reshuffling process as new developers take up new products they did not build to improve on it. This then leads to the next inference.

Inference 2

Rich media was not used in knowledge sharing activities in the core task of programming. This is because it did not fit the task characteristics of the core task, which is highly analysable. Rather the closer the support activity the media platform provided to the main task, the more likely the company being investigated would be adopted a media platform. It did not matter how rich the media was. However, from a theoretical standpoint. Media richness did matter. That was what led the company to choose a lean media which would support the task characteristics of their core task, in which inherent knowledge sharing processes are embedded.

Based on these inferences, it was necessary to find out from the respondent what would make rich media compatible with their line of work. The response was not positive. This was because software developers were already using media rich platforms such as Youtube to gain more knowledge about their trade on an individual basis. They have to continue to update their knowledge as their trade is quite dynamic. But trying to transpose the professional development activities into their firm to enhance knowledge sharing would be an overkill. This is because of 2 reasons.

1. **Information Overload:** The developers do not only access information needed to help them develop their codes, they also receive other relevant information not related to programming. This includes information gathered from attending meeting, reading reports and performing other tasks. Hence rich media will not enhance their work.
2. **Developer Apathy:** Developers feel that most information they receive is noise and not needed. An example given in the interview is the desire to introduce a new programming language to the team. In some cases the team spends six to eight months to study the language which becomes obsolete by the time they are done studying. The company decided to change that approach and encourage the introduction of new programming languages. But the aim was not to replace the existing language used by the teams, but to try their hands on a new product with a new team to see how it will fare in the market. Hence, the respondent felt that most new knowledge was noise and rich media platforms will enhance that noise, which may not result in productivity.

Therefore this findings indicates that media richness in media platforms does influence knowledge sharing in virtual software development teams when implementing codes.

DISCUSSION

As the media richness of media platforms evolved, so has the need to use media platforms to enhance knowledge sharing within virtual teams (see (Klitmøller & Lauring, 2013; Gibbs, Kim, & Boyraz, 2017; Batarseh, Usher, & Daspit, 2017)).

This need is also identified in the software development industry. This has led to investigations on how collaboration using media platforms can be enhanced in virtual teams in software firms (Storey, Zagalsky, & Filho, 2016). It has also led to investigations on how socio-cultural factors and knowledge sharing affect virtual teams among other investigations (see (Vornanen, 2017). This implies that research within this context will be on the increase as richer media platforms evolve.

However, in setting the conceptual scene to this chapter in section, it was alluded to that as the media richness of media platforms evolves, so will the need to share knowledge on that platform by computer programmers. But the reverse seems to be the case, based on the findings of this chapter. In the implementation of software codes, the task characteristics involved in software coding only permits lean media.

But the findings opens up opportunities into the need for a more micro- level analysis in evaluating the role of media richness in enhancing knowledge sharing for virtual software teams. At the moment research into software development teams are focused on the different aspects of the macro level of the team (see (Woodward & Vongswasdi, 2017; Andres, 2002)). The macro level here implies the software development team as a whole. In a particular team, without mentioning the team leader and the scrum master, there are personnel involved in drafting the requirement specifications, designers of the software (this includes interaction designers), those implementing or coding the software (these are front enders and back enders) and the and user experience professions (involved in testing the software). In some cases the software developer or the personnel implementing the software tests the software using a special programme. Each of these group of professionals have different task characteristics which define their sub-teams. Aside the user experience professionals, each of the other group of professionals can operate with other virtual teams conducting the same tasks. They will utilize different media platforms tailored to their task and their dynamics for working together will be different. There, the independent research into these groups, which is referred to as the micro level here, would be a very beneficial. The analysis should not only be on how they share knowledge but the impact of the knowledge sharing on the improvement of their tasks.

CONCLUSION

This chapter was driven by the need to understand the effectiveness of current media platforms used by virtual software teams to share knowledge as they programme software. The outcome of this research was that in the case studied, media richness did enable knowledge sharing. However, it was the lean media platform that facilitated the core task characteristics in software programming that was adopted. Rich media did not fit the core task characteristics. Therefore it was not used for knowledge sharing in the course of the core task. It served as a support for complementary task. The findings in this chapter cannot be generalized due to its small sample size. In order to make a generalization, a quantitative research with a large sample size will be needed.

REFERENCES

Andres, H. P. (2002). A comparison of face-to-face and virtual software development teams. *Team Performance Management: An International Journal*, *8*(1/2), 39–48. doi:10.1108/13527590210425077

Baehr, C. (2012). Incorporating user appropriation, media richness, and collaborative knowledge sharing into blended e-learning training tutorial. *IEEE Transactions on Professional Communication*, *55*(2), 175–184. doi:10.1109/TPC.2012.2190346

Batarseh, F. S., Usher, J. M., & Daspit, J. J. (2017). Collaboration cpapbility in virtual teams:Examining the influence on diversity and innovation. *International Journal of Innovation Management*, 21.

Bergiel, B. J., Bergiel, E. B., & Balsmeier, P. W. (2008). Nature of virtual teams: A summary of their advantages and disadvantages. *Management Research News*, *31*(2), 99–110. doi:10.1108/01409170810846821

Bindrees, M. A., Pooley, R. J., Ibrahim, I. S., & Taylor, N. K. (2014). Re-Evaluating Media Richness Theory in Software Development Settings. *Journal of Computer and Communications*, *02*(14), 37–51. doi:10.4236/jcc.2014.214004

Casey, V., & Richardson, I. (2006). Uncovering the reality within Virtual software teams. *GSD '06 Proceedings of the 2006 international workshop on Global software development for the practitioner,* 66-72.

Daft, R. L., & Lengel, R. H. (1986). Organizational Information requirements, Media Richness and Structural design. *Management Science*, *32*(5), 554–571. doi:10.1287/mnsc.32.5.554

DeRosa, D. (2014, November 21). *5 Tools every virtual leader needs*. Retrieved from Onpoint consulting: http://www.onpointconsultingllc.com/blog/2014/11/5-tools-every-virtual-leader-needs

Gibbs, J. L., Kim, H., & Boyraz, M. (2017). Virtual teams. In C. R. Scott, L. Lewis, R. L. Barker, J. Keyton, T. Kuhn, & P. Turner (Eds.), The International Encyclopedia of Organizational Communications (pp. 1-14). Wiley. doi:10.1002/9781118955567.wbieoc215

GitHub. (2017). *Guthub*. Retrieved from Github: https://github.com

Gyamfi, A. (2016). The Impact of Media Richness on the Usage of Web 2.0 Services for Knowledge Transfer. *International Journal of E-Services and Mobile Applications*, *8*(2), 21–37. doi:10.4018/IJESMA.2016040102

Herbsleb, J. D., & Moitra, D. (2001). Globalization and Software. *IEEE Software*, *18*(2), 16–20. doi:10.1109/52.914732

Kim, S., & Soergel, D. (2006). Selectng and measuring task characteristics as indpendent variables. The American Society of Information Science and Technology, 42(1).

King, W. R. (2009). Knowledge Management and Organizational Learning. *Annals of Information Systems, 4*.

Klitmøller, A., & Lauring, J. (2013). When global virtual teams share knowledge: Media Richness, cultural difference and language commonality. *Journal of World Business*, *48*(3), 398–406. doi:10.1016/j.jwb.2012.07.023

Lepsinger, R. (2015, April 27). *3 Companies with High-performing virtual teams*. Retrieved from Linkedin: https://www.linkedin.com/pulse/3-companies-high-performing-virtual-teams-rick-lepsinger

Ramesh, A., & Dennis, A. R. (2002). The Object-Oriented Team: Lessons for Virtual Teams from Global Software Development. *Proceedings of the 35th Hawaii International Conference on System Sciences (HICSS-35'02)*. IEEE. doi:10.1109/HICSS.2002.993876

Rus, I., Lindvall, M., & Sinha, S. S. (2001). *Knowledge Management in Software Engineering:A DACS State-of-the-Art Report*. Fraunhofer Center for Experimental Software Engineering Maryland and The University of Maryland.

Storey, M., Zagalsky, A., & Filho, F. F. (2016). How Social and Communications channels Shape and Challenge a Participatory Culture in Software development. *IEEE Transactions and Software, 43*(2).

Vornanen, M. (2017). *The impact of socio-cultural factors and knowledge sharing to the success of global software development*. Tampere: University of Tampere.

Warkentin, M. E., Sayeed, L., & Hightower, R. (1997). Virtual teams versus face-to-face teams: An exploratory study of a Web based conference system. *Decision Sciences*, *28*(4), 975–996. doi:10.1111/j.1540-5915.1997.tb01338.x

Woodward, I. C., & Vongswasdi, P. (2017). *More that unites than divides: Intergenerational communication preferences in the workplace. In Communication Research and Practice*. Taylor and Francis.

Workman, M., Kahnweiler, W., & Bommer, W. (2003). The effects of cognitive style and media richness on commitment to telework and virtual teams. *Journal of Vocational Behavior*, *63*(2), 199–219. doi:10.1016/S0001-8791(03)00041-1

Ying, A. T., Wright, J. L., & Abrams, S. (2005). Source code that talks: an exploration of Eclipse task comments and their implication to repository mining. *Proceedings in MSR '05 Proceedings of the 2005 international workshop on Mining software repositories* (pp. 1-5). St. Louis, MO: ACM.

Chapter 8
Impact of Media Richness on Reduction of Knowledge-Hiding Behavior in Enterprises

Somayeh Labafi
University of Tehran, Iran

Datis Khajeheian
University of Tehran, Iran

Idongesit Williams
Aalborg University, Denmark

ABSTRACT

Knowledge hiding is one of the major obstacles in the progression of organizations that hinder the use of tacit knowledge of employees. The negative impact of this behavior is more significant in enterprises and small firms, because they are more reliant on knowledge of their employees. For this reason, factors that influence on tendency of employees to expose and use their knowledge would be appreciated by managers of organizations. With the aid of a conceptual framework in a qualitative study, this paper investigates the effect of media richness on knowledge hiding. Thematic analysis is used to analyze transcribed interview data from employees in a software company in Iran. Findings of the analysis show that media richness significantly impacts on organizational learning and influences on knowledge hiding behavior in employees. This article suggests that entrepreneurs and managers of small firms should provide employees' access to rich media content.

DOI: 10.4018/978-1-5225-2956-9.ch008

INTRODUCTION

The discussion in this chapter is on the effect of media platforms, used in organizations, on Knowledge hiding. Organizations thrive on knowledge acquired both internally and externally. Some organizations or firms, such as fast-growing start-ups, have been impacted positively by the knowledge they acquire (Friedrichsen et al., 2017, Salamzadeh & Kirby, 2017). This acquired knowledge enables entrepreneurial firms to survive turbulent markets (Khajeheian, 2013; Yang & Gabrielsson, 2017; Khajeheian, 2017). This makes the knowledge acquired by the organization, acquired externally or internally, a vital asset for success of entrepreneurial firms to survive and successfully compete with other entrepreneurial firms (Emami & Dimov, 2017; García-Sánchez et al., 2017).

Many researches have been done to investigate knowledge acquiring from external sources in entrepreneurial firms (e.g., Grigoriou & Rothaermel, 2016; Khajeheian, 2016; Khajeheian & Tadayoni, 2016; Trantopoulos et al., 2017). However, few researches have been done in regard of knowledge inside the entrepreneurial firms, while this has been a major problem (Huang et al., 2008). However, organizations and firms have been having problems in the acquisition of internal knowledge (Labafi, 2017). One of the main reasons for this problem is knowledge hiding (Labafi, 2017). In order to maintain competitive advantage with other colleagues within the firm, employees of firms and organizations are known to hide knowledge.

In a previous research conducted by the first author, the effect of knowledge hiding on innovation in software companies was studied (Labafi, 2017). Twenty software engineers working in an Iranian software company were interviewed. Data extracted from these interviews were analyzed using thematic analysis inspired by Meier and Boivin (2000). Within the findings, the availability of the media—such as the internet—was attributed to reducing Knowledge hiding, which would hamper innovations (Labafi, 2017). This was because the software engineers could access knowledge that would enhance their work from the Internet. However, if one were to probe the concept further, one is tempted to find out if the media platforms used in organizations actually hinder or hamper knowledge hiding between colleagues within organizations and entrepreneurial firms. Therefore, data gathered from the previous research was re-evaluated using the same methodology to find out, if the media is enable or hinder knowledge hiding. The outcome of this research is not generalizable as it is focused on a single case within an industrial sector. However, the significance of this work is in the fact that it provokes more discussion and research into investigating the impact of media on knowledge hiding in different sub-sectors of an economy in any country.

OVERVIEW ON THE CONCEPT OF KNOWLEDGE HIDING

While knowledge sharing and knowledge have received a numerous attention from researchers and scholars (Demirkasimoglu, 2015; Serenko & Bontis, 2016; Kang, 2016), knowledge hiding has not given such attention. Based on Connelly et al. (2012) and Zhao et al. (2016), knowledge hiding has been classified in three ways. These are evasive hiding, rationalize hiding and playing dumb. These characteristics are enabled by factors such as distrust, interpersonal relationships, social exchange an organizational background. In organizational context, knowledge hiding is a major drawback in the flow of knowledge needed to perform the mission of the organization. *Knowledge hiding* in organizations can be defined as "an individual's deliberate effort to avoid or hide the knowledge requested by another person" (Labafi, 2017, p. 133).

Knowledge hiding can occur with respect to explicit knowledge and tacit knowledge. This is because, as Emami et al. (2016) argue, experience is an important factor in new value creation intention in entrepreneurial firms. However, knowledge gained by experience is a personal asset and it provides competitive advantage to the specific employee within the firm. Therefore, transferring such knowledge is not necessarily desirable, unless giving out the knowledge does not threaten the employee's value to the company. This idea is supported by Haldin-Herrgard (2000), who pointed to the difficulties in the diffusion of tacit knowledge in organizations and experience is a tacit type of knowledge that can be hidden easily by employees. Some scholars have also made the attempt to identify the challenge of the diffusion of tacit knowledge as psychological. Ahmadi et al (2012) identified that that there is a relationship between psychological characteristics of the employee and knowledge sharing behavior in organizations. Peng (2013) on the other hand emphasized the problem by showing that knowledge-based psychological ownership positively affects knowledge hiding.

However, there are other studies where the effect of knowledge hiding of different organizational desires have been studied. Cerne et al. (2014) investigated the relationship between Knowledge hiding, creativity and the replication of new knowledge. Tsai (2015) performed a similar investigation. Both scholarly articles took a point of departure by conducting their investigation within the context of an organization's capacity to successfully replicate new knowledge. Other studies such as Yukl and Falbe (1996) showed the influence on an individual's power on knowledge hiding. Also, Labafi (2017) shows that the media could mitigate against knowledge hiding. The context of this study was software industry. In that sector, there is the need for specialized knowledge and frequent update of skills which requires a flow of knowledge. And the knowledge referred to here was are those extracted online. This idea serves a basis for investigating if the presence of the media, for knowledge sharing, actually mitigates against knowledge hiding in an organization. This serves as the starting point for the conceptual design, presented in the next section.

However, Knowledge hiding is not necessarily negative. Greenberg et al. (2007) pointed out the positive side of knowledge hiding. For example, they referred to the "white lie" as a situation where employees hide their knowledge with a positive intention aimed at protecting the feeling of person requesting the knowledge; or to protect the confidentiality of an issue, or safeguard the interests of a third party.

Media richness positively effects on organizational learning by creating organizational communities of practice (OCoP) (Kirkman et al., 2013). Richer media are expected to be more effective at transmitting ambiguous, complex, or personal information than less rich media (Badger et al., 2013). Media richness may increase information acquisition (Dineen et al., 2007; Badger et al., 2013).

Peltokorpi (2015) studied the effect of media richness on reverse knowledge transfer in organizations and showed that interactive effects of media richness can improve communication in organizations and help to better knowledge transfer.

CONCEPTUAL FRAMEWORK

In order to investigate the phenomenon qualitatively, a conceptual framework was developed to enable the study. The concepts identified form the basis of the overall set of themes. In this framework, media richness considered as independent variable that effects on organizational learning as well as knowledge hiding behavior. This fits into the four dimensions of media richness proposed by Schmitz and Fulk (1991). These are, the ability of two-way communication, the ability to communicate a variety of cues (like verbal, symbolic, nonverbal), the ability to convey a sense of personal presence, and language variety (Schmitz & Fulk, 1991). The evolution also empowers knowledge workers with the ability to enjoy immediate feedback, multiple communication channels, and user different languages, deliver personal messages, and other similar possibilities (Fernandez et al., 2013). However, the richness of the media is not bereft of its downsides. Lin et al. (2013) in their study of the media richness theory; the use and gratification theory and intimacy in social networks, using Facebook as a case, concluded that due to the existing lack of intimacy, media richness is not sufficient to stick users to Facebook.

Also, organizational learning assumed to have an effect on knowledge hiding: "Organizations frequently communicate potentially ambiguous information about values, culture, and other organizational attributes. The central argument of media richness theory is that richer media will convey information that is complex, ambiguous, and unfamiliar to recipients more effectively than less rich media." (Badger et al., 2013, p. 686). Both, media richness and organizational learning, effect on knowledge hiding assumed as negative, that means they will reduce such behavior in the organization.

Although qualitative research can produce testable hypotheses (Patton et al., 2015), but in qualitative researches hypotheses are not tested. For this reason, some assumptions have been developed to form the themes in re-analysis and interpretation of collected interviews. These assumptions, that extracted from literature, are as follow:

- **Assumption 1:** Media richness positively effects on organizational learning.
- **Assumption 2:** Media richness negatively effects on knowledge hiding.
- **Assumption 3:** Organizational learning negatively effects on knowledge hiding.

METHODOLOGY

This research is designed as a qualitative study case study. The case here is a software company in Iran. Data was gathered using via face-to-face semi-structured interviews with employees, managers and staff of the software company. Interviews were used for data gathering data because it generates verbal data that can be analyzed to derive interpretations and meanings behind the phenomena being investigated. As this research is a development of Labafi (2017), collected data form her research has been used as secondary data., These data generated from a sample of 20 employees in an Iranian software development firm. The duration of each interview was between 40-60 minutes. The interviews were recorded and transcribed for further analysis. The sample was made up of 17 male and 3 female respondents. The age range of the

Figure 1. Primary research framework

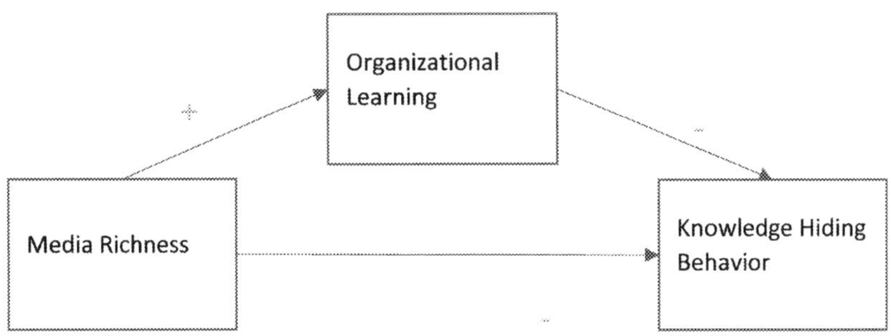

respondents was between 24 years and 35 years old. These respondents consisted of 12 bachelor degree graduates and 8 Master degree graduates.

The interviews were re-transcribed and analyzed. The re-Transcription of Interviews were reanalyzed based on the current research aim of the research. In the case of this chapter the generation of themes serves as a mean of interpreting and analyzing verbally generated data (Braun & Clarke, 2006). This method goes beyond data organization and leads to the interpretation of different aspects of the data expressed (Thomas, 2008). Based on this tradition, new and previous codes were carefully reviewed. Some of the codes were removed and replaced with new codes as a way of filtering out unneeded codes. In the previous study 530 codes were generated. In the current research 320 codes were based on the conceptual framework. The outcome of this analysis is reported in the next section.

FINDINGS

The procedures described by Meier and Boivin (2000) were followed to conduct the thematic analysis. By analyzing the codes obtained during research, researchers found in the following six main categories will be presented. The analysis produced 503 primary codes and identified 220 secondary codes within which these themes were worked through. Using conceptual similarities as a basis (Giorgi, 1985), the team members independently reduced the 220 secondary codes to 6 sub- themes. The following table shows procedure of data analysis and convert them to the main themes. However, based on the conceptual framework, emphasis is places on the three concepts, namely media, organizational learning and knowledge hiding.

PROPOSITIONS AND DISCUSSION

Findings emphasize on the importance of media richness, but as a mediator, not an independent variable like what has assumed.

In contrast with theoretical framework, media richness doesn't lead to organizational learning, nor it results to decrease in knowledge hiding behavior among employees. Media richness provides organizations with broader access to knowledge sources and facilitate knowledge acquiring for its members, but it cannot solely lead to acquisition of knowledge and removal of knowledge hiding.

Table 1. The identified themes

Themes	Sub Themes	Secondary Codes	Primary Codes
	Performance Management	Company pays higher salary for higher level of knowledge	3E14,4E16,6E11,6E19,10E12, 7E20, 7E19,5E13, 11E14, 14E7,17E11, 17E16, …
		In company there is no reward for sharing of knowledge.	
		Rewarding is for Having knowledge, not Sharing knowledge, so employees hide their knowledge.	
		Managers prefer to fire low skill employees.	
		Hiding knowledge secure a place in the firm	
		Company encourage knowledge rather than Collaborative work and cooperation	
Media	**Media as alternative knowledge source**	If hide my knowledge, others will get it from internet	3E11, 4E15, 8E21, 16E17, 17E 14, 9E13, 19E11, 2E15, 4E16, 4E18, ….
		Technical information is not secret	
		Internet made me needless to my colleagues' knowledge	
		The new technologies are useful for exposing new information.	
		Technology has reduced knowledge hiding.	
		Every person is not enable to use internet for working purposes.	
		Online Training courses are costly.	
		Technical information cannot be found on the Internet	
	Media and organizational learning	Understanding technical information need skill.	1E15, 1E17, 4E1, 4E6, 5E8, 8E12, 9E11, 9E 17, 11E10, 11E15, 14E2, ….
		Information is easy to access, but using it needs skill.	
		You can find what you need in the internet, if you know English.	
		All employees cannot use the information available on the Internet at work	

continued on following page

Table 1. Continued

Themes	Sub Themes	Secondary Codes	Primary Codes
Knowledge hiding	**Knowledge hiding and organizational learning**	I don't share my knowledge to be a frontier	1E2, 1E5, 2E6, 3E15, 4E11, 7E30, 8E23, 5E12, 7E13, 10E11, 10E14, 11E16, …
		More knowledge more secure job	
		Knowledge hiding makes communication ambiguous	
		Departments hide their knowledge by the excuse of specialization	
		Staff hide specialized information from coworker	
		Staff transfer less important information instead of technical information	
	complexity of specialized knowledge	Complexity of knowledge plays an important role in knowledge hiding	2E11, 3E3, 3E5, 3E6, 4E1, 12E10, 10E2, 10E4, 15E3, 16E12, 16E13, 17E14, …
		Software companies work with specialized information that is not usually found in the media.	
		Technical information not easily be transferred	
		Learning technical knowledge is time-consuming	
Organizational learning	**Organizational learning challenges**	The first reference to find a solution is a colleague	
		Staff prefer to participate in physical education trainings rather than learning from their fellow workers	4E11, 5E12, 6E11, 6E2, 7E4, 7E8, 2E9, 2E10, 19E14, 19E16, 20E7, 20E8, …
		cannot request training courses because it creates negative view	
		Learning is time-consuming and costly	
		Stress of firing, has caused no learning	
		Learning from colleague better than getting information from Internet	
		Is no learning for staff in company	
		Organizational communication is not provocative	

Proposition 1: In lack of organizational learning, knowledge hiding doesn't decrease significantly.

Social construction of technology can be employed for better understanding of this situation. Theory of social construction of technology argues that human action shapes technology (Burns et al., 2016) and technology is a product of the environment in which it is situated (Humphreys, 2005). This theory employed for organizations to shape how they use technological advances (Yousefikhah, 2017). By what we learnt from SCOT, we can propose that media richness doesn't lead to organizational learning without a social norm or agreement on how it should be used in organization.

Proposition 2: Media richness cannot replace human communication in working space, but it is complementary.

Also media richness doesn't lead to reduction of knowledge hiding behavior without a motivation from management or an encouraging motive that results achievement for holder of knowledge. Codes show that managerial practices can motivate employees to exploit capabilities of media for organization learning or to overlook it and keep their own knowledge as an asset for personal protection.

Proposition 3: To effective use of media richness, managers must encourage use of new media for organizational learning purposes.

The following model is proposed based on findings of this research. By this model, media richness is an intermediate factor that positively effects on knowledge hiding.

It has been discussed that the media based on its richness results to organizational learning (Kane, 2017). The framework based on the propositions derived from this research with respect to knowledge hiding challenges this assertion. The framework indicates that media richness should serve as a moderating factor, rather than an independent factor for it to have a positive influence on organizational learning. This finding is supported by Cai and Jun (2015) who also identified the moderating effect of media richness in information processing.

Figure 2. Proposed framework

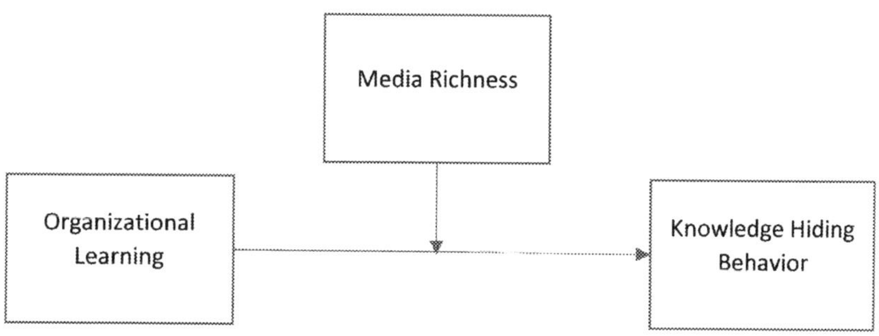

However, the utilization of the richness of the media to enable organizational learning and mitigate knowledge hiding is not without challenges. One of the obstacles in proper utilization of media richness can be explained by use of cognitive load theory. This theory argues that human beings are able to process a finite amount of cognitive resources (Sweller, 1988). So, the more information that an employee has to learn to perform his/her job, the more amount of information they need to process in working memory and it results to increase in mental workload. According to this theory, the more information a person has to learn in a short period of time, the more difficult it is to process that information in working memory, which results in higher mental workload (ibid). Mental workload is higher when people are not able to rely on schemas and must process more information in their working memory. This implies that experts, who have had the opportunity to develop schemas, will not need to process as much information in their working memory and will have a lower mental workload. Thus, many employees in industries such as software and media that are faced with an infinitive amount of information to be processed have difficulties in processing that information. In this case media richness compensates the capability of the mental process of information, even if they have been acquired from a less rich media. Therefore, the media serves as a source of learning. Therefore, entrepreneurs and managers of small firms should provide employees' access to rich media content because such opportunities will enhance organizational learning. If the SCOT approach is adopted, then the adoption of the task based media platform may help reduce knowledge hiding in entrepreneurial firms.

CONCLUSION

This research was conducted to find out if media platforms adopted in small firms or organizations can hinder or promote knowledge hiding. The findings, based on the case studied indicates that media platforms can actually promote knowledge hiding. However, this would be so if there was no conscious organizational learning process designed by which the media platform could be utilized. The chapter proposes a SCOT based approach to utilizing media platforms in organizations to mitigate knowledge hiding. But as stated earlier, the findings in this chapter cannot be generalized as it is a product from a single case. Therefore, the authors suggest further investigations into these relationships in different contexts, industries and environment. The propositions derived in this chapter can serve as a basis for a hypothesis for further evaluations. It is expected that future findings on this subject matter will help create knowledge for an efficient usage of media platforms to hinder knowledge hiding.

REFERENCES

Ahmadi, A. A., Daraei, M. R., Khodaie, B., & Salamzadeh, Y. (2012). Structural equations modeling of relationship between psychological empowerment and knowledge management practices (A case study: Social security organization staffs of Ardabil Province, Iran). *Journal of International Business Management*, *6*(1), 8–16.

Badger, J. M., Kaminsky, E. S., & Behrend, T. S. (2014). Media richness and information acquisition in internet recruitment. *Journal of Managerial Psychology*, *29*(7), 866–883. doi:10.1108/JMP-05-2012-0155

Braun, V., & Clarke, V. (2006). Using thematic analysis in psychology. *Qualitative Research in Psychology*, *3*(2), 77–101. doi:10.1191/1478088706qp063oa

Burns, T. R., Corte, U., & Machado, N. (2016). The sociology of creativity: PART III: Applications–The sociocultural contexts of the acceptance/rejection of innovations. *Human Systems Management*, *35*(1), 11–34. doi:10.3233/HSM-150852

Cai, S., & Jun, M. (2015). Relationship between Information Richness and Exchange Outcomes: Moderating Effects of Media Richness and Governance Mechanisms. *International Journal of Information Systems and Supply Chain Management*, *8*(1), 1–21.

Černe, M., Nerstad, C. G., Dysvik, A., & Škerlavaj, M. (2014). What goes around comes around: Knowledge hiding, perceived motivational climate, and creativity. *Academy of Management Journal*, *57*(1), 172–192. doi:10.5465/amj.2012.0122

Connelly, E. C., Zweig, D., Webster, J., & Trougakos, J.P. (2012). Knowledge hiding in organization. *Journal of Organizational Behavior, 33*, 64-88.

Demirkasimoglu, N. (2015). Knowledge Hiding in Academia: Is Personality a Key Factor? *International Journal of Higher Education*, *5*(1), 128. doi:10.5430/ijhe.v5n1p128

Dineen, B. R., Ling, J., Ash, S. R., & DelVecchio, D. (2007). Aesthetic properties and message customization: Navigating the dark side of web recruitment. *The Journal of Applied Psychology*, *92*(2), 356–372. doi:10.1037/0021-9010.92.2.356 PMID:17371084

Emami, A., & Dimov, D. (2017). Degree of innovation and the entrepreneurs' intention to create value: a comparative study of experienced and novice entrepreneurs. *Eurasian Business Review*, 1-22.

Emami, A., Dimov, D., & Paolucci, E. (2016). *Impact of opportunity confidence on new value creation intention: Does experience matter?*. Academic Press.

Fernandez, V., Simo, P., Sallan, J. M., & Enache, M. (2013). Evolution of online discussion forum richness according to channel expansion theory: A longitudinal panel data analysis. *Computers & Education*, *62*(0), 32–40. doi:10.1016/j.compedu.2012.10.020

Friedrichsen, M., Zarea, H., Tayebi, A., & Abad, F. A. S. (2017). Competitive strategies of knowledge and innovation commercialization: A unified SWOT and fuzzy AHP approach. *AD-Minister*, (30), 45-72.

García-Sánchez, E., García-Morales, V. J., & Bolívar-Ramos, M. T. (2017). The influence of top management support for ICTs on organisational performance through knowledge acquisition, transfer, and utilisation. *Review of Managerial Science*, *11*(1), 19–51. doi:10.1007/s11846-015-0179-3

Greenberg, J., Brinsfield, C. T., & Edwards, M. S. (2007). *Silence as deviant work behavior: The peril of words unspoken*. Symposium presented at the annual meeting of the Society for Industrial and Organizational Psychology, New York, NY.

Grigoriou, K., & Rothaermel, F. T. (2016). Organizing for knowledge generation: Internal knowledge networks and the contingent effect of external knowledge sourcing. *Strategic Management Journal*.

Haldin-Herrgard, T. (2000). Difficulties in diffusion of tacit knowledge in organizations. *Journal of Intellectual Capital*, *1*(4), 357–365. doi:10.1108/14691930010359252

Huang, X., Gattiker, T. F., & Schwarz, J. L. (2008). Interpersonal trust formation during the supplier selection process: The role of the communication channel. *Journal of Supply Chain Management*, *44*(3), 53–75. doi:10.1111/j.1745-493X.2008.00066.x

Humphreys, L. (2005). Reframing social groups, closure, and stabilization in the social construction of technology. *Social Epistemology*, *19*(2-3), 231–253. doi:10.1080/02691720500145449

Kane, G. C. (2017). The evolutionary implications of social media for organizational knowledge management. *Information and Organization*, *27*(1), 37–46. doi:10.1016/j.infoandorg.2017.01.001

Kang, S. W. (2016). Knowledge withholding: Psychological hindrance to the innovation diffusion within an organisation. *Knowledge Management Research & Practice*, *14*(1), 144–149. doi:10.1057/kmrp.2014.24

Khajeheian, D. (2013). New venture creation in social media platform; towards a framework for media entrepreneurship. In *Handbook of social media management* (pp. 125–142). Springer Berlin Heidelberg. doi:10.1007/978-3-642-28897-5_8

Khajeheian, D. (2016). Audience commodification: A source of innovation in business models. *Technology Innovation Management Review*, *6*(8), 40–47.

Khajeheian, D. (2017). Media entrepreneurship: a consensual definition. *AD-Minister*, (30), 91-113.

Khajeheian, D., & Tadayoni, R. (2016). User innovation in public service broadcasts: Creating public value by media entrepreneurship. *International Journal of Technoloy Transfer and Commercialisation*, *14*(2), 117–131. doi:10.1504/IJTTC.2016.081635

Kirkman, B. L., Cordery, J. L., Mathieu, J., Rosen, B., & Kukenberger, M. (2013). Global organizational communities of practice: The effects of nationality diversity, psychological safety, and media richness on community performance. *Human Relations*, *66*(3), 333–362. doi:10.1177/0018726712464076

Labafi. (2017). Knowledge hiding as an obstacle of innovation in organizations a qualitative study of software industry. *AD-Minister, 30*, 131-145.

Lin, Y. H., Lee, W. H., & Giang, C. M. (2016). *The Formation of Facebook Stickiness: The Perspectives of Media Richness Theory*. Use & Gratification Theory and Intimacy.

Patton, D. U., Hong, J. S., Patel, S., & Kral, M. J. (2015). A systematic review of research strategies used in qualitative studies on school bullying and victimization. *Trauma, Violence & Abuse*, *18*(1), 3–16. doi:10.1177/1524838015588502 PMID:26092753

Peltokorpi, V. (2015). Corporate language proficiency and reverse knowledge transfer in multinational corporations: Interactive effects of communication media richness and commitment to headquarters. *Journal of International Management*, *21*(1), 49–62. doi:10.1016/j.intman.2014.11.003

Peng, H. (2013). Why and when do people hide knowledge? *Journal of Knowledge Management*, *17*(3), 398–415. doi:10.1108/JKM-12-2012-0380

Salamzadeh, A., & Kirby, D. A. (2017). New venture creation: How start-ups grow?. *AD-Minister*, (30), 9-30.

Serenko, A., & Bontis, N. (2016). Understanding counterproductive knowledge behavior: Antecedents and consequences of intra-organizational knowledge hiding. *Journal of Knowledge Management*, *20*(6), 1199–1224. doi:10.1108/JKM-05-2016-0203

Thomas, D. (2008). *A general inductive approach for qualitative data analysis*. University of Auckland.

Trantopoulos, K., von Krogh, G., Wallin, M. W., & Woerter, M. (2017). External Knowledge and Information Technology: Implications for Process Innovation Performance. *Management Information Systems Quarterly*, *41*(1), 287–300.

Yang, M., & Gabrielsson, P. (2017). Entrepreneurial marketing of international high-tech business-to-business new ventures: A decision-making process perspective. *Industrial Marketing Management*, *64*, 147–160. doi:10.1016/j.indmarman.2017.01.007

Yousefikhah, S. (2017). Sociology of innovation: Social construction of technology perspective. *AD-Minister*, (30), 31-43.

Yukl, G., Kim, H., & Falbe, C. M. (1996). Antecedents of influence outcomes. *The Journal of Applied Psychology*, *81*(3), 309–317. doi:10.1037/0021-9010.81.3.309

Zhao, H., He, P., Sheard, G., & Wan, P. (2016). Workplace ostracism and knowledge hiding in service organizations. *International Journal of Hospitality Management*, *59*, 84–94. doi:10.1016/j.ijhm.2016.09.009

Chapter 9
Knowledge Swarms and Experiential Hives™:
A Compelling Vision for On-Demand Mobile Knowledge Mentoring – Nation Building and Transforming Mentors Into Multipliers

Philip Donald Marsh
Knowledge Mentoring Institute (Pty) Ltd., South Africa

ABSTRACT

We stand at the dawn of the greatest evolutionary disruption in the potential for large-scale human learning and development through the rapid convergence of truly transformational communication, cooperation and collaboration technologies and capabilities. The knowledge force is increasingly made up of very diverse employee profiles with differences in not only age and gender, but changing cultural norms and values, pervasive belief systems and large disparities in educational backgrounds. Highly individualised learning styles and behavioural characteristics and a host of other potential societal learning dividers, also magnify the challenge of building truly reflexive and responsive high-impact learning organisations. This chapter introduces the pressing need for a significant step-change in the way we approach company and community learning on a large scale and attempts to offer research-based insights and empirical evidence into media-enriching solutions such as mobile knowledge mentoring which will change the nature and experience of learning forever.

DOI: 10.4018/978-1-5225-2956-9.ch009

BACKGROUND

Metaphorically speaking, we are on the fluid face of a very rapidly swelling wave in a mega-surge of unpredictable change. The demands of, and on the multiple stakeholders engaged in the global organisational learning and critical knowledge transfer landscape are changing so rapidly that we need drastic transformation in the way we approach this learning, not only in the future, but right now.

The *internet of everything* (IoE) coupled with the exciting opportunities created by *machine learning* and the inexorable and accelerating convergence of modern disruptive communication and collaboration technologies present unparalleled learning opportunities. At the same time, the tsunami-like transformational forces and the mercurial *new world of work*, as described by the Gartner Watchlist Report (2010), present learning challenges of an unprecedented nature and scale.

Describing the modern learner as "overwhelmed, distracted and impatient", the research by established industry leaders such as Bersin by Deloitte (2014)[1] and infographic authors Tauber and Johnson (2014) indicates that the modern learner will both require and demand a new way of *learning empowerment* and enablement. Combinations of highly engaging and *experientially-rewarding* learning technologies and engagement methodologies will be required, providing *on-demand learning* solutions, anywhere and anytime.

Generational differences alone, as described by Dittman (2005) account for a significant element of the "disconnect" between the young, ambitious and socially hyper-connected graduates of today. While their senior managers and subject matter experts are generally more qualified, knowledgeable, experienced and connected, they are also far less technologically inclined and social media-oriented and will need to engage far more enthusiastically in previously unfamiliar learning tools, techniques and technologies, if they want to remain relevant.

The unacceptably high incidence of predictable, repetitive and increasingly costly mistakes in all business and public sectors, indicates that our long-cherished traditional and theoretical models of teaching, learning and knowledge sharing are ineffective and unsustainable. The traditional focus and reliance on old teaching methods and *searchable chunked content* in the form of policies, procedures and training manuals have just not worked. The rules and systems-oriented approach to organisational learning and knowledge exchange, which included the almost mechanistic gathering, capturing, packaging and sharing of large amounts of disconnected information without context, have been shown to offer sub-optimal learning and knowledge transfer.

An article in the Wall Street Journal by Davenport (June 2015), a founding father of both the Knowledge Management movement and the concept of the Learning Organisation, asked the quintessential question – "*Whatever happened to knowledge management*?"

This challenge of effectively sharing and transferring knowledge to the somewhat exuberant and overly confident modern learners is not a new phenomenon. The journey of managing and monitoring the achievement of real *competence* and *capability* has been very well described by Dunning and Kruger (1999) as shown in Figure 1.

Part of the problem appears to be the chaotic dynamics of the *new world of work* and the demands of the *modern learner* in this new fluid-like learning frontier. The added complexity of highly mobile and often remotely situated staff, who move between offices and often nomadically from project to project, or client to client, creates large knowledge sharing disconnects between the sources and seekers of learning.

When coupled with the inordinate wastage and loss of billable person-hours due to *traffic and travel* related challenges, the potential cost savings of an increasingly *dematerialised and disintermediated world of work* through mobile knowledge mentoring provides a very compelling argument. The unlockable value of connecting competent and committed specialists with new entrants and enabling and facilitating their collaborations on *common knowledge needs* in the cloud and via mobile devices, and not solely in grandiose corporate office parks, presents a global opportunity of unparalleled scale.

Figure 1. The Dunning-Kruger effect

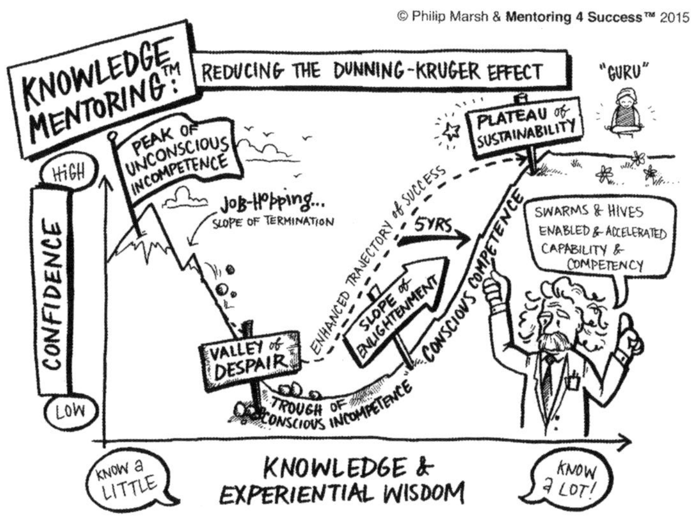

Global studies by some of the world's most respected research institutions such as Bersin by Deloitte (2014)[2], the American Management Association (2010) and the U.S. Department of Labor (1999) as far back as the turn of the 21st century, showed the need for radical change in the way we address the obvious learning disconnect and the often questionable impact and difficulty in quantifying the real return on investment of current learning and training modalities.

Multiple sources, including Gartner (2010), www.trainingindustry.com and www.reportlinker.com estimate that the annual global training spend in 2015 was upwards of US$ 350bn; the actual figure is unknown since individualised, self-selected/self-financed and "informal" training initiatives are excluded from these statistics.

The urgent need for increased media richness in the organisational learning initiatives in developing countries and underprivileged communities, is multiplied several factors over where the so-called "curse of knowledge" is often prevalent. This phenomenon describes the unintended inability of the *source of the knowledge* to grasp the depth of disconnect between themselves and the *seekers of the knowledge.* The situation is exacerbated even further in multi-cultural societies and developing countries which are largely dependent on "ex-pat" knowledge and skills and where potential cultural and societal learning differences could be experienced.

This heightened potential for differences in the cultural interpretations and perceptions of behavioural-based learning modalities, often creates an unintentional *cognitive dissonance* amongst learners. A conscious or subconscious form of *cognitive rebellion* is often the result of possible cultural disconnects with either the message, or the messenger, and is generally caused through a level of pre-associated comfort with prior learning experiences, or discomfort with the facilitator style and relationship, or long-established personal beliefs.

These on-going challenges of rapid transformation on a continental scale, are coupled with massive shifts in the way we need to work and the apparent *compression of time*, where there is an urgent need to do more, in less time, with fewer highly skilled and experienced people. The ability to package, teach, learn, share, and transfer scarce and critical skills and knowledge, and also develop strategic relationships, acquire valuable experiences and learn important lessons, presents a daunting, yet increasingly critical need among the ambitious and mobile younger generation.

By way of example, in the two decades of rapid transformation in South Africa, the Minister of Higher Education and Training, the Honourable Blade Nzimande told a Department of Labour (DoL) Employment Equity (EE) and Transformation Indaba gala dinner on 18 April 2013 that *"South Africa has spent R57 billion over the past 10 years through the Sector Education and Training Authorities (SETAs) in various training programmes, but the country does not have much to show for this investment"*(Source Marsh (2016, 2017)). The attempt to *effectively potentiate* the next generation of managers and experts through *outcomes-based* and *unit standards* aligned training material has produced very poor results. Clearly, a far better media enriching model is urgently required at a global level.

There has never been a more critical moment than the present, to find more successful and sustainable solutions for organisational learning and knowledge exchange for our next generation of knowledge-workers, leaders and specialists. Through radically transforming our traditional approach to individual and organisational learning and dramatically improving *media richness* as originally described by Daft and Lengel (1986) and the quality and impact of the learning message through collaborative learning techniques and technologies, we stand at the dawn of an amazing learning journey.

Mobile knowledge mentoring (enabled context) and micro-learning (enabled content) technologies now offer large and dispersed organisations the holy-grail of true learning organisational capabilities such as reflexive agility and intuitive responsiveness at a scale never previously possible. *Design thinking* on-demand is now a reality.

KNOWLEDGE SWARMS AND EXPERIENTIAL HIVES™

The *Knowledge Swarms and Experiential Hives*™ model as depicted in Figure 2 was first presented by chapter author Marsh (2015) at the 2015 Global Knowledge Management Congress in Mumbai, India. The model introduced the compelling need for increasing media richness and large-scale collaborative learning through sector-based, *societal swarming* and learning initiatives. Highly dispersed *knowledge needs-driven* projects such as national development plans and major science projects produce wonderful opportunities to test and prove new ideas in *dispersed and decentralised* collaboration environments.

The previously unattainable benefits of swarming *knowledge seekers*, connecting and collecting knowledge, experience and relationships from the vastly *distributed cognition* of a nation's current *knowledge sources* collaborating effectively in *experiential hives*, will be a key differentiator of the successful and sustainable nations of the future. The concept of accessing and mobilising distributed cognition as suggested by Hutchins (1991) is now not only possible, but essential. The aspirant *digital natives,* as first documented by Prensky (2001), will expect their learning to *be on-demand, just-in-time, just-enough and just-for-them* and this will only be made possible through media-rich mobile learning technologies and almost ubiquitous access to *context enriching* mentors.

In a media and knowledge-enriched environment, where the *value of context* must win over the *volume of content* for knowledge and experience to be shared, the *experientially-based value chain* of an entire nation's *intellectual treasure*

Figure 2. The Knowledge Swarms and Experiential Hives Model

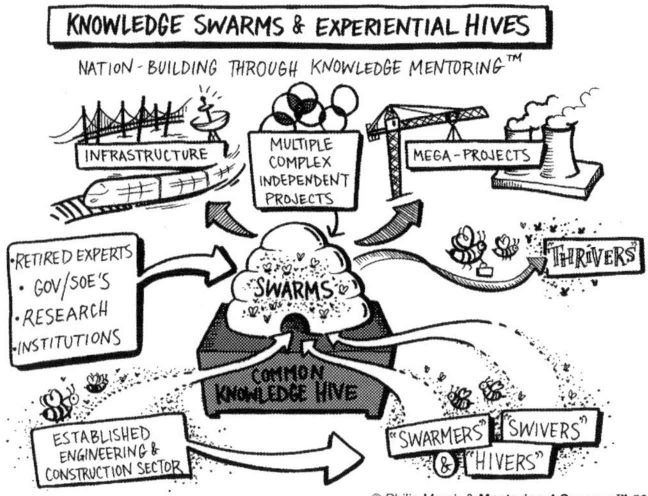

could easily be mobilised in dynamically structured and peer reviewed common knowledge focused *experiential hives*; this could enable *nation-building through mobile knowledge mentoring* on a national level.

The retired and/or currently active corporate executives and subject matter experts, including recently retrenched high-value knowledge sources could be strategically engaged in these common knowledge *experiential hives*; this could be further cascaded through the layers of currently engaged and employed managers, technical personnel and operational staff who would add a different dimension of operational value via client or community feedback. These common knowledge *experiential hives* could be accessed by thousands of young graduates and young candidate professionals, and potentially, thousands of unemployed graduates, who could communicate, cooperate and collaborate in needs-based *knowledge swarms*, connected to media enriching engagement tools and technologies for the benefit of entire nations. It would not only improve the productivity and performance of the employed, but also the *employability and potential* of the poor and unemployed, who become increasingly *unemployable* through disconnection to their initial lines of study and passion.

The key role players and participants in the *Knowledge Swarms and Experiential Hives*™ model as proposed by the author Marsh (2015) model are as follows:

1. **The Swarmers:** They are made up of the inexperienced, or less experienced, employed and/or unemployed graduates, across the various employment sectors, who are connected in self-selecting and needs-driven swarms, to the experiential

hives, as well as the other swarmers using combinations of physical, mobile and cloud-based platforms;

2. **The Swivers:** They are made up of highly experienced and/or professionally registered middle to senior managers and technical experts across the various sectors, who are similarly connected to the various role players through the same physical and technological enablers;
3. **The Hivers:** They are made up of external experts/global experts/recently retired or retrenched local experts and other volunteered and accessible subject matter specialists, connected through the same enablers to the role players;
4. **The Thrivers:** They are made up of the pro-active and newly empowered **Swarmers,** who are now able to start their own small self-employment opportunities and new enterprise development initiatives and offer their products and / or services to an existing employer base, or directly to the markets themselves, once again connected through the same physical and technological enablers;
5. **The Drivers:** They are made up of the complex inter-play of other committed stakeholder organisations and entities, such as government, academia, business, state-owned or controlled entities, professional bodies and skills development authorities, who are able to monitor and evaluate impact via the rich data and meta-data which is produced via the mobile App and cloud-based collaborations of the first four groups;
6. **The Sponsors and Suppliers:** They are made up of all the providers of capital, labour, plant, products, services and materials and who represent a critical source of potential funding and incentivisation for the success and sustainability of the *Knowledge Swarms and Experiential Hives*™ model. This group of stakeholders gain approved and selective access to the data analytics in the multiple dashboards and only participate via financial or knowledge contribution to the experiential hives and are not part of the active collaborations.

Knowledge needs-based and mobile App enabled swarming and accessibility to common knowledge experiential hives and the rich data associated with these, offers a scalable knowledge sharing and knowledge transfer environment that has never been possible before. Authors Falkvinge (2013), Iacoban, Reynolds and Brewster (2003) and Miller (2007) have all identified the compelling need to both understand and harness the empowering and enabling opportunities of these complex societal swarming algorithms in order to fully unlock the knowledge sharing potential of the swarms and the associated hives. Mobile learning and mobile knowledge mentoring technologies provide the ideal platform to enable this needs-driven knowledge-in-an-instant expert collaboration.

Whenever there is an urgent need for knowledge from selected experts or colleagues, or where the wisdom of the collaborative needs to be mobilised, almost on-demand, in order to interpret a complex set of circumstance not covered in the "rule book", mobile knowledge mentoring provides a very elegant and instantaneous knowledge-laboratory for the co-development of an innovative and optimised solution. Situationally relevant context-on-demand, liberated through the experiential wisdom of the mobilised knowledge swarms and experiential hives can provide immediate access to critical knowledge in-the-moment-of-need. If we extrapolate this potential knowledge-exchange value chain even further, then the ability to collectively share experiential wisdom immediately after-the-moment-of-awe must surely rate as one of the most priceless media enriching organisational learning opportunities ever conceived.

Activating the Quorum Sensor

An example of these knowledge exchanges could be the posting of a profound new experientially-based safety rule, which could save lives on a construction mega-project. Another example could include insights into a problematic (or preferred) supplier or sub-contractor on a similar mega-project or in a major corporate office complex, where risks could be instantly reduced and money saved (or opportunities exploited). These triggers can serve as effective *quorum sensors* to mobilise the hyper-connected players in the model and activate the *swarming algorithms* of the *knowledge-conscious*. This enables an almost instant change in large-scale group sentiment and associated behaviour. Indeed, tracking and monitoring changes in individual and group sentiments and behavioural dynamics is already part of the *new science* of evaluating mobile media richness and the impact of modern organisational learning.

The devastating droughts in the USA and Southern Africa and the destructive fires in the USA and Australia provide spectacular examples of how the quorum sensor of a dire societal need can mobilise in an instant, massive community collaborations and relief efforts, without any rules, remuneration or recognition.

Indeed, the author and his wife have been in two life-threatening situations while touring on motorcycles with friends, in southern Montana in the USA in 2012, and the Gariep Dam area in South Africa in 2015. Surrounded by uncontrolled and unpredictable bush and forest fires in swirling winds, it was only the locals' ability to communicate, cooperate and collaborate effectively on a *common outcome* that saved the day. The almost clockwork-like ability of the swarming helpers to coordinate, connect and collect critical information and resources in an instant, using social collaboration platforms, is something that no national emergency or relief agency can achieve alone. This previously disconnected collection of players swarmed almost in an instant, driven by the societal quorum sensor of saving the lives of some hitherto unknown people, and then once the mission and common outcome was achieved, they de-swarmed equally quickly (and quite probably have never had the need to regroup in that same swarm formation again).

The incredible potential of this life-saving gift is also available as a solution for nation-building on a grand scale. If one considers the many thousands of collective years of profound knowledge, strategic relationships and experiential wisdom lost to the world each year with the retirement and/or retrenchment of the *scarce and critical skills and knowledge-rich* baby boomers and X-generation, the media enriching mobile knowledge mentoring potential provides a powerful and compelling solution. If a set of pressing *common societal knowledge-needs* was effectively matched with a *common purpose-driven response* from those with the knowledge, experience and relationships, real nation-building could become citizen-led, scalable and a sustainable solution of national proportion. The tools and technologies to connect, collect and to collaborate already exist and the stage is most certainly set; it merely requires the willingness and enablement of the role players and actors.

Nation-Building Through Mobile Knowledge Mentoring

The value proposition of this exciting and entertaining convergence of multiple media-enriching technological and communication capabilities promises to unlock, for the first time, the real potential of our future generations, by truly engaging multiple stakeholders in both *content filtered* and *context rich* learning collaborations.

The author's own *5 Cs Holacratic Contribution Model*™ shown in Figure 3 is a nation-building philosophy, which connects the knowledge sharing benefits and *multiplying value-chain* of effective collaboration between a cascading hierarchy of players - *colleagues, companies, communities, countries and continents.* The 5 Cs model represents a media enriching and mobility-driven, multi-stakeholder solution and underpins the potential of the *ubiquitous cyber-sage* (on-line or mobile knowledge mentor) and the vast potential of *2nd life career opportunities* for retiring or retrenched experts and other knowledge specialists, who are increasingly healthy, active and living longer productive lives.

The nation-building opportunity of re-tapping into this knowledge-rich base is built into the original *Knowledge Swarms and Experiential Hives – nation-building through knowledge mentoring"* model from author Marsh (2015, 2016). Retired and/or retrenched experts and other experienced people have a continued opportunity to add value to themselves, their communities and their countries, through pro-active participation in *experiential hives* grouped into *common knowledge themes, fields* and *networks* using media enriching mobile learning and knowledge mentoring technologies. These in turn can be linked to powerful *big data analytics* and *engagement dashboards*, providing previously undreamt of opportunities to manage, measure, motivate, monitor and mentor the *learning potentiation* and progression of large groups of ambitious young learners, and most importantly, those from disadvantaged backgrounds.

The transformational turbulence of our *new world of work,* pressurised by the apparent compression of time and increasingly constrained by our over-crowded and centralised infrastructural limitations and all the associated logistical and transport challenges, begs for a better solution.

Mobile knowledge mentoring, which enables both *real-time/synchronous* collaboration as well as *on-demand/a-synchronous* gathering, packaging, sharing and exchange, offers a unique *dematerialisation* and *disintermediation* solution never before possible. Organisations and individuals are rapidly embracing the fact that instant access to the *trusted knowledge network* is far more valuable than simply being present at a desk, or glazing over in yet another drawn out meeting. Indeed, instant access to the *trusted common knowledge networks* will potentially cut billions of dollars of unnecessary wastage out of our over-strained transport and infrastructural budgets as well as our aging and under-performing learning and development systems.

Another significant benefit of the new mobile knowledge mentoring era is the removal of the *agents of interference* and all those organisational or political *gate keepers* and *knowledge hoarders* who intentionally or unintentionally add so much friction to the path of *effective knowledge flow* in organisations and communities.

The *5 Cs Holacratic Contribution Model* is deceptively simple and merely requires that the various *actors* on the *cascading stages of collaboration* nurture a knowledge-driven culture embodied in three simple questions, which must be asked by each of the actors each day – *what do I know?, what do I need?...and what can I share?*

The modern learner and thus potential mentee is far more concerned about social cohesion than their predecessors, as indicated by Tovey and Atlee (2008). If given an opportunity to uplift a community or colleague, they will generally do so without hesitation. Mobile learning and mobile Apps in particular, provide the most significant global opportunity ever created, to "share the love" (knowledge), not just between those fortunate enough to be employed, but also with the unemployed graduates and youth of the world as well. This very real opportunity of *enhancing employability, skills development, capacity building* and *potential job creation* through on-demand access to *ubiquitous knowledge networks* provides a nation building opportunity that must not be missed.

The attractiveness and ability for potential *knowledge funders* such as donor agencies, government grants, corporate sponsors, industry stakeholders and even advertisers to occupy relevant, contextualised and *prime-time* real estate on the screens of the rapidly growing millions of mobile learners and mobile knowledge

Figure 3. The 5 C's Holacratic Contribution Model

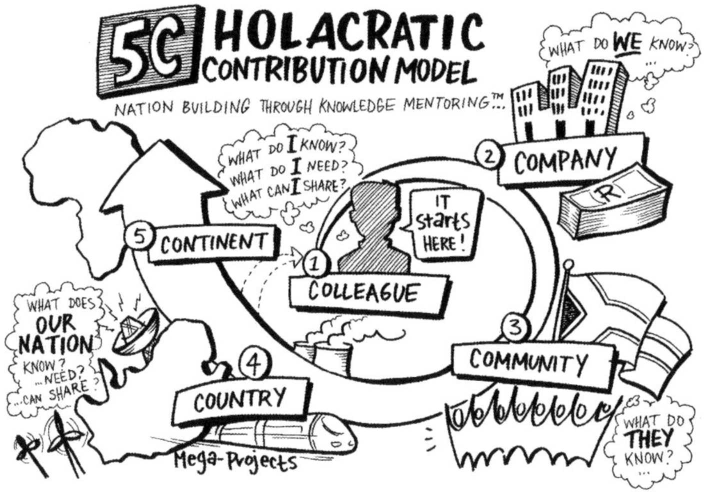

mentoring partnerships, is driving the technology to new heights of interactivity and experiential learning. It provides an exciting opportunity for socially-conscious organisations, who wish to demonstrate an explicit commitment to large-scale societal empowerment and upliftment by participating meaningfully in nation building initiatives. In particular, the potential for sponsoring mobile learning and knowledge mentoring initiatives for individuals and groups of unemployed and disabled people takes nation building to a new level of integrity.

This potential pool of nation building funding, will in turn, provide an equally exciting opportunity to recognise, remunerate and reward those truly committed high-performance knowledge contributors and collaborators who are peer reviewed and evaluated by the knowledge seekers themselves, and by so doing, this will drive increased interest, improved collaborative commitment and ultimately underpin sustainable scalability through increased social cohesion.

The well-governed and transparently monitored access to this *knowledge funding fuel* could unlock the true potential of the author's original *Nation Building through Mobile Knowledge Mentoring*™ model at a company, community, or country-level, on an unprecedented scale. It could change the mostly-failed company and community-based, *skills-only* training and development initiatives which are traditionally based on working memory only and a tick box style of *content and competency* development. Mobile knowledge mentoring enables the *critical context* and *capability* space and thus develops both long-term and long-lasting memory through heightened episodic engagement. This will be the essential ingredient for the successful and sustainable capacity-building needs of developing societies in the future.

What the *Knowledge Management* (KM) and *High Performance Learning Organisation* (HPLO) fraternities have attempted to solve with their big budget consulting and technology solutions for almost 20 years (with generally disappointing results), could now become an everyday reality as a direct consequence of being able to address real *societal knowledge needs* and the demands of the modern millennial learner through mobile knowledge mentoring.

A critical success factor will be understanding and embracing the nature and needs of the *modern mobile millennial learner*, who represent the highly aspirant and mercurial knowledge swarmers and offering them *experientially engaging* mobile learning solutions that fully unlock the end-to-end opportunities of the whole *societal knowledge rich* value chain.

Mobile Knowledge Mentoring and the Modern Mobile Millennial Learners

The consistent hallmark of all highly developed and successful civilizations has been the ability to teach, learn, share and pass on the collective community *knowledge gains* such as important life skills, health matters, brilliant discoveries, academic achievements, technical inventions and the general *experiential wisdom*, from the one generation to the next.

The *new world of work* and the concept of the *modern mobile millennial learner* are not fads, but rather a *fundamental step-change* in both societal and individual learner needs and expectations. If ignored, they will precipitate the end game of any organisation, which sticks rigidly to the comfort of a well-worn past, as the *learning unattractiveness* of the organisation will travel far beyond the perimeter walls of the lush office park.

Experience globally over the past two decades has proven that what worked for our parents and the baby-boomer generation, does not work with millennial learners. Not only is the *time to learn, to practice, to assimilate feedback* and *to perfect*, no longer available, but the inexorable demand is to do it all completely differently anyway.

Notwithstanding the huge advances and benefits of our technologically enabled age, the internet and Smartphones in particular, have created confusion as to what *represents information* and what *constitutes knowledge* – so an expert/peer-reviewed filtration process is essential in the more complex and knowledge intensive environments which require high degrees of cognitive reasoning and not just content regurgitation.

All micro-learning and mobile knowledge mentoring initiatives in future will need to be well-crafted combinations of learning experiences which are *granular* in nature and *context rich* in order to achieve any effective media richness. They will consist of high impact and focused "content with context" *knowledge nuggets* made up of short, sharp and inspirational learning moments. Traditional *chunked* learning materials and training workshops stretched into lengthy and often boring training modules and courses will soon be a relic of the past – even in the more rigorous academic institutions and environments.

Context over *content* is the new learning mantra and *anywhere/anytime* learning and knowledge mentoring removes the traditional restraints of *fixed time, specialist dependent* and *location-restricted* learning and will be the game-changer for empowering and enabling both the high-performance learning organisations of the future, as well as the empowerment of previously disadvantaged communities.

Neuroscience and Mobile Knowledge Mentoring

To validate this mobile knowledge mentoring approach further, on-going research in the neuroscience of learning by authors such as Carey (2014), Rizzolatti and Laila (2004) and Quiroga (2012) shows that *episodic* and *experiential learning* is far more important than the historical focus on *semantic, systems* and *rule-based training*, which has in the main shown to achieve consistently poor results.

Abundant research in this area provides key insights for learning and development professionals and practitioners alike, as well as all the potential knowledge mentors and mentees engaged in any form of human capital enhancement and talent acceleration initiatives.

According to Bersin[iii] by Deloitte (2016), the overwhelmed, distracted and impatient modern learner and knowledge mentee demands a learning environment that is *untethered, on-demand, collaborative* and *empowering* (Source Marsh (2016)). The need for an enhanced learning experience and self-exploration process is often closely associated with the so-called *quarter-life crisis*, during which young millennials start their struggle with rapidly cumulating adult responsibilities and their need to ensure both secured employment and future earning progression.

To add to the challenge, the observed employee learning patterns of the Y-Generation (Millennials) and the on-going research by authors such as Dittman (2005), Codrington (2011) and Prensky (2001) into the generation of so-called *digital natives* and the imminent arrival of the Z-Generation (Post-Millennials) indicate that three conclusive absolutes will permeate the new employee learning fabric:

1. Highly individualised and personalised learning profiles and solutions will be demanded,
2. Hyper-connected, anywhere, anytime mobile social collaboration will be the norm; and
3. Societal upliftment through shared learning (knowledge) will be a generational expectation.

Any learning and development initiatives, or indeed mentoring relationships which do not cater for these modern learner dynamics will be ineffective and probably discarded, irrespective of corporate policy, training protocols and performance management expectations.

Scarce and critical skills, knowledge, experience and relationships are not acquired through formalised and structured training interventions alone; they are gained and synthesised on an almost daily basis in multiple combinations and associations of day-to-day interactions with the world and the need *to know* or *to ask* or *to share* in a real-time environment is essential to our accelerated, integrated human development.

If information and media richness theory (or MRT) as introduced by Daft and Lengel (1986) is a measure of the increasing effectiveness of a framework of communication and collaboration mediums to reproduce the information sent over it (with the full contextual and experiential wisdom originally intended by the source), it is essential that the technologies and methodologies used in future learning and knowledge mentoring initiatives cater for optimised learning and memory formation. This will not be achieved solely through the *WOW* factor of gamification, interactive augmented reality and animated 3D learning simulations alone, and will need to address multiple sensory components of the *learning journey* which the neurosciences have shown us are so critical to effective knowledge sharing, learning and memory formation.

Effective knowledge mentoring using media rich learning modalities must take into account that, the only way to objectively validate effective knowledge transfer and assess the quality and depth of new understanding, is to observe the learner actually explaining and teaching their new knowledge to someone else. The brain systems, associations and neurochemistry involved in the act of actually consolidating and synthesising one's own perceptions, interpretations, reasoning, memories, emotions, language, gestures and the act of actually "showing another with an intent to teach and capacitate" will create both long-term and long-lasting memory, as well as provide an opportunity to correct any areas still requiring further learning or experience.

This optimised learning process as represented in Figure 4 is an important and long overdue movement away from the classical teaching methods and classroom style of learning, which tended to focus more on mobilising working memory only through rote memorisation activities and outmoded study methods.

Media richness and accuracy in the message of critical communications becomes even more important when there is a significantly heightened sense of urgency and/or the environment is emotionally charged. The limbic system in our brains, which governs our *fight, freeze or flight* survival response to a threatening stimulus (as well as our long-term memories), will often make very different decisions to the ones our rational pre-frontal cortex may make, if given time to deliberate and reason through the options.

Figure 4. Optimising learning and memory formation through episodic learning

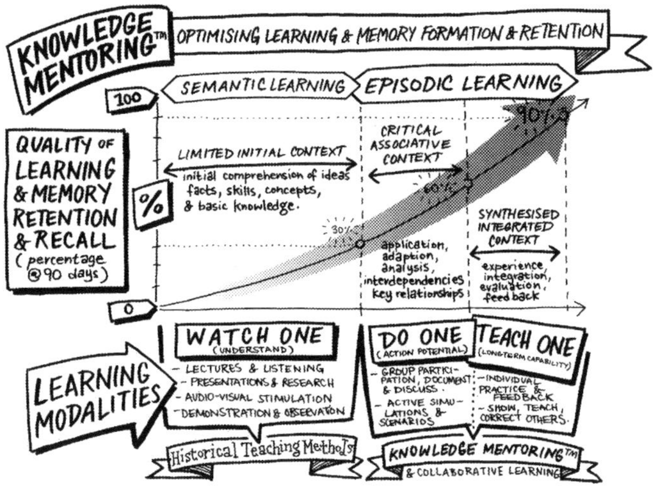

The work by Kahneman (2013) provides wonderful evidence of the importance and benefit of having someone like a mentor to help manage and reduce the potentially negative consequences of "fast brain thinking" only. Unless a life-threatening situation exists which generally triggers emotionally charged, System 1 type survival thinking only, a more considered response generally produces a far better result. Unfortunately inexperience and uncertainty often precipitates emotional immaturity in younger employees and consequently fast brain thinking only, and therefore access to the experiential wisdom and maturity of a trusted knowledge network and experiential hive could be a capability and career enhancing benefit to millions of young learners.

Mobile Knowledge Mentoring and Microlearning

Historical knowledge-sharing and knowledge-transfer constraints such as constant diary changes, limited internal capability and capacity, job security fears, strained budgets, lack of time, location and distance separation and even cognitive distance, become increasingly less significant with the mobile media-rich learning and sharing technologies and techniques available.

The almost magical value propositions now contained in the various *new ways of learning* through microlearning and mobile knowledge mentoring for all sizes of organisations and all sizes of budgets as presented in compelling arguments in the multiple research publications by industry leaders such as Grovo (2017), Bersin by Deloitte (2014, 2015, 2017)[3], Overton and Dixon (2016) and Penfold (2106) are arguably as critical to business continuity as cash-flow is.

Micro learning solution provider Grovo.com estimates that microlearning is 50% cheaper to produce, 300% fatser to develop and increases information and memeory retention by 20%. When combined with the benefit of a mobile knowledge mentor, the potential to create the ultimate high-impact learning organisation becomes a very real possibility. Here, the focus moves away from traditional course content and curricula curation and moves into *contextual conversations of understanding and situational relevance* with a mobile knowledge mentor and collaborative knowledge network, supported with just enough focused content to be effective.

Bersin by Deloitte (2015)[iii] and the GSM Report (2015)[4] estimate that between 12% and 15% of all global learning is already offered via mobile and with mobile learning comes the reality of large group collaborative learning. Mobile knowledge mentoring and quite literally, 24/7 access to *common knowledge on tap*, offers a metaphorical *knowledge pub for the insatiably thirsty*. When coupled with the fact that as much as 25% of our "standard working day" is often taken up with traveling, during which time we could be more productively engaged in *mobile learning* and *mobile mentoring moments*, this mobile media enriching solution represents the best opportunity we have ever had to truly empower and enable future generations.

The modern learner, and by implication, the *modern mentor* and the *modern mentee*, have a potential communication, cooperation and collaboration *learning profile* unlike any previous generations.

The trick will be to ensure that we don't move rapidly from the *information age* into the *knowledge/collaboration age* and then almost immediately into the *sensory saturation age*, of which there are already increasingly alarming indications of occurrence.

Mobile Knowledge Mentoring and the Cyber-Sage

Mobile knowledge mentoring provides the essential *collaborative context* as opposed to pure content driven learning and presents the game-changing gift and opportunity of almost ubiquitous access to a k*nowledge mentor* and *cyber-sage*. It provides the massively scalable opportunity to connect those who have the knowledge and experiential wisdom, with those who desperately need it, and for them to collaborate on common needs, development goals and interests on a cascading value-chain of colleague, company, community or even country-level, on demand, anywhere and anytime.

Traditional teaching and learning methods have tended to rely heavily on the gathering and packaging of structured content which is then taught with an overriding emphasis on a more *semantic learning* approach.

The modern mobile millennial learner and the opportunities of enhanced *episodic* and *experiential learning* associated with mobile knowledge mentoring and access to a knowledge network and/or cyber-sage, will take scalable learning and development to a level never before dreamt of. If media richness in learning is a measure of the increasing effectiveness of the actual transfer of knowledge, then mobile knowledge mentoring and the opportunities of the cyber-sage must represent the very highest levels of human learning potential.

The remaining section of this chapter deals with some of the characteristics and benefits of this exciting new media enriching learning opportunity and the magnificent *journey to insight* for both organisational and societal learning which can be unlocked through them.

Mobile Knowledge Mentoring and the Wisdom of the Collective

- **Overconfidence Bias:** One of the real challenges associated with content-based training and single expert teacher/mentor led learning is the perception that both *message* and *messenger* must be correct. It brings into play the potential for *overconfidence bias* as described by Dobelli (2014) and the fact that the so-called experts and potential mentors may suffer from heightened levels of self-confidence, even bordering on overconfidence, and their perceived rank in the conversation generally earns them a far higher degree of *blind-knowledge acceptance*.
- **Chauffeur Knowledge:** A closely associated challenge is something that Dobelli (2014) terms *chauffeur knowledge*, which manifests when someone plays the role of the *convincing subject matter journalist* and enthusiastically extols the profound knowledge and experiential wisdom of others, with the inherent human potential to either misinterpret, misrepresent or multiply the original knowledge constructs.
- **Alternative Options Blindness:** Another drawback of single partnership-based and small-group learning initiatives is the potential for limited collective experience and what could be termed *alternative option blindness*, which "without fingerprints", unintentionally eradicates alternative options and the potential for innovation and abstract thinking. Humans are very quick to adopt comfort zones and settle into the stories and associations that resonate with them most readily and this can have the effect of restricting the full learning potential of the single-partnership mentee.
- **Knowledge Facade:** Favourable circumstances, inappropriate influence and even plain good luck can often be found in the conversations and anecdotal evidence describing some individuals' meteoric rise to fame and fortune. These same people are then catapulted onto the conference and keynote presenters' circuits as perceived experts, with no real competence, capability or ingenious methodological reasoning behind their *knowledge*

facade. Unchecked by a collaborative forum and peer review process, these individuals can be detrimental, if not downright destructive, to the careers of the learners and mentees allocated to them in isolation, as it is quite possible to simply pass-on and perpetuate poor practice and bad habits.

- **Contextual Correctness:** Mobile knowledge mentoring provides a scalability option to include multiple and varied expert collaborators, who provide an instantaneous filter and peer review feedback system which ensures accuracy and *contextual correctness* between multiple sources and multiple seekers. The subsequent perceptions, interpretations and reasoning processes that are triggered within an expert and peer-reviewed learning collaborative are infinitely more valuable than any single knowledge source alone. Access to new ways of thinking and the multiple experiences contained in the varied connections and neural associations of others, helps to make *sense and meaning* out of what often appears to be chaos to the less experienced learner.
- **Sense-Making and Meaning:** The potential to extract some form of meaningful insight and intuitive reasoning out of chaos was originally described by Kurtz and Snowden (2003) in their seminal work on sense-making and the Cynefin model. As organisations and environments transition from *controlled* into *complicated* states of existence, standardised training on the rules and systems used and supported by adequate training processes and content generally suffices. In these states, the ability to *categorise* and *analyse* the problem quickly and respond via documented policies and procedures is generally the accepted best practice. However, once the state deteriorates into more *complex* and even *chaotic* states of random disorder, the ability to *effectively probe* the situation, as well as the actual *speed of action*, based purely on gut feel, intuitive reasoning and experiential wisdom, are the critical ingredients for survival or success. There can be no stronger argument for collaborative mobile knowledge mentoring than the work on *sense-making* by authors such as Weick (1988) and there are many fine examples of the value of the "wisdom of the crowd" which lend empirical support to the argument for the wide-spread implementation of pervasive mobile knowledge mentoring collectives, on both organisational as well as a societal levels.
- **Cyber-Sage Pool:** This *on-demand* and *in-the-moment* access to knowledge and wisdom and the almost instantaneous contextual feedback available through the vast potential of an enabled and hyper-connected *cyber-sage pool,* takes media richness in organisational learning to new levels of exponential value creation in human learning and potential.

The Importance of Trust in Learning and Mobile Knowledge Mentoring

- **Trust-Based Learning:** Developing real trust for effective learning and knowledge mentoring in multi-cultural and multi-generational companies and communities is no mean feat. Researchers Bergh, Thorgen and Wincent (2011) and Seyfried (2014) have shown the critical nature of *trust-based learning* and the micro-mechanisms and processes that are required to build trust over time. Mobile knowledge mentoring almost uniquely offers the social learning platform and engagement space so critical to ensuring effective *commitment, companionship, competence* and *capability* development. The research also indicates that *social learning* and *knowledge network collaboration* drives and fosters powerful human experiences of increased cognitive and emotional connectivity amongst the participating knowledge networks and would thus help to drive and improve the *social cohesion* agenda so critical to our global nation-building needs, on all levels of interpretation.
- **Mentors Into Multipliers:** The modern learner and mentee is generally a proven, highly collaborative and accomplished on-line and/or mobile gamer – witness the success of the global cyber-gaming platforms such as League of Legends, Warcraft and Counter-Strike, which are now multi-billion dollar businesses and celebrated (and respected) gaming cults. The magnificent knowledge sharing potential of the concept of e*cho trust* as described by Burt (2001) is intrinsic in the Millennial DNA. For example, if Mentor A assists Mentee B, and if Mentee B knows and has a trusting relationship with Mentee C, then Mentee C will trust and accept advice from Mentor A, even if they have never met, due to the association-based *perception of trust* developed within collaborative groups focused on common goals. This introduces the exciting potential of achieving real organisational and societal empowerment scalability by transforming *mentors into multipliers* and thereby providing an elegantly practical solution to the very complex problem of an aging *expert knowledge-force*.

Mobile Knowledge Mentoring and Leveraging Social Network Analytics

- **Strength of Weak Ties:** The power of *social networks* as described by Cross and Parker (2004) and the significant unlockable value contained in the work by Granovetter (1973) on the *strength of weak ties* also presents an unprecedented knowledge connection, collection, communication, cooperation and collaboration opportunity of great potential. Mobile knowledge mentoring and access to the wisdom of the trusted, yet possibly mostly unknown, *mobile knowledge mentors* and the concept of the *cyber-sage*, will accelerate learning and development at an unprecedented pace across the entire globe. The ability to tap into the knowledge, experience and relationships of a trusted *friend of a friend*, almost on-demand, represents a level of distributed cognition never previously available.

- **Value of Weak Signals and Reflexive Agility:** The equally unlockable value of the *weak signals* contained in the data and meta-data of large group employee learning and knowledge exchange collaborations are like hidden organisational treasure. This represents metaphorical *gold dust* to any executive decision making on future staffing and learning needs. Modern mobile knowledge mentoring technologies and dashboards underpin the potential for real reflexive agility and intuitive responsiveness and offer an effective enabler of this vast potential for the first time.
- **Design Thinking Enablement:** The modern *design thinking* approach to organisational learning and effectiveness is fully enabled via mobile knowledge mentoring; *Needs discovery* (active empathy), *affinity thinking* (connecting the dots), *intuitive design* (engaging the experience), *reflexive agility* (launch-listen-learn) and *benefits realisation* (continuous iteration) achieve a new level of capability with mobile knowledge mentoring.
- **Knowledge-Based Decision Support:** The real game-changing capabilities to measure, manage, motivate, monitor and mentor the *real knowledge needs* and *collective learning insights* of the collaborative, present an unparalleled opportunity for learning and development initiatives to evolve beyond mere tracking and reporting exercises. The previously uncharted realm of individualised *learner needs* and *trends prediction* is now a reality, transforming learner interaction and engagement statistics into a new category of *knowledge-based decision support.*

Mobile Knowledge Mentoring and Rich Engagement Analytics

- **Positive Peer Pressure:** One of the greatest on-going challenges experienced by the author over almost 20 years in a multitude of large group structured mentoring and critical knowledge sharing interventions, is the uncertainty of the actual level of volunteered commitment and honesty of the available knowledge mentors and other sources of experiential wisdom. Metaphorically speaking, it is quite possible in traditional mentoring initiatives for uncommitted and disengaged mentors to share only their *bathroom song*, and get away with it unnoticed (and still be rewarded for their contribution), whilst when placed in a positive peer reviewed and monitored space, they are far more likely to share their *"Pavarotti" song* with the other participants.

- **Social Loafers and Knowledge Hoarders:** Mobile knowledge mentoring offers the ability and benefits of monitoring *rich engagement analytics,* which quickly exposes the so-called *social loafers*, knowledge hoarders and other low contribution collaborators. This group usually represents those more reluctant and reticent participants, who under their own agenda, always find the minimum acceptable level of contribution and engagement possible and progressively contribute less and less as the group becomes accustomed and de-sensitised to their lack of involvement.
- **Value of Collaborative Effort:** Performance management and incentivisation systems of the future will no longer focus on the traditional key performance areas and HR driven competencies of individuals alone, but rather on the value of the contribution and *collaborative efforts of the collective* and mobile engagement analytics will provide this critical knowledge. The ability to unlock the full potential value of the knowledge exchange in collaborative networks through mobile knowledge mentoring is truly staggering.

Mobile Knowledge Mentoring Through Gamification and Funification

- **Emotional Stimulus:** Industrial psychologists and organisational learning specialists have known for a long time that we think and learn better with the inclusion of *dramatics* and *emotions* in the learning modality, as opposed to quantitative constructs and rational concepts alone, as these limbic connections are the mobilisers of quality long-term memory.
- **Gamification and Funification:** Derryberry (2008), Muntean (2011) and Kapp (2012) have all demonstrated the critical nature of fun and building gaming and play into the learning space of the millennials and mobile learning and knowledge mentoring provides an ideal platform to achieve this in an on-demand model. Almost magically, just as societal norms demand it, micro learning, mobile learning and mobile knowledge mentoring offers and unlocks the essential ingredients of game-based recognition and reward through;
    - Participation, social collaboration status and associated inclusiveness (belonging);
    - Gamification and funification with instant gratification and incentivisation (reward);

  - Progression and advancement for peer-valued contribution and collaboration (recognition);
  - Positive peer-to-peer pressure and non-destructive competitiveness (achievement).
- **Knowledge Badging:** Mobile knowledge mentoring also offers the status-enhancing opportunity of recognising *knowledge contribution* through *knowledge status badging* for valued collaborators and contributors using fun "contribution recognising" titles such as *Explorers, Adventurers, Masters, Knights* and *Wizards*. It provides an objective, fair and transparent *learning recognition* opportunity and a media enriching experience, which stimulates the reward systems of the participants' brains and encourages learners, mentees and mentors to share their best "Pavarotti songs" and real learning needs and expectations, thus transforming a traditional emphasis on *pushed content only* into a highly individualised and context rich *pulled sense-making* learning strategy.

Mobile Knowledge Mentoring Reduces Domain Dependence

- **Cognitive Encasement:** It is the author's experience that a high-level of *domain dependency* often exists amongst the expert knowledge base of the aging baby boomers. *"This is the way we have always done it…so why do it differently now?"* is arguably one of the most demoralising retorts that any aspirant and enthusiastic young learner has to endure.
- **Pathway Dependence:** The neurological pathways and memories developed and reinforced over time, with ever increasing levels of usage and comfort with the potentially limiting, but trusted theory and practical experience of the knowledge source, create unintended inhibitors to "thinking out of the box".
- **Collaborative Comfort:** A mobile knowledge mentoring environment provides an enabled collaboration space where the potential discomfort of being perceived to "challenge the old ram in the room" is removed and innovative young minds can pro-actively challenge the status quo and engage in meaningful collaboration on *organisational pain points* which may otherwise remain as the accepted *de facto consequences* of a more traditional existence.
- **Alternative Realities:** An added advantage is that *multi-disciplinary* and *multi-generational* teams can be quickly and easily constructed and the subsequent treasures of alternative opinions, complementary academic constructs and worldly experiences makes for a media rich learning cocktail that is not possible in domain dominated environments.

Mobile Knowledge Mentoring Reduces Familiarity Bias

- **Intentional Comfort Framing:** In teacher dependent training and single partnership-only based mentoring initiatives, the risk of reduced media richness and lower levels of effective knowledge exchange is significantly increased. This is due to a natural *familiarity bias* associated with the higher levels of comfort with which the teachers and mentors may have intentionally and *selectively framed* their world view and own experiences in the specific subject area.
- **Selective Perception and Recall:** Dobelli (2014) shows that the perceived rich pictures, mental models and neural associations, which come to mind so readily when discussing a point, may in fact simply be those which are most easily recalled or constructed and may not in fact include solid reasoning and sound judgement, often unintentionally perpetuating poor or at least less than ideal practice.
- **Guided Exploration:** Mobile knowledge mentoring dilutes and reduces this risk, as multiple collaborating views and experiences can expand on the initial knowledge base and significantly enhance the evolving *learning product,* with a far more holistic and varied input and knowledge base.

Mobile Knowledge Mentoring Scalability-Enhancing Technologies

- **The Knowledge Pulse:** In a relatively short space of time, mobile communication and collaboration technologies have evolved significantly from the early social chat and gaming platforms into more value adding sports, news and key financial information applications and now into highly sophisticated and full blown business engagement and decision support mobile Apps. The authors organisation has developed two revolutionary mobile knowledge mentoring Apps known as *myKnowledgeMentor*™ and *myMentorAccelerator*™ which are enterprise scale mobile solutions for enhanced decision support through accessing the collaboration and engagement analytics of the constantly fluctuating *knowledge pulse* of the organisation.
- **Mobile Mentoring Moments:** Mobile knowledge mentoring and learning offers the massive potential of *mobile mentoring moments* where traditional massive open on-line courses, or moocs, can be granulated into context rich *mini moocs*, giving instantaneous and ubiquitous on-demand learning and mentoring insights to millions. The explosion in on-line and mobile

learning content, coupled with the plethora of *modern learning enablers* available in the gamification, animation, simulation and augmented reality space is producing new business and learning behaviours never experienced previously.

- **Return on Knowledge Mentoring:** Behavioural psychologists, learning specialists and software coders are already collaborating on developing the complex algorithms that will track shifts in learner sentiments, values and behaviours, using combinations of word selection and usage and a host of other multi-dimensional engagement analytics. This will potentially unlock the holy grail of measuring a meaningful *return on knowledge mentoring investment* (ROKMI) as described by Marsh (2014) which evaluates the quantifiable value the mentee's new knowledge, experience and relationships add to themselves and the lives of others, on a cascading 6 point scale.
- **Group Think:** In the very near future, serious digital learning disruptors, such as the *Group Think: Team Edition* displayed in the Ultralife Personal Augmentation Spa product line in the Museum of the Future in Dubai, will allow teams of between 6 to 12 people to connect cognitively via a personal augmentation implant into their brains, and share experiences and *common thought associations* not possible through the current vagaries of human communication and interpretation.
- **Ubiquitous Learning:** When coupled with artificial intelligence (AI), the *internet of things* (IoT) and rapidly emerging machine learning (ML) capabilities, the new levels of accelerated human learning and knowledge mentoring possible in the very near future is now bordering on what only a few years ago would have been viewed as full blown science fiction.

Mobile Knowledge Mentoring Nurtures Personalisation and Personification

- **The Human Connection:** Humans inherently prefer learning from stories and anecdotes, rather than from statistics and rules. We have been evolving far longer as humans in terms of vertical and horizontal learning and knowledge sharing capabilities, than modern learning technologies and systems have been available. The ability to nurture and appeal to deeply connecting human psychological characteristics such as *personalisation* and *personification* are dramatically enhanced in the mobile knowledge mentoring world. The modern mobile millennial learner will gladly invest their own time and money in improving their own mobile learning experience, if given the option.

- **Career Enhancement:** Research by Bersin[iii] by Deloitte indicates that besides knowledge badging and other recognition and reward options available, this level of personal investment increases even further if associated with professional advancement or credit. Mobile learning and knowledge mentoring offers an exciting solution for on-demand, full process, professional registration support mentoring to the millions of graduates struggling with professional candidacy and learnership requirements. It provide exactly the same benefits to the professional mentors in terms of validating continuing professional development (CPD) requirements, and thus a powerful win-win is activated in mobile knowledge mentoring.
- **Learning Relatedness:** Mobile knowledge mentoring technologies also provide an ideal application for recording and sharing one's own unique and preferred learning profile, which cannot easily be achieved in more traditional learning interventions. It offers an opportunity to personalise and personify the *total learning experience* and achieve a level of media richness and human connection never before possible. A large variety of value-adding learning and behavioural assessments can be selected by participants collaborating in large dispersed groups and built into the mobile knowledge mentoring experience. This facilitates the opportunity for mentors and mentees who have no previous relationship or knowledge of each other, to develop a far better understanding of the learning and behavioural dynamics involved and thereby enhancing the mutual respect and general *relatedness* of the partnership and the group.

Mobile Knowledge Mentoring and Common Knowledge Exchange Frameworks

- **Sharing Knowledge at a Distance:** For the first time, mobile knowledge mentoring offers the modern learner and mobile mentee the ability to communicate, cooperate and collaborate remotely and in decentralised groups at the very highest levels of committed and self-volunteered engagement possible; this represents the highest test for media richness theory which is sharing and transferring knowledge at a distance. The limited downside of a reduced face-to-face interaction and the ability to read and interpret feedback from both body language and facial expressions using our highly attuned fusiform gyri (brain system for facial and expression recognition), is fairly easily overcome by using *common knowledge exchange* frameworks to harmonise the thinking.

- **Knowledge Pools:** One example is using a knowledge mentoring technique developed by the author, which involves ever increasing *knowledge pools* as shown in Figure 5 which are constantly topped up through on-going collaboration and shared experiences. The scalability potential is substantial and makes use of a similar phenomenon to that which engineers refer to as the *free surface effect* – a powerful *hydraulic happening*, where unconstrained water in the hull of a roll-on/roll-off ferry for example, will easily tip the ferry over in rough weather, as a result of the unrestrained fluid force generated. The simple solution of creating waffle-like segments restrains the water in many much smaller segments and its potentially destructive effect is nullified. The concept of *knowledge pools* was developed by the author and drives an opposite condition which makes use of the positive potential of the *free knowledge effect,* where unrestrained collaborations and shared experiences are leveraged using mobile knowledge mentoring enablers and thereby benefit far more than just those involved in the actual experience. Once again, this transforms *knowledge mentoring* into *knowledge multiplying.*
- **Knowledge Asset Structuring:** Another extremely useful media enriching and knowledge sharing technique is the author's *knowledge asset structuring* model as shown in Figure 6, which has been successfully used in many major organisations to ensure high degrees of consistency during the gathering, packaging and sharing of large-scale knowledge mentoring interventions.

Figure 5. Knowledge pools and the free knowledge effect

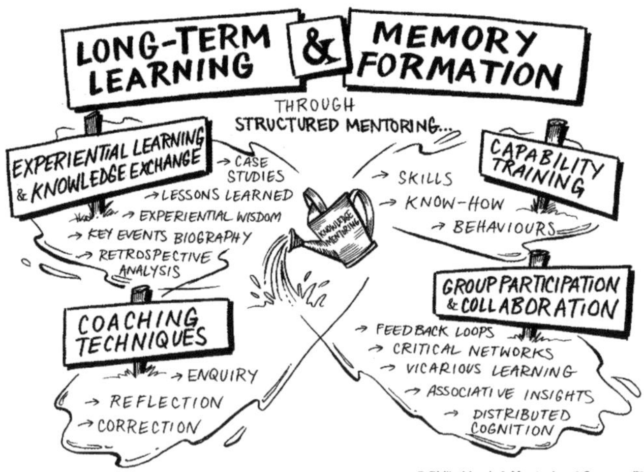

Figure 6. Knowledge asset structuring model

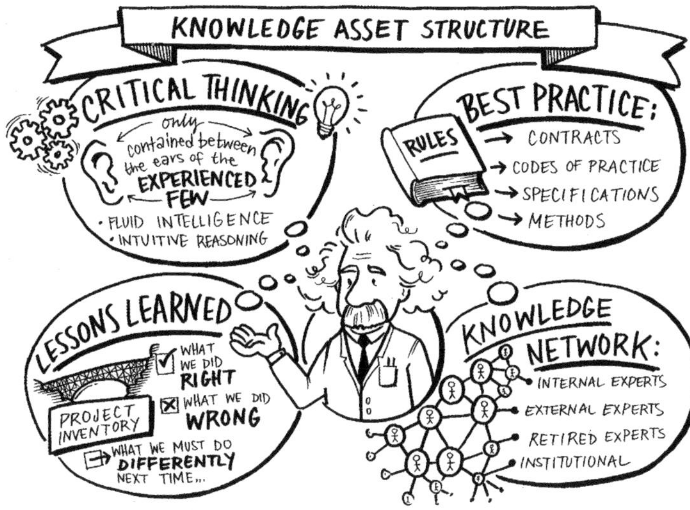

Mobile Knowledge Mentoring Transforms Competencies Into Capabilities

- **Capability Realisation:** The ultimate aim of effectively validating any media enriching learning initiative must be to assess whether the learner has migrated from a simple *closed content-driven* and semantic learning type *competency level*, to a far more experiential learning and context driven *capability realisation* level. This is the acid test of any critical knowledge transfer intervention as shown in Figure 7 and essentially evaluates whether a seeker of knowledge has been effectively empowered to a desired degree of *self-sustainability* and *own-capability realisation*.

CONCLUSION

The ability to participate in multi-modality learning opportunities and to collaborate and innovate on common knowledge needs and challenges and to make a valued contribution to out-of-date processes and practices (unlike the "grin and bear it/ that is the way we have always done it" Silent and Baby Boomer generations), creates a compelling new opportunity for enhancing employee engagement and staff retention strategies.

Figure 7. Capability realisation through critical knowledge transfer

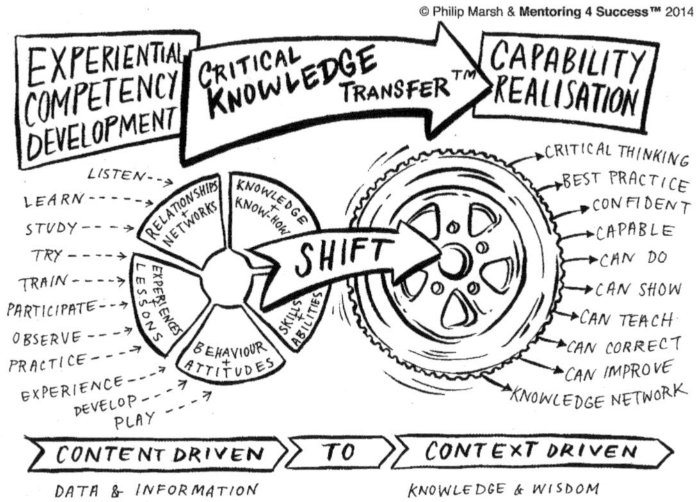

The reflexive agility and intuitive responsiveness that mobile knowledge mentoring potentially unlocks and unleashes in medium to large organisations is truly staggering and the early adopters will surely have a level of competitive advantage which no capital purchase can ever compete with.

A move towards *objective practicality* and away from *obsessive perfection* and the ability to experiment, launch, listen and learn faster in a trusted and safer environment will be a critical shift in future approaches to evaluating media richness and effectiveness in all learning initiatives. The enabler of true design thinking is mobile knowledge mentoring.

The *learning loops* and feedback systems connected through mobile knowledge mentoring provide a *progressive value-monitoring system* which takes the evaluation of *media richness in organisational learning* to a whole new level of integrity, truth and meaning.

In a transforming world embracing higher levels of social consciousness and a welcome shift in corporate focus away from "profits at all costs" to include social and environment issues, organisational and societal learning will become increasingly inextricably intertwined. Knowledge Swarms and Experiential Hives™ provides an elegant learning solution for the global empowerment challenge and mobile knowledge mentoring and the value of the cyber-sage could just offer the most viable and scalable solution yet.

REFERENCES

American Management Association, Training, Articles and White Papers. (2010). *The Bottom Line on Improperly Trained Leaders.* Retrieved from http://www.amanet.org/training/articles/the-bottom-line-on-improperly-trained-leaders.aspx

Bergh, P., Thorgren, S., & Wincent, J. (2011). Entrepreneurs Learning Together -The Importance of Building Trust for Learning and Exploiting Business Opportunities. *The International Entrepreneurship and Management Journal, 7*(1), 17–37. doi:10.1007/s11365-009-0120-9

Burt, R. S. (2001). *Bandwidth and echo: trust, information, and gossip in social networks.* Academic Press.

Carey, B. (2014). *How we Learn – the surprising truth about when, where and why it happens.* Random House Publishing Group.

Codrington, G. (2011). *Mind in the Gap, Understanding the different generations –You're your past, you're your generation, choose your future.* Penguin South Africa.

Cross, R. L., & Parker, A. (2004). *The Hidden Power of Social Networks: Understanding how Work Really Gets Done.* Harvard Business School Press.

Daft, R. L., & Lengel, R. H. (1986). Organizational information requirements, media richness and structural design. *Management Science, 32*(5), 554–571. doi:10.1287/mnsc.32.5.554

Davenport, T. (2015). *Wall Street Journal.* Retrieved from https://www.linkedin.com/pulse/whatever-happened-knowledge-management-tom-davenport

Derryberry, A. (2008). *Serious Games: Online games for learning.* Retrieved from https://www.semanticscholar.org/paper/Serious-games-online-games-for-learning-Derryberry/c9bd36db4fc2f95d4b53aa2021337d0e2ee7ac4f

Dittman, M. (2005). *Generational Differences at Work - A psychologist studies ways to help traditionalists, baby boomers, gen Xers and millennials work better together, despite their generational differences.* American Psychological Association.

Dobelli, R. (2014). *The art of thinking clearly.* Farrar, Straus and Giroux.

Falkvinge, R. (2013). *Swarmwise: The Tactical Manual to Changing the World.* Retrieved from https://falkvinge.net/files/2013/04/Swarmwise-2013-by-Rick-Falkvinge-v1.1-2013Sep01.pdf

Granovetter, M. S. (1973). The strength of weak ties. *American Journal of Sociology*, *78*(6), 1360–1380. doi:10.1086/225469

Greve, N. (2011, Nov 11). Civil Engineering shortage leads to infrastructure deterioration. *Engineering News*.

Grovo. (2017). *Future-proof your workforce with microlearning*. Retrieved from http://blog.grovo.com/ebook-futureproof-workforce-microlearning/

GSM Association Report. (2015). *The Mobile Economy (Europe 2015)*. Retrieved from http://www.gsma.com/mobileeconomy/archive/GSMA_ME_Europe_2015.pdf

Hutchins, E. (1991). *The social organization of distributed cognition*. Retrieved from https://www.researchgate.net/publication/232427152_The_social_organization_of_distributed_cognition

Iacoban, R., Reynolds, R. G., & Brewster, J. (2013). *Cultural swarms: Modeling the impact of culture on social interaction and problem solving*. In *2003 IEEE Swarm Intelligence Symposium, SIS 2003 - Proceedings* (pp. 205-211). Institute of Electrical and Electronics Engineers Inc. DOI: doi:10.1109/SIS.2003.1202270

Johnson, D. (2017). *High Impact Learning Organisation: Maturity Model*. Bersin by Deloitte. Retrieved from http://www.bersin.com/Practice/Detail.aspx?docid=20893

Kahneman, D. (2013). *Thinking Fast and Slow*. Farrar, Straus and Giroux.

Kapp, K. M. (2012). *The Gamification of Learning and Instruction: Game-based methods and strategies for training and education*. Wiley.

Kruger, J., & Dunning, D. (1999). Unskilled and Unaware of It: How Difficulties in Recognizing Ones Own Incompetence Lead to Inflated Self-Assessments. *Journal of Personality and Social Psychology*, *77*(6), 1121–1134. doi:10.1037/0022-3514.77.6.1121 PMID:10626367

Kurtz, C. F., & Snowden, D. J. (2003). *The new dynamics of strategy: Sense-making in a complex and complicated world*. Retrieved from http://alumni.media.mit.edu/~brooks/storybiz/kurtz.pdf

Marsh, P. (2014). *Nation Building through Knowledge Mentoring – a framework to bridge the global scarce and critical skills and knowledge crisis*. Self-Published.

Marsh, P. (2016). *Knowledge Swarms and Experiential Hives – a nation building solution to address the scarce and critical skills and knowledge crisis in the engineering and construction sector*. Civil Engineering Journal – June Edition.

Marsh, P. (2017). *A Glimpse Into The Communication Challenges Faced By HardHat Professionals*. Retrieved from http://www.thhp.co.za/glimpse-communication-hhp

Marsh, P. (2015). Conference Proceedings. *Knowledge Swarms and Experiential Hives™ – the critical and emergent role of the ageing knowledge expert in the engineering and construction sectors of developing nations*. Global Knowledge Management Congress, Mumbai, India.

Miller, P. (2007). *The genius of Swarms*. Retrieved from http://ngm.nationalgeographic.com/2007/07/swarms/miller-text

Muntean, C. I. (2011). *Raising engagement in e-learning through gamification*. Retrieved from http://www.icvl.eu/2011/disc/icvl/documente/pdf/met/ICVL_ModelsAndMethodologies_paper42.pdf

O'Leonard, K. (2014). *The Corporate Learning Factbook 2014: Benchmarks, Trends and Analysis of the U.S. Training Market*. Bersin by Deloitte.

Overton, L., & Dixon, G. (2016). *Preparing for the Future of Learning – a changing Perspective for L & D Leaders*. Towards Maturity; In-Focus Report. Retrieved from https://www.cipd.co.uk/Images/preparing-for-the-future-of-learning_2016-a-changing-perspective-for-l-and-d-leaders_tcm18-13846.pdf

Penfold, S. (2016). *Profile of the modern learner – helpful facts and stats – infographic*. Elucidat Blog. Retrieved from https://blog.elucidat.com/modern-learner-profile-infographic/

Prensky, M. (2001). *On the Horizon - Digital Natives, Digital Immigrants*. MCB University Press. Retrieved from http://www.marcprensky.com/writing/Prensky%20-%20Digital%20Natives,%20Digital%20Immigrants%20-%20Part1.pdf

Quiroga, R. Q. (2012). Concept cells: The building blocks of declarative memory functions. *Nature Reviews Neuroscience*. Retrieved from https://www.researchgate.net/publication/228114707_Concept_cells_the_building_blocks_of_declarative_memory_functions

Report, G. (2010). *Watchlist: Continuing Changes in the Nature of Work, 2010 – 2020*. Retrieved from https://www.gartner.com/doc/1331623/watchlist-continuing-changes-nature-work

Rizzolatti, G., & Laila, C. (2004). The mirror-neuron system. *Annual Review of Neuroscience*, *27*(1), 169–192. doi:10.1146/annurev.neuro.27.070203.144230 PMID:15217330

Seyfried, C. (2014). Trust-Based Learning and Its Importance in Intercultural Education. *CLCWeb: Comparative Literature and Culture, 16*(3). https://doi.org/10.7771/1481-4374.2515

Taub, T., & Johnson, D. (2015). *Meet the Modern Learner (Infographic)*. Bersin by Deloitte. Retrieved from https://www.bersin.com/Practice/Detail.aspx?id=18071

Tovey, M., & Atlee, T. (2008). *Co-intelligence, Collective Intelligence and Conscious Evolution – Creating a Prosperous World at Peace*. Retrieved from https://archive.org/stream/CollectiveIntelligenceCreatingAProsperousWorldAtPeace/Complete_022508-cFinal1420_djvu.txt

US Department of Labour. (1999). *Futurework: Trends and Challenges for work in the 21st Century*. Cornel University ILR School.

Weick, K. E. (1995). *Sensemaking in organisations*. University of Michigan. SAGE Publications.

ENDNOTES

1 Wang-Audia & Tauber (2014), Meet the Modern Learner: Engaging the overwhelmed, distracted and impatient employee, https://www.bersin.com/Practice/Detail.aspx?id=18066.

2 O'Leonard (2014). The Corporate Learning Factbook 2014: Benchmarks, Trends, and Analysis of the U.S. Training Market, http://www.bersin.com/corporate-learning-factbook-2014.

3 http://www.bersin.com.

4 GSM Asociation Report, 2015 The mobile economy.

Chapter 10
Governance Choice in Open Innovation:
The Antecedent Role of External Source Choice

Mehdi Bagherzadeh
NEOMA Business School, France

Sabine Brunswicker
Purdue University, USA

ABSTRACT

To increase the incentive for external sources to form interactive relationships, some firms selectively reveal their internally developed knowledge for free. However, 'selective revealing' is in conflict with the firm's interest in control over IP and challenges the governance of knowledge flows in open innovation. Taking a behavioral perspective, this paper proposes a complementary role of 'selective revealing' and 'behavioral control' and its relationship with a firm's source choice. We draw upon a sample of 125 large firms in the United States and Europe to statistically support the proposed complementarity. Results suggest that in value chain-centric and competitor relationships, firms may opt for guided revealing. In contrast, firms primarily engaged with universities are unable to establish guided revealing as a governance mechanism.

DOI: 10.4018/978-1-5225-2956-9.ch010

INTRODUCTION

The flourishing literature on open innovation suggests that firms should transcend their organizational boundaries to propel their own innovation activities through purposive use of inflows and outflows of knowledge (Bagherzadeh Niri, 2016, (Chesbrough, 2003; West & Bogers, 2014; West, Salter, Vanhaverbeke, & Chesbrough, 2014; Wikhamn, 2013). Scholars have presented empirical evidence that this strategic choice is viable for many types of firms, but it is particularly adopted by large firms (Chesbrough & Brunswicker, 2014). The notion of open innovation relates to a variety of external actors, ranging from customers, suppliers, universities, to competitors (Laursen & Salter, 2006). To benefit from these actors, firms utilize a variety of 'open innovation practices', such as alliance relationships (Felin & Zenger, 2014) or innovation contests (Afuah & Tucci, 2012; Kathan, Hutter, Füller, & Hautz, 2015). When engaging in these practices, some firms give up control over innovation-related knowledge, and engage in what scholars refer to as selective revealing or selective sharing (Dahlander & Gann, 2010; Jarvenpaa & Välikangas, 2014). They decide to purposively and selectively share internal problem or solution-related knowledge, and accept that they will no longer maintain control over these critical resources.

The role of selective revealing[1] is particularly important in light of the fact that open innovation is best conceptualized as an interactive problem solving process (West & Bogers, 2014). Taking a problem-oriented view, open innovation implies an interactive problem solving process with mutual knowledge flows between the focal firm and the external knowledge actors (Nickerson & Zenger, 2004). The shift towards selective revealing within such interactive problem solving relationships creates tensions in the *governance of knowledge flows* in open innovation, in particular with respect to two governance dimensions: *control* over the process of creating and utilizing intellectual assets, and *incentives* for knowledge creation and sharing (Majchrzak, Jarvenpaa, & Bagherzadeh, 2014). Selective revealing has negative effects on control, as the focal firm cannot exclude the external source from using the shared knowledge (Kathan et al., 2015). Selective revealing may also facilitate the process of governing knowledge flows. Sharing motivates external actors to engage more deeply in the knowledge exchange, to invest their own time and resources, or even to strategically align their own activities more closely with the focal firms (Alexy, George, & Salter, 2013).

In light of this contradictory logic, this paper complements the current discussion towards 'control', which is dominated by a focus on control over legal intellectual property rights (IPR), with a behavioral perspective. Taking an organizational control theory lens, we argue that there is an alternative control mechanism that is less concerned with the *direct* control of (potentially emerging or existing) know-how, and its usage through legal ownership and usage rights. Instead of controlling the ownership or usage of intellectual assets, firms may opt for *behavioral control* (Kirsch, 1996), which allows firms to mutually monitor, evaluate, and influence the routines, procedures, and activities carried out during knowledge exchange processes in open innovation.

Behavioral control creates an opportunity to control the processes of how innovation-related knowledge is created, and establishes formal routines for how knowledge and information are used and shared, even without legal exclusion rights. However, the shift towards behavioral control maybe bounded by a firm's source choices (Grimpe & Sofka, 2009). Each external actor has its own characteristic that can affect the need for selective revealing as well as behavioral control when interacting with them. Building on the results of an exploratory study introducing and conceptualizing behavioral control as governance mechanism of knowledge flows (Bagherzadeh & Brunswicker, 2016), this paper aims to elaborate more on the interplay between two governance mechanisms – revealing/sharing and behavioral control – and the antecedent role of a firm's source choice. Thus, this paper starts with four governance modes, that represent different combinations of selective revealing and behavioral control and explicate how each mechanism individually supports the governance of knowledge flows along two governance dimensions: incentives, and control. Next, we discuss the antecedent role of a firm's source choice that may affect which governance choice a firm opts for. Using a sample of 125 large firms in Europe and the U.S. collected via an international open innovation survey in 2012, we empirically explore the antecedent role of a firm's source choice in the selection of governance mode (4 modes). Our results indicate that certain source choices, namely those that are inherently agnostic to behavioral control, are hardly associated with what we refer to as "guided revealing" where firms combine selective revealing with behavioral control.

THEORY AND CONCEPTUAL DEVELOPMENT

Recent contributions highlight the existence of a two-way interaction between the focal firm and external knowledge sources (West & Bogers, 2014), which can be best conceptualized as an interactive problem solving process. This interactive process implies mutual knowledge flows between the focal firm and external knowledge sources. These knowledge flows are important, because potential technological solution knowledge is usually unknown to the focal firm (Felin & Zenger, 2014). In addition, the focal firm regularly lacks the ability to assess external knowledge and technological areas. Thus, both the focal firm and the external source have to deeply engage in knowledge sharing and exchange. Only powerful incentives can motivate the external source to engage in knowledge creation and sharing relevant to the innovation problem. In addition to the need for incentives that support knowledge creation and sharing, control over the process of knowledge creation and utilization is essential in governing open innovation (Nickerson & Zenger, 2004). A governance mechanism for open innovation, defined as *a control mechanism which coordinates and safeguards knowledge flows* across organizational boundaries (Schroeder & Wagner, 2012) needs to support two governance dimensions: 1) *Incentives* for knowledge creation and sharing across organizational boundaries and 2) *Control* over the creation and usage of IP – both existing and emerging.

Selective Revealing as Purposive Governance Mechanism

When engaged in selective revealing and sharing, firms waive legal control rights over their prior internal intellectual assets and make them available for free to their external sources (Jarvenpaa & Välikangas, 2014). They lack the ability to exclude the external source from using the revealed knowledge. Existing literature on selective revealing highlights that it can create both direct and indirect benefits (Ness, 2009). But it may also have negative implications (Henkel, Schöberl, & Alexy, 2014). In the following section, we discuss the positive and negative effects of selective revealing, with respect to 1) incentives, and 2) control.

- **Incentives for Knowledge Creation and Sharing:** When selectively revealing knowledge to the external source, the focal firm automatically waives control over emerging knowledge that successfully integrates non-proprietary assets that are free for use. Thus, the external firm may be able to establish control over new knowledge through legal ownership or control rights (Leiponen, 2008). As put forward by Aghion and Tirole (1994), the shift of power to establish potential legal control and exclusion rights over IP towards the external source creates incentives to invest in *additional* resources for creation of *new knowledge*. As a result, the 'action' potential to establish control rights over emerging solutions can positively affect the external knowledge sources' incentives to invest time and resources to make additional *efforts and investments*. If the external innovation partners share their own internal know-how with the focal firm, it increases the ability to co-create new knowledge through knowledge integration (Majchrzak, Cooper, & Neece, 2004), to develop solutions that integrate the 'revealed' assets, and to integrate the newly created know-how from the external source (Henkel, Baldwin, & Shih, 2013). Sharing knowledge with the focal firm creates additional opportunities for the external partner to appropriate value from newly created knowledge that integrates the focal firm's and the external actors' know-how, either in joint value constellations, or individually (Adner

& Kapoor, 2010). When turning to agency theory, we find further support that selective revealing can create incentives for knowledge sharing through the alignment of incentives. Such an alignment may have positive effects on the behavior of the external knowledge sources. Agency theory argues that, in agency relationships, tensions and an unwillingness to share knowledge because of the existence of information asymmetry, can be solved by aligning incentives between partners (Eisenhardt, 1989). A focal firm may reveal the existing knowledge to align incentives between themselves and the external knowledge sources. By selective revealing, the focal firm provides the external knowledge source with some information about their goals for open innovation, and their needs with respect to relevant technological knowledge areas and knowledge. As a result of this selective revealing, the focal firm can decrease cost for incentives alignment, which in turn motivates the outsider to engage in extensive knowledge sharing.

- **Control Over IP Creation and Utilization:** While selective revealing can create incentives for external knowledge sources to engage in knowledge creation and sharing, we argue that it has negative effects on the second governance dimension, namely control over IP creation and utilization. When the focal firm waives control rights, the external knowledge sources may act opportunistically by seeking self-interest at the expense of the focal firm's knowledge (Alexy et al., 2013). Consequently, there is a high level of uncertainty with respect to the question of what IP is created by the external source, and how it is used (Niri & Brunswicker, 2014). However, when turning to the external source, selective revealing creates positive effects on control over IP creation and use. External firms can use the existing internal IP of the focal firm for free, without infringing any ownership rights. In short, the control effects for the focal firm are negative. Table 1 summarizes the supportive and negative effects of selective revealing on two governance dimensions with respect to focal firms and external knowledge sources.

Due to the negative implications of selective revealing with respect to control over IP creation and utilization, the focal firm is exposed to a challenge task: It needs to identify other means to 'channel' and control IP creation and utilization. Literature on collaborative innovation and organizational control highlights that structure of control over the external partners behavior, instead of IP itself, can play an important role in attenuating control problems over IP (Pisano, 1989; Teece, 1986). Here, we propose a theoretical shift from control over the actual intellectual assets, through formal and informal IP rights, towards a behavioral control dimension. In the next section, we will expound on the supportive and negative influences of behavioral control as an alternative governance mechanism, using the previously identified governance dimensions.

Table 1. Supportive and negative effects of selective revealing on two governance dimensions

	Governance Dimensions	
	Incentives for Knowledge Creation and sharing	**Control Over IP Creation and Utilization**
Focal Firms		Creating uncertainty regarding what IP is created by external source, and how it is used due to potential opportunistic behavior of external knowledge sources (-)
External Knowledge Sources	• Generating incentives for external knowledge sources to engage in knowledge creation and sharing (+) • Generating incentives for external knowledge sources to engage in knowledge sharing	• Control over the creation of emerging IP and freedom of usage (+) • Free usage of the existing internal IP of the focal firm (+)

Note: (+) = Supportive effect of selective revealing on governance dimensions; (-) = Negative effect of selective revealing on governance dimensions.

Behavioral Control as an Alternative Governance Mechanism

- Behavioral control is defined as a mechanism by which firms can mutually monitor, evaluate, and direct the routines, procedures, and activities that take place during interactive open innovation (Kirsch, 1996; Koza & Lewin, 1998). Behavioral control affects both governance dimensions.
- **Incentives for Knowledge Creation and Sharing:** Behavioral control clarifies the 'routines', 'processes', and 'procedures', in which new knowledge is created and shared. It makes the interactive open innovation process more transparent. Open innovation activities, particularly if they are interactive in nature, are characterized by information asymmetry regarding each other's goals and intentions. These asymmetries increase the cost of valuing partners and increase the uncertainty in the relationship (Eisenhardt, 1989). This situation creates barriers for engaging in knowledge sharing, and investment in knowledge creation, for both partners. These asymmetries and uncertainties can be overcome by establishing behavioral control mechanisms for influencing, monitoring, and directing the open innovation process. As a result, both the focal firm and external knowledge sources have more transparency about knowledge flows and learn more regarding the partner's capabilities and knowledge (Schnackenberg & Tomlinson, 2014).
- **Control Over IP Creation and Utilization:** Behavioral control may also positively affect the control of both the creation and utilization of IP. Control over the process may create an *indirect* mechanism of control by shaping the

interactive problem solving processes, subsuming formal routines, informal norms, and values. Behavioral control gives focal firms the opportunity to observe, assess, and influence activities and decisions by formally and informally prescribing procedures and methods of how IP is created and utilized (Kirsch, 1996). Behavioral control mechanisms provide an action to potentially direct the behavior of the partner firms' behavior. In addition to directing the actual problem solving process, it allows control of the process of IP utilization (Fauchart & Von Hippel, 2008). Fauchart and Von Hippel's study on norm-based IP models shows how chefs rely largely on norm-based intellectual property control systems to protect their IP related to their recipes: They defined norms and processes about sharing and utilization of intellectual properties (Fauchart & Von Hippel, 2008). The supportive effects of behavioral control on governance dimensions are summarized in Table 2.

Four Choices for Governance of Knowledge Flows in Open Innovation

Four different governance choices, proposed by Bagherzadeh and Brunswicker (2016), differ in terms of the degree of selective revealing and behavioral control. Based on our theoretical examination of the supportive and negative effects of selective revealing and behavioral control, these four governance choices differ in the way they support incentives for knowledge creation and sharing, and control over IP creation and utilization in our two governance dimensions (see Table 3).

Table 2. Supportive of behavioral control on two governance dimensions

	Governance Dimensions	
	Incentives for Knowledge Creation and Sharing	**Control Over IP Creation and Utilization**
Focal Firms	Creating incentives for firms to engage in knowledge sharing and creation by increasing transparency (+)	Reducing the uncertainty of opportunistic behavior with respect to IP creation and usage through routines and procedures (+) Indirectly controlling existing and emerging IP and their application by controlling the processes and routines in which IP is created and used (+)
External Knowledge Sources	Creating incentives for external knowledge sources to engage in knowledge sharing and creation by increasing transparency (+)	Indirectly controlling existing and emerging IP and their application by controlling the processes and routines in which IP is created and used (+)

Note: (+) = Supportive effect of selective revealing on governance dimensions

Table 3. Four governance choices and their supportive role in two governance dimensions

		Selective Revealing	
		Low	**High**
Behavioral Control	**High**	Mode 3: Full Control • Incentive (M) • Control (H)	Mode 4: Guided Revealing • Incentive (H) • Control (M)
	Low	Mode 1: IP usage control • Incentive (L) • Control (M)	Mode 2: Selective Revealing • Incentive (M) • Control (L)

Note: (L) = low level of support; (M) = medium level of support; (H) = high level of support

- **IP Usage Control:** In this governance choice, the focal firm has high level of control over intellectual property usage, and minimal control over the process of knowledge creation and utilization. They do not selectively reveal their internal know-how. Thus, we argue that it establishes sufficient control over existing and emerging IP, and its utilization. At the same time, this governance choice creates minimal incentive for external knowledge sources to engage in knowledge creation and sharing. As a result of the external partner took little effort to invest additional time and resources to create new knowledge, and both partners tried to reduce the sharing of knowledge in the interactive problem solving process.
- **Selective Revealing/Sharing:** This governance choice provides firms with a low level of direct control over existing and jointly created intellectual assets, because they waive legal control rights over some of their internal IP, and potentially also over IP that are created in the interactive relationship. They also do not establish behavioral control mechanism. We argue that selective revealing may establish a strong incentive for the external knowledge source to engage in knowledge sharing and the creation of knowledge that integrate the free and non-proprietary know-how of the focal firm with their newly generated know-how. However, selective revealing significantly reduces the ability to control the usage of the existing and jointly created knowledge for the focal firm, as there is no legal IP mechanism in place, and the focal firm does not establish behavioral or norm-based control activities.
- **Full Control:** Full control creates high level of direct and indirect control over the knowledge flows, as it combines direct controls over IP assets as well as behavioral control over the process. However, the ability to motivate external knowledge sources to engage in extensive knowledge sharing is limited, because the focal firm does not share their internal assets for free

and does not allocate greater legal control and exclusion rights to the external firm.

- **Guided Revealing/Sharing:** This governance choice equips the focal firm and external knowledge sources with high indirect control over intellectual assets, since behavioral control allows them to control and direct the process in which knowledge flows take place. At the same time, there is no control right over existing or emerging intellectual properties. This mode generates strong incentives for knowledge creation and sharing. This governance choice can also indirectly generate some level of control over IP creation and usage through behavioral control mechanisms.

Source Choice and Its Antecedents Role for Governance Choice

The case examples in the literature illustrate that innovating firms opt for different governance modes based on their interaction with different external sources (Ness, 2009; White, 2005). This suggests that each external source has characteristics that can affect the need for selective revealing, as well as behavioral control, when interacting with them. For example, information asymmetry in interactions with competitors leads to the focal firm perceiving a high level of partnering uncertainty. As a result, they seek for means to establish strong incentives for knowledge sharing and strategic alignment (Ritala & Hurmelinna-Laukkanen, 2013)

In the following section, we will explore the nature and boundary conditions of each type of external source. We also elaborate upon the potential relationship and association between these boundary conditions and the firm's preferred mechanisms to govern knowledge flows across (Summarized in Table 4).

- **Universities:** Universities and public research organizations are led by the norms and values of science. Following the notion of science being a public good, they intend to publish and share new discoveries within their scientific community (Perkmann et al., 2013). This situation can increase the level of uncertainty in collaborations with universities and research centers regarding the usage of shared and jointly created knowledge. At the same time, the recent discussion on university-industry relationships highlights the 'third mission' of academic institutions and public research organizations in fostering commercialization and technology transfer. Among other factors, this has increased the interest of universities to maintain control over intellectual assets, and results in a stronger emphasis on formal IP rights and legal control of IP usage through licensing (Dechenaux, Thursby,

& Thursby, 2011). However, there is little interest in exploring joint value creation opportunities with one single focal firm. Thus, if the focal firm is revealing internal problem or solution related knowledge to the university, it may not create a strong incentive effect for university to create and share new knowledge for, and with, the focal firm only.

Additionally, interactions with universities and research organizations are characterized by a high level of technological novelty and uncertainty (Dechenaux et al., 2011). This suggests that firms seek behavioral control over the scientific process of discovery in order to understand commercial opportunities that result from emerging IP. However, the values and norms of the academic community usually make the establishment of such control mechanism very difficult, or even impossible. Thus, both IP control and behavioral control are crucial for focal firms when engaging in interaction with universities and research centers.

- **Value-Chain Partners:** Firms engage in interaction with their value chain to access important information about needs, ideas, and requirements of customers and users (Brunswicker & Vanhaverbeke, 2014). Incentive effects play an important role for both suppliers and customers (Enkel, Perez-Freije, & Gassmann, 2005). As a result, cultivating their suppliers' and customers' motivation to engage in knowledge sharing and creation is a pivotal task for the focal firm. Selective revealing may generate such incentive effects, because it gives firms the opportunity to use the shared knowledge without cost, and also explore additional opportunities for creating value from it, even within the value chain relationship. Interaction with value chain partners is regularly related to knowledge and technologies for existing products and markets that maintain a low level of product and market uncertainty (Brunswicker & Vanhaverbeke, 2014). Thus, there are opportunities to quickly exploit the knowledge created within these relationships. Thus, there is a need for control over behavior of value chain partners regarding the application and sharing of existing and emerging intellectual assets with other firms.
- **Competitors:** Competitors are generally unwilling to collaborate with firms that need their knowledge, since they consider them as risky partners (Ritala & Hurmelinna-Laukkanen, 2013). Therefore, competitors have little incentive to share knowledge with them (Alexy et al., 2013). Selective revealing can create such incentives, because it allows the competitor establishing control over the revealed knowledge. At the same time, information asymmetry in interactions with competitors makes for a high level of partnering uncertainty.

As a result, there is a risk that competitors will act opportunistically and follow their own objectives at the expense of the focal firm's knowledge. It forces the focal firm to have control over the behaviors of their competitors in interactive open innovation, in order to control the direct application of existing and emerging intellectual properties, since they do not have any control over IP.

EMPIRICAL STUDY

Sample and Data Collection

This paper draws upon a firm-level survey database of 125 large firms in the United States and Europe, which was conducted in Fall 2012. The data includes a new 23-item measurement instrument with comprehensive questions for different types of open innovation practices, selective revealing, that improves upon previous survey-based researches on open innovation (Chesbrough & Brunswicker, 2014). Thus, our

Table 4. Interrelation between source choice and governance choice

External Sources	Governance Dimensions		Governance Choice
	Incentives	Control Over IP	
Universities	Control over IP may motivate the university create new knowledge; however, due to the interest to utilize this know-how in a broad way rather than just within one particular university-industry relationships, the creation of incentives through selective revealing is limited	Following the norms and values of science, universities aim to contribute to the public good, and freely share knowledge without control rights attached; this implies that firms seek strong control over the actual knowledge assets through formal IP rights	IP usage control or even full control
Value-Chain partners	Selective revealing may create strong direct incentives for the value-chain partner; since they have several opportunities for collaboration along the value chain	There is a risk of opportunistic behavior of other firms since focal firms' knowledge can be shared with them by value chain partners	Guided revealing
Competitors	Limited incentives are perceived by competitors to interact with other firms since they consider them as risky partner	There is a risk of opportunistic behavior of competitors regarding focal firms' knowledge.	Guided revealing

empirical study significantly advances existing Eurostat Community Innovation Survey (CIS)-based empirical examinations of open innovation, which are mostly concerned with search and sourcing (Faems, Van Looy, & Debackere, 2005; Grimpe & Sofka, 2009; Laursen & Salter, 2006; Laursen & Salter, 2014). Our sample is a cross-industry sample of large stock market listed firms with annual revenues in excess of $250 million and more than 1000 employees. This sampling frame was used to address the void that there is no survey on open innovation for very large firms that examines the adoption of multiple complementary open innovation practices (Chesbrough & Brunswicker, 2014).

98 firms (Out of 125 firms-78%) apply open innovation practices and none of them have abandoned it. 42 firms (out of 98) were excluded from analysis because of missing values (39 firms), at least, on one of the variables related to selective revealing and behavioral control, and being outlier (3 firms). Finally, we used a sample of 56 firms for our empirical study in the current paper. The sample, utilized in this study, is the same as the sample used by Bagherzadeh and Brunswicker (2016).

Table 5. Final sample characteristics

Industry Group (n=53)	**Firm Age (as of 2012, n=51)**		
Mining and Construction	5.7%	< 25 years	21.6%
Manufacturing (Low-tech)	5.7%	25-75 years	21.6%
Manufacturing (Medium-low tech)	13.2%	76-100 years	13.7%
Manufacturing (Medium-high tech)	30.2%	> 101 years	43.1%
Manufacturing (High-tech)	15.1%		
Transportation, communication, electric, gas, and sanitary services	9.4%		
Wholesales trade and retail	11.3%		
Finance, insurance, real state, and services	9.4%		
No. of Employees (in 2011, n=51)	**OI Duration (as of 2012, n=51)**		
1000-4000	29.4%	< 2.5	31.4%
4001-8000	17.6%	2.5-5	19.6%
8001-24000	25.5%	5-10	17.6%
24001-200000	27.5%	10-90	31.4%

Adapted from Bagherzadeh and Brunswicker, 2016.

Note: n differs since all data on sample characteristics was not available for all firms; OI=Open Innovation

Measures and Variables

Based on definition of constructs adopted in this paper, we applied perceptual measures in order to operationalize them.

- **External Knowledge Sources in Open Innovation:** We measure the source choice by focusing on the relevance of a particular external source in a firm's open innovation activities including (1) customers, (2) suppliers, (3) competitors, and (4) universities. We assessed the source choice by asking "how important were the following external sources in your firm's open innovation activities?" and collecting responses on a seven-point Likert scale from 1 (not important) to 7 (very important).
- **Selective Revealing:** This construct refers to the degree of selectively revealing and sharing internally developed knowledge to external partners without any direct financial rewards. We assessed the degree of selective revealing and sharing by asking the question "how regularly have you revealed internal knowledge to outsiders without any direct financial compensation?" and rating the responses on a seven-point Likert scale where 1 refers to "not revealed" and 7 refers to "frequently revealed" (Bagherzadeh & Brunswicker, 2016).
- **Behavioral Control:** This construct reflects to what extent firms are able to monitor and control routines, procedures, and activities of their partners that take place in interactive open innovation. In this paper like the exploratory study conducted by Bagherzadeh and Brunswicker (2016), behavioral control was operationalized as a composite measure by two items as proxy that asked respondents to indicate on a seven-point Likert scale 1) "how important were joint venture activities with external partners in open innovation?", and 2) "how important were idea and startup competitions in open innovation?" where 1 refers to "not important" and 7 refers to "very important". The second scale was used as a reverse scale for measuring behavioral control.

STATISTICAL ANALYSIS AND RESULTS

Descriptive Statistics

The results of descriptive analysis are summarized in Table 6. The mean for the interaction with competitors is 2.48 shows that competitors are not considered as critical external sources of open innovation for large firms. The average interaction level with customers, suppliers, and universities are 5.58, 4.63, and 4.63 respectively,

Table 6. Descriptive statistics

Variable	Mean	Median	SD	Minimum	Maximum
Customers (n=42)	5.57	6.00	1.35	2.00	7.00
Suppliers (n=42)	4.60	5.00	1.61	2.00	7.00
Competitors (n=42)	2.48	2.00	1.58	1.00	6.00
Universities (n=42)	4.67	5.00	1.78	1.00	7.00
Selective revealing/sharing (n=56)	3.09	3.00	1.47	1.00	7.00
Behavioral control (n=56)	4.22	4.00	1.33	1.00	7.00

indicating that these external sources are important in open innovation activities of large firms. The results also show, on average, selective revealing and sharing is modest frequent for large firms and they consider behavioral control as a somehow important governance mechanism.

Governance Choices (Selective Revealing/ Sharing and Behavioral Control)

The study, conducted by Bagherzadeh and Brunswicker (2016) applied the Chi-square test to see whether or not firms with a high level of engagement in selective revealing and sharing tend to engage in a high level of behavioral control in open innovation activities. Table 7 shows the results of the Chi- square test. It shows that there is an association between the level of selective revealing and behavioral control adopted by large firms. This result shows that, to counteract the negative effects of selective revealing on the two governance dimensions (incentives and control over IP), in particular in terms of loss of control over the IP and its usage, focal firms

Table 7. Chi-square test: relationship between governance mechanisms

<table>
<tr><th colspan="2" rowspan="2"></th><th colspan="2">Selective Revealing/Sharing</th></tr>
<tr><th>Low</th><th>High</th></tr>
<tr><td rowspan="2">Behavioral Control</td><td>High</td><td>Full control
Obs. 18, Exp. 21.9</td><td>Guided revealing
Obs. 16, Exp. 12.1</td></tr>
<tr><td>Low</td><td>IP usage control
Obs. 18, Exp. 14.1</td><td>Selective revealing
Obs. 4, Exp. 7.9</td></tr>
<tr><td colspan="2">Chi square, df, (p-value)</td><td colspan="2">4.851, df=1, (0.028)</td></tr>
</table>

Adopted from Bagherzadeh and Brunswicker, 2016:112.

Note: Obs. = Observed frequency of firms; Exp: = Expected frequency of firms, n=56; df = degree of freedom tend to apply guided revealing as a governance choice in order to have control over the behavior of their external knowledge sources.

An Empirical Typology of External Knowledge Sourcing in Large Firms

Our explorative analysis, in the current paper, is concerned with the relationship with a firm's source choice and the role of selective revealing and behavioral control in interactions with these sources. To do so, we introduce an empirical typology of source choices of open innovation in large firms. It helps us to discuss how the nature of the interrelationships with different sources is associated with a firm's choice of combining selective revealing and behavioral control. We applied two steps cluster analysis (hierarchical and non- hierarchical methods) in a sequential way to classify firms that use similar external sources into homogeneous clusters (Hair, Anderson, Tatham, & Black, 1998). Ward's method and the squared Euclidian distance measure were applied for hierarchical cluster analysis. Then, we applied a non- hierarchical cluster analysis technique (K-means) to develop the final clusters based on the results of hierarchical method as starting point. The result of analysis indicated three clusters which is consistent with the previous research (Grimpe & Sofka, 2009). Table 8 shows the mean of interaction with four external knowledge sources for each cluster.

Cluster 1 - Value Chain-Centric: Firms in this cluster engage in relatively a high level of interaction with customers and suppliers compared to other external knowledge sources. They do not rely on the interaction with competitors in their open innovation activities.

Cluster 2 - Ecosystem: Firms in this cluster are characterized by relatively a high level of interaction with customers, suppliers and universities. They follow a balanced approach for open innovation related to customers, suppliers and

Table 8. Three clusters of firms based on their external knowledge sourcing strategy

Variables	C1: Value Chain-Centric (n=17)	C2: Ecosystem (n=15)	C3: University-Centric (n=10)	F-Value, (df=2)
Customers	6.06	5.93	4.20	9.78**
Suppliers	4.82	5.60	2.70	18.70**
Competitors	1.29	4.27	1.80	57.17**
Universities	4.47	4.13	5.80	3.22*

Note: C = Cluster; n = Number of firms in each cluster; df = degree of freedom; * $p < 0.1$; ** $p < 0.001$

Table 9. Chi-square test: source choice and its antecedent role for governance choice

		Source Choice (Three Clusters)		
		Value Chain-Centric (n=17)	**Ecosystem (n=15)**	**University-Centric (n=10)**
Governance Choices	IP usage control	Obs. 3, Exp. 4.5	Obs. 2, Exp. 3.9	Obs. 6, Exp. 2.6
	Selective revealing	Obs. 1, Exp. 1.6	Obs. 3, Exp. 1.4	Obs. 0, Exp. 1
	Full control	Obs. 7, Exp. 5.7	Obs. 3, Exp. 5	Obs. 4, Exp. 3.3
	Guided revealing	Obs. 6, Exp. 5.3	Obs. 7, Exp. 4.6	Obs. 0, Exp. 3.1
Chi square, df, (p-value)	14.345, df=6, (0.026)			

universities compared to cluster 1 and 3. Competitors also play an important role in their open innovation strategy.

Cluster 3 - University-Centric: Firms in this cluster show a high preference for universities in comparison to other external sources (customers, suppliers, and competitors). In this cluster, competitors do not play an important role in their open innovation activities.

Source Choice and Its Antecedent Role for Governance Choice

The Chi-square test was applied to statistically examine whether there is a relationship between external knowledge sourcing (three clusters) and governance choices (four governance choices). An overview of the results is summarized in Table 9.

The results reveal that all of firms (n=13) that adopt guided revealing are related to cluster 1 (Value chain-centric) and 2 (Ecosystem). Firms in cluster 3 (University-centric) do not apply guided revealing as a governance choice in their open innovation activities. In cluster 1 and 2, the number of firms that apply guided revealing is higher than expected.

Most of the firms (6 firms out of 11) that adopt IP usage control are in cluster 3. They show a relatively high degree of interaction with universities. In cluster 3, the number of firms (n=6) that applied IP usage control is higher than expected. In cluster 1 and 2, the number of firms that relied on IP usage control is lower than expected.

Our exploration of the association between the firm's source choice and its governance choices suggests that the preferred governance choice is different across three clusters. Results indicates that firms with a high level of interaction with competitors or the emphasis of value chain partners (customers and suppliers) tend to adopt *guided revealing* to govern knowledge flows. On the other hand, firms with high level of interaction with universities preferred to adopt *IP usage control or full control*. The Chi-squared test shows, the differences in adopting governance choices are statistically significant across three clusters (Chi-square=14.345 with p-value=0.026).

To sum up, firms that intensively interact with market related partners such as customers, suppliers or competitors but not with universities tend to adopt guided revealing as governance choice. In contrast, firms that lean towards universities as key open innovation partner and little interaction with market-related partners pay high attention to formal IP control and are less inclined to selectively reveal internal knowledge for free. This suggests that the incentive effects of selective revealing are limited when working with universities in open innovation, as potential incentive effects may support new knowledge creation but not necessarily knowledge sharing along the interactive relationship with scientific partners. However, our results suggest that firms may struggle to establish behavioral control mechanism when interacting with universities, as scientific values and norms make it difficult to establish routines for control over the research process.

DISCUSSION, IMPLICATIONS, AND LIMITATIONS

In this paper we aim to advance our conceptual understanding about the governance of knowledge flows in interactive open innovation activities. Such interactive relationships challenge established theoretical assumptions with respect to two critical governance dimensions, namely 1) incentives for knowledge creation and sharing and 2) control over IP creation and utilization. We complement the existing theoretical discussion on control of IP, which is primarily focused on the value creation and appropriation mechanism related to the static 'outcome' of the problem solving process, with a behavioral and process-oriented dimension of control. Taking an organizational perspective, control is not just related to the static outcome (the IP asset) but also to the actions and activities required for creating a new IP asset and the processes of coordinating the usage of IP. We theoretically explicate four governance choices, proposed by Bagherzadeh and Brunswicker (2016) that combines selective revealing and behavioral control: 1) IP usage control, 2) selective revealing, 3) full control, and 4) guided revealing. Guided revealing presents an alternative governance mechanism that may positively affect both incentives and control. Selective revealing of internal IP assets motivates the external partner to create new knowledge, and share the knowledge with the focal firm. In addition, guided revealing creates new indirect mechanism for controlling the creation and usage of IP. By establishing behavioral control mechanism, the focal firm is able to direct both the nature of the knowledge creation (e.g. by prescribing the methods to be used, etc.) and thus, indirectly steering the strategic alignment with the partner. In addition, it also prescribes the mechanism for using and sharing established intellectual properties (Fauchart & Von Hippel, 2008).

In addition, we advance our understanding of how different governance mechanisms are associated with a firm's source choice. When empirically exploring the interrelation, we learn that those firms that engage in competitor or value chain -centric open innovation relationships put a greater emphasis on selective revealing in order to nurture knowledge creation and sharing along these relationships. At the same, they also seem to be able to opt for open innovation practices that allow for behavioral control. Interestingly, interactions with universities are hardly associated with guided revealing. This suggests that the incentive effects of selective revealing are limited with focusing on interactions with universities, and firms are not intended to establish control over the innovation process through behavioral control. In sum, this paper advances existing theoretical and empirical contributions to the literature on governance in open innovation conceptualized as an interactive problem solving process taking by taking and organizational control perspective (West and Bogers, 2014). In addition, it also contributes to the discussion on governance of knowledge flows by exploring the role of external sources in governance selection.

ACKNOWLEDGMENT

The authors acknowledge the support of Professor Henry Chesbrough and the Garwood Center for Corporate Innovation at University of California at Berkeley, CA, for conducting this research.

REFERENCES

Adner, R., & Kapoor, R. (2010). Value creation in innovation ecosystems: How the structure of technological interdependence affects firm performance in new technology generations. *Strategic Management Journal*, *31*(3), 306–333. doi:10.1002/smj.821

Afuah, A., & Tucci, C. L. (2012). Crowdsourcing as a solution to distant search. *Academy of Management Review*, *37*(3), 355–375. doi:10.5465/amr.2010.0146

Aghion, P., & Tirole, J. (1994). The management of innovation. *The Quarterly Journal of Economics*, *109*(4), 1185–1209. doi:10.2307/2118360

Alexy, O., George, G., & Salter, A. J. (2013). Cui bono? The selective revealing of knowledge and its implications for innovative activity. *Academy of Management Review*, *38*(2), 270–291. doi:10.5465/amr.2011.0193

Bagherzadeh, M., & Brunswicker, S. (2016). Governance of Knowledge Flows in Open Exploration: The Role of Behavioral Control. In T. K. Das (Ed.), *Decision Making in Behavioral Strategy (DMBS)*. IAP.

Bagherzadeh Niri, M. (2016). *Governance of inter-organizational collaborations when engaged in open innovation* (Unpublished PhD dissertation/thesis). University of Ramon Llull, Barcelona, Spain.

Brunswicker, S., & Vanhaverbeke, W. (2014). Open Innovation in Small and Medium-Sized Enterprises (SMEs): External Knowledge Sourcing Strategies and Internal Organizational Facilitators. *Journal of Small Business Management.*

Chesbrough, H. (2003). *Open innovation: The new imperative for creating and profiting from technology*. Harvard Business Press.

Chesbrough, H., & Brunswicker, S. (2014). A Fad or a Phenomenon?: The Adoption of Open Innovation Practices in Large Firms. *Research-Technology Management*, *57*(2), 16–25.

Dahlander, L., & Gann, D. M. (2010). How open is innovation? *Research Policy*, *39*(6), 699–709. doi:10.1016/j.respol.2010.01.013

Dechenaux, E., Thursby, J., & Thursby, M. (2011). Inventor moral hazard in university licensing: The role of contracts. *Research Policy*, *40*(1), 94–104. doi:10.1016/j.respol.2010.09.015

Eisenhardt, K. M. (1989). Agency theory: An assessment and review. *Academy of Management Review*, *14*(1), 57–74.

Enkel, E., Perez-Freije, J., & Gassmann, O. (2005). Minimizing market risks through customer integration in new product development: Learning from bad practice. *Creativity and Innovation Management*, *14*(4), 425–437. doi:10.1111/j.1467-8691.2005.00362.x

Faems, D., Van Looy, B., & Debackere, K. (2005). Interorganizational collaboration and innovation: Toward a portfolio approach*. *Journal of Product Innovation Management*, *22*(3), 238–250. doi:10.1111/j.0737-6782.2005.00120.x

Fauchart, E., & Von Hippel, E. (2008). Norms-based intellectual property systems: The case of French chefs. *Organization Science*, *19*(2), 187–201. doi:10.1287/orsc.1070.0314

Felin, T., & Zenger, T. R. (2014). Closed or open innovation? Problem solving and the governance choice. *Research Policy*, *43*(5), 914–925. doi:10.1016/j.respol.2013.09.006

Grimpe, C., & Sofka, W. (2009). Search patterns and absorptive capacity: Low-and high-technology sectors in European countries. *Research Policy*, *38*(3), 495–506. doi:10.1016/j.respol.2008.10.006

Hair, J. F., Anderson, R. E., Tatham, R. L., & Black, W. C. (1998). *Multivariate analysis*. Englewood: Prentice Hall International.

Henkel, J., Baldwin, C. Y., & Shih, W. (2013). IP Modularity: Profiting from innovation by aligning product architecture with intellectual property. *California Management Review*, *55*(4), 65–82. doi:10.1525/cmr.2013.55.4.65

Henkel, J., Schöberl, S., & Alexy, O. (2014). The emergence of openness: How and why firms adopt selective revealing in open innovation. *Research Policy*, *43*(5), 879–890. doi:10.1016/j.respol.2013.08.014

Jarvenpaa, S. L., & Välikangas, L. (2014). Opportunity Creation in Innovation Networks: Interactive revealing practices. *California Management Review*, *57*(1), 67–87. doi:10.1525/cmr.2014.57.1.67

Kathan, W., Hutter, K., Füller, J., & Hautz, J. (2015). Reciprocity vs. Free-Riding in Innovation Contest Communities. *Creativity and Innovation Management*, *24*(3), 537–549. doi:10.1111/caim.12107

Kirsch, L. J. (1996). The management of complex tasks in organizations: Controlling the systems development process. *Organization Science*, *7*(1), 1–21. doi:10.1287/orsc.7.1.1

Koza, M. P., & Lewin, A. Y. (1998). The co-evolution of strategic alliances. *Organization Science*, *9*(3), 255–264. doi:10.1287/orsc.9.3.255

Laursen, K., & Salter, A. (2006). Open for innovation: The role of openness in explaining innovation performance among UK manufacturing firms. *Strategic Management Journal*, *27*(2), 131–150. doi:10.1002/smj.507

Laursen, K., & Salter, A. J. (2014). The paradox of openness: Appropriability, external search and collaboration. *Research Policy*, *43*(5), 867–878. doi:10.1016/j.respol.2013.10.004

Leiponen, A. (2008). Control of intellectual assets in client relationships: Implications for innovation. *Strategic Management Journal*, *29*(13), 1371–1394. doi:10.1002/smj.715

Majchrzak, A., Cooper, L. P., & Neece, O. E. (2004). Knowledge reuse for innovation. *Management Science*, *50*(2), 174–188. doi:10.1287/mnsc.1030.0116

Majchrzak, A., Jarvenpaa, S. L., & Bagherzadeh, M. (2014). A Review of Interorganizational Collaboration Dynamics. *Journal of Management*.

Ness, H. (2009). Governance, negotiations, and alliance dynamics: Explaining the evolution of relational practice. *Journal of Management Studies*, *46*(3), 451–480. doi:10.1111/j.1467-6486.2008.00818.x

Nickerson, J. A., & Zenger, T. R. (2004). A knowledge-based theory of the firm—The problem-solving perspective. *Organization Science*, *15*(6), 617–632. doi:10.1287/orsc.1040.0093

Niri, M. B., & Brunswicker, S. (2014). Joint exploration with the enemy– revealing needed?. *Proceedings of the 1st ISPIM Americas Innoavtion Forum*.

Perkmann, M., Tartari, V., McKelvey, M., Autio, E., Broström, A., DEste, P., & Hughes, A. et al. (2013). Academic engagement and commercialisation: A review of the literature on university–industry relations. *Research Policy*, *42*(2), 423–442. doi:10.1016/j.respol.2012.09.007

Pisano, G. P. (1989). Using equity participation to support exchange: Evidence from the biotechnology industry. *Journal of Law Economics and Organization*, 109–126.

Ritala, P., & Hurmelinna-Laukkanen, P. (2013). Incremental and radical innovation in coopetition—the role of absorptive capacity and appropriability. *Journal of Product Innovation Management*, *30*(1), 154–169. doi:10.1111/j.1540-5885.2012.00956.x

Schnackenberg, A. K., & Tomlinson, E. C. (2014). Organizational Transparency A New Perspective on Managing Trust in Organization-Stakeholder Relationships. *Journal of Management*, 0149206314525202.

Schroeder, A., & Wagner, C. (2012). Governance of open content creation: A conceptualization and analysis of control and guiding mechanisms in the open content domain. *Journal of the American Society for Information Science and Technology*, *63*(10), 1947–1959. doi:10.1002/asi.22657

Teece, D. J. (1986). Profiting from technological innovation: Implications for integration, collaboration, licensing and public policy. *Research Policy*, *15*(6), 285–305. doi:10.1016/0048-7333(86)90027-2

West, J., & Bogers, M. (2014). Leveraging External Sources of Innovation: A Review of Research on Open Innovation. *Journal of Product Innovation Management*, *31*(4), 814–831. doi:10.1111/jpim.12125

West, J., Salter, A., Vanhaverbeke, W., & Chesbrough, H. (2014). Open innovation: The next decade. *Research Policy*, *43*(5), 805–811. doi:10.1016/j.respol.2014.03.001

White, S. (2005). Cooperation Costs, Governance Choice and Alliance Evolution. *Journal of Management Studies*, *42*(7), 1383–1412. doi:10.1111/j.1467-6486.2005.00548.x

Wikhamn, B. R. (2013). Two Different Perspectives on Open Innovation–Libre versus Control. *Creativity and Innovation Management*, *22*(4), 375–389. doi:10.1111/caim.12035

ENDNOTE

1 We use selective revealing and sharing synonymously for free revealing and sharing as well.

Chapter 11
Cyber-Security Intelligence Gathering:
Issues With Knowledge Management

Ezer Osei Yeboah-Boateng
Ghana Technology University College, Ghana

Elvis Akwa-Bonsu
Detectware, Ghana

ABSTRACT

Recently, KM has found applications in cyber-security. Though the actionable information gathered is intangible, they are used to improve knowledge sharing in organizations. Key cyber-security objectives are to prevent, detect and respond to threats. Using open-sharing of vulnerabilities and exploits, cyber risks could be mitigated through info-sharing. Cyber-intelligence is perceived as a process and a product, with outcomes being alerts that solicit explicit responses, leading to mitigation of possible threats. Using the Scrum approach, relevant articles and databases were reviewed, towards improving mitigation strategies. A virtual machine experiment utilized various tools to gather intelligence. Results from footprinting were used to design a KM-based Cyber-Intelligence Gathering model that incorporates Lewin's Change Theory. It is intuitive and serves as an effective mitigation strategy for most organizations, especially SMEs. The implication is that knowledge sharing could be harnessed to create a pool of mitigation resources for most enterprises in developing economies.

DOI: 10.4018/978-1-5225-2956-9.ch011

INTRODUCTION

All attacks follow certain stages. By observing those stages during an attack progression and then creating immediate protections to block those attack methods, organizations can achieve a level of closed-loop intelligence that can block and protect across this attack kill chain. (Sager, 2014, p. 1)

Knowledge Management (KM) techniques have found applications in all spheres in technology based organizations, and in recent times with cyber-security (Tisdale, 2015). In spite of the intangible nature of the actionable information, often gathered from knowledge capturing activities, they can be employed to improve information sharing and management in organizations (Belsis, Kokolakis, & Kiountouzis, 2005). Managing enterprise networks require the use of knowledge management methods employed in the gathering of information, open-sharing of vulnerabilities and related exploits, as well as hotfixes from vendors.

Knowledge is defined as a "fluid mix of framed experiences, values, contextual information and expert insights ... [which] is often embedded .... in documents or repositories [such as] organizational processes and practices" (Davenport & Prusak, 2000). Knowledge management is utilized in the collection, organization, analysis and collaborative sharing of the vast amount of information to the cybersecurity professionals, national security agents, and business community, etc.

Often, most IT professionals have perceived cyber-security as a mere technical problem. However, in recent times researchers are highlighting that a holistic cyber-security endeavors involve business concerns, governance and compliance issues, as well as organizational psychology (Tisdale, 2015) (Yeboah-Boateng, 2013a).

As businesses utilize the opportunities offered by ICTs, they are also exposed to cybersecurity challenges, such as vulnerabilities and threats. These vulnerabilities are flaws and weaknesses, which are typically inherent within the systems design, configurations and operations (Yeboah-Boateng, 2013a). When these susceptibilities are not properly dealt with, they can be exploited by various threats. "Whenever they are attacked [businesses] are adversely affected by way of loss of revenues, loss of customer confidence, loss of investor confidence, loss of resources, loss of credibility, cost related to dealing with the security breaches, cost of mitigation, as well as possible business closure, etc." (Yeboah-Boateng, 2013a, p. 1).

In 2014, for example, studies uncovered that major vulnerabilities, known for many years, which had been dormant were then being exploited. The situation was exacerbated as those exploited breaches in turn facilitated other possible intrusions or incidents (Bradley, Alvarez, Kuhn, & McMillen, 2015). In essence, vulnerabilities – be they unknown or undisclosed or undiscovered – there must be best efforts employed to limit the extent of impact in the event of incident or attack.

In cyber-security related endeavors, the quality of data validation and dissemination of the information gathered are key. There's the need to exchange information in managing vulnerabilities (such as Day-Zero vulnerabilities), threats, incidents, etc. (Dandurand & Serrano, 2013). Generally, KM analytics can be used for effective management of these actionable information in mitigating the possible risks to the organizations. Aspects of KM lend their support to cyber-security management, including information gathering on vulnerabilities and associated patches, data analytics, collaboration and information sharing (Forbes & Ahmed, 2011).

In today's ubiquitous business environments, information sharing raises various concerns amidst social media and networks. How do organizations strike a perfect balance in sharing information and the need for real-time intelligence gathering? How does "Bring-Your-Own-Devices" (BYOD) impact on the knowledge management principles? What roles are users playing in knowledge management in respect of cyber-security? How are the user fulfilling their knowledge management roles in respect of cyber-security?

Using the Scrum methodology, we gleaned through extensive literature of key articles, databases, and authorities, towards improving the cyber-team's mitigation strategies, whilst minimizing the possibilities of exploitation (Yeboah-Boateng, 2013a). Typically, the agile development model requires extreme agility with the usual characteristics of dynamic Security Operations Center (SOC) culture and real-time communications. This study is an exploratory survey of cyber-security vulnerabilities and knowledge management practices employed in patch management. Sources of data have been employing use cases of domestic, transnational and global literature as well as databases on vulnerabilities discovery and reports, exploits and attacks, and hotfixes.

A conceptual model cataloging or detailing the taxonomy of concerns emanating from intelligence capturing, storage and transfer is developed to assist in strategic mitigation measures. The essence of the model is to facilitate transforming knowledge gathered into business value decisions (Kankanhalli & Tan, 2008). The model also seeks to explore the vulnerabilities information, find the entity relations amongst the key concepts and to proffer appropriate options for decision-making. The Knowledge Management based Cyber-Intelligence Gathering (KM-CIG) model is pivoted on the Kurt Lewin's Unfreeze-Refreeze model, to create and/or resolve the puzzles associated with gathering intelligence and using same to make major decision in the cyber-sphere.

Strategic Cyber-Intelligence has its roles and responsibilities in equipping Chief Technology Officers (CTOs) and Network Managers at all levels with insight and understanding of the state-of-the-art in cyber-crime, prevalence of vulnerabilities and threats posed to Information systems, and the mitigation measures employed to minimize the impact of cyber-risk. It calls for some pragmatic changes in approaches or methods used to collect data, policies formulated to prevent, detect and respond to these threats. In fact, the information gathered and processed is what knowledge management practitioners refer to as Actionable Information or simply, Knowledge.

"Intelligence is actionable knowledge derived from processed, or analyzed, data and information" (Intelligence & National Security Alliance, 2015, p. 2). It involves collecting, processing, analyzing, contextualizing and reporting threat information in support of strategic decision-making.

In this study, cyber-intelligence is deemed as the assessment of possible threat agent's motivations, capabilities and opportunities within the cyberspace, in order to provide appropriate measures for the enterprise systems, networks and facilities to sustain its business objectives (Intelligence & National Security Alliance, 2015). Cyber-intelligence with its associated knowledge sharing is vital to every security decision made by data subjects and owners, including the prospects of mitigation against mission-critical assets.

Problem Formulation

Dalziel (2015) posits that an organization ought to build an objective based, with measurable metrics kind of threat intelligence program. Though, he admits the mission-critical nature of cyber-intelligence to the organization, he purports that the vendor-proffered solutions are largely data, such as "bad Internet Protocols (IPs), or Application vulnerabilities, or malware signatures, or Uniform Resource Locations (URLs) blacklists, to botted nodes, or botnet C^2 servers, or social media data, etc." (Dalziel, 2015, p. 3)

To situate the discussion on cyber-intelligence gathering vis-à-vis Knowledge Management (KM), there's the need to distinguish between what constitutes, data, information and intelligence.

Data – typically come in the form of raw feed, "machine-readable feed, file, or service in XML, JSON, CSV, or API formats, Web service, etc." (Dalziel, 2015, p. 4). Information is processed data that is usually organized, structured and/or presented in context so as to make it meaningful or useful. Intelligence, on the other hand, is processed data or information obtained from analysis and evaluation that promotes strategic decision making. Explicitly, "Intelligence is data that has been refined, analyzed or processed such that it is Relevant, Actionable, and Valuable" (Dalziel, 2015, p. 4). For the purposes of this study, and in accordance with KM principles, the "data" which has been analyzed, refined and processed is no longer called "data" but "actionable information", otherwise known as Knowledge. Actionable, according to (Dalziel, 2015)must lead to two outcomes, namely:

1. An alert, or a prompt that solicits an explicit response or action or decision leading to mitigation of a possible threat or restoring a compromise;
2. An information that is relevant and evidential enough to warrant an non-action decision.

We herewith note that "indecision is itself a choice; not to decide, is to decide not to" (Graham, 2010, p. 149).

Knowledge Management involves complex, organizational dynamics, with interrelationships of multiple stakeholders that exist to create the vulnerabilities reports. The reports are often considered "overly binary based probabilistic" risk metrics as against intuitive based holistic "possibilistic" solutions (Yeboah-Boateng, 2013a). How do we consolidate on the vulnerabilities reports and deduce mitigation strategies?

In view of day-zero attacks, how do the stakeholders collaborate on day-zero vulnerabilities and associated patches; as time is of essence! There is the need for approaches or a model that facilitate early identification, dissemination and mitigation, considering the enormous datasets produced on daily or weekly basis in respect of intrusion attempts and/or incidents.

How are vulnerabilities identified and reported? Who are the actors in the organization in terms of cyber-intelligence? How do they monitor the threats based on classified assets?

Tisdale (2015, p. 191) posits that "cybersecurity is particularly a knowledge management problem" – in view of the big data, multitude of stakeholders, complexities and complications. Whereas the hackers' profile is constantly evolving to be more sophisticated, the end-users remain the weakest link in the security chain. The role of all and sundry within the organization cannot be over-emphasized. Indeed, "everyone becomes a stakeholder in cybersecurity" (Tisdale, 2015, p. 192).

In spite of the number of vendor-sponsored vulnerabilities vis-à-vis hotfixes sharing, there remains a considerable gap in sharing of cyber-intelligence amongst governmental, public and private sector practitioners. Effective, accurate and timely cyber-intelligence sharing has a huge gap, in terms of information quality.

Key Research Questions and Objectives

Key research questions and objectives for this study are presented hereunder:

- How can knowledge capturing and sharing activities be harnessed for mitigation of cybersecurity vulnerabilities?
- What are the cyber-intelligence concerns of knowledge management?

- How are the vulnerabilities reports consolidated and mitigation strategies deduced?
- How do the stakeholders collaborate on day-zero vulnerabilities and associated patches?

The objectives of the study are as follows:

- To assess the cyber-intelligence concerns with sharing gathered information for patch management;
- To design a knowledge management based cyber-intelligence gathering model to examine the dissemination of vulnerabilities and threats;
- To explore the roles of stakeholders in collaborating on day-zero vulnerabilities and associated patches.

Highlights of Findings

Key findings are the taxonomy of cyber-intelligence approaches to collaborative sharing. An intuitive strategic KM-based Cyber-Intelligence model aimed at assisting stakeholders as a guide in collecting, organizing, analyzing and sharing actionable information that could be harnessed to formulate appropriate mitigation strategy is proposed.

The model is useful in synthesizing vulnerabilities and threats information gathered from multiple sources; and subsequently, contextualized to deduce insights for possible remedies or patch management. It offers a concise overview of mitigation strategies aimed at gathering cyber-intelligence and providing insights into how vulnerabilities data and possible threats could be harnessed to support critical decisions.

Significance of the Chapter

The study's appeal with perspectives from knowledge management – knowledge capture and collaborative sharing is an enhancement to the discussion of cyber-security intelligence gathering, for which IT managers and researchers would find useful. Though cyber-intelligence theories are emergent, this research seeks to contribute to the body of knowledge with the strategic model of shared intelligence aimed at educating today's talents for tomorrow's threats (Intelligence & National Security Alliance, 2015).

Outline of the Chapter

This introductory section dealt with overview of cyber-intelligence and knowledge management concerns with collaborative sharing. Followed by related works on cyber-intelligence challenges, knowledge management capturing, collaborative sharing, Lewin's change theory, and patch management. Open source intelligence gathering and associated tools and techniques are discussed. By intuitive deductions and critical thinking the model is designed and its implications for strategic cyber-intelligence decision making follows, and then conclusion and recommendations.

LITERATURE REVIEW

Typically, intelligence is the same in terms of Tactics, Techniques and Procedures (TTPs), irrespective of its applied field. Cyber-intelligence is not different! It is often perceived as hostile or offensive in nature, especially as perceived as espionage operations, but its main purpose is for strategic defense against adversaries. In this study, we perceive intelligence as a tool in defense used for the resistance, recognition, recovery and, sometimes, redress (Endicott-Popovsky, 2013).

In view of the different sources, that intelligence data may be collected or gathered or captured, it may be fraught with inaccuracies or uncertainties. However, the output must be properly examined and contextualized (compared with some baseline to reach credible conclusions).

Intelligence is a multi-faceted "product resulting from information" gathering, capturing, classifying, estimating or appraising, examining, incorporating, explaining (OPSEC, 1991). It is characterized by non-ambiguous processing of data, though, the data gathered may be fraught of fuzzy or ambiguous data, and its ultimate output must not be fuzzy.

Traditionally, intelligence may be categorized as either strategic – long-term, or operational – near-term. For this study, both are bundled together for cyber-risk as some impacts of near-term may have long-term repercussions on the organizations, such as possible business closure (Yeboah-Boateng, 2013a).

Intelligence is used for competitive advantage. Cyber-Intelligence is a strategic tool used in ensuring that effective mitigation measures are planned and implemented for cyber-risk incidents and possibilities. Its intuitive nature makes it easy to use by all IT or NOC associates.

With a lot of dependence of businesses on IT and its infrastructures, cyber-intelligence has assume prominence, especially as a means to ensure governance and compliance with the customers data collected and used.

Typically, technology is utilized in the organization as an enabler, and as well, a value-adder (Mitchell, 2009). Today, the technology is used as a tool to stimulate or generate ideas, to develop strategies and to facilitate knowledge sharing (Mitchell, 2009).

Cyber-intelligence is simply issues surrounding information (or data) acquisition, processing and analysis as well as dissemination. The issues are multi-faceted, which raise a lot concerns; where are the sources? Who are the users and/or actors? What are the sensors and/or actuators? How are the data processed, and by whom? How are the information distributed and acted upon? (Clark, 2007).

It is an aid in planning and strategic decision-making, when one can reasonably predict the motivations of the threat agents, thereby appropriately instituting mitigation measures to deal with security challenges.

This exploratory study is about educating security professionals on mitigation measures, heretofore known as Intelligence on the unknown attacks, which seek to circumvent the latest updates "by changing signatures, targets and/or patterns of behavior" (Sager, 2014, p. 1).

Knowledge Management

Knowledge representation is a key component in the technological scheme of sharing knowledge. Diverse types of knowledge are prevalent, including tacit and explicit – which are traditionally named; then, social, declarative, procedural, causal, relational, etc. (Alavi & Leidner, 2001). Notably, information systems today utilize mainly the declarative and procedural dimensions in almost all systems (Ein-Dor, 2009). Thus, the intelligence gathered are presented in both declarative (contents) and procedural (controls) forms; e.g. HTML, XML, etc.

The main approaches adapted in gathering intelligence data is through "creation, exploration and interaction" with systems and the cyber-risk parameters (Farmer, 2009).

Knowledge management based cyber-intelligence is an emergent technological study with influence on "policy makers, practitioners, researchers and students (Chen, 2006, p. xi). We gathered data from diverse sources, be it from authoritative sources (e.g. OWASP, IC3, Symantec, FBI, etc.) or open sources (e.g. "TV-News" effect stories, journal articles, blogs, etc.), and in multiple formats and in huge volumes (Chen, 2006).

By definition, Knowledge discovery techniques are "non-trivial extraction of implicit, previously unknown, and potentially useful knowledge from data" (Chen, 2006). This was employed as a convenient but practical exploration of datasets gathered from end-users across various Internet platforms.

Kurt Lewin's Change Model

Kurt Lewin theorized a 3-stage model of change in information systems, which is also known as the Unfreezing-Change-Refreeze model (Luftman, 2004). It espouses that for effective knowledge sharing to take place, the organization would need to reject the status-quo and then, to replace the existing knowledge with the learned or newly acquired knowledge. In essence, it alludes to the dynamic nature of cyber-intelligence; as new vulnerabilities are recognized or discovered, almost on daily basis (e.g. Day-Zero vulnerabilities).

Similarly, it enjoins the end-users to adaptively re-evaluate the state of systems with respect to knowledge sharing. This, indeed, is the crux of the study; to facilitate with ease the cyber-security intelligence gathering about potential and possible known and unknown vulnerabilities and threats.

To recapitulate, the knowledge management principles involved are information capturing or gathering, processing of the collected information into usefully actionable information; as insights to resist, recognize, recover and retaliate on systems intrusions.

The Unfreezing component is an observation of the status-quo in information systems (Kaminski, 2011), for example. Here, systems administrators or network managers could rely on existing policies, current configurations, and patches. But, in reality, systems would require dynamic changes to policies (c.f. policy as a living document), system configuration may be remodeled to reflect changes in business operations, whilst, hotfixes, updates, or patches are constantly applied to ensure secured systems.

In this study, the actual process of change is the processing of intelligence and the insights (or knowledge) shared across the organization or industry as best practices, and finally, frozen as the norm. The cycle goes on and on.

Open Source Intelligence (OSINT)

OSINT is basically intelligence data available to the public (OPSEC, 1996). OSINT has` assumed prominence in the intelligence community with the emergence of the Internet and the Web especially. Today, various electronic databases exist as well as tools to gather and process them into usable and actionable intelligence.

It is not uncommon to gather some intellectual property, proprietary data, sensitive government data, or trade secrets from corporate websites.

Strategic Intelligence finds applications in marketing, policy formulation, investment, transition at nation-state governance, etc.

Intelligence is certainly broader than corporate espionage. Indeed, Intelligence is a process of Strategic problem solving which involves data gathering, processing, examining and decision-making that often impact the entity concerned, positively or adversely (McDowell, 2009). McDowell (2009) clearly articulates that Intelligence is used to resolve issues pertaining to threats, risks and competitive advantage. That's exactly the essence of this study.

The theory of Intelligence and its practice dates many hundreds of decades (c.f. the Biblical account of intelligence gathering in Numbers 13:1-14), yet its application to Knowledge Management is quite recent and sometimes unclear.

The strategic nature of intelligence encourages the use of "intuitive and creative thinking" in the analysis of intelligence data collected (McDowell, 2009, p. 6). McDowell (2009) dissects intelligence as encompassing process, activity as well as product. Intelligence is summed up as a tool used in gathering appropriate data, to solve a problem, and the need to have business continuity or disaster recovery, whilst anticipating the future state of the organization (McDowell, 2009).

Intelligence is often prefixed to indicate its purpose and location, such as "military, political, economic, or crime intelligence" (McDowell, 2009, p. 12).

In this study, we use Cyber-Intelligence to indicate that our scope is within the cyber-space or market.

We also utilize the threat agent fuzzy function (Yeboah-Boateng, 2013a) (Yeboah-Boateng, 2013b) given as

$$Threats \triangleq \tilde{F}(motivation, capability, opportunity, AssetValue)$$

and adapting McDowell's treatise on Intelligence roles, the above function is reformulated or recontextualized (Yeboah-Boateng, 2016) as follows:

$$Threats_{due\ to\ Intelligence} \triangleq \tilde{F}(Intentions, Capabilities, Limitations, Vulnerabilities)$$

In essence, the threats due to antagonists or adversaries is given as a fuzzy function of:

- **Motivations:** Which are the intentions of the antagonists or adversaries;
- **Capabilities:** Are the strengths, skills and tools at the disposal of the entities;

- **Opportunities:** Are the limitations posed by counter-intelligence or corrective or recovery measures put in place to deal with any eventualities;
- Asset Value (A_V) has inherent vulnerabilities which are often exploited to cause harm or risk.

The Cyber Kill Chain Model

This is a 7-step model developed by the Lockheed Martin's Computer Incident Response Team (CIRT) in 2010, to enhance cyber-security analysis appreciation of the adversary's TTPs (Lockheed Martin, 2010). The model is a framework for computer network attack (CNA) or computer network espionage (CNE), whereby the typical hacking process is categorized into various attack phases (Lockheed Martin, 2010) (Sager, 2014). The categories are as follows:

1. **Reconnaissance:** Or Footprinting – involves information gathering about the target, such as its network topology, applications, services, hardware and software mix, etc. (e.g. harvesting email addresses, articles, etc.);
2. **Weaponization:** Involves preparation and penetration plan for launching a backdoor and to execute an attack (e.g. creating deliverable payload);
3. **Delivery:** Involves the actual launching of the attack and injecting the backdoor (e.g. through emails, websites, USBs, etc.);
4. **Exploitation:** Involves triggering the backdoor; in other words, taking advantage of the situation exploit the susceptible systems (e.g. exploiting vulnerabilities with codes);
5. **Installation:** Involves installing a backdoor as a bootstrap and creating any associated remote access tools (e.g. installing malware on computing resources or assets);
6. **Command and Control (C&C):** Involves use of tools to establish remote access (e.g. remote manipulation of victim systems);
7. **Action on Objective:** Involves collection and exfiltration of information, or other actions against the target (e.g. with hands-on execution).

Though the Cyber Kill Chain model is a useful tool to comprehend the stages involved in cyber-attack, it seems to be emphasizing the status-quo; whereby perimeter based malware prevention is the norm (Engel, 2014). The above notwithstanding, this study utilizes the approach, especially the first phase in gathering intelligence.

Patch Management

The time between the discovery of an operating system or application vulnerability and the emergence of an exploit is getting shorter, sometimes only a matter of hours. This imposes pressures on IT managers to rapidly patch production systems which directly conflicts with configuration management best practices of quality assurance testing. Many organizations are struggling to keep current with the constant release of new patches and updates. At the same time, they are under pressure to provide near 100% availability of key business systems. (Voldal, 2003, p. 2)

NIST (2013, p. 2) defines patch management as the process of identifying, acquiring, installing and verifying patches for computing resources. Generally, patches are applied to correct vulnerabilities, and/or functional problems within the systems and applications, as well as installing new system features and enhancements.

Patch management may be complex and coupled with the exigencies of hotfixes to cure reported "day-zero" vulnerabilities, could impose undue challenges on the system administrators and the production systems. There are concerns of the timing to apply patches, which assets are prioritized, and the policies governing the enterprise patch management vis-à-vis configuration management. In spite of the urgency, all security patches must be subjected to change management request process for proper documentation and accounting (FlatIron Technologies, 2014).

Typically, the following process serves as a guide in applying a patch management: based on policies in place, precautions are taken before implementing the patches; there's the need to develop a test environment that mirrors the production system (e.g. using VMware); need to develop a backup or fallback plan; need to evaluate the patches and document changes to system configuration and the results of the test carried out; then to rollout the patches at set time.

METHODOLOGY

The intelligence life cycle theoretic serves as the key model in all intelligence operations; from planning and strategic direction, data acquisition (or information gathering or collection), data processing, data analytics, through to data distribution (or dissemination). Depending on the strategic focus of a particular intelligence operations, intelligence could be perceived as either a product, or a process, or sometimes, a party (or practice by persons, within an organization) that performs the operations. In this study, we use intelligence to connote those of a product as well as a process. In the cyber-space, the practicing entity is the security operations center (SOC) or the network monitoring team (in most organizations, it's embodied in the NOC).

Using the US-based Intelligence cycle, which is a 5-step process (Department of Defence (DoD), 2000) (Rocha, 2015) this study is focused on the second step of Collection. Typically, the intelligence data gathering involves multiplicity or redundancy of collecting assets or resources. In essence, all possible avenues of data gathering are targeted and collected with minimal possibility of failure to capture. Similarly, in this study's experiments, multiple tools and techniques (utilities) were employed in data gathering.

Data sources are varied; collecting both structured and unstructured datasets. The scope of strategic intelligence gathering (collection) is based on the "nature, extent and impact" of cyber-risk posed by these threats agents, e.g. antagonists or adversaries (McDowell, 2009, p. 22).

The requirements specification set the stage for effective and efficient collection and analysis of intelligence data. By employing the Agile Scrum methodology, we reviewed the end-user's needs, cognizance of the fact that end-users are the weakest link in the cyber-security chain. The objective is to gather first hand end-user needs on the system operations, configurations and perceived vulnerabilities.

The next step was in guesstimating the requirements. Here, we estimated how long it takes for the observation or to collect the logs (i.e. data). We then prioritized the computing resources (i.e. assets classification). The objective is how urgent and how critical are the computing resources to the business? (Yeboah-Boateng, 2013a).

Having appropriately classified the assets, the C-level officers (CxOs) share the main vision (objective) of the project or operations. To what extent would an attack impact on the business? Is it just cost of mitigation, or loss of revenue, or loss of customer and investor confidence?

Finally, from the datasets gathered (i.e. cyber-intelligence collected), the CxOs initiate the process towards unfreezing the status-quo. Using a feedback process, which is iterative, refreezing the lessons or insights from observations.

In this study, an experiment was setup with a virtual machine, rather than with a production network or system. The reasons are not far-fetched as some tools and exploits used could adversely impact on normal production operations.

Cybersecurity Intelligence Gathering (Lab Analysis)

The study's experiment was setup for illustrations and to demonstrate some of the intelligence gathered and used in designing the proposed model.

Laboratory Setup

All lab analyses were conducted using virtual machines with the host been Windows 10 professional. The virtual machines were Windows 7 Professional, ReUnion Linux and Kali Linux 2016 R2. We employed various tools and utilities, including Whois, Domain Dossier, Nmap, etc. Using the Cyber Kill Chain model as our guiding steps in this lab; and focusing on intelligence gathering (i.e. Reconnaissance), various vulnerabilities are identified, captured, analyzed, and in practice, subsequently, collaboratively shared as insights for further decision making.

As indicated earlier, this phase is basically for information gathering or foot printing, in which we study publicly available information about the target environment. These utilities serve as preliminary intelligence gathering tools. In practice, perimeter, gateway and/or end-point devices are used to prevent, detect and analyzed these datasets.

Figure 1. Windows 7 professional

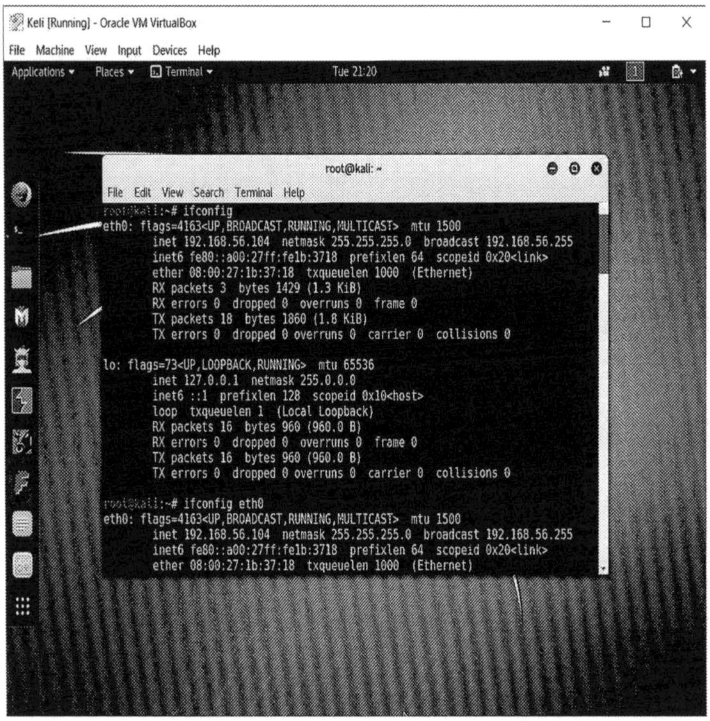

Figure 2. Kali Linux 2016R2

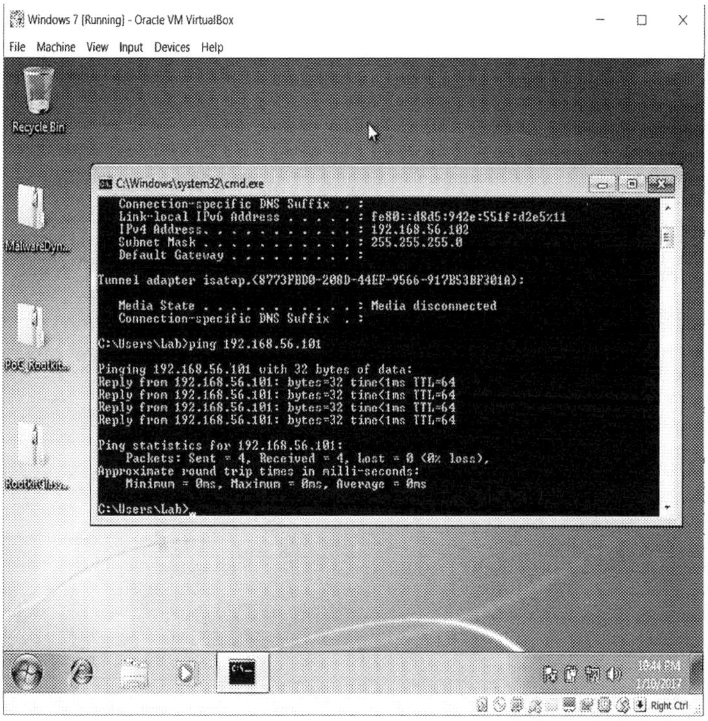

WHOIS

Whois is a command in Linux and Unix environments that produces details about an organizations presences online; i.e. domain registration name, date of expiration, name of the (registrant, email, telephone, country, update and expiring dates etc.), IP address netblock, traceroute, and open ports.

Domain Dossier

Domain Dossier works in similar fashion as the Whois but it's an online tool from https://centralops.net.co/domaindossier. Here, we can collect information such as domain whois records (very similar to whois), DNS records, Network Whois records, Traceroute and service scan.

Figure 3. Typical Whois results

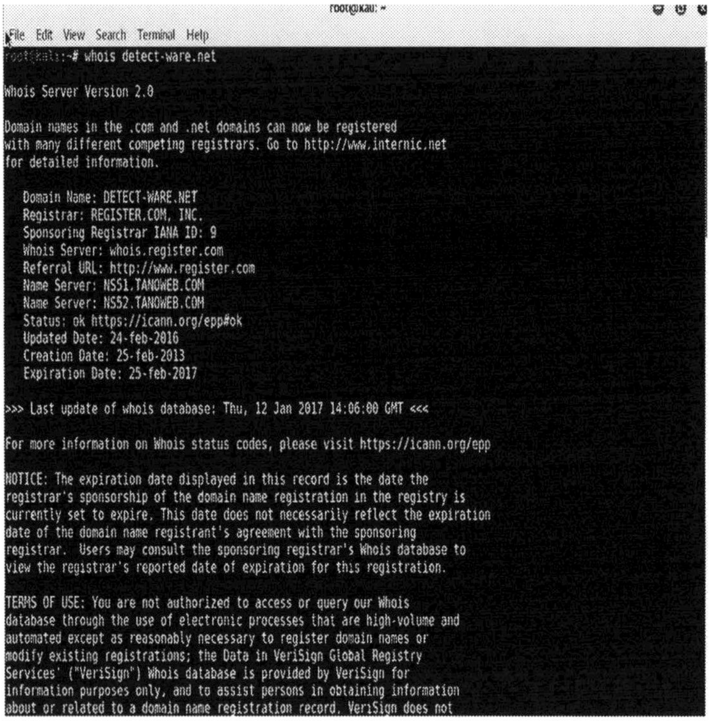

Domain Dossier Results

Address Lookup

- Canonical name: detect-ware.net.
- aliases
- addresses: 207.58.149.159

Domain Whois Record

Queried whois.internic.net with "dom detect-ware.net"...

```
Domain Name: DETECT-WARE.NET
Registrar: REGISTER.COM, INC.
Sponsoring Registrar IANA ID: 9
Whois Server: whois.register.com
Referral URL: http://www.register.com
```

Figure 4. Typical Whois results

Figure 5. Domain dossier

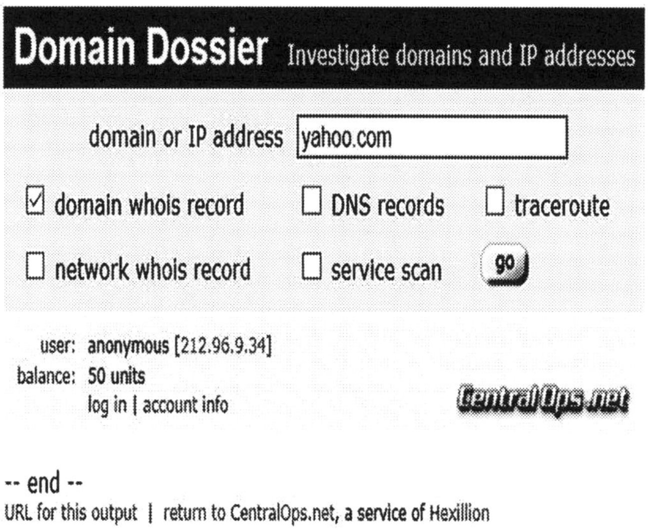

```
   Name Server: NS51.TANOWEB.COM
   Name Server: NS52.TANOWEB.COM
   Status: ok https://icann.org/epp#ok
   Updated Date: 24-feb-2016
   Creation Date: 25-feb-2013
   Expiration Date: 25-feb-2017
>>> Last update of whois database: Thu, 12 Jan 2017 14:12:47
GMT <<<
For more information on Whois status codes, please visit
https://icann.org/epp
```

Queried whois.register.com with "detect-ware.net"...

```
Domain Name: detect-ware.net
Registry Domain ID: 1782639993_DOMAIN_NET-VRSN
Registrar WHOIS Server: whois.register.com
Registrar URL: http://www.register.com
Updated Date: 2016-02-24T14:40:01Z
Creation Date: 2013-02-25T15:56:31Z
Registrar Registration Expiration Date: 2017-02-25T15:56:31Z
Registrar: Register.com, Inc.
Registrar IANA ID: 9
Registrar Abuse Contact Email: abuse@web.com
Registrar Abuse Contact Phone: +1.8773812449
Reseller:
Domain Status: ok http://icann.org/epp#OK
Registry Registrant ID:
Registrant Name: Elvis Koto
Registrant Organization:
Registrant Street: P.O.Box GH233
Registrant City: Accra
Registrant State/Province:
Registrant Postal Code: GH233
Registrant Country: GH
Registrant Phone: +233.0277723505
Registrant Phone Ext.:
Registrant Fax:
Registrant Fax Ext.:
Registrant Email: detectware@yahoo.com
Registry Admin ID:
```

```
Admin Name: Elvis Koto
Admin Organization:
Admin Street: P.O.Box GH233
Admin City: Accra
Admin State/Province:
Admin Postal Code: GH233
Admin Country: GH
Admin Phone: +233.0277723505
Admin Phone Ext.:
Admin Fax:
Admin Fax Ext.:
Admin Email: detectware@yahoo.com
Registry Tech ID:
Tech Name: Elvis Koto
Tech Organization:
Tech Street: P.O.Box GH233
Tech City: Accra
Tech State/Province:
Tech Postal Code: GH233
Tech Country: GH
Tech Phone: +233.0277723505
Tech Phone Ext.:
Tech Fax:
Tech Fax Ext.:
Tech Email: detectware@yahoo.com
Name Server: ns51.tanoweb.com
Name Server: ns52.tanoweb.com
DNSSEC: Unsigned
URL of the ICANN WHOIS Data Problem Reporting System: http://
wdprs.internic.net/
>>> Last update of WHOIS database: 2016-02-24T14:40:01Z <<<
```

Network Whois Record

Queried whois.arin.net with “n 207.58.149.159”...

```
NetRange:        207.58.128.0 - 207.58.191.255
CIDR:                     207.58.128.0/18
NetName:                SERVINT-CIDR-3
```

```
NetHandle:          NET-207-58-128-0-1
Parent:             NET207 (NET-207-0-0-0-0)
NetType:            Direct Allocation
OriginAS:
Organization:       ServInt (SRVN)
RegDate:            2004-04-29
Updated:            2012-03-02
Comment:            ADDRESSES WITHIN THIS BLOCK ARE NON-
PORTABLE
Ref:                https://whois.arin.net/rest/net/NET-
207-58-128-0-1
OrgName:            ServInt
OrgId:              SRVN
Address:            12001 Sunrise Valley Drive
Address:            Suite 350
City:               Reston
StateProv:          VA
PostalCode:         20191
Country:            US
RegDate:            1997-04-07
Updated:            2013-10-17
Ref:                https://whois.arin.net/rest/org/SRVN
OrgTechHandle:      NO178-ARIN
OrgTechName:        ServInt Engineering
OrgTechPhone:       +1-703-847-1381
OrgTechEmail:       ipdept@servint.com
OrgTechRef:         https://whois.arin.net/rest/poc/NO178-
ARIN
OrgNOCHandle:       MST329-ARIN
OrgNOCName:         MST
OrgNOCPhone:        +1-703-847-1421
OrgNOCEmail:        mst@servint.com
OrgNOCRef:          https://whois.arin.net/rest/poc/MST329-
ARIN
OrgAbuseHandle: ABUSE2161-ARIN
OrgAbuseName:       Abuse
OrgAbusePhone:      +1-703-847-1381
OrgAbuseEmail:      abuse@servint.com
OrgAbuseRef:        https://whois.arin.net/rest/poc/
ABUSE2161-ARIN
```

Table 1. DNS records

Name	Class	Type	Data	Time to Live	
detect-ware.net	IN	MX	preference: 0 exchange: detect-ware.net	14400s	(04:00:00)
detect-ware.net	IN	SOA	server: ns51.tanoweb.com email: dnsadmin@srv5.tanoweb.com serial: 2016091302 refresh: 86400 retry: 7200 expire: 3600000 minimum ttl: 86400	86400s	(1.00:00:00)
detect-ware.net	IN	NS	ns52.tanoweb.com	86400s	(1.00:00:00)
detect-ware.net	IN	NS	ns51.tanoweb.com	86400s	(1.00:00:00)
detect-ware.net	IN	A	207.58.149.159	14400s	(04:00:00)
159.149.58.207.in-addr.arpa	IN	PTR	srv5.tanoweb.com	86400s	(1.00:00:00)
149.58.207.in-addr.arpa	IN	SOA	server: ns.servint.com email: hostmaster@servint.com serial: 2011091823 refresh: 3600 retry: 600 expire: 2419200 minimum ttl: 10800	21600s	(06:00:00)
149.58.207.in-addr.arpa	IN	NS	ns2.servint.com	21600s	(06:00:00)
149.58.207.in-addr.arpa	IN	NS	ns.servint.com	21600s	(06:00:00)

Traceroute

Tracing route to detect-ware.net [207.58.149.159]... (see Table 2)

Service Scan

See Table 3.

Nmap

Nmap (Network Mapper) is a security scanner originally written by Gordon Lyon (also known by his pseudonym *Fyodor Vaskovich*). It's used to discover hosts and services on a computer network, thus creating a "map" of the network. Nmap operates at both the Network and Transport layers. By using raw sockets, Nmap sends specially crafted packets (or segments, depending on the layer concerned), to the target host and then analyzes the responses; to identify the hosts on the network,

Table 2. Traceroute results

Hop	rtt	rtt	rtt	IP Address	Fully Qualified Domain Name
1	0	0	1	208.101.16.73	49.10.65d0.ip4.static.sl-reverse.com
2	0	0	0	66.228.118.153	ae11.dar01.sr01.dal01.networklayer.com
3	0	0	0	173.192.18.254	ae14.bbr02.eq01.dal03.networklayer.com
4	0	0	0	80.239.195.177	dls-bb1-link.telia.net
5	31	31	31	62.115.137.44	ash-bb3-link.telia.net
6	31	31	31	80.91.248.159	ash-b1-link.telia.net
7	31	31	31	62.115.40.218	giglinx-ic-308514-ash-b1.c.telia.net
8	31	31	32	209.50.254.29	
9	48	54	56	209.50.254.33	
10	31	31	31	207.58.153.66	sc-sdv3557.servint.net
11	31	31	31	207.58.149.159	srv5.tanoweb.com
Trace complete					

services enabled, possible operating systems, firewalls, and Intrusion detection and prevention systems (IDS/IPS).

The features on Nmap are extensible by scripts that provide more advanced service detection, vulnerability detection, and other features. Nmap is also capable of adapting to network conditions including latency and congestion during a scan.

Nmap was originally a Linux-only utility, but it was ported to Windows, Solaris, HP-UX, BSD variants (including OS X), AmigaOS, and IRIX. Linux is the most popular platform, followed closely by Windows.

The following command was executed from our Kali linux (192.168.56.104-Attacker) against our Windows 7 (192.168.56.102-Victim) machine.

```
Nmap -sS -A 192.168.56.102
```

Other cyber Intelligence gathering techniques intended to gather intelligence on traffic flow, IDS and passive networks, include Remote Administrator Tools (RAT), Metaspliot, Keylogger, HoneyPots, firewall logs, IDS logs, Pcap files, nfdump, argus, nfsen, snort, bro, suricata, npad, p)f, iptables, OSSEC, colletd, graphite, etc.

Table 3. Service scan

FTP - 21	220---------- Welcome to Pure-FTPd [privsep] [TLS] ---------- 220-You are user number 1 of 50 allowed. 220-Local time is now 14:12. Server port: 21. 220-This is a private system - No anonymous login 220-IPv6 connections are also welcome on this server. 220 You will be disconnected after 15 minutes of inactivity. 220 Logout.
SMTP - 25	220-srv5.tanoweb.com ESMTP Exim 4.87 #1 Thu, 12 Jan 2017 14:12:58 +0000 220-We do not authorize the use of this system to transport unsolicited, 220 and/or bulk e-mail. 421 srv5.tanoweb.com lost input connection
HTTP - 80	HTTP/1.1 200 OK Date: Thu, 12 Jan 2017 14:12:58 GMT Server: Apache X-Powered-By: PHP/5.5.30 Set-Cookie: 5fa9302837f05e1dbd87045ec31d34e1=d60fb25fd7630262a7476410aba1297b; path=/ P3P: CP="NOI ADM DEV PSAi COM NAV OUR OTRo STP IND DEM" Set-Cookie: jf-grafeeze_tpl=jf-grafeeze; expires=Tue, 02-Jan-2018 14:12:58 GMT; Max-Age=30672000; path=/ Expires: Mon, 1 Jan 2001 00:00:00 GMT Last-Modified: Thu, 12 Jan 2017 14:12:58 GMT Cache-Control: post-check=0, pre-check=0 Pragma: no-cache Connection: close Content-Type: text/html; charset=utf-8
POP3 - 110	+OK Dovecot ready.
IMAP - 143	* OK [CAPABILITY IMAP4rev1 LITERAL+ SASL-IR LOGIN-REFERRALS ID ENABLE IDLE NAMESPACE STARTTLS AUTH=PLAIN AUTH=LOGIN] Dovecot ready.
HTTPS - 443	Certificate validation errors: RemoteCertificateNameMismatch Signature algorithm: sha256RSA Public key size: 2048 bits Issuer: CN="cPanel, Inc. Certification Authority", O="cPanel, Inc.", L=Houston, S=TX, C=US Subject: CN=srv5.tanoweb.com, OU=PositiveSSL, OU=Domain Control Validated Subject Alternative Name: DNS Name=srv5.tanoweb.com, DNS Name=www.srv5.tanoweb.com Serial number: 0C9D9443C096910238450F0BA998EEAC Not valid before: 2017-01-07 00:00:00Z Not valid after: 2018-01-07 23:59:59Z SHA1 fingerprint: B32B880CEA8C9363DF09FB334EE98E82C4CD0B39 HTTP/1.1 200 OK Date: Thu, 12 Jan 2017 14:12:59 GMT Server: Apache Last-Modified: Mon, 11 Jan 2016 23:47:05 GMT Accept-Ranges: bytes Content-Length: 111 Connection: close Content-Type: text/html

Figure 6. Nmap results

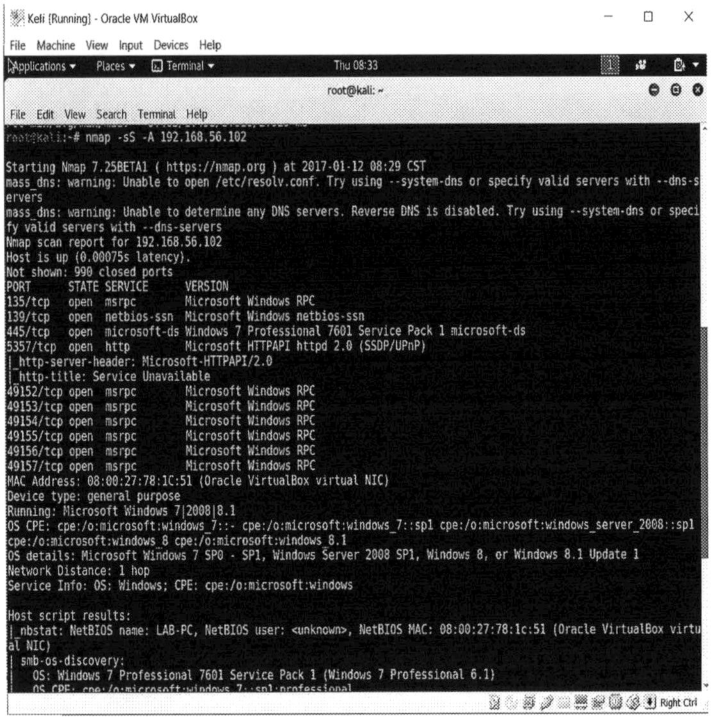

KM-BASED CYBER-INTELLIGENCE GATHERING (KM-CIG) MODEL

The KM-CIG model is 4 phased model that seeks to assist cyber-security professional with knowledge management based approaches in gathering cyber-security intelligence aimed at prevention, detection and recovery of cyber incidents and potential attacks. This study utilized intuitive reasoning and strategic thinking inspired from Kurt Lewin's Refreezing Change model, coupled with the Cyber Kill Chain model, to formulate a puzzle-like model for mitigating threats.

The demonstrations from the lab experiment are used in support of measures needed to proactively prevent, detect and (in the event of incident) recover from potential threats.

Figure 7. Conceptual framework
Adapted from McDowell, 2009, p.29.

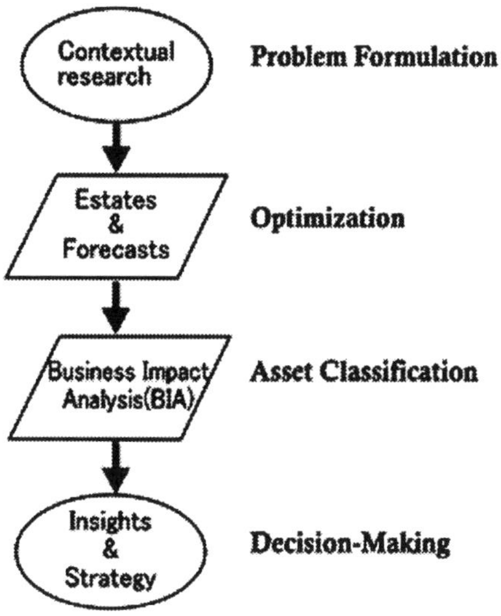

Figure 8. KM-Based Cyber-Intelligence Gathering (KM-CIG) model

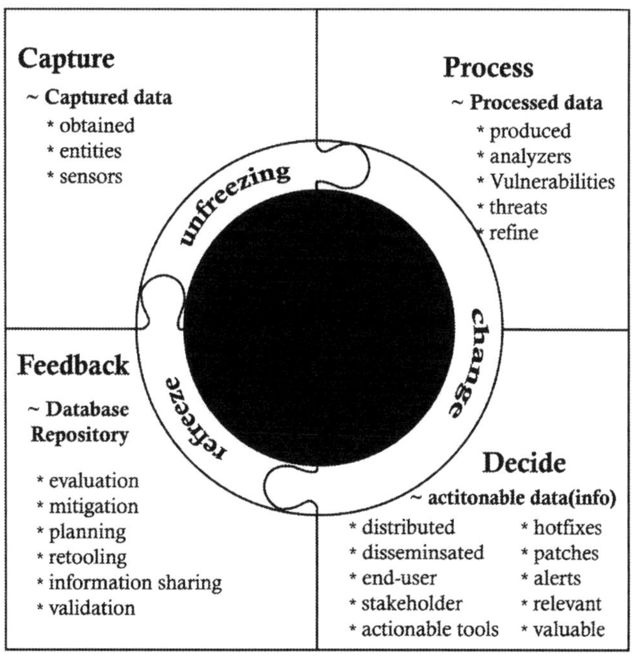

KM-based Cyber-Intelligence Gathering(km-CIG) Model

CONCLUSION

The agility of the Scrum methodology has been employed in this study to gather cyber-intelligence, which in turn was used to model the KM-CIG for decision making. Typically, the intelligence as a process involves the acquisition of data and its processing or refining to useable and actionable information (i.e. knowledge). Similarly, the intelligence as a product implies that the alerts that are produced informs network managers to be proactive in mitigation measures aimed at resistance, recognition, recovery and possibly, retaliation of intrusion or security incidents.

Some of the issues addressed include Day-Zero vulnerabilities, patch management, data inconsistencies, security and privacy, communications with end-users and stakeholders, organizational culture, Governance-Risk-and-Compliance (GRC), competitive advantage, business continuity plan, etc.

In addressing some of the issues raised earlier, we herewith offer the following guidance. The Intelligence – collected, classified, estimated, appraised, examined, incorporated, and explained must be validated. There would be need to create repositories of validated vulnerabilities and patches or hotfixes. New and updated vulnerabilities and/or hotfixes could be sent to practitioners via alerts; especially those that classified and benchmarked as serious. In view of the constant releases of hotfixes, new challenges are imposed on the practitioners, in conflict with patch management best practices and the need to avoid or mitigate exploitations.

Since cyber-intelligence, even as nascent, is evolving with the harnessing of knowledge management principles to gather appropriate intelligence data, the need for information quality cannot be over-emphasized. Among others, it must ensure that the intelligence data is contextualized, i.e. relevant –as the information must define the extent to which the data addresses or is usable for the cyber-intelligence decision making. Similarly, timeliness is of essence – as the currency of the data gathered must not be rendered "useless"; and in consonance with the accuracy of the information (Miller, 1996).

Future research will explore the use of social networks in facilitating the knowledge sharing and some associated concerns that would arise.

REFERENCES

Alavi, M., & Leidner, D. E. (2001). Review: Knowledge Management and Knowledge Management Systems: Conceptual Foundations and Research Issues. *Management Information Systems Quarterly*, *25*(1), 107. doi:10.2307/3250961

Belsis, P., Kokolakis, S., & Kiountouzis, E. (2005). Information Systems Security from a Knowledge Management Perspective. *Information Management & Computer Security*, *13*(3), 189–202. doi:10.1108/09685220510602013

Bradley, N., Alvarez, M., Kuhn, J., & McMillen, D. (2015). *IBM 2015 Cyber-Intelligence Index*. IBM Security Research.

Chen, H. (2006). *Intelligence and Security Informatics for International Security: Information Sharing & Data Mining*. Springer. doi:10.1007/11734628

Clark, J. R. (2007). *Intelligence and National Security: a Reference Handbook - Contemporary Military, Strategic and Security Issues*. Westport, CT: Praeger Security International.

Dalziel, H. (2015). *How to Define and Build an Effective Cyber Threat Intelligence Capability*. Syngress.

Dandurand, L., & Serrano, O. S. (2013). Towards Improved Cyber Security Information Sharing - Requirements for a Cyber Security Data Exhange and Collaboration Infrastructure (CDXI). In K. Podins, J. Stinissen, & M. Maybaum (Ed.), *2013 5th International Conference on Cyber Conflict*. NATO CCD COE Publications.

Davenport, T., & Prusak, L. (2000). *Working Knowledge: How Organizations Manage What They Know*. Boston, MA: Harvard Business School Press.

Department of Defence (DoD). (2000). *Doctrince for Intelligence Support to Joint Operations, Joint Publications 2-0*. Washington, DC: GPO.

Ein-Dor, P. (2009). Taxonomies of Knowledge. In M. E. Jennex (Ed.), Knowledge Management - Concepts, Methodologies, Tools and Applications (Vol. 1, pp. 163-170). Premier Reference, Information Science Reference, IGI Global.

Endicott-Popovsky, B. (2013). *Information Security and Risk Management in Context*. Retrieved from www.coursetalk.com/providers/coursera/courses/information-security-and-risk-management-in-context

Engel, G. (2014, November 18). Deconstructing The Cyber Kill Chain. *DarkReading*. Retrieved March 15, 2017, from www.darkreading.com/attacks-breaches/deconstructing-the-cyber-kill-chain/a/d-id/1317542

Farmer, W. M. (2009). Mathematical Knowledge Management. In M. E. Jennex (Ed.), Knowledge Management - Concepts, Methodologies, Tools and Applications (Vol. 1, pp. 2976-2983). Premier Reference, Information Science Reference, IGI Global.

FlatIron Technologies. (2014). *Overview of Patch Managemnet Best Practices for Information Systems*. FlatIron Technologies, LLC.

Forbes, L. H., & Ahmed, S. M. (2011). Information and Communications Technology - Building Information Modeling. In L. H. Forbes, & S. M. Ahmed (Eds.), Modern Construction: Lean Project Delivery and Integrated Practices. Taylor & Francis Group, LLC.

Graham, B. (2010). *Unto the Hills: A Daily Devotion*. Thomas Nelson, Inc.

Intelligence & National Security Alliance. (2015). *Cyber Intelligence: Preparing Today's Talents for Tomorrow's Threats*. INSA, Cyber Intelligence Task Force.

Kaminski, J. (2011). Theory Applied to Informatics - Lewin's Change Theory. *CJNI: Canadian Journal of Nursing Informatics, 6*(1). Retrieved from www.cjni.net/journal/?p=1210

Kankanhalli, A., & Tan, B. C. (2008). Knowledge Managemnet Metrics: A Review and Directions of Future Research. In M. E. Jennex (Ed.), Knowledge Management: Concepts, Methodologies, Tools and Applications (Vol. 6, pp. 3409-3420). IGI Global.

Lockheed Martin. (2010). *What We Do*. Lockheed Martin, Inc. Retrieved February 17, 2017, from Lockheed Martin's homepage: www.lockheedmartin.com/us/what-we-do/aerospace-defense/cyber-kill-chain.html

Luftman, J. N. (2004). *Managing the Information Technology Resources*. Pearson.

McDowell, D. (2009). *A Handbook for Practitioners, Managers and Users: Strategic Intelligence*. The Scarecrow Press, Inc.

Miller, H. E. (1996). The Multiple Dimensions of Information Quality. *Information Systems Management, 13*(2), 79–82. doi:10.1080/10580539608906992

Mitchell, H. (2009). Technology and Knowledge Management. In M. E. Jennex (Ed.), Knowledge Management - Concepts, Methodologies, Tools & Applications (Vol. 1, pp. 41-47). Premier Reference, Information Science Reference, IGI Global.

OPSEC. (1991). *Interagency OPSEC Support Staff- Compendium of OPSEC Terms*. Greenbelt, MD: IOSS.

OPSEC. (1996). *Operations Security: Intelligence Threats Handbook*. Interagency OPSEC Support Staff.

Rocha, L. (2015, August 15). *The 5 Steps of the Intelligence Cycle*. Retrieved from Security Monitoring, Threat Intelligence: www.countuponsecurity.com/2015/08/15/the-5-steps-of-the-intelligence-cycle/

Sager, T. (2014). *An Intelligent Approach to Attack Prevention*. SANS Institute.

Somppaya, M., & Scarfone, K. (2013). *Guide to Enterprise Patch Management Technologies*. National Institute for Standards & Technology.

Tisdale, S. M. (2015). Cybersecurity: Challenges from a Systems, Complexity, Knowledge Management and Business Intelligence Perspective. *Issues in Information Systems, 16*(III), 191–198.

Use Case Diagram Tutorials. (2015). Retrieved December 27, 2015, from www.creately.com/blog/diagrams/use-case-diagram-tutorial/

Voldal, D. (2003). *A Practical Methodology for Implementing Patch Management Process*. SANS Institute.

Yeboah-Boateng, E. O. (2013a). *Cyber-Security Challenges with SMEs in Developing Economies: Issues of Confidentiality, Integrity & Availablity (CIA)*. Aalborg University.

Yeboah-Boateng, E. O. (2013b, February). Fuzzy Similarity Measures Approach in Benchmarking Taxonomies of Threats against SMEs in Developing Economies. *Canadian Journal on Computing in Mathematics, Natural Sciences. Engineering in Medicine*, 34–44.

Yeboah-Boateng, E. O. (2016, October). Recontextualization of Discretized Cyber-Risk Functional Arguments with Fuzzy Polynomials. *International Journal on Computer Science and Engineering, 4*(10), 19–26.

Chapter 12
Knowledge Management:
Applications and Implications

Kijpokin Kasemsap
Suan Sunandha Rajabhat University, Thailand

ABSTRACT

This chapter indicates the overview of Knowledge Management (KM); KM and innovation; KM and human capital; KM and social capital; KM and Human Resource Management (HRM); the significant perspectives on KM; and the advanced issues of knowledge transfer, knowledge sharing, and knowledge mapping. KM is the advanced method toward better organizational performance through knowledge transfer and knowledge sharing, and involves various organizational factors, such as people, process, technology, and culture. Utilizing KM can enhance the execution of innovation, human capital, social capital, decision making, and HRM in modern organizations. Regarding KM perspectives, creating and distributing new knowledge through effective knowledge transfer and knowledge sharing have the potential to increase organizational performance and gain sustainable competitive advantage in the knowledge era.

INTRODUCTION

Knowledge is one of the most important drivers of innovation in the information-based society (Anzelak, Frankl, & Mayr, 2009). Information management systems generally enable the sharing and organization of information, thus increasing the available knowledge base for individuals (Kirsch, Hine, & Maybury, 2015). In modern organizations, productivity depends on the ability of managers to create the new knowledge and generate the smart actions (Tzortzaki & Mihiotis, 2014).

DOI: 10.4018/978-1-5225-2956-9.ch012

Knowledge is a critical asset and helps organizations solve problems (Martinez-Gil, 2015). The generation of knowledge needs to be embedded in corporate processes toward reducing the obstacles of collecting the multiple knowledge perspectives within the complex organizations (Vaidyanathan, 2008).

Knowledge management (KM) involves the strategies and processes designed to identify, capture, structure, value, obtain, and share an organization's intellectual assets to enhance its performance and competitiveness (Kasemsap, 2017a) regarding the cause of the change of processes and information systems in the company (Litvaj & Stancekova, 2015). The goals of KM are to enhance the performance of an organization and its profitability (Wang, Ding, Liu, & Li, 2016) and to support the creation, transfer, and application of knowledge (Gottschalk, 2007). Organizational knowledge creation is an essential process for companies in the knowledge age (Akbar & Tzokas, 2013).

The main challenge for a growing company is to remain innovative while introducing KM processes (Krumina, Krumins, & Rozentale, 2015). KM presents a systematic approach for searching and using knowledge in the interest of making value (Mráček & Mucha, 2015). Information technology (IT) systems for KM which improve management processes differ depending on whether the knowledge is centralized or decentralized (Ogiela, 2015). KM requires the integration between the IT systems and people who run the company as the method to attain innovation (Menaouer, Khalissa, Abdelbaki, & Abdelhamid, 2015). In the workplace, employees need IT which provides them with information and knowledge (Meroño-Cerdán, 2009). If information is omitted, the entire KM process becomes useless (Ogiela, 2013).

This chapter is based on a literature review of KM. The extensive literature of KM provides a contribution to practitioners and researchers by indicating the applications and implications of KM in order to maximize the impact of KM in the knowledge age.

BACKGROUND

The concept of KM is rooted in cognitive psychology and organizational theory (Bach, Lee, & Carroll, 2009) and concerns the creation of structures that combine the most advanced elements of technological resources and the essential input of human response and decision making (Raisinghani, 2008). The KM literature largely focuses on the explicit and formal representation of knowledge in the computer-based KM systems (Davison, Ou, & Martinsons, 2013). The ability to manage knowledge is increasingly important for securing and maintaining organizational success and surviving in the knowledge economy (Russ, 2010). KM becomes an integral business activity for organizations as they realize that competitiveness pivots around the effective KM (Wong, 2005).

In an era of business transition, the effective management of knowledge is proposed as a strategy that effectively utilizes organizational intangible assets (Lytras, Russ, Maier, & Naeve, 2008). As KM becomes increasingly important, organizations must strive to understand the dynamics of KM (Edwards-Buckingham, 2009). KM is considered as a key aspect in sustaining competitive advantage (Monticolo, Hilaire, Gomes, & Koukam, 2009). In order to build and sustain a competitive advantage, this knowledge must be protected within an organization's core businesses from discovery by competitors (Chilton & Bloodgood, 2014). KM typically takes the form of programs that are tied to organizational objectives and are intended to lead to the achievement of specific outcomes, such as shared intelligence, improved performance, and competitive advantage (Herschel, 2009).

Paraki (2006) defined KM as the efficient utilization of the intangible knowledge-related resources available in every sector of the economy to enhance the productivity of all factors of production. The acquisition of knowledge is the fastest way to generate knowledge, although the knowledge must have a certain degree of formalization and the source must be selected with care (Calvo-Mora, Navarro-García, & Periañez-Cristobal, 2015). Concerning KM, learning provokes the adoption of new beliefs, new relationships, modification, and reinforcement of behavior and values, as well as other types of more practical improvements (Leal-Rodríguez, Roldán, Ariza-Montes, & Leal-Millán, 2014).

APPLICATIONS AND IMPLICATIONS OF KNOWLEDGE MANAGEMENT

This section provides the overview of KM; KM and innovation; KM and human capital; KM and social capital; KM and human resource management (HRM); the significant perspectives on KM; and the advanced issues of knowledge transfer, knowledge sharing, and knowledge mapping.

Overview of Knowledge Management

KM is the process of capturing, organizing, and storing information of workers and groups within an organization (Kasemsap, 2017b). Based on the principles of KM, organizations develop and implement KM initiatives to improve the efficiency of business processes, increase the productivity of their services, and find the new solutions for their customers (Nguyen & Mohamed, 2011). Organizations require information for decision making that is relevant in the dynamic environments (Garcia-

Alvarez, 2015). Governments have created the innovative systems connecting people to information by focusing on KM practices (Carstens, Bean, & Barlow, 2009). Increased interaction, interdependency, and volatility on a global scale are rapidly changing local governments' external environment, their community characteristics, and their organizational orientation (Handzic, Lagumdzija, & Celjo, 2009).

As long as a dynamic process of knowledge reception, structuring, and transmission has been developed, organizations will tend to develop outputs with a higher added value on the market (Schmidt & Keil, 2013). The competitiveness of companies is determined to a great extent by the use of information and communication technology (ICT), which allows for the creation of value and the establishment of KM processes within the organization (Kuo & Ye, 2010). ICT is a key concept in obtaining and facilitating the creation of explicit knowledge by means of the collection, storage, aggregation, and transmission of quantitative data (Phang & Foong, 2010). Leaders of global businesses should organize ICT skills for organizational employees to enlarge their knowledge in global business (Kasemsap, 2014a).

Knowledge management performance evaluation (KMPE) is based on balanced scorecard (BSC) and fuzzy comprehension methods, which can simplify the evaluation process. KMPE has crucial effects in improving organizational performance (Wang et al., 2016). Li et al. (2014) proposed the new multi-criteria decision making (MCDM) method combining quality function deployment (QFD) with technique for order preference to evaluate the KM systems from the user's perspective. Kuo and Liang (2012) proposed the new performance evaluation method for tackling the fuzzy MCDM problems based on combining the VIKOR method (i.e., one of the most important MCDM tools) and interval-valued fuzzy sets. VIKOR ranks alternatives and determines the solution named compromise that is the closest to the ideal perspective.

Organizations establishing KM system have to ensure the good fit between task and technology, and to institutionalize knowledge-sharing culture within work contexts (El Said, 2015). Process management facilitates the creation of knowledge (Asif, de Vries, & Ahmad, 2013), as the processes include concepts, methods, and techniques to support the design, implementation, and analysis of the activities that generate the value. The information derived from the activities that establish the processes are transformed into knowledge (Weske, 2007). Process management facilitates the storage and the transfer of knowledge (Molina, Lloréns-Montes, & Ruiz-Moreno, 2007) while transforming it from tacit to explicit knowledge. The implementation of process management changes the structure of the company, making it more flexible (Calvo-Mora et al., 2015).

Knowledge Management and Innovation

The global economies thrive on the cutting-edge knowledge, which drives research and organizational innovation in competitive environments (Kasemsap, 2016a). KM is assumed to create value for organizations by applying their accumulated knowledge to their products and services outputs. Innovation is recognized as a key value creator for organizations in times of growth and can promote KM in the modern workplace. It is important because innovation of products, processes, and structures has been assessed as a critical component in the success of new-age firms. KM helps in identifying any gaps in the knowledge base and provides processes to fill the gaps in order to promote innovation.

Innovation is a direct outcome of KM effectiveness (Darroch & McNaughton, 2002) as well as being one of the main objectives for knowledge-creating companies toward obtaining competitive advantage (Nonaka & Takeuchi, 1995). KM keeps a smooth flow of knowledge and information used in the innovation process. KM allows for cooperation among various departments within the organization through online collaboration forums toward achieving organizational innovation. KM practices in the workplace should focus on making the application of the existing knowledge to the organizational activities more effective (Zack, McKeen, & Singh, 2009). KM, strategic orientation, and organizational innovation are correlated with organizational performance (Kasemsap, 2014b).

KM enhances a knowledge-oriented culture through which innovation can happen. KM provides organizational context to the body of knowledge in the organization and assists in steady growth of the knowledge base through gathering and capturing of explicit and tacit knowledge toward innovation. KM assists in building capacities and competencies that are required for the innovation process. Knowledge-sharing behavior positively mediates the relationships between organizational learning and organizational innovation and between KM and organizational innovation in the learning organizations (Kasemsap, 2014c).

KM provides many tools, processes, and platforms to ensure the integration of an organization's knowledge base toward organizational innovation. KM relates to organizational learning, communication, information systems, artificial intelligence, and intellectual assets (Lehaney, Clarke, Coakes, & Jack, 2004). KM-related innovations provide the essential pathways through which teachers, researchers, students, and KM professionals who are interested in applying KM theory (Buckley & Jakovljevic, 2013). Companies operating in the knowledge-based industrial markets should rely on external relationships and networks in order to complement their knowledge domains and develop innovations in an effective way (Martín-de Castro, 2015).

Open innovation, also known as external or networked innovation, refers to the external knowledge flowing into the company (i.e., inbound open innovation) and internal knowledge flowing out from the company (i.e., outbound open innovation) that the company can utilize while innovating new products and while introducing their own innovations to the market (Chesbrough, 2003). Open innovation is focused on revealing new ideas, reducing risk, increasing speed, and managing scarce resources. Under the open innovation paradigm, there is an important flow of external knowledge into the organization which turns into projects in cooperation with external partners and causes the incorporation of external technologies.

KM is a fundamental part of managing open innovations (Haapalainen & Kantola, 2015). Wallin and von Krogh (2010) introduced the process model to integrate knowledge in open innovation, involving five important steps (i.e., defining the innovation process steps, identifying relevant innovation knowledge, choosing an appropriate integration mechanism, creating effective governance mechanisms, and balancing incentives). Once open innovation is adopted, the organization's boundaries become permeable and that allows combining organizational resources (e.g., knowledge, technology, and employee) with the external co-operators.

Knowledge Management and Human Capital

Human capital includes the collective skills, knowledge, or other intangible assets of individuals that can be used to create economic value for the individuals, their employers, or their community (Kasemsap, 2017c). Organizational efforts have typically concentrated on the KM capabilities required for the externalization and codification of organizational knowledge and for the development of tacit knowledge embedded in human capital (Cohen & Olsen, 2015). Firms should implement both human capital (in terms of firm-level human capital and employee-level human capital) and competency recognized as the influential organizational assets for producing high-technology products and services in order to obtain sustainable competitive advantage in the global knowledge economy (Kasemsap, 2016b).

Knowledge remains tied to individuals (Haesli & Boxall, 2005), and is only available to the organization through employee motivation to contribute it (Zhou & Fink, 2003). Human capital-oriented KM focuses on ensuring employee commitment and motivating employees to share their knowledge in the workplace (Smedlund, 2008). IT and human capital-based KM are associated with the company's competitiveness (Andreeva & Kianto, 2012). The development of human capital relies on the sharing of tacit knowledge among employees, which provides the learning opportunities and helps transfer the skills toward gaining the improved job performance (Wang, Hult, Ketchen, & Ahmed, 2009).

Knowledge Management and Social Capital

Social capital is the network of relationships among individuals, companies, and institutions in a society, together with the associated norms of behavior, trust, and cooperation (Kasemsap, 2014d). Social capital can promote the improved performance of diverse groups, the growth of entrepreneurial firms, superior managerial performance, enhanced supply chain relations, the value derived from strategic alliances, and the evolution of communities (Kasemsap, 2017d).

Nahapiet and Ghoshal (1998) viewed social capital as the valuable asset of individual network structure and synthesized it into three main dimensions: cognitive, relational, and structural perspectives. The cognitive dimension covers norms, value evaluation, attitudes, and beliefs. The relational dimension refers to the degree of interaction and the quality of social relations (Jones, 2005). The structural dimension refers to network ties, configuration, stability among actors, network roles, rules, and precedents (Inkpen & Tsang, 2005) toward maintaining the social relationships with customers (von Friedrichs Grängsjö & Gummesson, 2006).

Accumulating social capital is helpful to enhance KM (Liu & Lee, 2015). Yli-Renko et al. (2001) indicated that the greater levels of social capital (e.g., social interaction, relationship quality, and customer network ties) will enhance the company's ability to evaluate the perceived knowledge, thus increasing both the company's motivation to exchange information and its opportunity for knowledge acquisition. Social capital provides the understanding of customers' requirements in order to develop the knowledge into the new products and services (Yli-Renko, Autio, & Tontti, 2002). Social capital should facilitate knowledge acquisition by creating the repeated interaction and increase the company's opportunity to access the knowledge (Rodan & Galunic, 2004).

Knowledge Management and Human Resource Management

In the modern organization, KM and HRM are positively associated (Theriou & Chatzoglou, 2008). HRM is essential as a structural mechanism in the development and adaptation of human capital to achieve sustainable competitive advantage (Jackson, Schuler, & Jiang, 2014). Through human resource practices, companies can influence and shape the skills, attitudes and behaviors of individuals, so that they can do their job better and achieve the objectives of the organization (Collins & Clark, 2003). Regarding HRM processes, conducting selection, encouraging active employee participation, organizing performance assessment, and establishing performance-related incentives are the effective work practices that are related, through their impact on the development and motivation of employees, toward gaining the improved organizational performance (Jiang, Takeuchi, & Lepak, 2013).

HRM systems are used to manage various types of knowledge assets in the workplace (Swart & Kinnie, 2013). The need for alignment of the HRM strategies is recognized as a mediator of KM for the company that links the goals of the company and its improved performance (Wang, Chiang, & Tung, 2012). Organizational learning, HRM, and KM capability are related to improved organizational performance in modern organizations (Kasemsap, 2015). Managing the knowledge employees, through strategic HRM, is essential for organizations to maximize their performance (Chuang, Jackson, & Jiang, 2016). Key factors for successful KM implementation include corporate culture, technological systems, ethical leadership, HRM practices, and organizational flexibility (Guadamillas-Gomez & Donate-Manzanares, 2009). HRM-related social interaction increases the strength of the relationship between KM skills and organizational performance (Hsiao, Chen, & Chang, 2011).

Significant Perspectives on Knowledge Management

KM can be a powerful tool if successfully implemented into an organizational structure (de Stricker, 2014). KM is critical for organizational learning, as KM processes can support organizational processes, such as individual learning and collective learning (King, Chung, & Haney, 2008). Interactive learning and subsequent innovation have become the important approaches to the economic growth (Lee, Chen, & Chen, 2015). Knowledge-based manufacturers can acquire and exploit knowledge to achieve the superior organization performance through creating an interactive learning framework (Yeunga, Laia, & Yeea, 2007). Gagnon et al. (2015) indicated that the development of a learning culture in an organization involves the continuous education of its members.

The extent of knowledge cooperation has a significant impact on the utilization of IT to support the interorganizational KM (Khandelwal & Gottschalk, 2004). IT and social-cultural variables are considered as the major components to support the KM processes (Okunoye, 2008). Analyzing the information and operational environments helps management in KM and activates the organization's awareness about the development needs of information systems (Kettunen, Hautala, & Kantola, 2009). The effective use of KM systems as an important condition can help managers recognize the new market opportunities (Hodgkinson & Healey, 2011).

Economic development is enhanced through the knowledge-based organizations to create new market and new industry platforms (Kasemsap, 2016c). KM is a functional set of behaviors, processes, and technologies that are designed for managing information more efficiently to improve learning, decision making, innovation, and other approaches toward business success (Kasemsap, 2016d). Lifelong learning and KM have become a fundamental goal of education policies, both at the national and international levels (Kasemsap, 2016e). The KM performance evaluation needs to assess how governance mechanisms and learning routines are deployed and to develop the KM capability that produces the desired performance outcomes (Chen & Fong, 2015).

In the workplace, managers should establish the contextual conditions to optimize the organization's use of KM practices through the design of important tools, such as HRM practices (Lin, 2011), setting the well-organized corporate culture (Donate & Guadamillas, 2010), the implementation of IT (Lin & Huang, 2008) and the establishment of organizational structures (Singh & Kant, 2009). KM seeks to design systems and strategies to make it possible to systematically take advantage of the knowledge generated within an organization (Pérez-Montoro, 2009). Effective KM is the key driver of new knowledge and new ideas to the innovation process, innovative products, services, and solutions (Kasemsap, 2016f).

IT and KM applications effectively improve the strategic tools for providing the direct link between customers and tourism organizations, thus encouraging the communication channels in global tourism (Kasemsap, 2016g). KM of a new product development (NPD) project team is critical for a company's competitive advantage, and incentive mechanism is one of the most effective KM drives (Zhang & Zhang, 2014). When knowledge depth and scope are insufficient, companies make the additional investments required to integrate the external knowledge from research and development (R&D) alliances with their internal knowledge stock (Caner & Tyler, 2015). Knowledge creation helps R&D personnel create the novel products, which increase the new product success (Chang, Hung, & Lin, 2014).

Organizational culture involves the values and behaviors that contribute to the unique social and psychological environment of an organization (Kasemsap, 2017e), and can enhance the implementation of KM (Sensuse, Cahyaningsih, & Wibowo, 2015). Organizational culture, organizational climate, and KM are positively related to job performance (Kasemsap, 2016h). Related KM studies show that the evolution of IT solutions can transform communities of practice (CoPs) into networks of practice in which individuals interact with others in the network who share similar interests despite geographic dispersion (Schneckenberg, 2009). CoPs help promote a growing cycle of knowledge sharing activities that allow for the members to regularly meet, reflect, and evolve in the KM environment (Kasemsap, 2016i).

Advanced Issues of Knowledge Transfer

Research on the intra-firm knowledge transfer has generally found a positive impact of knowledge inflows on the innovation of an organizational unit (Lai, Lui, & Tsang, 2016). Intra-firm knowledge transfer is essential for effective knowledge management, as it brings knowledge acquired by individuals and business units to the level of the whole organization (Maurer, Bartsch, & Ebers, 2011). Internal knowledge flows, including human resources and core technologies, can be transferred into external teams, and at the same time, external knowledge can be transferred into the internal teams (Lee et al., 2015).

The company's disseminative capability and the achievement of expert knowledge are positively related to knowledge transfer success (Schulze, Brojerdi, & von Krogh, 2014). Knowledge complexity and knowledge teachability can increase the likelihood of finding the value in person-to-person knowledge transfer (Brown, Dennis, Burley, & Arling, 2013). Innovation is related to the company's ability to diffuse knowledge throughout the organization so that the organization increases its absorptive capacity (Chew & Gottschalk, 2009). Absorptive capacity is an important determinant of knowledge transfer (Junni & Sarala, 2013).

Advanced Issues of Knowledge Sharing

KM approaches have been broadly considered to entail either a focus on organizing communities or a focus on the process of knowledge creation, sharing, and distribution (Leidner & Alavi, 2009). Knowledge-intensive companies need to organize their individual knowledge assets through knowledge sharing to create the collective knowledge resources (Swart, Kinnie, van Rossenberg, & Yalabik, 2014). Effective knowledge sharing depends on both knowledge leaders to develop a shared vision (Zhang & Cheng, 2015) and human collaboration (Mezghani, Exposito, & Drira, 2016). Efficient knowledge sharing also reinforces the company's absorptive capacity and drives the organizational learning processes which allow the company to adapt to the competitive environments (Schneckenberg, Truong, & Mazloomi, 2015).

Managers recognize the benefits of ICT-based knowledge sharing, whereas the practice of workers is revealed to privilege self-reliance and interpersonal knowledge sharing (Trusson, Doherty, & Hislop, 2014). Sharing knowledge through collaborative innovation is increasingly important (Fidel, Schlesinger, & Cervera, 2015). Employees who share knowledge generally engage more in creating, promoting, and implementing the innovations (Radaelli, Lettieri, Mura, & Spiller, 2014). The higher levels of internal knowledge sharing relate to the stronger entrepreneurial orientation (de Clercq, Dimov, & Thongpapanl, 2013). Companies with low levels of internal knowledge can greatly benefit from the optimal investment in the externally generated knowledge (Denicolai, Ramirez, & Tidd, 2014).

Knowledge sharing helps companies manage the accumulated experiences of employees and promotes teamwork in the resolution of problems and customer service requirements (Hu, Horng, & Sun, 2009). Both interaction and communication during knowledge sharing can reduce the uncertainty and can promote the positive cooperation among employees (Storey & Kelly, 2002). The use of knowledge exchange systems to facilitate the transfer of knowledge has become commonplace in modern organizations (Gressgård, 2015). Knowledge exchange results in innovation through the developed IT systems that enable both information and knowledge to effectively flow within the organization (Černe, Jaklič, & Škerlavaj, 2013). Radical innovation is positively affected by exploitative learning and by the knowledge sharing capability (Maes & Sels, 2014).

Zhang et al. (2015) indicated that social media enhances various opportunities regarding organizational learning. Social media can improve knowledge sharing in companies (Kaplan & Michael, 2010). Companies need to be connected to their technological business environment through social media because interacting with external sources of knowledge can effectively improve their capabilities about industry benchmark and competitive advantage (Kasemsap, 2014e).

Advanced Issues of Knowledge Mapping

Knowledge mapping is a managerial approach whose finality is to identify the patrimonies of know-how that are strategic in the actions of the trades in the organization (Menaouer et al., 2015). Knowledge mapping aims to provide the trade's critical knowledge of the company and constructs a roadmap to locate the information needed to make the best use of resources toward effective KM. Knowledge mapping illustrates how knowledge flows throughout an organization and allows for the indication of the importance of knowledge that must be preserved.

Lai et al. (2009) indicated that KM systems are more useful for knowledge sharing when the company develops personalization strategies and an adequate mapping of knowledge in storage devices. As knowledge storage practices are about filing, structuring, and gathering the information, their effect on performance becomes recognized when organizational members apply these initiatives (Cummings & Teng, 2003). Knowledge mapping enhances the domains of knowledge on where organizational efforts should be effectively made in terms of capitalization, sharing, and innovation.

FUTURE RESEARCH DIRECTIONS

The classification of the extensive literature in the domains of KM will provide the potential opportunities for future research. KM involves the comprehensive gathering of information or knowledge, its organization, development and analysis, and sharing it with the goal of effective utilization. Digital literacy is the ability to use ICT to find, evaluate, create, and communicate information, requiring both cognitive and technical skills (Kasemsap, 2017f). Electronic learning brings faster delivery, lower costs, more effective learning, and lower environmental impact in the modern learning environments (Kasemsap, 2017g). Organizational learning is the organization-wide continuous process that enhances its collective ability to accept, make sense of, and respond to the internal and external changes (Kasemsap, 2017h). Talent management is the organization's attempts to recruit, develop, and retain the high-potential people that they can find, afford, and hire (Kasemsap, 2017i). An examination of linkages among KM, digital literacy, electronic learning, organizational learning, and talent management in modern organizations would seem to be viable for future research efforts.

CONCLUSION

This chapter indicated the overview of KM; KM and innovation; KM and human capital; KM and social capital; KM and HRM; the significant perspectives on KM; and the advanced issues of knowledge transfer, knowledge sharing, and knowledge mapping. KM is the advanced method toward better organizational performance through knowledge transfer and knowledge sharing, and involves various organizational factors, such as people, process, technology, and culture. Utilizing KM can enhance the execution of innovation, human capital, social capital, decision making, and HRM in modern organizations. Regarding KM perspectives, creating and distributing new knowledge through effective knowledge transfer and knowledge sharing have the potential to increase organizational performance and gain sustainable competitive advantage in the knowledge era.

REFERENCES

Akbar, H., & Tzokas, N. (2013). An exploration of new product development's front-end knowledge conceptualization process in discontinuous innovations. *British Journal of Management, 24*(2), 245–263. doi:10.1111/j.1467-8551.2011.00801.x

Andreeva, T., & Kianto, A. (2011). Knowledge processes, knowledge-intensity and innovation: A moderated mediation analysis. *Journal of Knowledge Management, 15*(6), 1016–1034. doi:10.1108/13673271111179343

Anzelak, M., Frankl, G., & Mayr, H. C. (2009). Knowledge management for production. In M. Khosrow-Pour (Ed.), *Encyclopedia of information science and technology* (2nd ed.; pp. 2355–2360). Hershey, PA: IGI Global. doi:10.4018/978-1-60566-026-4.ch373

Asif, M., de Vries, H. J., & Ahmad, N. (2013). Knowledge creation through quality management. *Total Quality Management & Business Excellence*, *24*(5/6), 664–677. doi:10.1080/14783363.2013.791097

Bach, P. M., Lee, R. L., & Carroll, J. M. (2009). Knowledge management challenges in the non-profit sector. In M. Khosrow-Pour (Ed.), *Encyclopedia of information science and technology* (2nd ed.; pp. 2348–2354). Hershey, PA: IGI Global. doi:10.4018/978-1-60566-026-4.ch372

Brown, S. A., Dennis, A. R., Burley, D., & Arling, P. (2013). Knowledge sharing and knowledge management system avoidance: The role of knowledge type and the social network in bypassing an organizational knowledge management system. *Journal of the American Society for Information Science and Technology*, *64*(10), 2013–2023. doi:10.1002/asi.22892

Buckley, S., & Jakovljevic, M. (2013). *Knowledge management innovations for interdisciplinary education: Organizational applications*. Hershey, PA: IGI Global. doi:10.4018/978-1-4666-1969-2

Calvo-Mora, A., Navarro-García, A., & Periañez-Cristobal, R. (2015). Project to improve knowledge management and key business results through the EFQM excellence model. *International Journal of Project Management*, *33*(8), 1638–1651. doi:10.1016/j.ijproman.2015.01.010

Caner, T., & Tyler, B. B. (2015). The effects of knowledge depth and scope on the relationship between R&D alliances and new product development. *Journal of Product Innovation Management*, *32*(5), 808–824. doi:10.1111/jpim.12224

Carstens, D. S., Bean, L., & Barlow, J. (2009). Knowledge management in e-government. In M. Khosrow-Pour (Ed.), *Encyclopedia of information science and technology* (2nd ed.; pp. 2361–2367). Hershey, PA: IGI Global. doi:10.4018/978-1-60566-026-4.ch374

Černe, M., Jaklič, M., & Škerlavaj, M. (2013). Management innovation in focus: The role of knowledge exchange, organizational size, and IT system development and utilization. *European Management Review*, *10*(3), 153–166. doi:10.1111/emre.12013

Chang, J. J., Hung, K. P., & Lin, M. J. J. (2014). Knowledge creation and new product performance: The role of creativity. *R & D Management*, *44*(2), 107–123. doi:10.1111/radm.12043

Chen, L., & Fong, P. S. W. (2015). Evaluation of knowledge management performance: An organic approach. *Information & Management*, *52*(4), 431–453. doi:10.1016/j.im.2015.01.005

Chesbrough, H. (2003). *Open innovation: The new imperative for creating and profiting from technology*. Boston, MA: Harvard Business School Press.

Chew, E. K., & Gottschalk, P. (2009). Innovation and driven knowledge management. In E. Chew & P. Gottschalk (Eds.), *Information technology strategy and management: Best practices* (pp. 392–427). Hershey, PA: IGI Global. doi:10.4018/978-1-59904-802-4.ch011

Chilton, M. A., & Bloodgood, J. M. (2014). *Knowledge management and competitive advantage: Issues and potential solutions.* (pp. 1–387). Hershey, PA: IGI Global. doi:10.4018/978-1-4666-4679-7

Chuang, C., Jackson, S. E., & Jiang, Y. (2016). Can knowledge-intensive teamwork be managed? Examining the roles of HRM systems, leadership, and tacit knowledge. *Journal of Management, 42*(2), 524–554. doi:10.1177/0149206313478189

Cohen, J. F., & Olsen, K. (2015). Knowledge management capabilities and firm performance: A test of universalistic, contingency and complementarity perspectives. *Expert Systems with Applications: An International Journal, 42*(3), 1178–1188. doi:10.1016/j.eswa.2014.09.002

Collins, C. J., & Clark, K. D. (2003). Strategic human resource practices, top management team social networks, and firm performance: The role of human resource in creating organizational competitive advantage. *Academy of Management Journal, 46*(6), 740–751. doi:10.2307/30040665

Cummings, J. L., & Teng, B. S. (2003). Transferring R&D knowledge: The key factors affecting knowledge transfer success. *Journal of Engineering and Technology Management, 20*(1/2), 39–68. doi:10.1016/S0923-4748(03)00004-3

Darroch, J., & McNaughton, R. (2002). Examining the link between knowledge management practice and types of innovation. *Journal of Intellectual Capital, 3*(3), 210–222. doi:10.1108/14691930210435570

Davison, R. M., Ou, C. X. J., & Martinsons, M. G. (2013). Information technology to support informal knowledge sharing. *Information Systems Journal, 23*(1), 89–109. doi:10.1111/j.1365-2575.2012.00400.x

de Clercq, D., Dimov, D., & Thongpapanl, N. (2013). Organizational social capital, formalization, and internal knowledge sharing in entrepreneurial orientation formation. *Entrepreneurship Theory and Practice, 37*(3), 505–537. doi:10.1111/etap.12021 de Stricker, U. (2014). *Knowledge management practice in organizations: The view from inside*. Hershey, PA: IGI Global. doi:10.4018/978-1-4666-5186-9

Denicolai, S., Ramirez, M., & Tidd, J. (2014). Creating and capturing value from external knowledge: The moderating role of knowledge intensity. *R & D Management*, *44*(3), 248–264. doi:10.1111/radm.12065

Donate, M. J., & Guadamillas, F. (2010). The effect of organizational culture on knowledge management practices and innovation. *Knowledge and Process Management*, *17*(2), 82–94. doi:10.1002/kpm.344

Donate, M. J., & Sánchez de Pablo, J. D. (2015). The role of knowledge-oriented leadership in knowledge management practices and innovation. *Journal of Business Research*, *68*(2), 360–370. doi:10.1016/j.jbusres.2014.06.022

Edwards-Buckingham, C. D. (2009). Knowledge management as organizational strategy. In M. Khosrow-Pour (Ed.), *Encyclopedia of information science and technology* (2nd ed.; pp. 2343–2347). Hershey, PA: IGI Global. doi:10.4018/978-1-60566-026-4.ch371

El Said, G. R. (2015). Understanding knowledge management system antecedents of performance impact: Extending the task-technology fit model with intention to share knowledge construct. *Future Business Journal*, *1*(1/2), 75–87. doi:10.1016/j.fbj.2015.11.003

Fidel, P., Schlesinger, W., & Cervera, A. (2015). Collaborating to innovate: Effects on customer knowledge management and performance. *Journal of Business Research*, *68*(7), 1426–1428. doi:10.1016/j.jbusres.2015.01.026

Gagnon, M. P., Payne-Gagnon, J., Fortin, J. P., Pare, G., Cote, J., & Courcy, F. (2015). A learning organization in the service of knowledge management among nurses: A case study. *International Journal of Information Management*, *35*(5), 636–642. doi:10.1016/j.ijinfomgt.2015.05.001

Garcia-Alvarez, M. T. (2015). Analysis of the effects of ICTs in knowledge management and innovation: The case of Zara group. *Computers in Human Behavior*, *51*, 994–1002. doi:10.1016/j.chb.2014.10.007

Gottschalk, P. (2007). *Knowledge management systems: Value shop creation*. Hershey, PA: IGI Global. doi:10.4018/978-1-59904-060-8

Gressgård, L. J. (2015). Antecedents of knowledge exchange systems usage: Motivational and work environment factors. *Knowledge and Process Management*, *22*(2), 112–125. doi:10.1002/kpm.1471

Guadamillas-Gomez, F., & Donate-Manzanares, M. J. (2009). Knowledge management strategies implementation in innovation intensive firms. In D. Jemielniak & J. Kociatkiewicz (Eds.), *Handbook of research on knowledge-intensive organizations* (pp. 169–192). Hershey, PA: IGI Global. doi:10.4018/978-1-60566-176-6.ch011

Haapalainen, P., & Kantola, J. (2015). Taxonomy of knowledge management in open innovations. *Procedia Manufacturing*, *3*, 688–695. doi:10.1016/j.promfg.2015.07.307

Haesli, A., & Boxall, P. (2005). When knowledge management meets HR strategy: An exploration of personalization-retention and codification-recruitment configurations. *International Journal of Human Resource Management*, *16*(11), 1955–1975. doi:10.1080/09585190500314680

Handzic, M., Lagumdzija, A., & Celjo, A. (2009). Knowledge management technology in local government. In M. Khosrow-Pour (Ed.), *Encyclopedia of information science and technology* (2nd ed.; pp. 2373–2379). Hershey, PA: IGI Global. doi:10.4018/978-1-60566-026-4.ch376

Herschel, R. T. (2009). Chief knowledge officers. In M. Khosrow-Pour (Ed.), *Encyclopedia of information science and technology* (2nd ed.; pp. 527–531). Hershey, PA: IGI Global. doi:10.4018/978-1-60566-026-4.ch086

Hodgkinson, G. P., & Healey, M. P. (2011). Psychological foundations of dynamic capabilities: Reflexion and reflection in strategic management. *Strategic Management Journal*, *32*(13), 1500–1516. doi:10.1002/smj.964

Hsiao, Y. C., Chen, C. J., & Chang, S. C. (2011). Knowledge management capacity and organizational performance: The social interaction view. *International Journal of Manpower*, *32*(5/6), 645–660. doi:10.1108/01437721111158242

Hu, M. M., Horng, J., & Sun, Y. C. (2009). Hospitality teams: Knowledge sharing and service innovation performance. *Tourism Management*, *30*(1), 41–50. doi:10.1016/j.tourman.2008.04.009

Inkpen, A. C., & Tsang, E. W. K. (2005). Social capital, networks, and knowledge transfer. *Academy of Management Review*, *30*(1), 146–165. doi:10.5465/AMR.2005.15281445

Jackson, S. E., Schuler, R. S., & Jiang, K. (2014). An aspirational framework for strategic human resource management. *The Academy of Management Annals*, *8*(1), 1–56. doi:10.1080/19416520.2014.872335

Jiang, K., Takeuchi, R., & Lepak, D. P. (2013). Where do we go from here? New perspectives on the black box in strategic human resource management research. *Journal of Management Studies*, *50*(8), 1448–1480.

Jones, S. (2005). Community-based ecotourism: The significance of social capital. *Annals of Tourism Research*, *32*(2), 303–324. doi:10.1016/j.annals.2004.06.007

Junni, P., & Sarala, R. M. (2013). The role of absorptive capacity in acquisition knowledge transfer. *Thunderbird International Business Review*, *55*(4), 419–438. doi:10.1002/tie.21554

Kaplan, A. M., & Michael, H. (2010). Users of the world, unite! The challenges and opportunities of social media. *Business Horizons*, *53*(1), 59–68. doi:10.1016/j.bushor.2009.09.003

Kasemsap, K. (2014a). The role of social networking in global business environments. In P. Smith & T. Cockburn (Eds.), *Impact of emerging digital technologies on leadership in global business* (pp. 183–201). Hershey, PA: IGI Global. doi:10.4018/978-1-4666-6134-9.ch010

Kasemsap, K. (2014b). Strategic innovation management: An integrative framework and causal model of knowledge management, strategic orientation, organizational innovation, and organizational performance. In P. Ordóñez de Pablos & R. Tennyson (Eds.), *Strategic approaches for human capital management and development in a turbulent economy* (pp. 102–116). Hershey, PA: IGI Global. doi:10.4018/978-1-4666-4530-1.ch007

Kasemsap, K. (2014c). The role of knowledge sharing on organisational innovation: An integrated framework. In L. Al-Hakim & C. Jin (Eds.), *Quality innovation: Knowledge, theory, and practices* (pp. 247–271). Hershey, PA: IGI Global. doi:10.4018/978-1-4666-4769-5.ch012

Kasemsap, K. (2014d). The role of social capital in higher education institutions. In N. Baporikar (Ed.), *Handbook of research on higher education in the MENA region: Policy and practice* (pp. 119–147). Hershey, PA: IGI Global. doi:10.4018/978-1-4666-6198-1.ch007

Kasemsap, K. (2014e). The role of social media in the knowledge-based organizations. In I. Lee (Ed.), *Integrating social media into business practice, applications, management, and models* (pp. 254–275). Hershey, PA: IGI Global. doi:10.4018/978-1-4666-6182-0.ch013

Kasemsap, K. (2015). Developing a framework of human resource management, organizational learning, knowledge management capability, and organizational performance. In P. Ordoñez de Pablos, L. Turró, R. Tennyson, & J. Zhao (Eds.), *Knowledge management for competitive advantage during economic crisis* (pp. 164–193). Hershey, PA: IGI Global. doi:10.4018/978-1-4666-6457-9.ch010

Kasemsap, K. (2016a). The roles of knowledge management and organizational innovation in global business. In G. Jamil, J. Poças-Rascão, F. Ribeiro, & A. Malheiro da Silva (Eds.), *Handbook of research on information architecture and management in modern organizations* (pp. 130–153). Hershey, PA: IGI Global. doi:10.4018/978-1-4666-8637-3.ch006

Kasemsap, K. (2016b). Analyzing the roles of human capital and competency in global business. In S. Sen, A. Bhattacharya, & R. Sen (Eds.), *International perspectives on socio-economic development in the era of globalization* (pp. 1–29). Hershey, PA: IGI Global. doi:10.4018/978-1-4666-9908-3.ch001

Kasemsap, K. (2016c). Advocating entrepreneurship education and knowledge management in global business. In N. Baporikar (Ed.), *Handbook of research on entrepreneurship in the contemporary knowledge-based global economy* (pp. 313–339). Hershey, PA: IGI Global. doi:10.4018/978-1-4666-8798-1.ch014

Kasemsap, K. (2016d). The roles of e-learning, organizational learning, and knowledge management in the learning organizations. In E. Railean, G. Walker, A. Elçi, & L. Jackson (Eds.), *Handbook of research on applied learning theory and design in modern education* (pp. 786–816). Hershey, PA: IGI Global. doi:10.4018/978-1-4666-9634-1.ch039

Kasemsap, K. (2016e). The roles of lifelong learning and knowledge management in global higher education. In P. Ordóñez de Pablos & R. Tennyson (Eds.), *Impact of economic crisis on education and the next-generation workforce* (pp. 71–100). Hershey, PA: IGI Global. doi:10.4018/978-1-4666-9455-2.ch004

Kasemsap, K. (2016f). Creating product innovation strategies through knowledge management in global business. In A. Goel & P. Singhal (Eds.), *Product innovation through knowledge management and social media strategies* (pp. 330–357). Hershey, PA: IGI Global. doi:10.4018/978-1-4666-9607-5.ch015

Kasemsap, K. (2016g). The roles of information technology and knowledge management in global tourism. In A. Nedelea, M. Korstanje, & B. George (Eds.), *Strategic tools and methods for promoting hospitality and tourism services* (pp. 109–138). Hershey, PA: IGI Global. doi:10.4018/978-1-4666-9761-4.ch006

Kasemsap, K. (2016h). A unified framework of organizational perspectives and knowledge management and their impact on job performance. In A. Normore, L. Long, & M. Javidi (Eds.), *Handbook of research on effective communication, leadership, and conflict resolution* (pp. 267–297). Hershey, PA: IGI Global. doi:10.4018/978-1-4666-9970-0.ch015

Kasemsap, K. (2016i). Utilizing communities of practice to facilitate knowledge sharing in the digital age. In S. Buckley, G. Majewski, & A. Giannakopoulos (Eds.), *Organizational knowledge facilitation through communities of practice in emerging markets* (pp. 198–224). Hershey, PA: IGI Global. doi:10.4018/978-1-5225-0013-1.ch011

Kasemsap, K. (2017a). Investigating the roles of neuroscience and knowledge management in higher education. In S. Mukerji & P. Tripathi (Eds.), *Handbook of research on administration, policy, and leadership in higher education* (pp. 112–140). Hershey, PA: IGI Global. doi:10.4018/978-1-5225-0672-0.ch006

Kasemsap, K. (2017b). Mastering knowledge management in academic libraries. In B. Gunjal (Ed.), *Managing knowledge and scholarly assets in academic libraries* (pp. 27–55). Hershey, PA: IGI Global. doi:10.4018/978-1-5225-1741-2.ch002

Kasemsap, K. (2017c). The fundamentals of human capital. In A. Bhattacharya (Ed.), *Strategic human capital development and management in emerging economies* (pp. 59–89). Hershey, PA: IGI Global. doi:10.4018/978-1-5225-1974-4.ch004

Kasemsap, K. (2017d). The fundamentals of social capital. In G. Koç, M. Claes, & B. Christiansen (Eds.), *Cultural influences on architecture* (pp. 259–292). Hershey, PA: IGI Global. doi:10.4018/978-1-5225-1744-3.ch010

Kasemsap, K. (2017e). Exploring the role of organizational culture in modern organizations. In R. Styron Jr & J. Styron (Eds.), *Comprehensive problem-solving and skill development for next-generation leaders* (pp. 116–138). Hershey, PA: IGI Global. doi:10.4018/978-1-5225-1968-3.ch006

Kasemsap, K. (2017f). Digital storytelling and digital literacy: Advanced issues and prospects. In D. Loveless, P. Sullivan, K. Dredger, & J. Burns (Eds.), *Deconstructing the education-industrial complex in the digital age* (pp. 151–171). Hershey, PA: IGI Global. doi:10.4018/978-1-5225-2101-3.ch009

Kasemsap, K. (2017g). Electronic learning: Theory and applications. In P. Vu, S. Fredrickson, & C. Moore (Eds.), *Handbook of research on innovative pedagogies and technologies for online learning in higher education* (pp. 367–392). Hershey, PA: IGI Global. doi:10.4018/978-1-5225-1851-8.ch016

Kasemsap, K. (2017h). Organizational learning: Advanced issues and trends. In A. Bencsik (Ed.), *Knowledge management initiatives and strategies in small and medium enterprises* (pp. 42–66). Hershey, PA: IGI Global. doi:10.4018/978-1-5225-1642-2.ch003

Kasemsap, K. (2017i). Fundamentals of talent management: Capitalizing on intellectual assets. In M. Mupepi (Ed.), *Effective talent management strategies for organizational success* (pp. 260–282). Hershey, PA: IGI Global. doi:10.4018/978-1-5225-1961-4.ch017

Kettunen, J., Hautala, J., & Kantola, M. (2009). Knowledge management with partners in a dynamic information environment. In A. Cartelli & M. Palma (Eds.), *Encyclopedia of information communication technology* (pp. 503–509). Hershey, PA: IGI Global. doi:10.4018/978-1-59904-845-1.ch066

Khandelwal, V., & Gottschalk, P. (2004). Information technology support for interorganizational knowledge transfer: An empirical study of law firms in Norway and Australia. In M. Khosrow-Pour (Ed.), *Advanced topics in information resources management* (Vol. 3, pp. 262–274). Hershey, PA: Idea Group Publishing. doi:10.4018/978-1-59140-253-4.ch012

King, W. R., Chung, T. R., & Haney, M. H. (2008). Knowledge management and organizational learning. *Omega*, *36*(2), 167–172. doi:10.1016/j.omega.2006.07.004

Kirsch, P., Hine, A., & Maybury, T. (2015). A model for the implementation of industry-wide knowledge sharing to improve risk management practice. *Safety Science*, *80*, 66–76. doi:10.1016/j.ssci.2015.07.009

Krumina, I., Krumins, G., & Rozentale, S. (2015). Vidzeme region of Latvia: Knowledge management in micro enterprises. *Procedia: Social and Behavioral Sciences*, *213*, 781–786. doi:10.1016/j.sbspro.2015.11.475

Kuo, M. S., & Liang, G. S. (2012). A soft computing method of performance evaluation with MCDM based on interval-valued fuzzy numbers. *Applied Soft Computing*, *12*(1), 476–485. doi:10.1016/j.asoc.2011.08.020

Kuo, Y. K., & Ye, K. D. (2010). How employees' perception of information technology application and their knowledge management capacity influence organisational performance. *Behaviour & Information Technology*, *29*(3), 287–303. doi:10.1080/01449290701852166

Lai, J., Lui, S. S., & Tsang, E. W. K. (2016). Intrafirm knowledge transfer and employee innovative behavior: The role of total and balanced knowledge flows. *Journal of Product Innovation Management*, *33*(1), 90–103. doi:10.1111/jpim.12262

Lai, J. Y., Wang, C. T., & Chou, C. Y. (2009). How knowledge map fit and personalization affect success of KMS in high-tech firms. *Technovation*, *29*(4), 313–324. doi:10.1016/j.technovation.2008.10.007

Leal-Rodríguez, A. L., Roldán, J. L., Ariza-Montes, J. A., & Leal-Millán, A. (2014). From potential absorptive capacity to innovation outcomes in project teams: The conditional mediating role of the realized absorptive capacity in a relational learning context. *International Journal of Project Management*, *32*(6), 894–907. doi:10.1016/j.ijproman.2014.01.005

Lee, A. H. I., Chen, H. H., & Chen, S. (2015). Suitable organization forms for knowledge management to attain sustainable competitive advantage in the renewable energy industry. *Energy*, *89*, 1057–1064. doi:10.1016/j.energy.2015.06.047

Lehaney, B., Clarke, S., Coakes, E., & Jack, G. (2004). Knowledge management in more detail. In B. Lehaney, S. Clarke, E. Coakes, & G. Jack (Eds.), *Beyond knowledge management* (pp. 12–30). Hershey, PA: Idea Group Publishing. doi:10.4018/978-1-59140-180-3.ch002

Leidner, D., & Alavi, M. (2009). The role of culture in knowledge management: A case study of two global firms. In N. Kock (Ed.), *E-collaboration: Concepts, methodologies, tools, and applications* (pp. 1043–1063). Hershey, PA: IGI Global. doi:10.4018/978-1-60566-652-5.ch079

Li, M., Jin, L., & Wang, J. (2014). A new MCDM method combining QFD with TOPSIS for knowledge management system selection from the user's perspective in intuitionistic fuzzy environment. *Applied Soft Computing*, *21*(3), 28–37.

Lin, H. F. (2011). The effects of employee motivation, social interaction, and knowledge management strategy on KM implementation level. *Knowledge Management Research & Practice*, *9*(3), 263–275. doi:10.1057/kmrp.2011.21

Lin, T. C., & Huang, C. C. (2008). Understanding knowledge management system usage antecedents: An integration of social cognitive theory and task technology fit. *Information & Management*, *45*(6), 410–417. doi:10.1016/j.im.2008.06.004

Litvaj, I., & Stancekova, D. (2015). Knowledge management embedment in company, knowledge repositories, knowledge management significance and usage in company. *Procedia Economics and Finance*, *23*, 833–838. doi:10.1016/S2212-5671(15)00549-3

Liu, C. H., & Lee, T. (2015). Promoting entrepreneurial orientation through the accumulation of social capital, and knowledge management. *International Journal of Hospitality Management*, *46*, 138–150. doi:10.1016/j.ijhm.2015.01.016

Lytras, M. D., Russ, M., Maier, R., & Naeve, A. (2008). *Knowledge management strategies: A handbook of applied technologies.* (pp. 1–390). Hershey, PA: IGI Global. doi:10.4018/978-1-59904-603-7

Maes, J., & Sels, L. (2014). SME's radical product innovation: The role of internally and externally oriented knowledge capabilities. *Journal of Small Business Management, 52*(1), 141–163. doi:10.1111/jsbm.12037

Martín-de Castro, G. (2015). Knowledge management and innovation in knowledge-based and high-tech industrial markets: The role of openness and absorptive capacity. *Industrial Marketing Management, 47*, 143–146. doi:10.1016/j.indmarman.2015.02.032

Martinez-Gil, J. (2015). Automated knowledge base management: A survey. *Computer Science Review, 18*, 1–9. doi:10.1016/j.cosrev.2015.09.001

Maurer, I., Bartsch, V., & Ebers, M. (2011). The value of intra-organizational social capital: How it fosters knowledge transfer, innovation performance, and growth. *Organization Studies, 32*(2), 157–185. doi:10.1177/0170840610394301

Menaouer, B., Khalissa, S., Abdelbaki, B., & Abdelhamid, T. (2015). Towards a new approach of support innovation guided by knowledge management: Application on FERTIAL. *Procedia: Social and Behavioral Sciences, 210*, 260–269. doi:10.1016/j.sbspro.2015.11.366

Meroño-Cerdán, Á. L. (2009). Knowledge management systems as a framework for IT in knowledge management. In T. Torres-Coronas & M. Arias-Oliva (Eds.), *Encyclopedia of human resources information systems: Challenges in e-HRM* (pp. 611–616). Hershey, PA: IGI Global. doi:10.4018/978-1-59904-883-3.ch089

Mezghani, E., Exposito, E., & Drira, K. (2016). A collaborative methodology for tacit knowledge management: Application to scientific research. *Future Generation Computer Systems, 54*, 450–455. doi:10.1016/j.future.2015.05.007

Molina, L. M., Lloréns-Montes, J., & Ruiz-Moreno, A. (2007). Relationship between quality management practices and knowledge transfer. *Journal of Operations Management, 25*(3), 682–701. doi:10.1016/j.jom.2006.04.007

Monticolo, D., Hilaire, V., Gomes, S., & Koukam, A. (2009). An ontological approach to managing project memories in organizations. In N. Kock (Ed.), *E-collaboration: Concepts, methodologies, tools, and applications* (pp. 244–269). Hershey, PA: IGI Global. doi:10.4018/978-1-60566-652-5.ch022

Mráček, P., & Mucha, M. (2015). The use of knowledge management in marketing communication of small and medium-sized companies. *Procedia: Social and Behavioral Sciences*, *175*, 185–192. doi:10.1016/j.sbspro.2015.01.1190

Nahapiet, J., & Ghoshal, S. (1998). Social capital, intellectual capital, and the organization advantage. *Academy of Management Review*, *23*(2), 242–266.

Nguyen, H. N., & Mohamed, S. (2011). Leadership behaviors, organizational culture and knowledge management practices: An empirical investigation. *Journal of Management Development*, *30*(2), 206–221. doi:10.1108/02621711111105786

Nonaka, I., & Takeuchi, H. (1995). *The knowledge creating company: How Japanese companies create the dynamics of innovation*. New York, NY: Oxford University Press.

Ogiela, L. (2013). Semantic analysis and biological modeling in selected classes of cognitive information systems. *Mathematical and Computer Modelling*, *58*(5/6), 1405–1414. doi:10.1016/j.mcm.2012.12.001

Ogiela, L. (2015). Advanced techniques for knowledge management and access to strategic information. *International Journal of Information Management*, *35*(2), 154–159. doi:10.1016/j.ijinfomgt.2014.11.006

Okunoye, A. (2008). Managing information technology component of knowledge management: Outsourcing as a strategic option in developing countries. In F. Tan (Ed.), *Global information technologies: Concepts, methodologies, tools, and applications* (pp. 2774–2795). Hershey, PA: IGI Global. doi:10.4018/978-1-59904-939-7.ch200

Paraki, J. G. (2006). Knowledge management in telemedicine. In A. Lazakidou (Ed.), *Handbook of research on informatics in healthcare and biomedicine* (pp. 210–220). Hershey, PA: IGI Global. doi:10.4018/978-1-59140-982-3.ch027

Pérez-Montoro, M. (2009). Knowledge management in organizations. In T. Torres-Coronas & M. Arias-Oliva (Eds.), *Encyclopedia of human resources information systems: Challenges in e-HRM* (pp. 605–610). Hershey, PA: IGI Global. doi:10.4018/978-1-59904-883-3.ch088

Phang, M. M. S., & Foong, S. Y. (2010). Information communication technologies (ICTs) and knowledge sharing: The case of professional accountants in Malaysia. *World Journal of Science. Technology and Sustainable Development*, *7*(1), 21–35.

Radaelli, G., Lettieri, E., Mura, M., & Spiller, N. (2014). Knowledge sharing and innovative work behaviour in healthcare: A micro-level investigation of direct and indirect effects. *Creativity and Innovation Management*, *23*(4), 400–414. doi:10.1111/caim.12084

Raisinghani, M. S. (2008). Knowledge management of e-business initiatives within two global organizations: A comparative case study analysis. In F. Tan (Ed.), *Global information technologies: Concepts, methodologies, tools, and applications* (pp. 1780–1794). Hershey, PA: IGI Global. doi:10.4018/978-1-59904-939-7.ch128

Rodan, S., & Galunic, C. (2004). More than network structure: How knowledge heterogeneity influences managerial performance and innovativeness. *Strategic Management Journal*, *25*(6), 541–562. doi:10.1002/smj.398

Russ, M. (2010). *Knowledge management strategies for business development.* (pp. 1–446). Hershey, PA: IGI Global. doi:10.4018/978-1-60566-348-7

Schmidt, J., & Keil, T. (2013). What makes a resource valuable? Identifying the drivers of firm-idiosyncratic resource value. *Academy of Management Review*, *38*(2), 206–228. doi:10.5465/amr.2010.0404

Schneckenberg, D. (2009). Web 2.0 and the empowerment of the knowledge worker. *Journal of Knowledge Management*, *13*(6), 509–520. doi:10.1108/13673270910997150

Schneckenberg, D., Truong, Y., & Mazloomi, H. (2015). Microfoundations of innovative capabilities: The leverage of collaborative technologies on organizational learning and knowledge management in a multinational corporation. *Technological Forecasting and Social Change*, *100*, 356–368. doi:10.1016/j.techfore.2015.08.008

Schulze, A., Brojerdi, G., & von Krogh, G. (2014). Those who know, do. Those who understand, teach. Disseminative capability and knowledge transfer in the automotive industry. *Journal of Product Innovation Management*, *31*(1), 79–97. doi:10.1111/jpim.12081

Sensuse, D. I., Cahyaningsih, E., & Wibowo, W. C. (2015). Knowledge management: Organizational culture in Indonesian government human capital management. *Procedia Computer Science*, *72*, 485–494. doi:10.1016/j.procs.2015.12.130

Singh, M. D., & Kant, R. (2009). Selected knowledge management implementation issues: A sectorial analysis. *International Journal of Innovation and Learning*, *6*(5), 550–567. doi:10.1504/IJIL.2009.025065

Smedlund, A. (2008). The knowledge system of a firm: Social capital for explicit, tacit and potential knowledge. *Journal of Knowledge Management*, *12*(1), 63–77. doi:10.1108/13673270810852395

Swart, J., & Kinnie, N. (2013). Managing multidimensional knowledge assets: HR configurations in professional service firms. *Human Resource Management Journal*, *23*(2), 160–179. doi:10.1111/j.1748-8583.2012.00197.x

Swart, J., Kinnie, N., van Rossenberg, Y., & Yalabik, Z. Y. (2014). Why should I share my knowledge? A multiple foci of commitment perspective. *Human Resource Management Journal*, *24*(3), 269–289. doi:10.1111/1748-8583.12037

Theriou, G. N., & Chatzoglou, P. D. (2008). Enhancing performance through best HRM practices, organizational learning and knowledge management. *European Business Review*, *20*(3), 185–207. doi:10.1108/09555340810871400

Trusson, C. R., Doherty, N. F., & Hislop, D. (2014). Knowledge sharing using IT service management tools: Conflicting discourses and incompatible practices. *Information Systems Journal*, *24*(4), 347–371. doi:10.1111/isj.12025

Tzortzaki, A. M., & Mihiotis, A. (2014). A review of knowledge management theory and future directions. *Knowledge and Process Management*, *21*(1), 29–41. doi:10.1002/kpm.1429

Vaidyanathan, G. (2008). Networked knowledge management dimensions in distributed projects. In F. Tan (Ed.), *Global information technologies: Concepts, methodologies, tools, and applications* (pp. 2574–2597). Hershey, PA: IGI Global. doi:10.4018/978-1-59904-939-7.ch187

von Friedrichs Grängsjö, Y., & Gummesson, E. (2006). Hotel networks and social capital in destination marketing. *International Journal of Service Industry Management*, *17*(1), 58–75. doi:10.1108/09564230610651589

Wallin, M. W., & von Krogh, G. (2010). Organizing for open innovation: Focus on the integration of knowledge. *Organizational Dynamics*, *39*(2), 145–154. doi:10.1016/j.orgdyn.2010.01.010

Wang, C. L., Hult, G. T. M., Ketchen, D. J. Jr, & Ahmed, P. K. (2009). Knowledge management orientation, market orientation and firm performance. An integration and empirical examination. *Journal of Strategic Marketing*, *17*(2), 99–122. doi:10.1080/09652540902879326

Wang, J., Ding, D., Liu, O., & Li, M. (2016). A synthetic method for knowledge management performance evaluation based on triangular fuzzy number and group support systems. *Applied Soft Computing*, *39*, 11–20. doi:10.1016/j.asoc.2015.09.041

Wang, K. L., Chiang, C., & Tung, C. M. (2012). Integrating human resource management and knowledge management: From the viewpoint of core employees and organizational performance. *International Journal of Organizational Innovation*, *5*(1), 109–137.

Weske, M. (2007). *Business process management: Concepts, languages, architectures*. Berlin, Germany: Springer–Verlag.

Wong, K. Y. (2005). Critical success factors for implementing knowledge management in small and medium enterprises. *Industrial Management & Data Systems, 105*(3), 261–279. doi:10.1108/02635570510590101

Yeunga, A. C. L., Laia, K. H., & Yeea, R. W. Y. (2007). Knowledge and information technology management in supply chain integration. *International Journal of Production Research, 45*(11), 2459–2477.

Yli-Renko, H., Autio, E., & Sapienza, H. J. (2001). Social capital, knowledge acquisition, and knowledge exploitation in young technology-based firms. *Strategic Management Journal, 22*(6/7), 587–613. doi:10.1002/smj.183

Yli-Renko, H., Autio, E., & Tontti, V. (2002). Social capital, knowledge, and the international growth of technology-based new firms. *International Business Review, 11*(3), 279–304. doi:10.1016/S0969-5931(01)00061-0

Zack, M., McKeen, J., & Singh, S. (2009). Knowledge management and organizational performance: An exploratory survey. *Journal of Knowledge Management, 13*(6), 392–409. doi:10.1108/13673270910997088

Zhang, L., & Cheng, J. (2015). Effect of knowledge leadership on knowledge sharing in engineering project design teams: The role of social capital. *Project Management Journal, 46*(5), 111–124. doi:10.1002/pmj.21525

Zhang, L., & Zhang, Z. (2014). The effects of incentive mechanism on knowledge management performance in China: The moderating role of knowledge attributes. *Project Management Journal, 45*(2), 34–47. doi:10.1002/pmj.21403

Zhang, X., Gao, Y., Yan, X., Ordóñez de Pablos, P., Sun, Y., & Cao, X. (2015). From e-learning to social-learning: Mapping development of studies on social media-supported knowledge management. *Computers in Human Behavior, 51*, 803–811. doi:10.1016/j.chb.2014.11.084

Zhou, A. Z., & Fink, D. (2003). The intellectual capital web: A systematic linking of intellectual capital and knowledge management. *Journal of Intellectual Capital, 4*(1), 34–48. doi:10.1108/14691930310455379

ADDITIONAL READING

Ahern, T., Leavy, B., & Byrne, P. J. (2014). Knowledge formation and learning in the management of projects: A problem solving perspective. *International Journal of Project Management*, *32*(8), 1423–1431. doi:10.1016/j.ijproman.2014.02.004

Ambos, T. C., Nell, P. C., & Pedersen, T. (2013). Combining stocks and flows of knowledge: The effects of intra-functional and cross-functional complementarity. *Global Strategy Journal*, *3*(4), 283–299. doi:10.1111/j.2042-5805.2013.01063.x

Andersson, U., Buckley, P. J., & Dellestrand, H. (2015). In the right place at the right time!: The influence of knowledge governance tools on knowledge transfer and utilization in MNEs. *Global Strategy Journal*, *5*(1), 27–47. doi:10.1002/gsj.1088

Capaldo, A., & Petruzzelli, A. M. (2014). Partner geographic and organizational proximity and the innovative performance of knowledge-creating alliances. *European Management Review*, *11*(1), 63–84. doi:10.1111/emre.12024

Corfield, A., Paton, R., & Little, S. (2013). Does knowledge management work in NGOs? A longitudinal study. *International Journal of Public Administration*, *36*(3), 179–188. doi:10.1080/01900692.2012.749281

Eckardt, R., Skaggs, B. C., & Youndt, M. (2014). Turnover and knowledge loss: An examination of the differential impact of production manager and worker turnover in service and manufacturing firms. *Journal of Management Studies*, *51*(7), 1025–1057.

Ferguson, S., Burford, S., & Kennedy, M. (2013). Divergent approaches to knowledge and innovation in the public sector. *International Journal of Public Administration*, *36*(3), 168–178. doi:10.1080/01900692.2012.749278

Fernández-Álvarez, Ó. (2014). The gender perspective in managing knowledge through cross-curricular studies in higher education. *Procedia: Social and Behavioral Sciences*, *161*, 269–274. doi:10.1016/j.sbspro.2014.12.070

Frank, A. G., Ribeiro, J. L. D., & Echeveste, M. E. (2015). Factors influencing knowledge transfer between NPD teams: A taxonomic analysis based on a sociotechnical approach. *R & D Management*, *45*(1), 1–22. doi:10.1111/radm.12046

Huang, K. (2014). Knowledge sharing in a third-party-governed health and human services network. *Public Administration Review*, *74*(5), 587–598. doi:10.1111/puar.12222

Jasimuddin, S. M., Li, J., & Perdikis, N. (2015). Knowledge recipients, acquisition mechanisms, and knowledge transfer at Japanese subsidiaries: An empirical study in China. *Thunderbird International Business Review*, *57*(6), 463–479. doi:10.1002/tie.21698

Judrups, J. (2015). Analysis of knowledge management and e-learning integration models. *Procedia Computer Science*, *43*, 154–162. doi:10.1016/j.procs.2014.12.021

Khan, Z., Lew, Y. K., & Sinkovics, R. R. (2015). International joint ventures as boundary spanners: Technological knowledge transfer in an emerging economy. *Global Strategy Journal*, *5*(1), 48–68. doi:10.1002/gsj.1089

Kim, H., Hur, D., & Schoenherr, T. (2015). When buyer-driven knowledge transfer activities really work: A motivation–opportunity–ability perspective. *Journal of Supply Chain Management*, *51*(3), 33–60. doi:10.1111/jscm.12077

Ko, W. W., & Liu, G. (2015). Understanding the process of knowledge spillovers: Learning to become social enterprises. *Strategic Entrepreneurship Journal*, *9*(3), 263–285. doi:10.1002/sej.1198

Lee, J., & Fink, D. (2013). Knowledge mapping: Encouragements and impediments to adoption. *Journal of Knowledge Management*, *17*(1), 16–28. doi:10.1108/13673271311300714

Lonnqvist, A., & Laihonen, H. (2013). Managing regional development: A knowledge perspective. *International Journal of Knowledge-Based Development*, *4*(1), 50–63. doi:10.1504/IJKBD.2013.052493

Marabelli, M., & Newell, S. (2014). Knowing, power and materiality: A critical review and reconceptualization of absorptive capacity. *International Journal of Management Reviews*, *16*(4), 479–499. doi:10.1111/ijmr.12031

Matayong, S., & Mahmood, A. K. (2013). The review of approaches to knowledge management system studies. *Journal of Knowledge Management*, *17*(3), 472–490. doi:10.1108/JKM-10-2012-0316

Mohammed, A. (2015). Knowledge management process in several organizations: Analytical study of modeling and several processes. *Procedia Computer Science*, *65*, 726–733. doi:10.1016/j.procs.2015.09.017

Natek, S., & Lesjak, D. (2013). Improving knowledge management by integrating HEI process and data models. *Journal of Computer Information Systems*, *53*(4), 81–86. doi:10.1080/08874417.2013.11645653

O'Mahoney, J., Heusinkveld, S., & Wright, C. (2013). Commodifying the commodifiers: The impact of procurement on management knowledge. *Journal of Management Studies*, *50*(2), 204–235. doi:10.1111/joms.12008

Pandey, S. C., & Dutta, A. (2013). Role of knowledge infrastructure capabilities in knowledge management. *Journal of Knowledge Management*, *17*(3), 435–453. doi:10.1108/JKM-11-2012-0365

Purcarea, I., Espinosa, M., & Apetrei, A. (2013). Innovation and knowledge creation: Perspectives on the SMEs sector. *Management Decision*, *51*(5), 1096–1107. doi:10.1108/MD-08-2012-0590

Rabeh, H. A. D., Jimenéz-Jimenéz, D., & Martínez-Costa, M. (2013). Managing knowledge for a successful competence exploration. *Journal of Knowledge Management*, *17*(2), 195–207. doi:10.1108/13673271311315169

Regnér, P., & Zander, U. (2014). International strategy and knowledge creation: The advantage of foreignness and liability of concentration. *British Journal of Management*, *25*(3), 551–569. doi:10.1111/1467-8551.12054

Schoenherr, T., Griffith, D. A., & Chandra, A. (2014). Knowledge management in supply chains: The role of explicit and tacit knowledge. *Journal of Business Logistics*, *35*(2), 121–135.

Shu, C., Liu, C., Gao, S., & Shanley, M. (2014). The knowledge spillover theory of entrepreneurship in alliances. *Entrepreneurship Theory and Practice*, *38*(4), 913–940. doi:10.1111/etap.12024

Vance, C. M., Andersen, T., Vaiman, V., & Gale, J. (2014). A taxonomy of potential contributions of the host country national local liaison role in global knowledge management. *Thunderbird International Business Review*, *56*(2), 173–191. doi:10.1002/tie.21610

Wibowo, M. A., & Waluyo, R. (2015). Knowledge management maturity in construction companies. *Procedia Engineering*, *125*, 89–94. doi:10.1016/j.proeng.2015.11.014

Wiewiora, A., Murphy, G., Trigunarsyah, B., & Brown, K. (2014). Interactions between organizational culture, trustworthiness, and mechanisms for inter-project knowledge sharing. *Project Management Journal*, *45*(2), 48–65. doi:10.1002/pmj.21407

Yusuf, S., Baden, T., & Prieto-Godino, L. L. (2014). Bridging the gap: Establishing the necessary infrastructure and knowledge for teaching and research in neuroscience in Africa. *Metabolic Brain Disease*, *29*(2), 217–220. doi:10.1007/s11011-013-9443-x PMID:24166356

KEY TERMS AND DEFINITIONS

Human Capital: The individual's skill set regarding the scope of economic value.

Human Resource Management: The efficient application of skilled workforce in an organization.

Innovation: The powerful method of utilizing new thoughts and systems.

Knowledge Management: The practical execution of knowledge and organizational resources.

Knowledge Sharing: The procedure that enhances the distribution of knowledge.

Knowledge Transfer: The transmission of knowledge among companies or customers.

New Product Development: The innovative process concerning the design, development, and distribution of created products or services.

Social Capital: The association among individuals and substances that can be profitable.

Chapter 13
Adoption of E-Voting System to Enhance the Electoral Process in Developing Countries

Samuel Agbesi
Aalborg University, Denmark

ABSTRACT

Literature reviewed confirm challenges in the electoral process in developing countries like Ghana. These challenges are mainly Institutional and Technical challenges. The Institutional challenges come from the electoral commission, security agencies such as the Police, and civil society groups that are not well equipped to lend their full support to the electoral process, and also electoral challenges can be identified in three stages, pre-election, during election, and after election. And it is assumed that e-voting system when adopted will resolve this electoral challenges, but the system design should be approach from the Socio-technical perspective so that the system will not fail after implementation.

INTRODUCTION

This chapter discusses the challenges of the voting process in developing countries, using Ghana as a case study, and how e-voting systems can be adopted to solve this challenges. We define developing countries in this context as all sub-Saharan African countries. The chapter further discuss what developing countries need to do to have a successful adoption of e-voting system by discussing Roger's diffusion of innovation theory.

DOI: 10.4018/978-1-5225-2956-9.ch013

BACKGROUND

With the advancement in Information and Communication Technology (ICT), several developed countries such as Estonia, US etc., are transforming their electoral process using IT. Computerized systems area being used to replace the manual part of the electoral process to make it more efficient and reliable. But developing countries are still using the manual process in all aspect of its electoral process. Country like Ghana has only replaced it manual verification system with biometric verification device called the BVD machine, but the rest of the process is still manual. There are claims that this manual electoral process has challenges which impact on the final outcome of the results. Some of the problem associated with these manual process includes ballot stuffing, multiple voting, tampering of voting results, spoilt ballots due to wrong thumb printing, long queues at polling center and delays in vote counting (Nana Karikari-Apau, 2012). The perception of these manipulations results in violence during elections and post elections across the sub-saharan Africa, and this violence is as a result of mistrust of the current electoral process (Goldsmith, A., 2015; Adolfo, Eldridge Vigil, et al, 2012). In the past few years several elections context in Africa has been marred by election violence, few of these countries includes Côte d'Ivoire, Kenya, Nigeria, Zimbabwe, Cameroon, Democratic Republic of Congo, Liberia, Equatorial Guinea, Gambia, Guinea, Madagascar, Sierra Leone, Senegal and Uganda. Violence's such as widespread coercive intimidation of both candidates and voters including harassment, imprisonment and assassinations; violent riots and clashes between supporters or security elements of the competing political parties; and attacks on local party headquarters and party symbols (Goldsmith, A., 2015). All these violence was as a result of the mistrust of the manual electoral process. Hence using ICT in the form of Electronic Voting (E-voting) system in the electoral process is a call in the right direction.

HOW E-VOTING CAN BE USED TO ENHANCED ELECTORAL PROCESS IN DEVELOPING COUNTRIES

What Is Electronic Voting (E-Voting) System?

E-voting has been define as any electronic means of casting votes, storing votes and tallying of votes or system where election data is recorded, stored and process primarily as digital information (Tanzila Afrin, Prof.K.J.Satao, 2013; Mohammed Awad Ernst L. Leiss, 2011). E-voting system can be of several forms but the most prominent among all is the Internet voting (I-voting) and Direct Recording Electronics (DRE).

With I-voting, voters can vote at the comfort of their homes, offices etc. remotely once they have access to the internet and the voting occurs without the supervision of any election official. Whiles with DRE voting occurs with voters voting on a dedicated computer at a polling station or at a controlled location, and we term those as voting kiosk (Sanjay Kumar and Ekta Walia, 2011). DRE voting occurs under the supervision of election officials.

Success Stories of E-Voting Adoption in Estonia

E-voting system has been opined to be the way forward when it comes to democratic elections even though there are other studies that is against it use due to the security issues associated to the internet, which is the main backbone of I-voting. But the success stories of other developed countries, for example Estonia, cannot not be overlooked.

Estonia introduced e-voting system in the local election in 2005 and in parliamentary elections in 2007. The sole aim of the use of e-voting was to increase voter participation. The underlying factor for the success of Estonia e-voting system, known as e-elections, was the development of a complete well-functioning electronic states (e-state) (Tsahkna, A., 2013; Alvarez, R. M., Hall, T. E., & Trechsel, A. H., 2009), popularly known as e-Estonia. With e-Estonia the government has facilitate it citizen interactions with the state through electronic services like i-Voting, e-Tax, e-Business, e-Banking, e-Ticket, e-School, e-Governance, etc. (https://estonia.ee/). Furthermore studies shows that in the entire world it's only Estonia where ID cards with remote identification and binding digital signature functions are obligatory, and statistics shows that 70% of Estonia inhabitants are already card holders. Estonia citizens are issued with this government ID, called the eID card, with a scannable chip and a unique PIN number. Hence with this ID, it makes internet voting (I-Voting) possible (Madise U., Martens T, 2005; Plumer B., 2012). The eID was introduced in 2002, an Idea born by then Prime Minister in 1999. The eID is the primary document for the identification of all its citizenry and foreigners living in the country, and the card also contains electronic features that aid secure authentication and legally binding digital signature that can be used with nationwide online services (Kitsing, M., 2014; Vinkel, P., 2011). The eID by Estonia is by far the most highly developed national ID in the world. The national ID of Estonia has an embedded files with 2048-bit public key encryption, which allows it to be used as a proof of identity in any electronic transaction. The eID card is used frequently with the following e-services (https://e-estonia.com):

- As a national ID card for legal travel within the EU for Estonian citizens
- As the national health insurance card

- As proof of identification when logging into bank accounts from a home computer
- As a pre-paid public transport ticket in some part of the country
- For digital signatures
- For i-voting
- For accessing government databases to check one's medical records, file taxes, etc.
- For picking up e-Prescriptions

With the existence of these infrastructure it has made it possible for Estonia citizens to access state portals, a one-stop-shop for the dozens of state services, using their electronic Identification (eID) card, and also making it possible for internet voting (i-Voting). The Estonia e-voting allows any registered voter to cast their vote via any computer with internet connection from anywhere in the world without going to a particular polling station. There are two possible procedures to cast your vote in Estonia: physically going to the polling station to use a paper ballot or voting electronically (I-voting), and both methods are based on "two envelopes" system.

The following steps are used for the paper ballot:

1. The voter appears at the polling station and present an ID document for identification
2. The voter then receive the ballot paper and two envelopes.
3. The voter fills the ballot and put it in an envelope which has no reference to the individual voter's identity.
4. The voter then enclose this envelope into the outer envelope, and this outer envelope contains the personal details of the voter.
5. The envelope is send to the voter's polling division. The eligibility of the voter is determined by using the outer envelope. The outer envelope is opened, and the inner (anonymous) envelope is put into the ballot box.

The I-voting method follows the steps stated below:

1. The voter insert their ID card into the card reader attached with the computer to open the voting web page.
2. The voter verifies his/her identity by using the first pin code that comes with the ID card (there are two pin codes).
3. The central server checks the eligibility of the voter from the population register.
4. The Voter is show the candidate list for the appropriate electoral district if the voter is eligible vote.
5. The voter make the voting decision, which is encrypted.

6. The voter then confirm his/her voting choice with their digital signature by entering their second pin code of their ID card.
7. The digital signatures are removed at the stage of counting, and in the final stage, the members of the Estonian National Electoral Committee can open the anonymous e-votes for counting

From the above review it is obvious that Estonia are successful in the e-voting implementation because of three key factors:

- A well-functioning electronic state
- A reliable and secure Identity management system and
- Availability of internet access in most households in Estonia. Household internet penetration rate is 86% as at 2016 (The Statistics Portal, 2016).), making it possible for citizens to vote remotely from the comfort of their homes or offices.

Summary of Voting Process in Ghana

1. **Voter Reference List:** Contains the list of all voters name in a particular polling station. These names are sorted in alphabetical order.
    a. This is the first point of contact for a voter coming to cast his/her vote. The person in charge will take your Voters ID card and check your name from the voter reference list. The Electoral official will then tell the next EC official on the station the page in which to find the voters actual details (which include a barcode)
2. Voter goes to the next work station to check the next list which contains voters detail list with barcodes.
3. **BVD (Biometric Verification Device) Verification:** If the voter name is found in the list in step 1 and 2 he/she now need to be verified by the BVD (fingers verification).
    a. If a voter fingers cannot be verified by the BVD, the EC official will scan the barcode in the reference list in step 2 to prove your identity. All the party agents present must confirm you are on the reference list
4. Your fingers will be marked with an indelible ink (to signify you have been verify and ready to vote)
5. Presidential ballot is giving to the voter to thumb print in an enclose box to cast the vote
6. Second ballot paper for parliamentary votes is also giving to the voter to thumb print and cast the vote

Challenges in the Electoral Process

The challenges of the electoral process in Ghana can be categorized into Institutional, Human and Technological (Prince Botwe, 2016). Prince Botwe (2016) identified the institutional challenges emanating from the electoral commission, security agencies such as the Police, and civil society groups that are not well equipped to lend their full support and are not living to their responsibilities. Electoral challenges can be identified in three stages, pre-election, during election, and after election (Abdallah, M., 2013). Pre-election challenges include violence that erupt during political campaign period. During this period a lot of accusation and counter accusation of schemes to rigged the elections by political parties which results in violence among supporters of those political parties. In the recent 2016 elections in Ghana, there were rumors of Togolese citizens crossing the border to register to vote during the registration exercises. It caused the leading opposition party to call for cleaning of the voter registered, which resulted in several groups picketing at the premises of the Electoral Commissions headquarters and forcing the Police to intervene. The main challenge that surfaces during pre-election has to do with voter registration (credible voter register). This issue has been a re-occurring issue in every election year. There are always complain of duplicate registration either by accident or deliberate, voters assigned to wrong electoral area and ghost names still existing on the register. Secondly, there are also challenges associated with the conduct of the elections and these are a) Electorate manipulation, that is, manipulating the voting process and vote counting, b) Gerrymandering, that is, drawing of electoral boundaries to get a particle result, c) intimidation, d) attack on polling station and e) ballot stuffing (Alhaji Mohammed Salisu Baba).

Recent observational study conducted during the 2016 Presidential and Parliamentary elections in Ghana reveals some common challenges across multiple polling stations. Most polling station votes delayed due to some of the reasons below:

- Security personnel's who are to be at post at a polling station were not present at start of polls
- **Incomplete Voting Materials:** Most polling station delayed their voting because election materials such as indelible ink, ballot papers or voter reference list were not available at the polling station at the time voting was supposed to start. One particular polling station has as many as one hundred presidential ballot booklets missing at a polling station and this resulted in a hold up, because party agents prevented voting to begin unless those booklets are found. The assumption was that these booklets may be used to rig the votes at that polling station.

- **Missing Voters Name in the Voter Reference List:** Some voters could not find their names in the polling station where they are supposed to vote, even though check done (SMS to short code) prior to the elections confirm the existence of their names. This normally results in misunderstanding between the voters and the election officials at polling station. Some of these missing names were later found in another polling area - some polling stations were divided into two or three within the same location.

Two major challenges that was observed across some polling stations during vote counting were errors in sorting out ballot papers according to candidates and counting errors. Some polling station did not close polls early because voting did not begin on-time and secondly some of these polling station did not have proper lighting system which make sorting of the ballots difficult. It could not be confirm if the sorting errors was intentional or accidental since it happened for both top two political parties. Secondly, counting of the sorted ballot papers is done in the presence of the audience at the polling station who are present to observe the counting and they normally counts with the election official and the audience intentionally confuse the counting either by counting one ballot paper twice or skipping the ballot count. This two challenges has the potential to influence the outcome of an election for both Presidential and Parliamentary.

From the above discussion of the Ghanaian voting process and the associated challenges it is obviously adopting a new method to enhance the electoral process is in the right direction, and E-voting systems when adopted will go a long way to mitigate most of these challenges. But we must plan the adoption carefully and involved all stakeholders in other to have a sustainable e-voting systems. There are evidence to support that most Information System implementation are failing in developing countries due to inadequate research in the innovation and a failure to involve all stakeholders.

What Developing Countries Need to Do for Successful Adoption Of E-Voting

E-Voting as a Socio-Technical System

E-voting system is a social-technical system hence it implementation most be approach as such. Most IT (Information Technology) system only concentrate on the technical aspect of it implementation and ignore the social aspect of it, and this has resulted in many IT systems failing (Lucas, Henry C, 1975). The term Socio-Technical is from Social and Technical; Social system means the characteristics of people who will interact with the systems, example their attitudes, skill and values, their relationship with others, and their reward system etc. And the Technical system has to do with the processes, task and the technology needed to process input data into output (Bostrom, R., & Heinen, J., 1977). To have a successful e-voting implementation system designers should look into both the social and technical aspect of it. The use of Socio-Technical design approach is the best way to have a successful e-voting implementation and to have an assurance of it not failing. In this case failure means voters not accepting to use the e-voting systems and the e-voting system not performing as it was intended.

Diffusion of E-Voting System

In order to have a successful e-voting implementation in Ghana we need to have a strategy for diffusion this new system. When the citizens understands the benefits the new system has over the old one it will influence their behavioral intention towards it acceptance.

Rogers EM, (2003) define diffusion as "the process by which innovation is communicated over certain channels over time among the members of a social system". In this definition Rogers identified four elements, namely, Innovation, Communication channel, Time and Social systems. In this case we are much interested in the Innovation and the communication channel.

Innovation can be define as any new idea or product that can be perceived as new which can be used to replace an existing idea or product (Rogers EM, 2003). For example we can use e-voting system as a new systems that can be used to replace the current paper-ballot system. Newness of an idea or product does not always mean a new knowledge. The idea or innovation may exist, but if an individual or group of people has not tried to adopt it or reject it implementation, it can still be classified as a new innovation (Rogers EM, 2003). E-voting system has been use in other countries Like US, Estonia etc., but not in Ghana, hence in this context it is a new idea. For any innovation to be adopted individuals or entity looks at how the new idea or innovation will benefit them. Rogers identified five basic characteristics of innovation (Rogers EM, 2003);

- **Relatively Advantage:** That is, the degree by which the new idea is better than the one it is going to be replaced. It is assumed that the greater the perceived relative advantage the higher the rate of adoption. If e-voting systems is perceived to be convenient to use, resolve the vote rigging etc., voters may adopt it and use it.
- **Compatibility:** Is the degree to which an innovation is consistent with the values and norms of potential adopters. Innovation that is not consistent with the values and norms of potential adopters will be rejected.

- Complexity is the degree to which an innovation is perceived to be difficult in terms of it usage and understanding of the system. If an innovation is perceived be easier to understand and use it will be adopted faster. If E-voting system is perceived to be simple to understand and to use it will impact positively on the rate of it adoption.
- **Trialability:** Is the degree to which a new idea or innovation may be tried on limited or pilot basis. If an innovation can be tested on pilot basis it will reduce the uncertainty to potential adopters and will help them to understand the idea more during these experiments. If e-voting can be experimented on low priority elections like District and Municipal elections or Party internal elections, it will help adopters to learn from it and understand how it works better before it is introduce to a more high priority elections like Parliamentary and Presidential elections.
- Observability is the degree to which the results of an innovation is visible to the other members of the social system.

These characteristic discuss above have impact on the adoption of new ideas in this case e-voting system. If E-voting is more advantageous, it's compatible with the values and norms of Ghanaian society, and there is a possibility for it to be experimented on pilot basis, and the results of this experiment is visible to all and finally if the e-voting system will be easier to understand and use, then voters will be willing to use it.

The second component of the diffusion which is very important is the communication process. Rogers EM, (2003) define communication as the process by which parties create and share information together in order to reach a mutual understanding. This information sharing is concern with the new idea or the innovation. The method involved in the communication process is (a) an innovation, (b) an individual or unit that has knowledge and experience in using that innovation, (c) another unit or individual that have no knowledge of the innovation and experience in using it, (d) and finally a communication channel that will connect the two units (Rogers EM, 2003). This communication channel is the means by which this information is transferred from one individual or unit to another. This channel could be a mass media channel, for example Radio, TV, newspaper etc. Mass media is deem to be the most effective and rapid way of sending message to potential adopters of a new idea or innovation by creating awareness of the importance and benefits of the new idea (Rogers EM, 2003). There is also interpersonal channels that is deem to be more effective in persuading individuals in adopting a new idea. Interpersonal channels involves face-to-face of exchange of information between two or more individuals. Studies shows that most people evaluate an innovation base on the evaluation giving to them by individuals like themselves who have previously adopted that innovation, but not on a scientific studies (Rogers EM, 2003).

Hence in this context to have voters or potential adopters to accept this new idea or e-voting system faster, stakeholders need to have a communication strategy that can be used to communicate the importance of this new idea. Mass media, like Radio advert by the Electoral Commission, Newspaper articles and panel discussions on TV about the need to have e-voting system replacing the paper-base will go a long way to change the minds of voters in accepting e-voting system. Individuals that have used any form of e-voting in Universities or elsewhere can be employed to have a face-to-face conversation to the rural people to explain to them how the systems works, and also clear their doubts of any misconception about E-voting.

CONCLUSION

Literature reviewed confirm challenges in the electoral process in developing countries like Ghana. These challenges are mainly Institutional and Technical challenges. The Institutional challenges come from the electoral commission, security agencies such as the Police, and civil society groups that are not well equipped to lend their full support to the electoral process, and also electoral challenges can be identified in three stages, pre-election, during election, and after election. And it is assume that e-voting system when adopted will resolve this electoral challenges, but the system design should be approach from the Socio-technical perspective so that the system will not fail after implementation. Furthermore, in order to influence individuals in using this new idea we must find better ways to communicate the idea and it's benefits or value to potentials adopters through some communication medium. Studies has shown that mass media like Radio, Newspapers, Socio media etc. is most efficient way of reaching potential adopters with the new idea, but also interpersonal media is most effective in persuading individual adopters. From the experience from Estonia it is clear that the basic infrastructure to facilitate I-voting exist and conscious effort were made by policy makers to have this infrastructure available. For Ghana to be able to effectively implement secure e-voting, policy makers need to first and foremost implement a Citizens Identity Management System (CIDMS), and with Citizen Identity Card it can allow citizens to perform secure online transaction including e-voting.

REFERENCES

Abdallah, M. (2013). *Ghana's 2012 Elections: Lessons Learnt towards Sustaining Peace and Democratic Stability*. Accra: KAIPTC.

Adolfo, E. V., Söderberg Kovacs, M., Nyström, D., & Utas, M. (2012). *Electoral Violence in Africa*. Academic Press.

Afrin, & Satao. (2013). E-Voting System for on Duty Person Using RSA Algorithm with Kerberos Concept. *International Journal of Advanced Research in Computer Engineering & Technology*, *2*(7), 2258–2261.

Alvarez, R. M., Hall, T. E., & Trechsel, A. H. (2009). Internet voting in comparative perspective: The case of Estonia. *PS: Political Science & Politics*, *42*(03), 497–505.

Baba. (n.d.). *What is e-voting? Various types of e-voting, USA to Venezuela - Issues to consider*. Retrieved from www.danquahinstitute.org/docs/prospectsevotingghana.pdf

Bostrom, R., & Heinen, J. (1977). MIS Problems and Failures: A Socio-Technical Perspective. Part I: The Causes. *Management Information Systems Quarterly*, *1*(3), 17–32. doi:10.2307/248710

Botwe, P. (2016). *Tackling the Challenges of Election in Ghana*. Retrieved from https://www.modernghana.com/news/676158/tackling-the-challenges-of-election-in-ghana.html

Goldsmith, A. (2015). Electoral Violence in Africa Revisited. *Terrorism and Political Violence*, *27*(5), 818–837. doi:10.1080/09546553.2013.863184

Leiss. (2011). Internet voting in the USA: analysis and commentary. Transforming Government: People. *Process and Policy*, *5*(1), 45–55.

Karikari-Apau. (2012). *Ghana president re-elected, a result opposition claims was 'manipulated'*. Retrieved from http://edition.cnn.com/2012/12/09/world/africa/ghana-elections/

Kitsing, M. (2014). Internet Voting in Estonia. In *Proceedings of the 2014 Conference on Electronic Governance and Open Society: Challenges in Eurasia* (pp. 137-144). ACM.

Kumar, S., & Walia, E. (2011). Analysis of Electronic Voting System In Various Countries. *International Journal on Computer Science and Engineering*, *3*(5), 1825–1830.

Lucas, H. C. (1975). *Why information Systems Fail*. New York: Columbia University Press.

Madise, U., & Martens, T. (n.d.). *E-voting in Estonia 2005. The first practice of country- wide binding Internet voting in the world*. Retrieved from http://neu.e-voting.cc/wp-content/uploads/Proceedings%202006/1.1.madise_martens_e-voting_in_estonia.pdf

Plumer, B. (2012). *Estonia gets to vote online. Why can't America?*. Retrieved from http://www.washingtonpost.com/blogs/wonkblog/wp/2012/11/06/estonians-get-to-vote-online-why-cant-america/

Rogers, E. M. (2004). *Diffusion of Innovations* (5th ed.). New York, NY: Free Press.

The Statistics Portal. (2016). *Share of households with internet access in Estonia from 2005 to 2016*. Retrieved from https://www.statista.com/statistics/377683/household-internet-access-in-estonia/

Tsahkna, A. (2013). E-voting: Lessons from Estonia. *European View*, *12*(1), 59–66. doi:10.1007/s12290-013-0261-7

Vinkel, P. (2011). Internet voting in estonia. In *Nordic Conference on Secure IT Systems* (pp. 4-12). Springer Berlin Heidelberg.

Compilation of References

Abdallah, M. (2013). *Ghana's 2012 Elections: Lessons Learnt towards Sustaining Peace and Democratic Stability*. Accra: KAIPTC.

Adner, R., & Kapoor, R. (2010). Value creation in innovation ecosystems: How the structure of technological interdependence affects firm performance in new technology generations. *Strategic Management Journal*, *31*(3), 306–333. doi:10.1002/smj.821

Adolfo, E. V., Söderberg Kovacs, M., Nyström, D., & Utas, M. (2012). *Electoral Violence in Africa*. Academic Press.

Afrin, & Satao. (2013). E-Voting System for on Duty Person Using RSA Algorithm with Kerberos Concept. *International Journal of Advanced Research in Computer Engineering & Technology*, *2*(7), 2258–2261.

Afuah, A. (2013). Are network effects really all about size? The role of structure and conduct. *Strategic Management Journal*, *34*(3), 257–273. doi:10.1002/smj.2013

Afuah, A., & Tucci, C. L. (2012). Crowdsourcing as a solution to distant search. *Academy of Management Review*, *37*(3), 355–375. doi:10.5465/amr.2010.0146

Aghion, P., & Tirole, J. (1994). The management of innovation. *The Quarterly Journal of Economics*, *109*(4), 1185–1209. doi:10.2307/2118360

Ahmadi, A. A., Daraei, M. R., Khodaie, B., & Salamzadeh, Y. (2012). Structural equations modeling of relationship between psychological empowerment and knowledge management practices (A case study: Social security organization staffs of Ardabil Province, Iran). *Journal of International Business Management*, *6*(1), 8–16.

Akbar, H., & Tzokas, N. (2013). An exploration of new product development's front-end knowledge conceptualization process in discontinuous innovations. *British Journal of Management*, *24*(2), 245–263. doi:10.1111/j.1467-8551.2011.00801.x

Alavi, M., & Leidner, D. E. (2001). Review: Knowledge management and knowledge management systems: Conceptual foundations and research issues. *Management Information Systems Quarterly*, *25*(1), 107–136. doi:10.2307/3250961

Alexy, O., George, G., & Salter, A. J. (2013). Cui bono? The selective revealing of knowledge and its implications for innovative activity. *Academy of Management Review*, *38*(2), 270–291. doi:10.5465/amr.2011.0193

Alvarez, R. M., Hall, T. E., & Trechsel, A. H. (2009). Internet voting in comparative perspective: The case of Estonia. *PS: Political Science & Politics*, *42*(03), 497–505.

Alvarez, S. A., & Barney, J. B. (2007). Discovery and creation: Alternative theories of entrepreneurial action. *Entrepreneurship Journal*, *1*(1), 11–26.

Amaldoss, W., & Rapoport, A. (2005). Collaborative Product and Market Development: Theoretical Implications and Experimental Evidence. *Marketing Science*, *24*(3), 396–414. doi:10.1287/mksc.1040.0105

American Management Association, Training, Articles and White Papers. (2010). *The Bottom Line on Improperly Trained Leaders*. Retrieved from http://www.amanet.org/training/articles/the-bottom-line-on-improperly-trained-leaders.aspx

Amit, R., & Schoemaker, P. (1993). Strategic assets and organizational rent. *Strategic Management Journal*, *14*(1), 33–46. doi:10.1002/smj.4250140105

Anderson, M., & Gavan, C. (2016). *Developing effective educational experiences through learning analytics*. Hershey, PA: Information Science Reference. doi:10.4018/978-1-4666-9983-0

Andreeva, T., & Kianto, A. (2011). Knowledge processes, knowledge-intensity and innovation: A moderated mediation analysis. *Journal of Knowledge Management*, *15*(6), 1016–1034. doi:10.1108/13673271111179343

Andres, H. P. (2002). A comparison of face-to-face and virtual software development teams. *Team Performance Management: An International Journal*, *8*(1/2), 39–48. doi:10.1108/13527590210425077

Anothayanon, W. (2006). *Knowledge management and characteristics* (Ph.D.). Walden University. Retrieved from http://search.proquest.com/docview/304933585/abstract/9056B96088874587PQ/8?accountid=8144

Anzelak, M., Frankl, G., & Mayr, H. C. (2009). Knowledge management for production. In M. Khosrow-Pour (Ed.), *Encyclopedia of information science and technology* (2nd ed.; pp. 2355–2360). Hershey, PA: IGI Global. doi:10.4018/978-1-60566-026-4.ch373

Argote, L., & Hora, M. (2017, April). Organizational Learning and Management of Technology. *Special Issue On Management Of Technology*, *26*(4), 579–590.

Argyris, C., & Schön, D.A. (1978). Organizational Learning: A Theory of Action Perspective. *Reis, 77*(78/97), 345-348.

Argyris, C., & Schön, D. (1978). *Organizational Learning: A Theory of Action Perspective.* Reading, MA: Addison-Wesley.

Asif, M., de Vries, H. J., & Ahmad, N. (2013). Knowledge creation through quality management. *Total Quality Management & Business Excellence, 24*(5/6), 664–677. doi:10.1080/14783363.2013.791097

Athaide, G. A., & Klink, R. R. (2009). Managing Seller-Buyer Relationships during New Product Development. *Journal of Product Innovation Management, 26*(5), 566–577. doi:10.1111/j.1540-5885.2009.00681.x

Atuahene-Gima, K. (2005). Resolving the capability—rigidity paradox in new product innovation. *Journal of Marketing, 69*(4), 61–83. doi:10.1509/jmkg.2005.69.4.61

Baba. (n.d.). *What is e-voting? Various types of e-voting, USA to Venezuela - Issues to consider.* Retrieved from www.danquahinstitute.org/docs/prospectsevotingghana.pdf

Bach, P. M., Lee, R. L., & Carroll, J. M. (2009). Knowledge management challenges in the non-profit sector. In M. Khosrow-Pour (Ed.), *Encyclopedia of information science and technology* (2nd ed.; pp. 2348–2354). Hershey, PA: IGI Global. doi:10.4018/978-1-60566-026-4.ch372

Badger, J. M., Kaminsky, E. S., & Behrend, T. S. (2014). Media richness and information acquisition in internet recruitment. *Journal of Managerial Psychology, 29*(7), 866–883. doi:10.1108/JMP-05-2012-0155

Baehr, C. (2012). Incorporating user appropriation, media richness, and collaborative knowledge sharing into blended e-learning training tutorial. *IEEE Transactions on Professional Communication, 55*(2), 175–184. doi:10.1109/TPC.2012.2190346

Bagherzadeh Niri, M. (2016). *Governance of inter-organizational collaborations when engaged in open innovation* (Unpublished PhD dissertation/thesis). University of Ramon Llull, Barcelona, Spain.

Bagherzadeh, M., & Brunswicker, S. (2016). Governance of Knowledge Flows in Open Exploration: The Role of Behavioral Control. In T. K. Das (Ed.), *Decision Making in Behavioral Strategy (DMBS).* IAP.

Baldwin, C. Y., & Woodard, C. J. 2009. The architecture of platforms: a unified view. In Platforms, Markets and Innovation (pp. 19–44). Cheltenham, UK: Edward Elgar Publishing. doi:10.4337/9781849803311.00008

Bartlett-Bragg, A. (2009). Reframing practice: Creating social learning networks. *International Journal of Development and Learning in Organizations, 23*(4), 16–20. doi:10.1108/14777280910970747

Bartunek, J. (1984). Changing interpretive schemes and organizational restructuring: The example of a religious order. *Administrative Science Quarterly, 29*(3), 224–241. doi:10.2307/2393029

Batarseh, F. S., Usher, J. M., & Daspit, J. J. (2017). Collaboration cpapbility in virtual teams:Examining the influence on diversity and innovation. *International Journal of Innovation Management*, 21.

Battistella, C., De Toni, A. F., & Pessot, E. (2017). Open accelerators for start-ups success: A case study. *European Journal of Innovation Management*, *20*(1), 80–111. doi:10.1108/EJIM-10-2015-0113

Becker, J.-M., Klein, K., & Wetzels, M. (2012). Hierarchical Latent Variable Models in PLS-SEM: Guidelines for Using Reflective-Formative Type Models. *Long Range Planning*, *45*(5–6), 359–394. doi:10.1016/j.lrp.2012.10.001

Becker, W., & Dietz, J. (2004). R&D co-operation and innovation activities of firms: Evidence for the German manufacturing industry. *Research Policy*, *33*(2), 209–223. doi:10.1016/j.respol.2003.07.003

Belderbos, R., Carree, M., & Lokshin, B. (2004). Cooperative R&D and Firm Performance. *Research Policy*, *33*(10), 1477–1492. doi:10.1016/j.respol.2004.07.003

Belsis, P., Kokolakis, S., & Kiountouzis, E. (2005). Information Systems Security from a Knowledge Management Perspective. *Information Management & Computer Security*, *13*(3), 189–202. doi:10.1108/09685220510602013

Benner, M., & Tushman, M. (2003). Exploitation, exploration, and process management: The productivity dilemma revisited. *Academy of Management Review*, *28*(2), 238–256.

Bergh, P., Thorgren, S., & Wincent, J. (2011). Entrepreneurs Learning Together -The Importance of Building Trust for Learning and Exploiting Business Opportunities. *The International Entrepreneurship and Management Journal*, *7*(1), 17–37. doi:10.1007/s11365-009-0120-9

Bergiel, B. J., Bergiel, E. B., & Balsmeier, P. W. (2008). Nature of virtual teams: A summary of their advantages and disadvantages. *Management Research News*, *31*(2), 99–110. doi:10.1108/01409170810846821

Bernardez, M., Valdez Gomez, J. A., Uribe, A., & Santana, A. (2007). Coaching for new business creation. *International Journal of Coaching in Organizations*, *5*(3), 52–65.

Bindrees, M. A., Pooley, R. J., Ibrahim, I. S., & Taylor, N. K. (2014). Re-Evaluating Media Richness Theory in Software Development Settings. *Journal of Computer and Communications*, *02*(14), 37–51. doi:10.4236/jcc.2014.214004

Biyalogorsky, E., Boulding, W., & Staelin, R. (2006). Stuck in the past: Why managers persist with new product failures. *Journal of Marketing*, *70*(2), 108–121. doi:10.1509/jmkg.70.2.108

Boateng, R., Malik, A., & Mbarika, V. (2009). Web 2.0 and Organizational Learning: Conceptualizing the link, Americas Conference on Information Systems. *Proceedings of the Fifteenth Americas Conference on Information Systems*, 1-2.

Boateng, R., Malik, A., & Mbarika, V. (2009). Web 2.0 and Organizational Learning: Conceptualizing the Link. *AMCIS 2009 Proceedings*. Retrieved from http://aisel.aisnet.org/amcis2009/546

Bochenek, L., & Blili, S. (2013). Social Media Champions- Drivers and Sophistication Process of Social Media Strategic Management. *Social Media in Strategic Management*, 143-167.

Bostrom, R., & Heinen, J. (1977). MIS Problems and Failures: A Socio-Technical Perspective. Part I: The Causes. *Management Information Systems Quarterly*, *1*(3), 17–32. doi:10.2307/248710

Botwe, P. (2016). *Tackling the Challenges of Election in Ghana*. Retrieved from https://www.modernghana.com/news/676158/tackling-the-challenges-of-election-in-ghana.html

Boudreau, K. J., & Hagiu, A. (2009). Platform rules: multi-sided platforms as regulators. In Platforms, Markets and Innovation (pp. 163-191). Cheltenham, UK: Edward Elgar Publishing Limited. doi:10.4337/9781849803311.00014

Boudreau, K. (2010). Open platform strategies and innovation: Granting access vs. devolving control. *Management Science*, *56*(10), 1849–1872. doi:10.1287/mnsc.1100.1215

Bradley, N., Alvarez, M., Kuhn, J., & McMillen, D. (2015). *IBM 2015 Cyber-Intelligence Index*. IBM Security Research.

Braun, V., & Clarke, V. (2006). Using thematic analysis in psychology. *Qualitative Research in Psychology*, *3*(2), 77–101. doi:10.1191/1478088706qp063oa

Brown, S. A., Dennis, A. R., Burley, D., & Arling, P. (2013). Knowledge sharing and knowledge management system avoidance: The role of knowledge type and the social network in bypassing an organizational knowledge management system. *Journal of the American Society for Information Science and Technology*, *64*(10), 2013–2023. doi:10.1002/asi.22892

Brown, T., Davidsson, P., & Wiklund, J. (2001). An operationalization of Stevensons conceptualization of entrepreneurship as opportunity-based firm behavior. *Strategic Management Journal*, *22*(10), 953–968. doi:10.1002/smj.190

Brunswicker, S., & Vanhaverbeke, W. (2014). Open Innovation in Small and Medium-Sized Enterprises (SMEs): External Knowledge Sourcing Strategies and Internal Organizational Facilitators. *Journal of Small Business Management.*

Buckley, S., & Jakovljevic, M. (2013). *Knowledge management innovations for interdisciplinary education: Organizational applications*. Hershey, PA: IGI Global. doi:10.4018/978-1-4666-1969-2

Burns, T. R., Corte, U., & Machado, N. (2016). The sociology of creativity: PART III: Applications–The sociocultural contexts of the acceptance/rejection of innovations. *Human Systems Management*, *35*(1), 11–34. doi:10.3233/HSM-150852

Burt, R. S. (2001). *Bandwidth and echo: trust, information, and gossip in social networks*. Academic Press.

Cai, S., & Jun, M. (2015). Relationship between Information Richness and Exchange Outcomes: Moderating Effects of Media Richness and Governance Mechanisms. *International Journal of Information Systems and Supply Chain Management*, *8*(1), 1–21.

Calia, R. C., Guerrini, F. M., & Moura, G. L. (2007). Innovation networks: From technological development to business model reconfiguration. *Technovation, 27*(8), 426–432. doi:10.1016/j.technovation.2006.08.003

Calvo-Mora, A., Navarro-García, A., & Periañez-Cristobal, R. (2015). Project to improve knowledge management and key business results through the EFQM excellence model. *International Journal of Project Management, 33*(8), 1638–1651. doi:10.1016/j.ijproman.2015.01.010

Caner, T., & Tyler, B. B. (2015). The effects of knowledge depth and scope on the relationship between R&D alliances and new product development. *Journal of Product Innovation Management, 32*(5), 808–824. doi:10.1111/jpim.12224

Carey, B. (2014). *How we Learn – the surprising truth about when, where and why it happens.* Random House Publishing Group.

Carstens, D. S., Bean, L., & Barlow, J. (2009). Knowledge management in e-government. In M. Khosrow-Pour (Ed.), *Encyclopedia of information science and technology* (2nd ed.; pp. 2361–2367). Hershey, PA: IGI Global. doi:10.4018/978-1-60566-026-4.ch374

Carvalho, L. M. C., & Galina, S. V. (2015). The role of business incubators for start-ups development in Brazil and Portugal. *World Journal of Entrepreneurship, Management and Sustainable Development, 11*(4), 256–267.

Casey, V., & Richardson, I. (2006). Uncovering the reality within Virtual software teams. *GSD '06 Proceedings of the 2006 international workshop on Global software development for the practitioner,* 66-72.

Černe, M., Jaklič, M., & Škerlavaj, M. (2013). Management innovation in focus: The role of knowledge exchange, organizational size, and IT system development and utilization. *European Management Review, 10*(3), 153–166. doi:10.1111/emre.12013

Černe, M., Nerstad, C. G., Dysvik, A., & Škerlavaj, M. (2014). What goes around comes around: Knowledge hiding, perceived motivational climate, and creativity. *Academy of Management Journal, 57*(1), 172–192. doi:10.5465/amj.2012.0122

Chakravarthy, B. S. (1982). Adaptation: A promising metaphor for strategic management. *Academy of Management Review, 7*(1), 35–44.

Chang, J. J., Hung, K. P., & Lin, M. J. J. (2014). Knowledge creation and new product performance: The role of creativity. *R & D Management, 44*(2), 107–123. doi:10.1111/radm.12043

Chatti, M. A., Klamma, R., Jarke, M., & Naeve, A. (2007). The Web 2.0 Driven SECI Model Based Learning Process. In *Seventh IEEE International Conference on Advanced Learning Technologies, 2007. ICALT 2007* (pp. 780–782). https://doi.org/10.1109/ICALT.2007.256

Chen, H. (2006). *Intelligence and Security Informatics for International Security: Information Sharing & Data Mining*. Springer. doi:10.1007/11734628

Chen, L., & Fong, P. S. W. (2015). Evaluation of knowledge management performance: An organic approach. *Information & Management*, *52*(4), 431–453. doi:10.1016/j.im.2015.01.005

Chesbrough, H. (2006). Open innovation: A new paradigm for understanding industrial innovation. *Open innovation: Researching a new paradigm*, 1-12.

Chesbrough, H. (2003). *Open innovation: The new imperative for creating and profiting from technology*. Harvard Business Press.

Chesbrough, H., & Brunswicker, S. (2014). A Fad or a Phenomenon?: The Adoption of Open Innovation Practices in Large Firms. *Research-Technology Management*, *57*(2), 16–25.

Chew, E. K., & Gottschalk, P. (2009). Innovation and driven knowledge management. In E. Chew & P. Gottschalk (Eds.), *Information technology strategy and management: Best practices* (pp. 392–427). Hershey, PA: IGI Global. doi:10.4018/978-1-59904-802-4.ch011

Chilton, M. A., & Bloodgood, J. M. (2014). *Knowledge management and competitive advantage: Issues and potential solutions.* (pp. 1–387). Hershey, PA: IGI Global. doi:10.4018/978-1-4666-4679-7

Chiu, Y. T. H. (2009). How network competence and network location influence innovation performance. *Journal of Business and Industrial Marketing*, *29*(1), 46–55.

Chua, A. Y., & Banerjee, S. (2013). Customer knowledge management via social media: The case of Starbucks. *Journal of Knowledge Management*, *17*(2), 237–249. doi:10.1108/13673271311315196

Chuang, C., Jackson, S. E., & Jiang, Y. (2016). Can knowledge-intensive teamwork be managed? Examining the roles of HRM systems, leadership, and tacit knowledge. *Journal of Management*, *42*(2), 524–554. doi:10.1177/0149206313478189

Clark, J. R. (2007). *Intelligence and National Security: a Reference Handbook - Contemporary Military, Strategic and Security Issues.* Westport, CT: Praeger Security International.

Codrington, G. (2011). *Mind in the Gap, Understanding the different generations –You're your past, you're your generation, choose your future*. Penguin South Africa.

Cohen, J. F., & Olsen, K. (2015). Knowledge management capabilities and firm performance: A test of universalistic, contingency and complementarity perspectives. *Expert Systems with Applications: An International Journal*, *42*(3), 1178–1188. doi:10.1016/j.eswa.2014.09.002

Cohen, M. D., & Levinthal, D. A. (1990). Absorptive capacity: A new perspective on learning and innovation. *Administrative Science Quarterly*, *35*(1), 128–152. doi:10.2307/2393553

Cohen, S. L. (2013). *How to accelerate learning: Entrepreneurial ventures participating in accelerator programs*. The University of North Carolina at Chapel Hill.

Cohen, W. M., & Levinthal, D. A. (1989). Innovation and learning: The two faces of R&D. *The Economic Journal*, *99*(397), 569–596. doi:10.2307/2233763

Collins, C. J., & Clark, K. D. (2003). Strategic human resource practices, top management team social networks, and firm performance: The role of human resource in creating organizational competitive advantage. *Academy of Management Journal*, *46*(6), 740–751. doi:10.2307/30040665

Colombo, M. G., Laursen, K., Magnusson, M., & Rossi-Lamastra, C. (2011). Organizing inter-and intra-firm networks: What is the impact on innovation performance?. *Industry and Innovation*, *18*(6), 531–538. doi:10.1080/13662716.2011.601958

Colombo, M. G., Piva, E., & Rossi-Lamastra, C. (2013). Authorising employees to collaborate with communities during working hours: When is it valuable for firms? *Long Range Planning*, *46*(3), 236–257. doi:10.1016/j.lrp.2012.05.004

Connelly, E. C., Zweig, D., Webster, J., & Trougakos, J.P. (2012). Knowledge hiding in organization. *Journal of Organizational Behavior, 33*, 64-88.

Cook, N. (2008). *Enterprise 2. 0: How Social Software Will Change the Future of Work*. Gower Publishing, Ltd. Retrieved from http://www.google.com/books?hl=en&lr=&id=f4z5yPx8XUsC&oi=fnd&pg=PT8&dq=enterprise+2.0+Cook,+2008&ots=yew0KKSbhC&sig=HbEuDixrkGIGwkZFqIQdhnTfTJ0

Cook, S. D. N., & Yanow, D. (1993). Culture and Organizational Learning. *Journal of Management Inquiry*, *2*(4), 373–390. doi:10.1177/105649269324010

Cope, J. (2005). Toward a dynamic learning perspective of entrepreneurship. *Entrepreneurship Theory and Practice*, *29*(4), 373–397. doi:10.1111/j.1540-6520.2005.00090.x

Corsaro, D., Cantu, C., & Tunisini, A. (2012). Actors heterogeneity in innovation networks. *Industrial Marketing Management*, *41*(5), 780–789. doi:10.1016/j.indmarman.2012.06.005

Creswell, J. W. (2009). *Research design: Qualitative Quantitative and Mixed Methods Approaches*. Thousand Oaks, CA: SAGE Publications.

Crittenden, V. L., Esper, K., Karst, N., & Slegers, R. (2015). *Evolving entrepreneurical education, Innovation in the Babson Classroom*. Emerald Group Publishing Ltd.

Cross, R. L., & Parker, A. (2004). *The Hidden Power of Social Networks: Understanding how Work Really Gets Done*. Harvard Business School Press.

Cummings, J. L., & Teng, B.-S. (2003). Transferring R&D knowledge: The key factors affecting knowledge transfer success. *Journal of Engineering and Technology Management*, *20*(1–2), 39–68. doi:10.1016/S0923-4748(03)00004-3

D., R., & C., T. (2005). Exploring Entrepreneurial Learning: A Comparative Study of Technology Development and projects. *Journal of Business Venturing*, *20*(1), 137–164.

Daft, R. L., & Lengel, R. H. (1986). Organizational Information Requirements, Media Richness and Structural Design. *Management Science*, *32*(5), 554–571. doi:10.1287/mnsc.32.5.554

Daft, R. L., Lengel, R. H., & Trevino, L. K. (1987). Message Equivocality, Media Selection, and Manager Performance: Implications for Information Systems. *Management Information Systems Quarterly*, *11*(3), 355–366. doi:10.2307/248682

Dahlander, L., & Gann, D. M. (2010). How open is innovation? *Research Policy*, *39*(6), 699–709. doi:10.1016/j.respol.2010.01.013

Dalziel, H. (2015). *How to Define and Build an Effective Cyber Threat Intelligence Capability*. Syngress.

Dandurand, L., & Serrano, O. S. (2013). Towards Improved Cyber Security Information Sharing - Requirements for a Cyber Security Data Exhange and Collaboration Infrastructure (CDXI). In K. Podins, J. Stinissen, & M. Maybaum (Ed.), *2013 5th International Conference on Cyber Conflict*. NATO CCD COE Publications.

Darroch, J., & McNaughton, R. (2002). Examining the link between knowledge management practice and types of innovation. *Journal of Intellectual Capital*, *3*(3), 210–222. doi:10.1108/14691930210435570

Davenport, T. (2015). *Wall Street Journal*. Retrieved from https://www.linkedin.com/pulse/whatever-happened-knowledge-management-tom-davenport

Davenport, T., & Prusak, L. (2000). *Working Knowledge: How Organizations Manage What They Know*. Boston, MA: Harvard Business School Press.

Davila, A., Foster, G., & Jia, N. (2010). Building sustainable high-growth startup companies: Management systems as an accelerator. *California Management Review*, *52*(3), 79–105. doi:10.1525/cmr.2010.52.3.79

Davison, R. M., Ou, C. X. J., & Martinsons, M. G. (2013). Information technology to support informal knowledge sharing. *Information Systems Journal*, *23*(1), 89–109. doi:10.1111/j.1365-2575.2012.00400.x

de Clercq, D., Dimov, D., & Thongpapanl, N. (2013). Organizational social capital, formalization, and internal knowledge sharing in entrepreneurial orientation formation. *Entrepreneurship Theory and Practice*, *37*(3), 505–537. doi:10.1111/etap.12021

de Oliveira, R. A., & Filipe, T. (2011). *Are they helping? An examination of business incubators' impact on tenant firms*. University of Twente.

De Propris, L. (2002). Types of innovation and inter-firm co-operation. *Entrepreneurship & Regional Development*, *14*(4), 337–353. doi:10.1080/08985620210144974

de Stricker, U. (2014). *Knowledge management practice in organizations: The view from inside*. Hershey, PA: IGI Global. doi:10.4018/978-1-4666-5186-9

Dechenaux, E., Thursby, J., & Thursby, M. (2011). Inventor moral hazard in university licensing: The role of contracts. *Research Policy*, *40*(1), 94–104. doi:10.1016/j.respol.2010.09.015

Demirkasimoglu, N. (2015). Knowledge Hiding in Academia: Is Personality a Key Factor? *International Journal of Higher Education*, *5*(1), 128. doi:10.5430/ijhe.v5n1p128

Denicolai, S., Ramirez, M., & Tidd, J. (2014). Creating and capturing value from external knowledge: The moderating role of knowledge intensity. *R & D Management*, *44*(3), 248–264. doi:10.1111/radm.12065

Department of Defence (DoD). (2000). *Doctrince for Intelligence Support to Joint Operations, Joint Publications 2-0*. Washington, DC: GPO.

DeRosa, D. (2014, November 21). *5 Tools every virtual leader needs*. Retrieved from Onpoint consulting: http://www.onpointconsultingllc.com/blog/2014/11/5-tools-every-virtual-leader-needs

Derryberry, A. (2008). *Serious Games: Online games for learning*. Retrieved from https://www.semanticscholar.org/paper/Serious-games-online-games-for-learning-Derryberry/c9bd36db4fc2f95d4b53aa2021337d0e2ee7ac4f

Dineen, B. R., Ling, J., Ash, S. R., & DelVecchio, D. (2007). Aesthetic properties and message customization: Navigating the dark side of web recruitment. *The Journal of Applied Psychology*, *92*(2), 356–372. doi:10.1037/0021-9010.92.2.356 PMID:17371084

Dinur, A. (2009). *Critical context and international intrafirm best-practice transfers*. Academic Press.

Dittman, M. (2005). *Generational Differences at Work - A psychologist studies ways to help traditionalists, baby boomers, gen Xers and millennials work better together, despite their generational differences*. American Psychological Association.

Dixon, N. (1994). *The Organizational Learning Cycle: How We Can Learn Collectively*. London: McGraw-Hill Company.

Dixon, N. (2000). *Common Knowledge: How Companies Thrive by sharing what they know*. Boston: Harvard University Press.

Dobelli, R. (2014). *The art of thinking clearly*. Farrar, Straus and Giroux.

Dodgson, M. (1993). Organizational learning: A review of some literatures. *Organization Studies*, *14*(3), 375–394. doi:10.1177/017084069301400303

Donate, M. J., & Guadamillas, F. (2010). The effect of organizational culture on knowledge management practices and innovation. *Knowledge and Process Management*, *17*(2), 82–94. doi:10.1002/kpm.344

Donate, M. J., & Sánchez de Pablo, J. D. (2015). The role of knowledge-oriented leadership in knowledge management practices and innovation. *Journal of Business Research*, *68*(2), 360–370. doi:10.1016/j.jbusres.2014.06.022

Dosi, G. (1998). Sources, Procedures, and Microeconomic Effects of Innovation. *Journal of Economic Literature*, *26*, 1120–1171.

Duncan, R. B. (1972). Characteristics of organizational environments and perceived environmental uncertainty. *Administrative Science Quarterly*, *17*(3), 313–327. doi:10.2307/2392145

Dutta, K., & Crossan, M. (2005). Entrepreneurial Opportunities: Understanding the Process Using the 4I Organizational Learning Framework. *Entrepreneurship and Practice*, *29*(4), 425–449. doi:10.1111/j.1540-6520.2005.00092.x

Dziadkiewicz, A. (2015). Social media and start-ups. *Zarządzanie Mediami*, *3*(4), 257–267.

Eaton, B., Elaluf-Calderwood, S., Sørensen, C., & Yoo, Y. (2011). Dynamic Structures of Control and Generativity in Digital Ecosystem Service Innovation: The Cases of the Apple and Google Mobile App Stores. In *Information Systems and Innovation Group Working Paper Series*. The London School of Economics and Political Science.

Eckhardt, J., & Shane, S. (2003). Opportunities and Entrepreneurship. *Journal of Management*, *29*(3), 333–349. doi:10.1177/014920630302900304

Edwards-Buckingham, C. D. (2009). Knowledge management as organizational strategy. In M. Khosrow-Pour (Ed.), *Encyclopedia of information science and technology* (2nd ed.; pp. 2343–2347). Hershey, PA: IGI Global. doi:10.4018/978-1-60566-026-4.ch371

Ein-Dor, P. (2009). Taxonomies of Knowledge. In M. E. Jennex (Ed.), Knowledge Management - Concepts, Methodologies, Tools and Applications (Vol. 1, pp. 163-170). Premier Reference, Information Science Reference, IGI Global.

Eisenhardt, K. M. (1989). Agency theory: An assessment and review. *Academy of Management Review*, *14*(1), 57–74.

El Said, G. R. (2015). Understanding knowledge management system antecedents of performance impact: Extending the task-technology fit model with intention to share knowledge construct. *Future Business Journal*, *1*(1/2), 75–87. doi:10.1016/j.fbj.2015.11.003

ElAtia, S., Ipperciel, D., & Zaiane, O. R. (2017). *Data mining and learning analytics: applications in educational research*. Hoboken, New Jersey: John Wiley & Sons, Inc.

Emami, A., & Dimov, D. (2017). Degree of innovation and the entrepreneurs' intention to create value: a comparative study of experienced and novice entrepreneurs. *Eurasian Business Review*, 1-22.

Emami, A., Dimov, D., & Paolucci, E. (2016). *Impact of opportunity confidence on new value creation intention: Does experience matter?*. Academic Press.

Endicott-Popovsky, B. (2013). *Information Security and Risk Management in Context*. Retrieved from www.coursetalk.com/providers/coursera/courses/information-security-and-risk-management-in-context

Engel, G. (2014, November 18). Deconstructing The Cyber Kill Chain. *DarkReading*. Retrieved March 15, 2017, from www.darkreading.com/attacks-breaches/deconstructing-the-cyber-kill-chain/a/d-id/1317542

Enkel, E., Perez-Freije, J., & Gassmann, O. (2005). Minimizing market risks through customer integration in new product development: Learning from bad practice. *Creativity and Innovation Management, 14*(4), 425–437. doi:10.1111/j.1467-8691.2005.00362.x

Erbes, A., Robert, V., & Yoguel, G. (2010). Capacities, innovation and feedbacks in production networks in Argentina. *Economics of Innovation and New Technology, 19*(8), 719–741. doi:10.1080/10438590903040807

Erdélyi, P. (2010). *The Matter of Entrepreneurial Learning: A Literature Review*. Boston, MA: Northteastern University.

Esquivel, R. V. (2013). From a Local Chapter to a Regional Catalyzer (Innovations Case Narrative: New Ventures México). *Innovations, 8*(3-4), 93-104.

Faems, D., Van Looy, B., & Debackere, K. (2005). Interorganizational collaboration and innovation: Toward a portfolio approach*. *Journal of Product Innovation Management, 22*(3), 238–250. doi:10.1111/j.0737-6782.2005.00120.x

Falkvinge, R. (2013). *Swarmwise: The Tactical Manual to Changing the World.* Retrieved from https://falkvinge.net/files/2013/04/Swarmwise-2013-by-Rick-Falkvinge-v1.1-2013Sep01.pdf

Fallah, A., Sadeghi, M., & Saeedi, K. (2012). Understanding entrepreneurship and media management in Iran. *Advances in Environmental Biology*, 1777-1780.

Faria, P., Lima, F., & Santos, R. (2010). Cooperation in Innovation Activities: The Importance of Partners. *Research Policy, 39*(8), 1082–1092. doi:10.1016/j.respol.2010.05.003

Farmer, W. M. (2009). Mathematical Knowledge Management. In M. E. Jennex (Ed.), Knowledge Management - Concepts, Methodologies, Tools and Applications (Vol. 1, pp. 2976-2983). Premier Reference, Information Science Reference, IGI Global.

Fauchart, E., & Von Hippel, E. (2008). Norms-based intellectual property systems: The case of French chefs. *Organization Science, 19*(2), 187–201. doi:10.1287/orsc.1070.0314

Felin, T., & Zenger, T. R. (2014). Closed or open innovation? Problem solving and the governance choice. *Research Policy, 43*(5), 914–925. doi:10.1016/j.respol.2013.09.006

Fernandez, V., Simo, P., Sallan, J. M., & Enache, M. (2013). Evolution of online discussion forum richness according to channel expansion theory: A longitudinal panel data analysis. *Computers & Education, 62*(0), 32–40. doi:10.1016/j.compedu.2012.10.020

Ferrier, M. B. (2013). Media entrepreneurship: Curriculum development and faculty perceptions of what students should know. *Journalism & Mass Communication Educator, 68*(3), 222–241. doi:10.1177/1077695813494833

Fidel, P., Schlesinger, W., & Cervera, A. (2015). Collaborating to innovate: Effects on customer knowledge management and performance. *Journal of Business Research, 68*(7), 1426–1428. doi:10.1016/j.jbusres.2015.01.026

Fiol, M. C., & Lyles, M. A. (1985). Organizational learning. *Academy of Management Review*, *10*, 803–813.

FlatIron Technologies. (2014). *Overview of Patch Managemnet Best Practices for Information Systems*. FlatIron Technologies, LLC.

Forbes, L. H., & Ahmed, S. M. (2011). Information and Communications Technology - Building Information Modeling. In L. H. Forbes, & S. M. Ahmed (Eds.), Modern Construction: Lean Project Delivery and Integrated Practices. Taylor & Francis Group, LLC.

Ford, D., & Johnsen, T. (2001). Managing networks of supplier and customer relationships for technological innovation: initial case study. *17th IMP Conference Proceedings*.

Foss, N. J., Laursen, K., & Pedersen, T. (2011). Linking Customer Interaction and Innovation: The Mediating Role of New Organizational Practices. *Organization Science*, *22*(4), 980–999. doi:10.1287/orsc.1100.0584

Foss, N. J., Lyngsie, J., & Zahra, S. A. (2013). The Role of External Knowledge Sources and Organizational Design in the Process of Opportunity Exploitation. *Strategic Management Journal*, *34*(12), 1453–1471. doi:10.1002/smj.2135

Freytag, V. (2002). Innovation in co-operation and co-operation innovation. *18th IMP Conference Proceedings*.

Frick, J., & Laudal, T. (2016). *COLIBRI: Blended Learning In An Innovative Transnational Approach*. Paper presented at the Danning og Utdanning- mellom klassiske idealer og ytre relevans, Stavanger, Norway.

Friedrichsen, M., Zarea, H., Tayebi, A., & Abad, F. A. S. (2017). Competitive strategies of knowledge and innovation commercialization: A unified SWOT and fuzzy AHP approach. *AD-Minister*, (30), 45-72.

Fritsch, M., & Lukas, R. (2001). Who co-operates on R&D?. *Research Policy*, *30*(2), 297–312. doi:10.1016/S0048-7333(99)00115-8

Fuzi, A. (2015). Co-working spaces for promoting entrepreneurship in sparse regions: The case of South Wales. *Regional Studies. Regional Science*, *2*(1), 462–469.

Gagnon, M. P., Payne-Gagnon, J., Fortin, J. P., Pare, G., Cote, J., & Courcy, F. (2015). A learning organization in the service of knowledge management among nurses: A case study. *International Journal of Information Management*, *35*(5), 636–642. doi:10.1016/j.ijinfomgt.2015.05.001

Galbraith, C. S. (1990). Transferring Core Manufacturing Technologies in High-Technology Firms. *California Management Review*, *32*(4), 56–70. doi:10.2307/41166628

Galbraith, J. R. (1973). *Designing Complex Organizations* (1st ed.). Boston, MA: Addison-Wesley Longman Publishing Co., Inc.

Ganamotse, G. N., Samuelsson, M., Abankwah, R. M., Anthony, T., & Mphela, T. (2017). The Emerging Properties of Business Accelerators: The Case of Botswana, Namibia and Uganda Global Business Labs. *Journal of Entrepreneurship and Innovation in Emerging Economies*, *3*(1), 16–40. doi:10.1177/2393957516684469

Garcia, D. J. M. (2017). *Do cohorts accelerate? Startups accelerators and unentrepreneurial learning*. Doctoral dissertation.

Garcia-Alvarez, M. T. (2015). Analysis of the effects of ICTs in knowledge management and innovation: The case of Zara group. *Computers in Human Behavior*, *51*, 994–1002. doi:10.1016/j.chb.2014.10.007

García-Sánchez, E., García-Morales, V. J., & Bolívar-Ramos, M. T. (2017). The influence of top management support for ICTs on organisational performance through knowledge acquisition, transfer, and utilisation. *Review of Managerial Science*, *11*(1), 19–51. doi:10.1007/s11846-015-0179-3

Gawer, A. (2009). Platform dynamics and strategies: From products to services. *Platforms, Markets and Innovation*, 45-76.

Gawer, A., & Cusumano, M. A. (2002). *Platform Leadership How Intel, Palm, Cisco and Others Drive Industry Innovation*. Cambridge, MA: Harvard Press.

Gawer, A., & Cusumano, M. A. (2012). How companies become platform leaders. MIT. *Sloan Management Review*, 49.

Gemunden, H. G., Ritter, T., & Heydebreck, P. (1996). Network configuration and innovation success: An empirical analysis in German high-tech industries. *International Journal of Research in Marketing*, *13*(5), 449–462. doi:10.1016/S0167-8116(96)00026-2

Ghazawneh, A., & Henfridsson, O. (2010). Governing third-party development through platform boundary resources. *ICIS 2010 Proceedings*. AIS Electronic Library (AISeL).

Ghazawneh, A., & Henfridsson, O. (2013). Balancing Platform Control and External Contribution in Third-Party Development: The Boundary Resources Model. *Information Systems Journal*, (23), 173–192.

Gibb, A. A. (2002). In Pursuit of a New Enterprise and Entrepreneurship Paradigm for Learning: Creative Destruction, New Values, New Ways of Doing Things and New Combinations of Knowledge. *International Journal of Management Reviews*, *4*(3), 213–232. doi:10.1111/1468-2370.00086

Gibbs, J. L., Kim, H., & Boyraz, M. (2017). Virtual teams. In C. R. Scott, L. Lewis, R. L. Barker, J. Keyton, T. Kuhn, & P. Turner (Eds.), The International Encyclopedia of Organizational Communications (pp. 1-14). Wiley. doi:10.1002/9781118955567.wbieoc215

Girard, M., & Stark, D. (2002). Distributing intelligence and organizing diversity in new media projects. *Sociedade e Estado*, *17*(1), 153–192. doi:10.1590/S0102-69922002000100009

GitHub. (2017). *Guthub*. Retrieved from Github: https://github.com

Goldsmith, A. (2015). Electoral Violence in Africa Revisited. *Terrorism and Political Violence*, *27*(5), 818–837. doi:10.1080/09546553.2013.863184

Gottschalk, P. (2007). *Knowledge management systems: Value shop creation*. Hershey, PA: IGI Global. doi:10.4018/978-1-59904-060-8

Grabski, J. (2009). Making fashion in the city: A case study of tailors and designers in Dakar. *Senegal. Fashion Theory*, *13*(2), 215–242. doi:10.2752/175174109X414268

Graham, B. (2010). *Unto the Hills: A Daily Devotion*. Thomas Nelson, Inc.

Granovetter, M. S. (1973). The strength of weak ties. *American Journal of Sociology*, *78*(6), 1360–1380. doi:10.1086/225469

Greenberg, J., Brinsfield, C. T., & Edwards, M. S. (2007). *Silence as deviant work behavior: The peril of words unspoken*. Symposium presented at the annual meeting of the Society for Industrial and Organizational Psychology, New York, NY.

Gressgård, L. J. (2015). Antecedents of knowledge exchange systems usage: Motivational and work environment factors. *Knowledge and Process Management*, *22*(2), 112–125. doi:10.1002/kpm.1471

Greve, N. (2011, Nov 11). Civil Engineering shortage leads to infrastructure deterioration. *Engineering News*.

Grigoriou, K., & Rothaermel, F. T. (2016). Organizing for knowledge generation: Internal knowledge networks and the contingent effect of external knowledge sourcing. *Strategic Management Journal*.

Grimpe, C., & Sofka, W. (2009). Search patterns and absorptive capacity: Low-and high-technology sectors in European countries. *Research Policy*, *38*(3), 495–506. doi:10.1016/j.respol.2008.10.006

Grovo. (2017). *Future-proof your workforce with microlearning*. Retrieved from http://blog.grovo.com/ebook-futureproof-workforce-microlearning/

GSM Association Report. (2015). *The Mobile Economy (Europe 2015)*. Retrieved from http://www.gsma.com/mobileeconomy/archive/GSMA_ME_Europe_2015.pdf

Guadamillas-Gomez, F., & Donate-Manzanares, M. J. (2009). Knowledge management strategies implementation in innovation intensive firms. In D. Jemielniak & J. Kociatkiewicz (Eds.), *Handbook of research on knowledge-intensive organizations* (pp. 169–192). Hershey, PA: IGI Global. doi:10.4018/978-1-60566-176-6.ch011

Gyamfi, A. (2016). The Impact of Media Richness on the Usage of Web 2.0 Services for Knowledge Transfer. *Int. J. E-Services Mob. Appl.*, *8*(2), 21–37. https://doi.org/10.4018/IJESMA.2016040102

Gyamfi, A. (2016). The Impact of Media Richness on the Usage of Web 2.0 Services for Knowledge Transfer. *International Journal of E-Services and Mobile Applications*, *8*(2), 21–37. doi:10.4018/IJESMA.2016040102

Haag, M. (2010). *Personal knowledge development in online learning environments: A personal value perspective*. Retrieved from http://uobrep.openrepository.com/uobrep/handle/10547/134937

Haapalainen, P., & Kantola, J. (2015). Taxonomy of knowledge management in open innovations. *Procedia Manufacturing*, *3*, 688–695. doi:10.1016/j.promfg.2015.07.307

Haesli, A., & Boxall, P. (2005). When knowledge management meets HR strategy: An exploration of personalization-retention and codification-recruitment configurations. *International Journal of Human Resource Management*, *16*(11), 1955–1975. doi:10.1080/09585190500314680

Hagedorn, S. (2012). *How to Create on iBooks*. Author.

Hair, J. F., Anderson, R. E., Tatham, R. L., & Black, W. C. (1998). *Multivariate analysis*. Englewood: Prentice Hall International.

Hair, J. F., Hult, G. T. M., Ringle, C., & Sarstedt, M. (2013). *A Primer on Partial Least Squares Structural Equation Modeling (PLS-SEM)*. SAGE Publications.

Haldin-Herrgard, T. (2000). Difficulties in diffusion of tacit knowledge in organizations. *Journal of Intellectual Capital*, *1*(4), 357–365. doi:10.1108/14691930010359252

Handzic, M., Lagumdzija, A., & Celjo, A. (2009). Knowledge management technology in local government. In M. Khosrow-Pour (Ed.), *Encyclopedia of information science and technology* (2nd ed.; pp. 2373–2379). Hershey, PA: IGI Global. doi:10.4018/978-1-60566-026-4.ch376

Hannan, M. T., & Freeman, J. (1977). The population ecology of organizations. *American Journal of Sociology*, 82: Hannan, M. T., & Freeman, J. (1984). Structural inertia and organizational change. *American Sociological Review*, *49*(2), 149–164. doi:10.2307/2095567

Hanna, R., Rohm, A., & Crittenden, V. L. (2011). Were all connected: The power of the social media ecosystem. *Business Horizons*, *54*(3), 265–273. doi:10.1016/j.bushor.2011.01.007

Hansen, P. K., Gertsen, F., Larsen, J. H., & Frick, J. (2002). Does Efficiency and Project based Learning comply? Paper presented at the Norddesign 2002, Trondheim, Norway.

Hanseth, O., & Lyytinen, K. (2010). Design theory for dynamic complexity in information infrastructures: The case of building internet. *Journal of Information Technology*, *28*(1), 1–19. doi:10.1057/jit.2009.19

Hatum, A., & Pettigrew, A. M. (2006). Determinants of Organizational Flexibility: A Study in an Emerging Economy. *British Journal of Management*, *17*(2), 115–137. doi:10.1111/j.1467-8551.2005.00469.x

Henan, M. T., & Freeman, J. (1977). The Population Ecology of Organizations. *American Journal of Sociology*, *82*(5).

Henderson, R., & Clark, K. (1996). Architectural innovation: The reconfiguration of existing product technologies and the failure of established firms. *Administrative Science Quarterly*, *35*(1), 9–30. doi:10.2307/2393549

Henkel, J., Baldwin, C. Y., & Shih, W. (2013). IP Modularity: Profiting from innovation by aligning product architecture with intellectual property. *California Management Review*, *55*(4), 65–82. doi:10.1525/cmr.2013.55.4.65

Henkel, J., Schöberl, S., & Alexy, O. (2014). The emergence of openness: How and why firms adopt selective revealing in open innovation. *Research Policy*, *43*(5), 879–890. doi:10.1016/j.respol.2013.08.014

Henseler, J., Ringle, C. M., & Sinkovics, R. R. (2009). The use of partial least squares path modeling in international marketing. In New Challenges to International Marketing (Vol. 20, pp. 277–319). Emerald Group Publishing Limited. Retrieved from http://www.emeraldinsight.com/doi/abs/10.1108/S1474-7979%282009%290000020014

Herbsleb, J. D., & Moitra, D. (2001). Globalization and Software. *IEEE Software*, *18*(2), 16–20. doi:10.1109/52.914732

Herschel, R. T. (2009). Chief knowledge officers. In M. Khosrow-Pour (Ed.), *Encyclopedia of information science and technology* (2nd ed.; pp. 527–531). Hershey, PA: IGI Global. doi:10.4018/978-1-60566-026-4.ch086

Herzhoff, J. (2011). *Unfolding the Convergence Paradox: The Case of Mobile Voice-Over-IP in the UK* (Unpublished PhD Thesis). London School of Economics and Political Science.

Herzhoff, J., Elaluf-Calderwood, S., & Sørensen, C. (2010). Convergence, Conflicts, and Control Points: A Systems-Theoretical Analysis of Mobile VoIP in the UK. *Proceedings of joint 9th International Conference on Mobile Business (ICMB 2010) and 9th Global Mobility Roundtable (GMR 2010)*.

Heydebrand, W., & Miron, A. (2002). Constructing innovativeness in new-media start-up firms. *Environment & Planning A*, *34*(11), 1951–1984. doi:10.1068/a3558

Hinchcliffe, D. (2007). *The state of Enterprise 2.0*. Retrieved July 15, 2015, from http://www.zdnet.com/article/the-state-of-enterprise-2-0/

Hoag, A. (2008). Measuring Media Entrepreneurship 1. *The International Journal on Media Management*, *10*(2), 74–80. doi:10.1080/14241270802000496

Hodgkinson, G. P., & Healey, M. P. (2011). Psychological foundations of dynamic capabilities: Reflexion and reflection in strategic management. *Strategic Management Journal*, *32*(13), 1500–1516. doi:10.1002/smj.964

Hong, K. S. (2002). Relationships between students and instructional variables with satisfaction and learning from a Web-based course. *The Internet and Higher Education*, *5*(3), 267–281. doi:10.1016/S1096-7516(02)00105-7

Hsiao, Y. C., Chen, C. J., & Chang, S. C. (2011). Knowledge management capacity and organizational performance: The social interaction view. *International Journal of Manpower*, *32*(5/6), 645–660. doi:10.1108/01437721111158242

Huang, X., Gattiker, T. F., & Schwarz, J. L. (2008). Interpersonal trust formation during the supplier selection process: The role of the communication channel. *Journal of Supply Chain Management, 44*(3), 53–75. doi:10.1111/j.1745-493X.2008.00066.x

Huber, G. P. (1991). A Theory of the Effects of Advanced Information Technologies on Organizational Design, Intelligence, and Decision Making. *Academy of Management Review, 15*, 47–71.

Hull, R., Coombs, R., & Peltu, M. (2000). Knowledge management practices for innovation: An audit tool for improvement. *International Journal of Technology Management, 20*(5-8), 633–656. doi:10.1504/IJTM.2000.002885

Hu, M. M., Horng, J., & Sun, Y. C. (2009). Hospitality teams: Knowledge sharing and service innovation performance. *Tourism Management, 30*(1), 41–50. doi:10.1016/j.tourman.2008.04.009

Humphreys, L. (2005). Reframing social groups, closure, and stabilization in the social construction of technology. *Social Epistemology, 19*(2-3), 231–253. doi:10.1080/02691720500145449

Hutchins, E. (1991). *The social organization of distributed cognition.* Retrieved from https://www.researchgate.net/publication/232427152_The_social_organization_of_distributed_cognition

Hwang, J., Kim, E., & Kim, S. (2009). Factors affecting open technological innovation in open source software companies in Korea. *Innovation-Management Policy & Practice, 11*(3), 279–290. doi:10.5172/impp.11.3.279

Iacoban, R., Reynolds, R. G., & Brewster, J. (2013). *Cultural swarms: Modeling the impact of culture on social interaction and problem solving.* In *2003 IEEE Swarm Intelligence Symposium, SIS 2003 - Proceedings* (pp. 205-211). Institute of Electrical and Electronics Engineers Inc. Doi:10.1109/SIS.2003.1202270

Ibrus, I. (2015). The replacement of media policies with (media) entrepreneurship policies: A view from Europes periphery. *International Journal of Digital Television, 6*(3), 311–318. doi:10.1386/jdtv.6.3.311_1

Inemek, A., & Matthyssens, P. (2013). The impact of buyer–supplier relationships on supplier innovativeness: An empirical study in cross-border supply networks. *Industrial Marketing Management, 42*(4), 580–594. doi:10.1016/j.indmarman.2012.10.011

Inkpen, A. C., & Dinur, A. (1998). Knowledge Management Processes and International Joint Ventures. *Organization Science, 9*(4), 454–468. doi:10.1287/orsc.9.4.454

Inkpen, A. C., & Tsang, E. W. K. (2005). Social capital, networks, and knowledge transfer. *Academy of Management Review, 30*(1), 146–165. doi:10.5465/AMR.2005.15281445

Intelligence & National Security Alliance. (2015). *Cyber Intelligence: Preparing Today's Talents for Tomorrow's Threats.* INSA, Cyber Intelligence Task Force.

Jackson, S. E., Schuler, R. S., & Jiang, K. (2014). An aspirational framework for strategic human resource management. *The Academy of Management Annals*, *8*(1), 1–56. doi:10.1080/19416520.2014.872335

Jarvenpaa, S. L., & Välikangas, L. (2014). Opportunity Creation in Innovation Networks: Interactive revealing practices. *California Management Review*, *57*(1), 67–87. doi:10.1525/cmr.2014.57.1.67

Jiang, K., Takeuchi, R., & Lepak, D. P. (2013). Where do we go from here? New perspectives on the black box in strategic human resource management research. *Journal of Management Studies*, *50*(8), 1448–1480.

Johnson, D. (2017). *High Impact Learning Organisation: Maturity Model.* Bersin by Deloitte. Retrieved from http://www.bersin.com/Practice/Detail.aspx?docid=20893

Jones, S. (2005). Community-based ecotourism: The significance of social capital. *Annals of Tourism Research*, *32*(2), 303–324. doi:10.1016/j.annals.2004.06.007

Jorde, T. M., & Teece, D. J. (1990). Innovation and Cooperation: Implications for Competition and Antitrust. *The Journal of Economic Perspectives*, *4*(3), 75–96. doi:10.1257/jep.4.3.75

Juárez, B., III. (2013). *Building innovation-based entrepreneurial communities: an assessment of practitioners' interactions with academically driven curriculum* (Doctoral dissertation). Massachusetts Institute of Technology.

Junni, P., & Sarala, R. M. (2013). The role of absorptive capacity in acquisition knowledge transfer. *Thunderbird International Business Review*, *55*(4), 419–438. doi:10.1002/tie.21554

Kahneman, D. (2013). *Thinking Fast and Slow*. Farrar, Straus and Giroux.

Kaiser, C., & Bodendorf, F. (2012). Mining consumer dialog in online forums. *Internet Research*, *22*(3), 275–297. doi:10.1108/10662241211235653

Kamasak, R., Yavuz, M., & Ozturk, T. Y. (2016). *Reducing Risk Through Strategic Flexibility and Implementation Leadership in High-Velocity Markets Global Business Strategies in Crisis, Contributions to Management Science*. Springer International Publishing AG 2017.

Kaminski, J. (2011). Theory Applied to Informatics - Lewin's Change Theory. *CJNI: Canadian Journal of Nursing Informatics, 6*(1). Retrieved from www.cjni.net/journal/?p=1210

Kane, G. C. (2017). The evolutionary implications of social media for organizational knowledge management. *Information and Organization*, *27*(1), 37–46. doi:10.1016/j.infoandorg.2017.01.001

Kang, S. W. (2016). Knowledge withholding: Psychological hindrance to the innovation diffusion within an organisation. *Knowledge Management Research & Practice*, *14*(1), 144–149. doi:10.1057/kmrp.2014.24

Kankanhalli, A., & Tan, B. C. (2008). Knowledge Managemnet Metrics: A Review and Directions of Future Research. In M. E. Jennex (Ed.), Knowledge Management: Concepts, Methodologies, Tools and Applications (Vol. 6, pp. 3409-3420). IGI Global.

Kaplan, A. M., & Michael, H. (2010). Users of the world, unite! The challenges and opportunities of social media. *Business Horizons*, *53*(1), 59–68. doi:10.1016/j.bushor.2009.09.003

Kapp, K. M. (2012). *The Gamification of Learning and Instruction: Game-based methods and strategies for training and education*. Wiley.

Karikari-Apau. (2012). *Ghana president re-elected, a result opposition claims was 'manipulated'*. Retrieved from http://edition.cnn.com/2012/12/09/world/africa/ghana-elections/

Karkoulian, S., Canaan Messarra, L., & McCarthy, R. (2013). The intriguing art of knowledge management and its relation to learning organizations. *Journal of Knowledge Management*, *17*(4), 511–526. doi:10.1108/JKM-03-2013-0102

Kasemsap, K. (2014a). The role of social networking in global business environments. In P. Smith & T. Cockburn (Eds.), *Impact of emerging digital technologies on leadership in global business* (pp. 183–201). Hershey, PA: IGI Global. doi:10.4018/978-1-4666-6134-9.ch010

Kasemsap, K. (2014b). Strategic innovation management: An integrative framework and causal model of knowledge management, strategic orientation, organizational innovation, and organizational performance. In P. Ordóñez de Pablos & R. Tennyson (Eds.), *Strategic approaches for human capital management and development in a turbulent economy* (pp. 102–116). Hershey, PA: IGI Global. doi:10.4018/978-1-4666-4530-1.ch007

Kasemsap, K. (2014c). The role of knowledge sharing on organisational innovation: An integrated framework. In L. Al-Hakim & C. Jin (Eds.), *Quality innovation: Knowledge, theory, and practices* (pp. 247–271). Hershey, PA: IGI Global. doi:10.4018/978-1-4666-4769-5.ch012

Kasemsap, K. (2014d). The role of social capital in higher education institutions. In N. Baporikar (Ed.), *Handbook of research on higher education in the MENA region: Policy and practice* (pp. 119–147). Hershey, PA: IGI Global. doi:10.4018/978-1-4666-6198-1.ch007

Kasemsap, K. (2014e). The role of social media in the knowledge-based organizations. In I. Lee (Ed.), *Integrating social media into business practice, applications, management, and models* (pp. 254–275). Hershey, PA: IGI Global. doi:10.4018/978-1-4666-6182-0.ch013

Kasemsap, K. (2015). Developing a framework of human resource management, organizational learning, knowledge management capability, and organizational performance. In P. Ordoñez de Pablos, L. Turró, R. Tennyson, & J. Zhao (Eds.), *Knowledge management for competitive advantage during economic crisis* (pp. 164–193). Hershey, PA: IGI Global. doi:10.4018/978-1-4666-6457-9.ch010

Kasemsap, K. (2016a). The roles of knowledge management and organizational innovation in global business. In G. Jamil, J. Poças-Rascão, F. Ribeiro, & A. Malheiro da Silva (Eds.), *Handbook of research on information architecture and management in modern organizations* (pp. 130–153). Hershey, PA: IGI Global. doi:10.4018/978-1-4666-8637-3.ch006

Kasemsap, K. (2016b). Analyzing the roles of human capital and competency in global business. In S. Sen, A. Bhattacharya, & R. Sen (Eds.), *International perspectives on socio-economic development in the era of globalization* (pp. 1–29). Hershey, PA: IGI Global. doi:10.4018/978-1-4666-9908-3.ch001

Kasemsap, K. (2016c). Advocating entrepreneurship education and knowledge management in global business. In N. Baporikar (Ed.), *Handbook of research on entrepreneurship in the contemporary knowledge-based global economy* (pp. 313–339). Hershey, PA: IGI Global. doi:10.4018/978-1-4666-8798-1.ch014

Kasemsap, K. (2016d). The roles of e-learning, organizational learning, and knowledge management in the learning organizations. In E. Railean, G. Walker, A. Elçi, & L. Jackson (Eds.), *Handbook of research on applied learning theory and design in modern education* (pp. 786–816). Hershey, PA: IGI Global. doi:10.4018/978-1-4666-9634-1.ch039

Kasemsap, K. (2016e). The roles of lifelong learning and knowledge management in global higher education. In P. Ordóñez de Pablos & R. Tennyson (Eds.), *Impact of economic crisis on education and the next-generation workforce* (pp. 71–100). Hershey, PA: IGI Global. doi:10.4018/978-1-4666-9455-2.ch004

Kasemsap, K. (2016f). Creating product innovation strategies through knowledge management in global business. In A. Goel & P. Singhal (Eds.), *Product innovation through knowledge management and social media strategies* (pp. 330–357). Hershey, PA: IGI Global. doi:10.4018/978-1-4666-9607-5.ch015

Kasemsap, K. (2016g). The roles of information technology and knowledge management in global tourism. In A. Nedelea, M. Korstanje, & B. George (Eds.), *Strategic tools and methods for promoting hospitality and tourism services* (pp. 109–138). Hershey, PA: IGI Global. doi:10.4018/978-1-4666-9761-4.ch006

Kasemsap, K. (2016h). A unified framework of organizational perspectives and knowledge management and their impact on job performance. In A. Normore, L. Long, & M. Javidi (Eds.), *Handbook of research on effective communication, leadership, and conflict resolution* (pp. 267–297). Hershey, PA: IGI Global. doi:10.4018/978-1-4666-9970-0.ch015

Kasemsap, K. (2016i). Utilizing communities of practice to facilitate knowledge sharing in the digital age. In S. Buckley, G. Majewski, & A. Giannakopoulos (Eds.), *Organizational knowledge facilitation through communities of practice in emerging markets* (pp. 198–224). Hershey, PA: IGI Global. doi:10.4018/978-1-5225-0013-1.ch011

Kasemsap, K. (2017a). Investigating the roles of neuroscience and knowledge management in higher education. In S. Mukerji & P. Tripathi (Eds.), *Handbook of research on administration, policy, and leadership in higher education* (pp. 112–140). Hershey, PA: IGI Global. doi:10.4018/978-1-5225-0672-0.ch006

Kasemsap, K. (2017b). Mastering knowledge management in academic libraries. In B. Gunjal (Ed.), *Managing knowledge and scholarly assets in academic libraries* (pp. 27–55). Hershey, PA: IGI Global. doi:10.4018/978-1-5225-1741-2.ch002

Kasemsap, K. (2017c). The fundamentals of human capital. In A. Bhattacharya (Ed.), *Strategic human capital development and management in emerging economies* (pp. 59–89). Hershey, PA: IGI Global. doi:10.4018/978-1-5225-1974-4.ch004

Kasemsap, K. (2017d). The fundamentals of social capital. In G. Koç, M. Claes, & B. Christiansen (Eds.), *Cultural influences on architecture* (pp. 259–292). Hershey, PA: IGI Global. doi:10.4018/978-1-5225-1744-3.ch010

Kasemsap, K. (2017e). Exploring the role of organizational culture in modern organizations. In R. Styron Jr & J. Styron (Eds.), *Comprehensive problem-solving and skill development for next-generation leaders* (pp. 116–138). Hershey, PA: IGI Global. doi:10.4018/978-1-5225-1968-3.ch006

Kasemsap, K. (2017f). Digital storytelling and digital literacy: Advanced issues and prospects. In D. Loveless, P. Sullivan, K. Dredger, & J. Burns (Eds.), *Deconstructing the education-industrial complex in the digital age* (pp. 151–171). Hershey, PA: IGI Global. doi:10.4018/978-1-5225-2101-3.ch009

Kasemsap, K. (2017g). Electronic learning: Theory and applications. In P. Vu, S. Fredrickson, & C. Moore (Eds.), *Handbook of research on innovative pedagogies and technologies for online learning in higher education* (pp. 367–392). Hershey, PA: IGI Global. doi:10.4018/978-1-5225-1851-8.ch016

Kasemsap, K. (2017h). Organizational learning: Advanced issues and trends. In A. Bencsik (Ed.), *Knowledge management initiatives and strategies in small and medium enterprises* (pp. 42–66). Hershey, PA: IGI Global. doi:10.4018/978-1-5225-1642-2.ch003

Kasemsap, K. (2017i). Fundamentals of talent management: Capitalizing on intellectual assets. In M. Mupepi (Ed.), *Effective talent management strategies for organizational success* (pp. 260–282). Hershey, PA: IGI Global. doi:10.4018/978-1-5225-1961-4.ch017

Kathan, W., Hutter, K., Füller, J., & Hautz, J. (2015). Reciprocity vs. Free-Riding in Innovation Contest Communities. *Creativity and Innovation Management*, *24*(3), 537–549. doi:10.1111/caim.12107

Katz, M., & Shapiro, C. (1994). Systems competition and network effects. *The Journal of Economic Perspectives*, *8*(2), 93–115. doi:10.1257/jep.8.2.93

Kettunen, J., Hautala, J., & Kantola, M. (2009). Knowledge management with partners in a dynamic information environment. In A. Cartelli & M. Palma (Eds.), *Encyclopedia of information communication technology* (pp. 503–509). Hershey, PA: IGI Global. doi:10.4018/978-1-59904-845-1.ch066

Khajeheian, D. (2017). Media entrepreneurship: a consensual definition. *AD-Minister*, (30), 91-113.

Khajeheian, D. (2013). New venture creation in social media platform; towards a framework for media entrepreneurship. In *Handbook of social media management* (pp. 125–142). Springer Berlin Heidelberg. doi:10.1007/978-3-642-28897-5_8

Khajeheian, D. (2016). Audience commodification: A source of innovation in business models. *Technology Innovation Management Review*, *6*(8), 40–47.

Khajeheian, D. (2017). Media entrepreneurship: A consensual definition. *Administer*, *30*, 91–113.

Khajeheian, D., & Tadayoni, R. (2016). User innovation in public service broadcasts: Creating public value by media entrepreneurship. *International Journal of Technoloy Transfer and Commercialisation*, *14*(2), 117–131. doi:10.1504/IJTTC.2016.081635

Khandelwal, V., & Gottschalk, P. (2004). Information technology support for interorganizational knowledge transfer: An empirical study of law firms in Norway and Australia. In M. Khosrow-Pour (Ed.), *Advanced topics in information resources management* (Vol. 3, pp. 262–274). Hershey, PA: Idea Group Publishing. doi:10.4018/978-1-59140-253-4.ch012

Kim, S., & Soergel, D. (2006). Selectng and measuring task characteristics as indpendent variables. The American Society of Information Science and Technology, 42(1).

Kim, J. H., & Wagman, L. (2014). Portfolio size and information disclosure: An analysis of startup accelerators. *Journal of Corporate Finance*, *29*, 520–534. doi:10.1016/j.jcorpfin.2014.10.017

Kim, P. (2014). *Massive open online courses: The MOOC revolution*. New York: Routledge.

Kim, W. (2015). The current transition in management of technology education: The case of Korea. *Technological Forecasting and Social Change*, *100*, 5–20. doi:10.1016/j.techfore.2015.03.018

King, W. R. (2009). Knowledge Management and Organizational Learning. *Annals of Information Systems, 4*.

King, W. R., Chung, T. R., & Haney, M. H. (2008). Knowledge management and organizational learning. *Omega*, *36*(2), 167–172. doi:10.1016/j.omega.2006.07.004

Kirkman, B. L., Cordery, J. L., Mathieu, J., Rosen, B., & Kukenberger, M. (2013). Global organizational communities of practice: The effects of nationality diversity, psychological safety, and media richness on community performance. *Human Relations*, *66*(3), 333–362. doi:10.1177/0018726712464076

Kirsch, L. J. (1996). The management of complex tasks in organizations: Controlling the systems development process. *Organization Science*, *7*(1), 1–21. doi:10.1287/orsc.7.1.1

Kirsch, P., Hine, A., & Maybury, T. (2015). A model for the implementation of industry-wide knowledge sharing to improve risk management practice. *Safety Science*, *80*, 66–76. doi:10.1016/j.ssci.2015.07.009

Kirzner, I. M. (1973). *Competition and entrepreneurship*. Chicago, IL: University of Chicago Press.

Kitsing, M. (2014). Internet Voting in Estonia. In *Proceedings of the 2014 Conference on Electronic Governance and Open Society: Challenges in Eurasia* (pp. 137-144). ACM.

Kjersdam, F., & Enemark, S. (1997). The Aalborg experiment project innovation in university education (3rd ed.). Faculty of Technology and Science Aalborg University Press.

Klitmøller, A., & Lauring, J. (2013). When global virtual teams share knowledge: Media Richness, cultural difference and language commonality. *Journal of World Business*, *48*(3), 398–406. doi:10.1016/j.jwb.2012.07.023

Kohler, T. (2016). Corporate accelerators: Building bridges between corporations and startups. *Business Horizons*, *59*(3), 347–357. doi:10.1016/j.bushor.2016.01.008

Kojo, I., & Nenonen, S. (2016). Typologies for co-working spaces in Finland–what and how? *Facilities*, *34*(5/6), 302–313. doi:10.1108/F-08-2014-0066

Kolb, D. (1984). *Experiential Learning: Experience as the Source of Learning and Development*. Prentice Hall inc.

Kolmos, A., Fink, F. K., & Krogh, L. (2004). *The Aalborg PBL Model: Progress, Diversity and Challenges*. Aalborg, Denmark: Aalborg University Press.

Koo, C., Wati, Y., & Jung, J. J. (2011). Examination of how social aspects moderate the relationship between task characteristics and usage of social communication technologies (SCTs) in organizations. *International Journal of Information Management*, *31*(5), 445–459. doi:10.1016/j.ijinfomgt.2011.01.003

Koza, M. P., & Lewin, A. Y. (1998). The co-evolution of strategic alliances. *Organization Science*, *9*(3), 255–264. doi:10.1287/orsc.9.3.255

Kruger, J., & Dunning, D. (1999). Unskilled and Unaware of It: How Difficulties in Recognizing Ones Own Incompetence Lead to Inflated Self-Assessments. *Journal of Personality and Social Psychology*, *77*(6), 1121–1134. doi:10.1037/0022-3514.77.6.1121 PMID:10626367

Krumina, I., Krumins, G., & Rozentale, S. (2015). Vidzeme region of Latvia: Knowledge management in micro enterprises. *Procedia: Social and Behavioral Sciences*, *213*, 781–786. doi:10.1016/j.sbspro.2015.11.475

Kumar, S., & Walia, E. (2011). Analysis of Electronic Voting System In Various Countries. *International Journal on Computer Science and Engineering*, *3*(5), 1825–1830.

Kuo, M. S., & Liang, G. S. (2012). A soft computing method of performance evaluation with MCDM based on interval-valued fuzzy numbers. *Applied Soft Computing*, *12*(1), 476–485. doi:10.1016/j.asoc.2011.08.020

Kuo, Y. K., & Ye, K. D. (2010). How employees' perception of information technology application and their knowledge management capacity influence organisational performance. *Behaviour & Information Technology*, *29*(3), 287–303. doi:10.1080/01449290701852166

Kurtz, C. F., & Snowden, D. J. (2003). *The new dynamics of strategy: Sense-making in a complex and complicated world.* Retrieved from http://alumni.media.mit.edu/~brooks/storybiz/kurtz.pdf

Labafi. (2017). Knowledge hiding as an obstacle of innovation in organizations a qualitative study of software industry. *AD-Minister, 30*, 131-145.

Lai, J. Y., Wang, C. T., & Chou, C. Y. (2009). How knowledge map fit and personalization affect success of KMS in high-tech firms. *Technovation, 29*(4), 313–324. doi:10.1016/j.technovation.2008.10.007

Lai, J., Lui, S. S., & Tsang, E. W. K. (2016). Intrafirm knowledge transfer and employee innovative behavior: The role of total and balanced knowledge flows. *Journal of Product Innovation Management, 33*(1), 90–103. doi:10.1111/jpim.12262

Lall, S., Bowles, L., & Baird, R. (2013). Bridging the "Pioneer Gap": The Role of Accelerators in Launching High-Impact Enterprises. *Innovations, 8*(3-4), 105-137.

Langley, A. (1999). Strategies for theorizing from process data. *Academy of Management Review, 24*(4), 691–710.

Larusson, J. A., & White, B. (2014). *Learning analytics: from research to practice.* New York: Springer. doi:10.1007/978-1-4614-3305-7

Laursen, K., & Salter, A. (2006). Open for Innovation: The role of openness in explaining innovative performance among UK manufacturing firms. *Strategic Management Journal, 27*(2), 131–150. doi:10.1002/smj.507

Laursen, K., & Salter, A. J. (2014). The paradox of openness: Appropriability, external search and collaboration. *Research Policy, 43*(5), 867–878. doi:10.1016/j.respol.2013.10.004

Leal-Rodríguez, A. L., Roldán, J. L., Ariza-Montes, J. A., & Leal-Millán, A. (2014). From potential absorptive capacity to innovation outcomes in project teams: The conditional mediating role of the realized absorptive capacity in a relational learning context. *International Journal of Project Management, 32*(6), 894–907. doi:10.1016/j.ijproman.2014.01.005

Lee, A. H. I., Chen, H. H., & Chen, S. (2015). Suitable organization forms for knowledge management to attain sustainable competitive advantage in the renewable energy industry. *Energy, 89*, 1057–1064. doi:10.1016/j.energy.2015.06.047

Lehaney, B., Clarke, S., Coakes, E., & Jack, G. (2004). Knowledge management in more detail. In B. Lehaney, S. Clarke, E. Coakes, & G. Jack (Eds.), *Beyond knowledge management* (pp. 12–30). Hershey, PA: Idea Group Publishing. doi:10.4018/978-1-59140-180-3.ch002

Leidner, D., & Alavi, M. (2009). The role of culture in knowledge management: A case study of two global firms. In N. Kock (Ed.), *E-collaboration: Concepts, methodologies, tools, and applications* (pp. 1043–1063). Hershey, PA: IGI Global. doi:10.4018/978-1-60566-652-5.ch079

Leiponen, A. (2008). Control of intellectual assets in client relationships: Implications for innovation. *Strategic Management Journal, 29*(13), 1371–1394. doi:10.1002/smj.715

Leiss. (2011). Internet voting in the USA: analysis and commentary. Transforming Government: People. *Process and Policy*, *5*(1), 45–55.

Lepsinger, R. (2015, April 27). *3 Companies with High-performing virtual teams*. Retrieved from Linkedin: https://www.linkedin.com/pulse/3-companies-high-performing-virtual-teams-rick-lepsinger

Leroy, F., & Ramanatsoa, B. (1997). The cognitive and Behavioral dimensions of organizational learning in a merger: An empirical stud. *Journal of Management Studies*, *34*(4), 871–894. doi:10.1111/1467-6486.00076

Levinthal, D. (1991). Organizational adaptation and environmental selection: Interrelated processes of change. *Organization Science*, *2*(1), 140–144. doi:10.1287/orsc.2.1.140

Lien, B. Y. H., Hung, R. Y. Y., Yang, B., & Li, M. (2006). Is the learning organization a valid concept in the Taiwanese context? *International Journal of Manpower*, *27*(2), 189–203. doi:10.1108/01437720610666209

Li, M., Jin, L., & Wang, J. (2014). A new MCDM method combining QFD with TOPSIS for knowledge management system selection from the user's perspective in intuitionistic fuzzy environment. *Applied Soft Computing*, *21*(3), 28–37.

Lin, H. F. (2011). The effects of employee motivation, social interaction, and knowledge management strategy on KM implementation level. *Knowledge Management Research & Practice*, *9*(3), 263–275. doi:10.1057/kmrp.2011.21

Lin, T. C., & Huang, C. C. (2008). Understanding knowledge management system usage antecedents: An integration of social cognitive theory and task technology fit. *Information & Management*, *45*(6), 410–417. doi:10.1016/j.im.2008.06.004

Linton, J. D. (2000). The role of relationships and reciprocity in the implementation of process innovation. *Engineering Management Journal*, *12*(3), 34–38. doi:10.1080/10429247.2000.114 15080

Lin, Y. H., Lee, W. H., & Giang, C. M. (2016). *The Formation of Facebook Stickiness: The Perspectives of Media Richness Theory*. Use & Gratification Theory and Intimacy.

Litvaj, I., & Stancekova, D. (2015). Knowledge management embedment in company, knowledge repositories, knowledge management significance and usage in company. *Procedia Economics and Finance*, *23*, 833–838. doi:10.1016/S2212-5671(15)00549-3

Liu, C. H., & Lee, T. (2015). Promoting entrepreneurial orientation through the accumulation of social capital, and knowledge management. *International Journal of Hospitality Management*, *46*, 138–150. doi:10.1016/j.ijhm.2015.01.016

Lockheed Martin. (2010). *What We Do*. Lockheed Martin, Inc. Retrieved February 17, 2017, from Lockheed Martin's homepage: www.lockheedmartin.com/us/what-we-do/aerospace-defense/cyber-kill-chain.html

Lopez, J. M., Frick, J., Kirikova, M., Solé-Pareta, J., Pedersen, J. M., & Tran, N. (2015). The Colibri Project: Overcoming diversity in blended e-learning activity preparation *Proceedings of the 43rd SEFI Annual Conference 2014: Diversity in engineering education: an opportunity to face the new trends of engineering*. SEFI: European Association for Engineering Education.

Lowry, P. B., & Gaskin, J. (2014). Partial Least Squares (PLS) Structural Equation Modeling (SEM) for Building and Testing Behavioral Causal Theory: When to Choose It and How to Use It. *IEEE Transactions on Professional Communication*, *57*(2), 123–146. doi:10.1109/TPC.2014.2312452

Lucas, H. C. (1975). *Why information Systems Fail*. New York: Columbia University Press.

Luftman, J. N. (2004). *Managing the Information Technology Resources*. Pearson.

Lumpkin, G. T., & Lichtenstein, B. B. (2005). The role of entrepreneurial learning in the opportunity-recognition. *Entrepreneurship Theory and Practice*, *29*(4), 451–472. doi:10.1111/j.1540-6520.2005.00093.x

Lundberg, C. (1995). Conceptual issues in organizational learning. *The International Journal of Organizational Analysis*, *3*(1), 7–19. doi:10.1108/eb028821

Lytras, M. D., Russ, M., Maier, R., & Naeve, A. (2008). *Knowledge management strategies: A handbook of applied technologies*. (pp. 1–390). Hershey, PA: IGI Global. doi:10.4018/978-1-59904-603-7

MacNeil, H. J., & Schoonmaker, M. G. (2017). Breaking the Entrepreneurial Glass Ceiling: An Examination of Gender Differences in the Early-Stage Accelerator Environment. In *United States Association for Small Business and Entrepreneurship Conference Proceedings* (p. 1222). United States Association for Small Business and Entrepreneurship.

Madise, U., & Martens, T. (n.d.). *E-voting in Estonia 2005. The first practice of country- wide binding Internet voting in the world*. Retrieved from http://neu.e-voting.cc/wp-content/uploads/Proceedings%202006/1.1.madise_martens_e-voting_in_estonia.pdf

Maes, J., & Sels, L. (2014). SME's radical product innovation: The role of internally and externally oriented knowledge capabilities. *Journal of Small Business Management*, *52*(1), 141–163. doi:10.1111/jsbm.12037

Mahoney, J. T., & Qian, L. (2013). Market frictions as building blocks of an organizational economics approach to strategic management. *Strategic Management Journal*, *34*(9), 1019–1041. doi:10.1002/smj.2056

Majchrzak, A., Cooper, L. P., & Neece, O. E. (2004). Knowledge reuse for innovation. *Management Science*, *50*(2), 174–188. doi:10.1287/mnsc.1030.0116

Majchrzak, A., Jarvenpaa, S. L., & Bagherzadeh, M. (2014). A Review of Interorganizational Collaboration Dynamics. *Journal of Management*.

Marais, S. J., & Schutte, C. S. L. (2009, October). The development of open innovation models to assist the innovation process. *23rd Annual SAIIE Conference, Conference Proceedings*, 96.

March, J. G., & Simon, H. A. (1958). *Organizations*. Hoboken, NJ: Wiley.

Marquardt, M. J. (2002). *Building the learning organization: Mastering the 5 elements for corporate learning*. Palo Alto, CA: Davies-Black Publishing, Inc.

Marsh, P. (2015). Conference Proceedings. *Knowledge Swarms and Experiential Hives™ – the critical and emergent role of the ageing knowledge expert in the engineering and construction sectors of developing nations*. Global Knowledge Management Congress, Mumbai, India,

Marsh, P. (2017). *A Glimpse Into The Communication Challenges Faced By HardHat Professionals*. Retrieved from http://www.thhp.co.za/glimpse-communication-hhp

Marsh, P. (2014). *Nation Building through Knowledge Mentoring – a framework to bridge the global scarce and critical skills and knowledge crisis*. Self-Published.

Marsh, P. (2016). *Knowledge Swarms and Experiential Hives – a nation building solution to address the scarce and critical skills and knowledge crisis in the engineering and construction sector*. Civil Engineering Journal – June Edition.

Martín-de Castro, G. (2015). Knowledge management and innovation in knowledge-based and high-tech industrial markets: The role of openness and absorptive capacity. *Industrial Marketing Management*, *47*, 143–146. doi:10.1016/j.indmarman.2015.02.032

Martinez-Gil, J. (2015). Automated knowledge base management: A survey. *Computer Science Review*, *18*, 1–9. doi:10.1016/j.cosrev.2015.09.001

Matlay, H. (2000). Organizational learning in small learning organizations Education + Training. London. *EDEXEL*, *42*(4/5), 202–210.

Maurer, I., Bartsch, V., & Ebers, M. (2011). The value of intra-organizational social capital: How it fosters knowledge transfer, innovation performance, and growth. *Organization Studies*, *32*(2), 157–185. doi:10.1177/0170840610394301

McAfee, A. P. (2006). Enterprise 2.0: The dawn of emergent collaboration. *Management of Technology and Innovation*, *47*(3). Retrieved from http://www.citeulike.org/group/2518/article/797161

McDowell, D. (2009). *A Handbook for Practitioners, Managers and Users: Strategic Intelligence*. The Scarecrow Press, Inc.

McQuiggan, S., Kosturko, L., McQuiggan, J., & Sabourin, J. (2015). *Mobile learning: a handbook for developers, educators, and learners*. Hoboken, NJ: John Wiley & Sons, Inc. doi:10.1002/9781118938942

Means, B., Bakia, M., & Murphy, R. (2014). *Learning online: what research tells us about whether, when and how*. New York: Routledge.

Menaouer, B., Khalissa, S., Abdelbaki, B., & Abdelhamid, T. (2015). Towards a new approach of support innovation guided by knowledge management: Application on FERTIAL. *Procedia: Social and Behavioral Sciences*, *210*, 260–269. doi:10.1016/j.sbspro.2015.11.366

Mention, A. L. (2011). Co-operation and co-opetition as open innovation practices in the service sector: Which influence on innovation novelty?. *Technovation*, *31*(1), 44–53. doi:10.1016/j.technovation.2010.08.002

Meroño-Cerdán, Á. L. (2009). Knowledge management systems as a framework for IT in knowledge management. In T. Torres-Coronas & M. Arias-Oliva (Eds.), *Encyclopedia of human resources information systems: Challenges in e-HRM* (pp. 611–616). Hershey, PA: IGI Global. doi:10.4018/978-1-59904-883-3.ch089

Mezghani, E., Exposito, E., & Drira, K. (2016). A collaborative methodology for tacit knowledge management: Application to scientific research. *Future Generation Computer Systems*, *54*, 450–455. doi:10.1016/j.future.2015.05.007

Miller, P. (2007). *The genius of Swarms.* Retrieved from http://ngm.nationalgeographic.com/2007/07/swarms/miller-text

Miller, D. (1996). A preliminary typology of organizational learning: Synthesizing the literature. *Journal of Management*, *22*(3), 485–505. doi:10.1177/014920639602200305

Miller, H. E. (1996). The Multiple Dimensions of Information Quality. *Information Systems Management*, *13*(2), 79–82. doi:10.1080/10580539608906992

Milliken, F. J. (1987, January). Three Types of Perceived Uncertainty about the Environment: State, Effect, and Response Uncertainty. *Academy of Management Review*, *12*(1), 133–143.

Minniti, M., & Bygrave. (2001). A dynamic model of entrepreneurial learning. *Entrepreneurship Theory and Practice*, *25*(3), 5–16.

Miotti, L., & Sachwald, F. (2003). Co-operative R&D: Why and with whom? An integrated framework of analysis. *Research Policy*, *32*(8), 1481–1499. doi:10.1016/S0048-7333(02)00159-2

Mitchell, H. (2009). Technology and Knowledge Management. In M. E. Jennex (Ed.), Knowledge Management - Concepts, Methodologies, Tools & Applications (Vol. 1, pp. 41-47). Premier Reference, Information Science Reference, IGI Global.

Molina, L. M., Lloréns-Montes, J., & Ruiz-Moreno, A. (2007). Relationship between quality management practices and knowledge transfer. *Journal of Operations Management*, *25*(3), 682–701. doi:10.1016/j.jom.2006.04.007

Monteiro, E. (1998). Scaling information infrastructure: The case of the next generation IP in Internet. *The Information Society*, *14*(3), 229–245. doi:10.1080/019722498128845

Monticolo, D., Hilaire, V., Gomes, S., & Koukam, A. (2009). An ontological approach to managing project memories in organizations. In N. Kock (Ed.), *E-collaboration: Concepts, methodologies, tools, and applications* (pp. 244–269). Hershey, PA: IGI Global. doi:10.4018/978-1-60566-652-5.ch022

Mráček, P., & Mucha, M. (2015). The use of knowledge management in marketing communication of small and medium-sized companies. *Procedia: Social and Behavioral Sciences*, *175*, 185–192. doi:10.1016/j.sbspro.2015.01.1190

Mueller, S., Volery, T., & von Siemens, B. (2012). What Do Entrepreneurs Actually Do? An Observational Study of Entrepreneurs Everyday Behavior in the Start-Up and Growth Stages. *Entrepreneurship Theory and Practice*, *36*(5), 995–1017. doi:10.1111/j.1540-6520.2012.00538.x

Muntean, C. I. (2011). *Raising engagement in e-learning through gamification.* Retrieved from http://www.icvl.eu/2011/disc/icvl/documente/pdf/met/ICVL_ModelsAndMethodologies_paper42.pdf

Murovec, N., & Prodan, I. (2009). Absorptive capacity, its determinants, and influence on innovation output: Cross-cultural validation of the structural model. *Technovation*, *29*(12), 859–872. doi:10.1016/j.technovation.2009.05.010

Murphy, G., & Salomone, S. (2013). Using social media to facilitate knowledge transfer in complex engineering environments: A primer for educators. *European Journal of Engineering Education*, *38*(1), 70–84. doi:10.1080/03043797.2012.742871

Musser, J., & O'Reilly, T. (2007). *Web 2.0: Principles and Best Practices*. O'Reilly Media.

Nahapiet, J., & Ghoshal, S. (1998). Social capital, intellectual capital, and the organization advantage. *Academy of Management Review*, *23*(2), 242–266.

Narasimhan, O., Rajiv, S., & Dutta, S. (2006). Absorptive capacity in high-technology markets: The competitive advantage of the haves. *Marketing Science*, *25*(5), 510–524. doi:10.1287/mksc.1060.0219

Ness, H. (2009). Governance, negotiations, and alliance dynamics: Explaining the evolution of relational practice. *Journal of Management Studies*, *46*(3), 451–480. doi:10.1111/j.1467-6486.2008.00818.x

Nguyen, H. N., & Mohamed, S. (2011). Leadership behaviors, organizational culture and knowledge management practices: An empirical investigation. *Journal of Management Development*, *30*(2), 206–221. doi:10.1108/02621711111105786

Nickerson, J. A., & Zenger, T. R. (2004). A knowledge-based theory of the firm—The problem-solving perspective. *Organization Science*, *15*(6), 617–632. doi:10.1287/orsc.1040.0093

Nieto, M. J., & Santamaria, L. (2007). The importance of diverse collaborative networks for the novelty of product innovation. *Technovation*, *27*(6-7), 367–377. doi:10.1016/j.technovation.2006.10.001

Nigam, A. (2014). What Can Design Thinkers Learn from Entrepreneurs?. *Design Management Review*, *25*(3), 28–29.

Niri, M. B., & Brunswicker, S. (2014). Joint exploration with the enemy– revealing needed?. *Proceedings of the 1st ISPIM Americas Innoavtion Forum.*

Nonaka, I. (1994). A dynamic theory of organizational knowledge creation. Organization Science, 5, 14–37.

Nonaka, I. (1988). Creating organizational order out of chaos: Self-renewal in Japanese firms. *California Management Review*, *30*(Spring), 57–73. doi:10.2307/41166514

Nonaka, I. (1994). A dynamic theory of organizational knowledge creation. *Organization Science*, *5*(1), 14–37. doi:10.1287/orsc.5.1.14

Nonaka, I., & Krogh, G. V. (2009). Perspective—Tacit Knowledge and Knowledge Conversion: Controversy and Advancement in Organizational Knowledge Creation Theory. *Organization Science*, *20*(3), 635–652. doi:10.1287/orsc.1080.0412

Nonaka, I., & Takeuchi, H. (1995). *The knowledge creating company: How Japanese companies create the dynamics of innovation.* New York, NY: Oxford University Press.

Nonaka, I., & Takeuchi, H. (1995). *The Knowledge-creating Company: How Japanese Companies Create the Dynamics of Innovation.* Oxford University Press.

Nonaka, I., Takeuchi, H., & Umemoto, K. (1996). A theory of organizational knowledge creation. *International Journal of Technology Management*, *11*(7), 833–845.

Nonaka, I., Toyama, R., & Konno, N. (1998). Leading Knowledge Creation: A New framework for dynamic Knowledge Management. *Proceedings at the 2nd Annual Knowledge Management Conference.*

Nonaka, I., Toyama, R., & Konno, N. (2000). SECI, Ba and Leadership: A Unified Model of Dynamic Knowledge Creation. *Long Range Planning*, *33*(1), 5–34. doi:10.1016/S0024-6301(99)00115-6

Nooteboom, B. (2000). Learning by interaction: absorptive capacity, cognitive distance and governance. *Journal of Management and Governance, 4*(1-2), 69-92.

O'Leonard, K. (2014). *The Corporate Learning Factbook 2014: Benchmarks, Trends and Analysis of the U.S. Training Market.* Bersin by Deloitte.

O'Reilly, T. (2005). *What is Web 2.0?.* O'Reilly Media. Available: http://tinyurl.com/743r5

Ogiela, L. (2013). Semantic analysis and biological modeling in selected classes of cognitive information systems. *Mathematical and Computer Modelling*, *58*(5/6), 1405–1414. doi:10.1016/j.mcm.2012.12.001

Ogiela, L. (2015). Advanced techniques for knowledge management and access to strategic information. *International Journal of Information Management*, *35*(2), 154–159. doi:10.1016/j.ijinfomgt.2014.11.006

Okamuro, H. (2007). Determinants of successful R&D cooperation in Japanese small businesses: The impact of organizational and contractual characteristics. *Research Policy*, *36*(10), 1529–1544. doi:10.1016/j.respol.2006.12.008

Okunoye, A. (2008). Managing information technology component of knowledge management: Outsourcing as a strategic option in developing countries. In F. Tan (Ed.), *Global information technologies: Concepts, methodologies, tools, and applications* (pp. 2774–2795). Hershey, PA: IGI Global. doi:10.4018/978-1-59904-939-7.ch200

OPSEC. (1991). *Interagency OPSEC Support Staff- Compendium of OPSEC Terms*. Greenbelt, MD: IOSS.

OPSEC. (1996). *Operations Security: Intelligence Threats Handbook*. Interagency OPSEC Support Staff.

Overton, L., & Dixon, G. (2016). *Preparing for the Future of Learning – a changing Perspective for L & D Leaders*. Towards Maturity; In-Focus Report. Retrieved from https://www.cipd.co.uk/Images/preparing-for-the-future-of-learning_2016-a-changing-perspective-for-l-and-d-leaders_tcm18-13846.pdf

Panahi, S., Watson, J., & Partridge, H. (2012). Social Media and Tacit Knowledge Sharing: Developing a Conceptual Model. In *World Academy of Science, Engineering and Technology* (pp. 1095–1102). Paris, France: World Academy of Science, Engineering and Technology (WASET). Retrieved from http://www.waset.org/journals/waset/v64/v64-208.pdf

Paraki, J. G. (2006). Knowledge management in telemedicine. In A. Lazakidou (Ed.), *Handbook of research on informatics in healthcare and biomedicine* (pp. 210–220). Hershey, PA: IGI Global. doi:10.4018/978-1-59140-982-3.ch027

Paroutis, S., & Saleh, A. A. (2009). Determinants of knowledge sharing using Web 2.0 technologies. *Journal of Knowledge Management*, *13*(4), 52–63. doi:10.1108/13673270910971824

Patton, D. U., Hong, J. S., Patel, S., & Kral, M. J. (2015). A systematic review of research strategies used in qualitative studies on school bullying and victimization. *Trauma, Violence & Abuse*, *18*(1), 3–16. doi:10.1177/1524838015588502 PMID:26092753

Pauwels, C., Clarysse, B., Wright, M., & Van Hove, J. (2016). Understanding a new generation incubation model: The accelerator. *Technovation*, *50*, 13–24. doi:10.1016/j.technovation.2015.09.003

Pedersen, J. M., Şükrü, M., Frick, J., & Mank, L. (2016). *Colibri: An International Blended Learning Experience based on Real-World Problems*. Paper presented at the PAEE/ALE2016, Minho, Portugal.

Peltokorpi, V. (2015). Corporate language proficiency and reverse knowledge transfer in multinational corporations: Interactive effects of communication media richness and commitment to headquarters. *Journal of International Management*, *21*(1), 49–62. doi:10.1016/j.intman.2014.11.003

Penfold, S. (2016). *Profile of the modern learner – helpful facts and stats – infographic*. Elucidat Blog. Retrieved from https://blog.elucidat.com/modern-learner-profile-infographic/

Peng, H. (2013). Why and when do people hide knowledge? *Journal of Knowledge Management*, *17*(3), 398–415. doi:10.1108/JKM-12-2012-0380

Pérez-Montoro, M. (2009). Knowledge management in organizations. In T. Torres-Coronas & M. Arias-Oliva (Eds.), *Encyclopedia of human resources information systems: Challenges in e-HRM* (pp. 605–610). Hershey, PA: IGI Global. doi:10.4018/978-1-59904-883-3.ch088

Perkmann, M., Tartari, V., McKelvey, M., Autio, E., Broström, A., DEste, P., & Hughes, A. et al. (2013). Academic engagement and commercialisation: A review of the literature on university–industry relations. *Research Policy*, *42*(2), 423–442. doi:10.1016/j.respol.2012.09.007

Pfeffer, J., & Salancik, G. R. (1978). *The external control of organizations: A resource dependence perspective*. New York: Harper & Row.

Pham, M. H. T. (2011). Blog ambition: Fashion, feelings, and the political economy of the digital raced body. *Camera Obscura*, *26*(176), 1–37. doi:10.1215/02705346-2010-013

Phang, M. M. S., & Foong, S. Y. (2010). Information communication technologies (ICTs) and knowledge sharing: The case of professional accountants in Malaysia. *World Journal of Science. Technology and Sustainable Development*, *7*(1), 21–35.

Piller, F. T., & Walcher, D. (2006). Toolkits for idea competitions: A novel method to integrate users in new product development. *R & D Management*, *36*(3), 307–318. doi:10.1111/j.1467-9310.2006.00432.x

Pisano, G. (1994). Knowledge, integration, and the locus of learning: An empirical analysis of process development. *Strategic Management Journal*, *15*(S1), 85–100. doi:10.1002/smj.4250150907

Pisano, G. P. (1989). Using equity participation to support exchange: Evidence from the biotechnology industry. *Journal of Law Economics and Organization*, 109–126.

Pittaway, L., & Thorpe, R. (2012). A framework for entrepreneurial learning: A tribute to Jason Cope. *Entrepreneurship & Regional Development*, *24*(9-10), 837–859. doi:10.1080/08985626.2012.694268

Plumer, B. (2012). *Estonia gets to vote online. Why can't America?*. Retrieved from http://www.washingtonpost.com/blogs/wonkblog/wp/2012/11/06/estonians-get-to-vote-online-why-cant-america/

Politis, D. (2005). The process of entrepreneurial learning: A conceptual framework. *Entrepreneurship Theory and Practice*, *29*(4), 399–424. doi:10.1111/j.1540-6520.2005.00091.x

Powell, W. W. (1990). Neither market no hierarchy: Networks form of organisation. *Research in Organizational Behavior*, *12*, 295–336.

Prensky, M. (2001). *On the Horizon - Digital Natives, Digital Immigrants*. MCB University Press. Retrieved from http://www.marcprensky.com/writing/Prensky%20-%20Digital%20Natives,%20Digital%20Immigrants%20-%20Part1.pdf

Price, R. (2004). The role of service providers in establishing networked regional business accelerators in Utah. *International Journal of Technology Management*, *27*(5), 465–474. doi:10.1504/IJTM.2004.004283

Quiroga, R. Q. (2012). Concept cells: The building blocks of declarative memory functions. *Nature Reviews Neuroscience*. Retrieved from https://www.researchgate.net/publication/228114707_Concept_cells_the_building_blocks_of_declarative_memory_functions

Radaelli, G., Lettieri, E., Mura, M., & Spiller, N. (2014). Knowledge sharing and innovative work behaviour in healthcare: A micro-level investigation of direct and indirect effects. *Creativity and Innovation Management*, *23*(4), 400–414. doi:10.1111/caim.12084

Radojevich-Kelley, N., & Hoffman, D. L. (2012). Analysis of accelerator companies: An exploratory case study of their programs, processes, and early results. *Small Business Institute Journal*, *8*(2), 54–70.

Rae, D. (2011). *Entrepreneurial learning: Practice, experience and theory. Paper presented at Entrepreneurial learning and education: From theory to practice*. British Academy of Management.

Rae, D. a. W. (2015). *Entrepreneurial Learning: New Perspectives in Research, Education and Practice*. Routledge Studies in Entrepreneurship.

Raheem, S., & Akhuemonkhan, I. A. (2014). Enterprise development through incubation management. *Developing Country Studies*, *4*(18), 67-82.

Raisinghani, M. S. (2008). Knowledge management of e-business initiatives within two global organizations: A comparative case study analysis. In F. Tan (Ed.), *Global information technologies: Concepts, methodologies, tools, and applications* (pp. 1780–1794). Hershey, PA: IGI Global. doi:10.4018/978-1-59904-939-7.ch128

Ramesh, A., & Dennis, A. R. (2002). The Object-Oriented Team: Lessons for Virtual Teams from Global Software Development. *Proceedings of the 35th Hawaii International Conference on System Sciences (HICSS-35'02)*. IEEE. doi:10.1109/HICSS.2002.993876

Rampersad, G., Quester, P., & Troshani, I. (2010). Managing innovation networks: Exploratory evidence from ICT, biotechnology and nanotechnology networks. *Industrial Marketing Management*, *39*(5), 793–805. doi:10.1016/j.indmarman.2009.07.002

Ratinho, T. (2011). The role of Business Incubators in Facilitating Firm Development. In *Are They Helping? An Examination of Business Incubators' Impact on Tenant Firms*. University of Twente.

Ravasi, D., & Turati, C. (2005). Exploring Entrepreneurial Learning: A Comparative Study of Technology Development and projects. *Journal of Business Venturing*, *20*(1), 137–164.

Reddick, C. G., Chatfield, A. T., & Ojo, A. (2017). A social media text analytics framework for double-loop learning for citizen-centric public services: A case study of a local government Facebook use. *Government Information Quarterly*, *34*(1), 110–125. doi:10.1016/j.giq.2016.11.001

Reimann, P. (2016). *Measuring and visualizing learning in the information-rich classroom*. New York, NY: Routledge.

Report, G. (2010). *Watchlist: Continuing Changes in the Nature of Work, 2010 – 2020.* Retrieved from https://www.gartner.com/doc/1331623/watchlist-continuing-changes-nature-work

Rese, A., & Baier, D. (2011). Success factors for innovation management in networks of small and medium enterprises. *R & D Management*, *41*(2), 138–155. doi:10.1111/j.1467-9310.2010.00620.x

Rickman, T. A., & Cosenza, R. M. (2007). The changing digital dynamics of multichannel marketing: The feasibility of the weblog: text mining approach for fast fashion trending. *Journal of Fashion Marketing and Management*, *11*(4), 604–621. doi:10.1108/13612020710824634

Riis, J. O., & Frick, J. (1990). *Organizational Learning: A Neglected Dimension of Production Management Systems design.* Paper presented at the Advanceds In Production Management Systems, Helsinki, Finland.

Ritala, P., & Hurmelinna-Laukkanen, P. (2013). Incremental and radical innovation in coopetition—the role of absorptive capacity and appropriability. *Journal of Product Innovation Management*, *30*(1), 154–169. doi:10.1111/j.1540-5885.2012.00956.x

Rizzolatti, G., & Laila, C. (2004). The mirror-neuron system. *Annual Review of Neuroscience*, *27*(1), 169–192. doi:10.1146/annurev.neuro.27.070203.144230 PMID:15217330

Robley, C., Felsen, B., & Spatz, S. (2010). *Making your eBook. The author's guide to eBook publishing, design, distribution, and marketing*. Academic Press.

Rocha, L. (2015, August 15). *The 5 Steps of the Intelligence Cycle*. Retrieved from Security Monitoring, Threat Intelligence: www.countuponsecurity.com/2015/08/15/the-5-steps-of-the-intelligence-cycle/

Rodan, S., & Galunic, C. (2004). More than network structure: How knowledge heterogeneity influences managerial performance and innovativeness. *Strategic Management Journal*, *25*(6), 541–562. doi:10.1002/smj.398

Rogers, E. M. (2004). *Diffusion of Innovations* (5th ed.). New York, NY: Free Press.

Rogova, E. (2014). The effectiveness of business incubators as the element of the universities spin-off strategy in Russia. *International Journal of Technology Management & Sustainable Development*, *13*(3), 265–281. doi:10.1386/tmsd.13.3.265_1

Romano, N. C., Donovan, C., Chen, H., & Nunamaker, J. F. (2003). A methodology for analyzing web-based qualitative data. *Journal of Management Information Systems*, *19*(4), 213–246. doi: 10.1080/07421222.2003.11045741

Rubera, G., & Kirca, A. H. (2012). Firm innovativeness and its performance outcomes: A meta-analytic review and theoretical integration. *Journal of Marketing*, *76*(3), 130–147. doi:10.1509/jm.10.0494

Rus, I., Lindvall, M., & Sinha, S. S. (2001). *Knowledge Management in Software Engineering:A DACS State-of-the-Art Report.* Fraunhofer Center for Experimental Software Engineering Maryland and The University of Maryland.

Russ, M. (2010). *Knowledge management strategies for business development.* (pp. 1–446). Hershey, PA: IGI Global. doi:10.4018/978-1-60566-348-7

Sager, T. (2014). *An Intelligent Approach to Attack Prevention.* SANS Institute.

Sakr, N. (2016). Survival or sustainability? Contributions of innovatively managed news ventures to the future of Egyptian journalism. *Journal of Media Business Studies*, *13*(1), 45–59. doi:10.1080/16522354.2015.1125608

Salamzadeh, A., & Kirby, D. A. (2017). New venture creation: How start-ups grow?. *AD-Minister*, (30), 9-30.

Salamzadeh, A., & Radovic Markovic, M. (2016). *Business Accelerators as Champions to achieve Resilient Growth: A Revolutionary Trend in a Developing Country.* International Scientific Conference on Impact of Economic Policies on Attaining Resilient Growth, Belgrade, Serbia.

Salamzadeh, A. (2015 a). *Innovation Accelerators: Emergence of Startup Companies in Iran. 60th Annual ICSB World Conference*, Dubai, UAE.

Salamzadeh, A. (2015 b). New Venture Creation: Controversial Perspectives and Theories. *Economic Analysis*, *48*(3/4), 101–109.

Salamzadeh, A., & Kawamorita, H. (2017). The enterprising communities and startup ecosystem in Iran. *Journal of Enterprising Communities*, *11*(4).

Salamzadeh, A., & Kirby, D. A. (2017). Startup Companies: How startups grow?. *AD-minister*, *30*(1), 9–29.

Sanchez, R., & Mahoney, J. (1996). Modularity, flexibility, and knowledge management in product organization and design. *Strategic Management Journal*, *17*(1), 63–76. doi:10.1002/smj.4250171107

Sarasvathy, S., Dew, N., Velamuri, S., & Venkataraman, S. (2003). Three Views of Entrepreneurial Opportunity. International Handbook Series on Entrepreneurship, 141-160.

Schmidt, J., & Keil, T. (2013). What makes a resource valuable? Identifying the drivers of firm-idiosyncratic resource value. *Academy of Management Review*, *38*(2), 206–228. doi:10.5465/amr.2010.0404

Schmidt, S. M., & Cummings, L. L. (1976). Organizational environment, differentiation and perceived environmental uncertainty. *Decision Sciences*, *7*(3), 447–467. doi:10.1111/j.1540-5915.1976.tb00692.x

Schnackenberg, A. K., & Tomlinson, E. C. (2014). Organizational Transparency A New Perspective on Managing Trust in Organization-Stakeholder Relationships. *Journal of Management*, 0149206314525202.

Schneckenberg, D. (2009). Web 2.0 and the empowerment of the knowledge worker. *Journal of Knowledge Management*, *13*(6), 509–520. doi:10.1108/13673270910997150

Schneckenberg, D., Truong, Y., & Mazloomi, H. (2015). Microfoundations of innovative capabilities: The leverage of collaborative technologies on organizational learning and knowledge management in a multinational corporation. *Technological Forecasting and Social Change*, *100*, 356–368. doi:10.1016/j.techfore.2015.08.008

Schroeder, A., & Wagner, C. (2012). Governance of open content creation: A conceptualization and analysis of control and guiding mechanisms in the open content domain. *Journal of the American Society for Information Science and Technology*, *63*(10), 1947–1959. doi:10.1002/asi.22657

Schulze, A., Brojerdi, G., & von Krogh, G. (2014). Those who know, do. Those who understand, teach. Disseminative capability and knowledge transfer in the automotive industry. *Journal of Product Innovation Management*, *31*(1), 79–97. doi:10.1111/jpim.12081

Schumpeter, J. A. (1975). *Capitalism, socialism and democracy*. New York: Harper.

Seawright, J., & Gerring, J. (2008). Case Selection Techniques in Case Study Research A Menu of Qualitative and Quantitative Options. *Political Research Quarterly*, *61*(2), 294–308. doi:10.1177/1065912907313077

Senge, P. M. (2010). *The Fifth Discipline: The Art & Practice of the Learning Organization*. Crown Publishing Group.

Senge, P., Roberts, C., Ross, R., Smith, B., & Kleiner, A. (1994). *The fifth discipline field book*. New York: Currency/Doubleday.

Sensuse, D. I., Cahyaningsih, E., & Wibowo, W. C. (2015). Knowledge management: Organizational culture in Indonesian government human capital management. *Procedia Computer Science*, *72*, 485–494. doi:10.1016/j.procs.2015.12.130

Serenko, A., & Bontis, N. (2016). Understanding counterproductive knowledge behavior: Antecedents and consequences of intra-organizational knowledge hiding. *Journal of Knowledge Management*, *20*(6), 1199–1224. doi:10.1108/JKM-05-2016-0203

Seyfried, C. (2014). Trust-Based Learning and Its Importance in Intercultural Education. *CLCWeb: Comparative Literature and Culture*, *16*(3). https://doi.org/10.7771/1481-4374.2515

Shane, S. 2. (2003). A General Theory of Entrepreneurship. Edward Elgar.

Shane, S., & Venkataraman, S. (2000, January). The Promise of Entrepreneurship as a Field of Research. *Academy of Management Review*, *25*(1), 217–226.

Shang, S. S. C., Li, E. Y., Wu, Y.-L., & Hou, O. C. L. (2011). Understanding Web 2.0 service models: A knowledge-creating perspective. *Information & Management*, *48*(4–5), 178–184. doi:10.1016/j.im.2011.01.005

Shapiro, C. a. R. (2013). *Creating Accessible iBooks Textbooks with iBooks*. Author.

Shaw, B. (1994). User–supplier links and innovation. In M. Dodgson & R. Rothwell (Eds.), *The Handbook of Industrial Innovation*. Cheltenham, UK: Edward Elgar.

Shepherd, C. (2011). Does social media have a place in workplace learning?. *Strategic Direction*, *27*(2), 3–4. doi:10.1108/02580541111103882

Sigrist, B. (1999). Entrepreneurial Opportunity Recognition, Paper presented at the annual UIC/AMA Symposium at the Marketing/Entrepreneurship Interface, Sofia-Antipolis, France.

Singh, M. D., & Kant, R. (2009). Selected knowledge management implementation issues: A sectorial analysis. *International Journal of Innovation and Learning*, *6*(5), 550–567. doi:10.1504/IJIL.2009.025065

Smedlund, A. (2008). The knowledge system of a firm: Social capital for explicit, tacit and potential knowledge. *Journal of Knowledge Management*, *12*(1), 63–77. doi:10.1108/13673270810852395

Smirnova, M. M., Podmetina, D., Väätänen, J., & Torkkeli, M. (2012). Collaborative approaches to new product development: The case of Russia. *International Journal of Entrepreneurship and Innovation Management*, *15*(1/2), 91–107. doi:10.1504/IJEIM.2012.044078

Somppaya, M., & Scarfone, K. (2013). *Guide to Enterprise Patch Management Technologies*. National Institute for Standards & Technology.

Stagars, M. (2015). The lean start-up changed everything. In *University Startups and Spin-Offs* (pp. 15–27). Apress.

Stevenson, H. H., & Jarillo, J. C. (1990). A paradigm of entrepreneurship: Entrepreneurial management. *Strategic Management Journal*, *11*, 17–27.

Storey, M., Zagalsky, A., & Filho, F. F. (2016). How Social and Communications channels Shape and Challenge a Participatory Culture in Software development. *IEEE Transactions and Software*, *43*(2).

Suddaby, R. F. W., & Foster, W. M. (2017, January). History and Organizational Change. *Journal of Management*, *43*(1), 19–38. doi:10.1177/0149206316675031

Swart, J., & Kinnie, N. (2013). Managing multidimensional knowledge assets: HR configurations in professional service firms. *Human Resource Management Journal*, *23*(2), 160–179. doi:10.1111/j.1748-8583.2012.00197.x

Swart, J., Kinnie, N., van Rossenberg, Y., & Yalabik, Z. Y. (2014). Why should I share my knowledge? A multiple foci of commitment perspective. *Human Resource Management Journal*, *24*(3), 269–289. doi:10.1111/1748-8583.12037

Swink, M. (2006). Building collaborative innovation capability. *Research Technology Management*, *49*(2), 37–47.

Tan. (2011). Research on the relationship between knowledge search and innovation performance—based on the view of organization learning. *Science and Technology Management Research*, *2011*, 166-170.

Taub, T., & Johnson, D. (2015). *Meet the Modern Learner (Infographic)*. Bersin by Deloitte. Retrieved from https://www.bersin.com/Practice/Detail.aspx?id=18071

Teece, D. (1998). Capturing value from knowledge assets: The new economy, markets for know-how, and intangible assets. *California Management Review*, *40*(3), 55–79. doi:10.2307/41165943

Teece, D. J. (1986). Profiting from technological innovation: Implications for integration, collaboration, licensing and public policy. *Research Policy*, *15*(6), 285–305. doi:10.1016/0048-7333(86)90027-2

Teece, D. J. (1992). Competition, cooperation, and innovation: Organizational arrangements for regimes of rapid technological progress. *Journal of Economic Behavior & Organization*, *18*(1), 1–25. doi:10.1016/0167-2681(92)90050-L

Tether, B. (2002). Who co-operates for innovation, and why. An empirical analysis. *Research Policy*, *31*(6), 947–967. doi:10.1016/S0048-7333(01)00172-X

The Statistics Portal. (2016). *Share of households with internet access in Estonia from 2005 to 2016*. Retrieved from https://www.statista.com/statistics/377683/household-internet-access-in-estonia/

Theriou, G. N., & Chatzoglou, P. D. (2008). Enhancing performance through best HRM practices, organizational learning and knowledge management. *European Business Review*, *20*(3), 185–207. doi:10.1108/09555340810871400

Thomas, D. (2008). *A general inductive approach for qualitative data analysis*. University of Auckland.

Tidd, J., Bessant, J., & Pavitt, K. (1997). *Managing Innovation: Integrating Technological, Market and Organisational Change*. Chichester, UK: Wiley.

Tilson, D., Lyytinen, K., & Sørensen, C. (2010). Research commentary -- Digital infrastructures: The missing IS research agenda. *Information Systems Research, 21*(4), 748-759.

Tilson, D., Sørensen, C., & Lyytinen, K. (2012). *Change and Control Paradoxes in Mobile Infrastructure Innovation – The Android and iOS Mobile Operating Systems Cases System Science*. HICSS.

Tisdale, S. M. (2015). Cybersecurity: Challenges from a Systems, Complexity, Knowledge Management and Business Intelligence Perspective. *Issues in Information Systems*, *16*(III), 191–198.

Tiwana, A., Konsynski, B., & Bush, A. A. (2010). Platform evolution: Coevolution of platform architecture, governance, and environmental dynamics. *Information Systems Research*, *21*(4), 675–687. doi:10.1287/isre.1100.0323

Torbert, W. (2000). A developmental approach to social science: A model for analyzing Charles Alexanders scientific contributions. *Journal of Adult Development*, *7*(4), 255–267. doi:10.1023/A:1009515512330

Tovey, M., & Atlee, T. (2008). *Co-intelligence, Collective Intelligence and Conscious Evolution – Creating a Prosperous World at Peace.* Retrieved from https://archive.org/stream/CollectiveIntelligenceCreatingAProsperousWorldAtPeace/Complete_022508-cFinal1420_djvu.txt

Trantopoulos, K., von Krogh, G., Wallin, M. W., & Woerter, M. (2017). External Knowledge and Information Technology: Implications for Process Innovation Performance. *Management Information Systems Quarterly*, *41*(1), 287–300.

Trossen, D., & Fine, C. (2005). *Value Chain Dynamics in the Communication Industry*. MIT Communications Futures Program. Retrieved from http://cfp.mit.edu/docs/core/edgedec2005.pdf

Trusson, C. R., Doherty, N. F., & Hislop, D. (2014). Knowledge sharing using IT service management tools: Conflicting discourses and incompatible practices. *Information Systems Journal*, *24*(4), 347–371. doi:10.1111/isj.12025

Tsahkna, A. (2013). E-voting: Lessons from Estonia. *European View*, *12*(1), 59–66. doi:10.1007/s12290-013-0261-7

Tuli, K. R., Kohli, A. K., & Bharadwaj, S. G. (2007). Rethinking customer solutions: From product bundles to relational processes. *Journal of Marketing*, *71*(3), 1–17. doi:10.1509/jmkg.71.3.1

Tuusjärvi, E., & Möller, K. (2009). Multiplicity of norms in inter-company cooperation. *Journal of Business and Industrial Marketing*, *24*(7), 519–528. doi:10.1108/08858620910986758

Tzortzaki, A. M., & Mihiotis, A. (2014). A review of knowledge management theory and future directions. *Knowledge and Process Management*, *21*(1), 29–41. doi:10.1002/kpm.1429

Ulaga, W., & Eggert, A. (2005). Relationship value in business markets: The construct and its dimensions. *Journal of Business-To-Business Marketing*, *12*(1), 73–99. doi:10.1300/J033v12n01_04

Ulrich, K. (1995). The role of product architecture in the manufacturing firm. *Research Policy*, *24*(3), 419–440. doi:10.1016/0048-7333(94)00775-3

US Department of Labour. (1999). *Futurework: Trends and Challenges for work in the 21st Century.* Cornel University ILR School.

Use Case Diagram Tutorials. (2015). Retrieved December 27, 2015, from www.creately.com/blog/diagrams/use-case-diagram-tutorial/

Vaidyanathan, G. (2008). Networked knowledge management dimensions in distributed projects. In F. Tan (Ed.), *Global information technologies: Concepts, methodologies, tools, and applications* (pp. 2574–2597). Hershey, PA: IGI Global. doi:10.4018/978-1-59904-939-7.ch187

Van de Ven, A., & Polley, D. (1991). Learning while innovating. *Organization Science*, *3*, 91–116.

Vinkel, P. (2011). Internet voting in estonia. In *Nordic Conference on Secure IT Systems* (pp. 4-12). Springer Berlin Heidelberg.

Volberda, H. W. (1996). Toward the Flexible Form: How to Remain Vital in Hypercompetitive Environments. *Organization Science*, *7*(4), 359–374. doi:10.1287/orsc.7.4.359

Voldal, D. (2003). *A Practical Methodology for Implementing Patch Management Process*. SANS Institute.

von Friedrichs Grängsjö, Y., & Gummesson, E. (2006). Hotel networks and social capital in destination marketing. *International Journal of Service Industry Management*, *17*(1), 58–75. doi:10.1108/09564230610651589

Vornanen, M. (2017). *The impact of socio-cultural factors and knowledge sharing to the success of global software development*. Tampere: University of Tampere.

Vuori, V., & Okkonen, J. (2012). Refining information and knowledge by social media applications: Adding value by insight. *Vine*, *42*(1), 117–128. doi:10.1108/03055721211207798

Wallin, M. W., & von Krogh, G. (2010). Organizing for open innovation: Focus on the integration of knowledge. *Organizational Dynamics*, *39*(2), 145–154. doi:10.1016/j.orgdyn.2010.01.010

Wang, F. (2016). *Social Media, Entrepreneurs and Accelerators: Examining the Role of Brands and Networks* (Doctoral dissertation). Rensselaer Polytechnic Institute.

Wang, C. L., Hult, G. T. M., Ketchen, D. J. Jr, & Ahmed, P. K. (2009). Knowledge management orientation, market orientation and firm performance. An integration and empirical examination. *Journal of Strategic Marketing*, *17*(2), 99–122. doi:10.1080/09652540902879326

Wang, C., & Ahmed, P. (2004). The development and validation of the organizational innovativeness construct using confirmatory factor analysis. *European Journal of Innovation Management*, *7*(4), 303–313. doi:10.1108/14601060410565056

Wang, C., & Ahmed, P. (2007). Dynamic capabilities - A review and research agenda. *International Journal of Management Reviews*, *9*(1), 31–51. doi:10.1111/j.1468-2370.2007.00201.x

Wang, C., & Chugh, H. (2014). Entrepreneurial Learning: Past Research and Future Challenges. *International Journal of Management Reviews*, *16*(1), 24–61. doi:10.1111/ijmr.12007

Wang, J., Ding, D., Liu, O., & Li, M. (2016). A synthetic method for knowledge management performance evaluation based on triangular fuzzy number and group support systems. *Applied Soft Computing*, *39*, 11–20. doi:10.1016/j.asoc.2015.09.041

Wang, K. L., Chiang, C., & Tung, C. M. (2012). Integrating human resource management and knowledge management: From the viewpoint of core employees and organizational performance. *International Journal of Organizational Innovation*, *5*(1), 109–137.

Warkentin, M. E., Sayeed, L., & Hightower, R. (1997). Virtual teams versus face-to-face teams: An exploratory study of a Web based conference system. *Decision Sciences*, *28*(4), 975–996. doi:10.1111/j.1540-5915.1997.tb01338.x

Weerawardena, J., & Mavondo, F. T. (2011). Capabilities, innovation and competitive advantage. *Industrial Marketing Management*, *40*(8), 1220–1223. doi:10.1016/j.indmarman.2011.10.012

Weiblen, T., & Chesbrough, H. W. (2015). Engaging with startups to enhance corporate innovation. *California Management Review*, *57*(2), 66–90. doi:10.1525/cmr.2015.57.2.66

Weick, K. E. (1982). *Management of Organizational Change among Loosely Coupled Element. In Change in Organizations: New Perspectives in Theory, Research, and Practice* (pp. 375–408). San Francisco, CA: Jossey-Bass.

Weick, K. E. (1995). *Sensemaking in organisations*. University of Michigan. SAGE Publications.

Weick, K., & Roberts, K. (1993). Collective mind in organizations: Heedful interrelating on flight decks. *Administrative Science Quarterly*, *38*(3), 357–381. doi:10.2307/2393372

Welch, J. (2012). The power of collaboration. *Economic Development Journal*, *11*(4), 36–55.

Weske, M. (2007). *Business process management: Concepts, languages, architectures*. Berlin, Germany: Springer–Verlag.

Westerlund, M., & Rajala, R. (2010). Learning and innovation in inter-organizational network collaboration. *Journal of Business and Industrial Marketing*, *25*(6), 435–442. doi:10.1108/08858621011066026

West, J., & Bogers, M. (2013). Leveraging external sources of innovation: A review of research on open innovation. *Journal of Product Innovation Management*.

West, J., & Bogers, M. (2014). Leveraging External Sources of Innovation: A Review of Research on Open Innovation. *Journal of Product Innovation Management*, *31*(4), 814–831. doi:10.1111/jpim.12125

West, J., Salter, A., Vanhaverbeke, W., & Chesbrough, H. (2014). Open innovation: The next decade. *Research Policy*, *43*(5), 805–811. doi:10.1016/j.respol.2014.03.001

White, S. (2005). Cooperation Costs, Governance Choice and Alliance Evolution. *Journal of Management Studies*, *42*(7), 1383–1412. doi:10.1111/j.1467-6486.2005.00548.x

Wikhamn, B. R. (2013). Two Different Perspectives on Open Innovation–Libre versus Control. *Creativity and Innovation Management*, *22*(4), 375–389. doi:10.1111/caim.12035

Wiklund, J. D. S. (2003). Aspiring for, and achieving growth: The moderating role of resources and opportunities. *Journal of Management Studies*, *20*, 71–91.

Wild, F. (2016). *Learning analytics in R with SNA, LSA, and MPIA*. New York, NY: Springer Berlin Heidelberg. doi:10.1007/978-3-319-28791-1

Williamson, O. (1992). Markets, hierarchies, and the modern corporation: An unfolding perspective. . *Journal of Economic Behavior & Organization*, *17*(3), 335–352. doi:10.1016/S0167-2681(95)90012-8

Wong, K. Y. (2005). Critical success factors for implementing knowledge management in small and medium enterprises. *Industrial Management & Data Systems*, *105*(3), 261–279. doi:10.1108/02635570510590101

Woodard, C. J., Ramasubbu, N., Tschang, F. T., & Sambamurthy, V. (2013). (forthcoming). Design Capital and Design Moves: The Logic of Digital Business Strategy. *MISQ Special Issue: Digital Business Strategy: Toward a Next Generation of Insights.*

Woodard, J. (2008). Architectural Control Points. *Third International Conference on Design Science Research in Information Systems and Technology (DESRIST 2008)*, Atlanta, GA.

Woodward, I. C., & Vongswasdi, P. (2017). *More that unites than divides: Intergenerational communication preferences in the workplace. In Communication Research and Practice*. Taylor and Francis.

Workman, M., Kahnweiler, W., & Bommer, W. (2003). The effects of cognitive style and media richness on commitment to telework and virtual teams. *Journal of Vocational Behavior*, *63*(2), 199–219. doi:10.1016/S0001-8791(03)00041-1

Wuyts, S., Dutta, S., & Stremersch, S. (2004). Portfolios of interfirm agreements in technology-intensive markets: Consequences for innovation and profitability. *Journal of Marketing*, *68*(2), 88–100. doi:10.1509/jmkg.68.2.88.27787

Yang, M., & Gabrielsson, P. (2017). Entrepreneurial marketing of international high-tech business-to-business new ventures: A decision-making process perspective. *Industrial Marketing Management*, *64*, 147–160. doi:10.1016/j.indmarman.2017.01.007

Yeboah-Boateng, E. O. (2013a). *Cyber-Security Challenges with SMEs in Developing Economies: Issues of Confidentiality, Integrity & Availablity (CIA)*. Aalborg University.

Yeboah-Boateng, E. O. (2013b, February). Fuzzy Similarity Measures Approach in Benchmarking Taxonomies of Threats against SMEs in Developing Economies. *Canadian Journal on Computing in Mathematics, Natural Sciences. Engineering in Medicine*, 34–44.

Yeboah-Boateng, E. O. (2016, October). Recontextualization of Discretized Cyber-Risk Functional Arguments with Fuzzy Polynomials. *International Journal on Computer Science and Engineering*, *4*(10), 19–26.

Yeunga, A. C. L., Laia, K. H., & Yeea, R. W. Y. (2007). Knowledge and information technology management in supply chain integration. *International Journal of Production Research*, *45*(11), 2459–2477.

Ying, A. T., Wright, J. L., & Abrams, S. (2005). Source code that talks: an exploration of Eclipse task comments and their implication to repository mining. *Proceedings in MSR '05 Proceedings of the 2005 international workshop on Mining software repositories* (pp. 1-5). St. Louis, MO: ACM.

Yin, R. K. (2009). *Case study research: Design and methods* (Vol. 5). Sage.

Yli-Renko, H., Autio, E., & Sapienza, H. J. (2001). Social capital, knowledge acquisition, and knowledge exploitation in young technology-based firms. *Strategic Management Journal*, *22*(6/7), 587–613. doi:10.1002/smj.183

Yli-Renko, H., Autio, E., & Tontti, V. (2002). Social capital, knowledge, and the international growth of technology-based new firms. *International Business Review*, *11*(3), 279–304. doi:10.1016/S0969-5931(01)00061-0

Yoo, Y., Henfridsson, O., & Lyytinen, K. (2010). The new organizing logic of digital innovation: An agenda for information systems research. *Information Systems Research*, *21*(4), 724–735. doi:10.1287/isre.1100.0322

Yousefikhah, S. (2017). Sociology of innovation: Social construction of technology perspective. *AD-Minister*, (30), 31-43.

Yukl, G., Kim, H., & Falbe, C. M. (1996). Antecedents of influence outcomes. *The Journal of Applied Psychology*, *81*(3), 309–317. doi:10.1037/0021-9010.81.3.309

Zack, M., McKeen, J., & Singh, S. (2009). Knowledge management and organizational performance: An exploratory survey. *Journal of Knowledge Management*, *13*(6), 392–409. doi:10.1108/13673270910997088

Zahra, S. A., Korri, J. S., & Yu, J. (2005). *Cognition and international entrepreneurship: Implications for research on international opportunity recognition and exploitation*. Management Department Faculty Publications. Paper 113.

Zahra, S. A., & George, G. (2002). Absorptive capacity: A review, reconceptualization, and extension. *Academy of Management Review*, *27*(2), 185–203.

Zhang, L., & Cheng, J. (2015). Effect of knowledge leadership on knowledge sharing in engineering project design teams: The role of social capital. *Project Management Journal*, *46*(5), 111–124. doi:10.1002/pmj.21525

Zhang, L., & Zhang, Z. (2014). The effects of incentive mechanism on knowledge management performance in China: The moderating role of knowledge attributes. *Project Management Journal*, *45*(2), 34–47. doi:10.1002/pmj.21403

Zhang, X., Gao, Y., Yan, X., Ordóñez de Pablos, P., Sun, Y., & Cao, X. (2015). From e-learning to social-learning: Mapping development of studies on social media-supported knowledge management. *Computers in Human Behavior*, *51*, 803–811. doi:10.1016/j.chb.2014.11.084

Zhao, H., He, P., Sheard, G., & Wan, P. (2016). Workplace ostracism and knowledge hiding in service organizations. *International Journal of Hospitality Management*, *59*, 84–94. doi:10.1016/j.ijhm.2016.09.009

Zhou, A. Z., & Fink, D. (2003). The intellectual capital web: A systematic linking of intellectual capital and knowledge management. *Journal of Intellectual Capital*, *4*(1), 34–48. doi:10.1108/14691930310455379

Zhou, K. Z. W. F. (2010). Technological capability, strategic flexibility, and product innovation. *Strategic Management Journal*, *31*(5), 547–561.

About the Contributors

Albert Gyamfi has a PhD in Knowledge Management from Aalborg University, Denmark. He is a consultant and an expert who has researched into media richness and web applications for knowledge management process and organisational learning.He is currently attached to Centre for Communication, Media and Information Technologies (CMI), Aalborg University Copenhagen.

Idongesit Williams is a Post-Doctoral researcher at Center for Communication, Media and Information Technologies (CMI) located at Aalborg University Copenhagen. He holds a Bachelor in Physics, a Master degree in Information and Communications Technologies and a Ph.D. He has since 2010 researched into Knowledge Management, Organizational Learning, socio-economic, socio-technical related to Information and Communications Technologies. He has authored more than 20 research publications, including journal papers, books, book chapters, conference papers and magazine articles. He is the co-editor of the Book, The African Mobile Story. He has organized conferences like the CMI annual conference and the CMI/GTUC conferences.

* * *

Elvis Akwa-Bonsu, MSc, CWSP, CWE, OSCP, CMFP, is a Cyber Security Expert and Researcher. Elvis is the Head of Intelligence at Detectware, a private cyber-security firm in Accra, Ghana. With 18 years of corporate experience, Elvis focuses on offensive, destructive, and defensive technology that affect and protect enterprises. He frequently speaks on the subject of security standards, penetration testing/auditing, digital investigations, attack techniques, wireless security, covert channel communications, network security monitoring, Packet Analysis, Malware Analysis, steganography, incident response, malware analysis, Honeypots, vulnerability analysis, virtualization, cloud computing security, business continuity and security awareness.

Eric Ansong is currently a PhD in Information Systems candidate in the University of Ghana Business School where he received his MPhil degree in Management Information Systems. Eric also holds a Bachelor of Arts degree in Information Studies from University of Ghana. He has played important roles in several research projects including serving as a research assistant on the DANIDA sponsored Problem-Based Learning (PBL)/E-Learning project at the University of Ghana. His research interests include ICT innovations in teaching and learning, technology-mediated teaching and learning, Social Media Marketing, Knowledge management systems and Information Systems Security.

Mehdi Bagherzadeh is an Assistant Professor of Innovation Management at NEOMA Business School, Department of Strategy & Entrepreneurship, Paris, France. He has completed his Ph.D. in Management Sciences (Innovation Management) with distinction "Cum Laude" from ESADE Business School, Barcelona, Spain from which he also obtained a master of research degree in Management Sciences. Also, he is a research fellow at the Research Center for Open Digital Innovation (RCODI), Purdue University, Indiana, United States. He was a visiting scholar at the RCODI, Purdue University and at the Marshall School of Business, the University of Southern California between December 2014 and September 2015. His specific research interests revolve around governance dynamics of open and collaborative innovation projects and its effect on innovation performance.

Richard Boateng is a technology researcher who focuses on developing, promoting and protecting ideas and concepts into sustainable projects of commercial value and development impact. Richard is an Associate Professor of Information Systems and the Head of the Department of Operations and Management Information systems at the University of Ghana Business School. He is also the Coordinator for the Building Stronger Universities Programme on E-learning and Problem-based Learning at the university. He is the associate editor of the Information Technologies & International Development Journal and also serves on the editorial board of the Information Development Journal.

Sabine Brunswicker is an Associate Professor for Innovation and the Scientific Director of the Research Center for Open Digital Innovation at Purdue University, Indiana, United States. She also serves as Visiting Professor at ESADE Business School, Barcelona, Spain, and as Strategic Advisor Open Innovation at the Fraunhofer Society, Stuttgart, Germany. She is an internationally recognized innovation researcher with a particular interest in open digital innovation and ecosystems. She is interested in emerging models of open and distributed innovation, and her current research is focused on the role of transparency and control over innovation-related knowledge and information in these emerging models.

Alexander Chekanov is a PhD Researcher in Management Sciences at ESADE Business School-URL. His research focuses on technological platform's architecture/ ecosystems, their design and evolution, with a special emphasis, among others, on the video game industry and healthcare sector.

Jan Frick is a Professor at the UIS Business School, University of Stavanger. His main interests are in Industrial Engineering /Operation Management /Entrepreneurship and the application in Industry. He has previously worked at research institutions such as SINTEF, Rogaland Research Institute and other collaborative industrial institutions. Prof. Frick has managed several Norwegian and international research projects and coordinated industrial collaboration networks. He is also manager of Beinesdalen Utvikling AS.

Kijpokin Kasemsap received his BEng degree in Mechanical Engineering from King Mongkut's University of Technology, Thonburi, his MBA degree from Ramkhamhaeng University, and his DBA degree in Human Resource Management from Suan Sunandha Rajabhat University. Dr. Kasemsap is a Special Lecturer in the Faculty of Management Sciences, Suan Sunandha Rajabhat University, based in Bangkok, Thailand. Dr. Kasemsap is a Member of the International Economics Development and Research Center (IEDRC), the International Foundation for Research and Development (IFRD), and the International Innovative Scientific and Research Organization (IISRO). Dr. Kasemsap serves on an International Advisory Board for International Journal of Productivity Management and Assessment Technologies (IJPMAT), International Journal of ICT Research in Africa and the Middle East (IJICTRAME), International Journal of Knowledge Society Research (IJKSR), International Journal of Virtual and Personal Learning Environments (IJVPLE), Journal of Cases on Information Technology (JCIT), International Journal of Virtual Communities and Social Networking (IJVCSN), International Journal of Handheld Computing Research (IJHCR), International Journal of Knowledge Management (IJKM), International Journal of Information and Communication Technology Education (IJICTE), International Journal of Interactive Communication Systems and Technologies (IJICST), International Journal of E-Health and Medical Communications (IJEHMC), International Journal of Reliable and Quality E-Healthcare (IJRQEH), International Journal of Wireless Networks and Broadband Technologies (IJWNBT), International Journal of Interdisciplinary Telecommunications and Networking (IJITN), International Journal of Technology and Human Interaction (IJTHI), International Journal of Hyperconnectivity and the Internet of Things (IJHIoT), and International Journal of Advanced Pervasive and Ubiquitous Computing (IJAPUC). Dr. Kasemsap is the sole author of over 250 peer-reviewed international publications and book chapters on business, education, and information technology. Dr. Kasemsap is included in the TOP 100 Professionals–2016 and in the 10th edition of 2000 Outstanding Intellectuals of the 21st Century by the International Biographical Centre, Cambridge, England.

Datis Khajeheian is an assistant professor of media management in the University of Tehran, Iran and a visiting lecturer in the Center for Communication, Media and Information Technologies in Aalborg University, Denmark. He has a PhD in Media Management and an M.A in Entrepreneurship with a specialty in New Venture Creation. Focused on media entrepreneurship as his main area of interest, Datis is head of the special interest group of "Emerging Media Markets" in the European Media Management Association. He has been author of numerous articles in English and Persian and has served in editorial roles in several academic journals.

Somayeh Labafi earned a Ph.D. in media management, she is a lecturer at the University of Tehran. Her research interests are media management, social media, media strategy, knowledge management and qualitative methods. She has written over 25 scientific articles in Iranian and international journals.

Philip Donald Marsh is the founder and CEO of the Knowledge Mentoring Institute (Pty) Ltd Group of Companies in South Africa (formerly the Knowledge Management Institute), collectively providing critical knowledge transfer solutions such as structured mentoring and knowledge mentoring™ programmes to major corporations and the public sector. Philip is one of the foremost experts on knowledge management, structured mentoring and knowledge mentoring in Southern Africa and has established a high public and professional profile as a respected thought leader and executive advisor to large organisations and government entities on a variety of knowledge-based "strategic sustainability / competitive knowledge advantage" solutions. Philip is the author of "Nation Building through Knowledge Mentoring™ - a framework to bridging the global scarce and critical skills and knowledge crisis" and a regular contributor to the 'Civil Engineering journal and Engineering Weekly publication in South Africa. Philip received a 2015 Global Knowledge Management Leadership award, at the Global KM Congress in Mumbai, India, in July 2015, for his paper and presentation entitled "Knowledge Swarms and Experiential Hives – the critical and emergent role of the ageing knowledge experts in the engineering and construction sectors of developing countries" and is a sought after conference and key note speaker, both locally and internationally Philip designed and conceptualized the development of the innovative new mobile knowledge mentoring Apps which he has trademarked as myKnowledgeMentor™ and myMentorAccelerator™, a game changer to empower and enable the "Modern Learner" to communicate, cooperate and collaborate better with peers and experts. Philip also sits on the Education and

Training Panel of the South African Institution of Civil Engineers (SAICE) and has collaborated on several working committees with key academic, business and government stakeholders to address the potential Structured Workplace Learning (SWL) and Work Integrated earning (WIL) challenges posed by the South African National Development Plan (NDP). Philip holds the following qualifications and professional designations - B.Sc(Eng); Pr.Eng; Dipl.Bus.Man; G.D.E; M.S.A.I.C.E; M.I.C.E; M.I.Struct.E; C. Eng; A.I.P.M; CKM.

Edna Owusu-Bempah is an MPhil in Management Information Systems graduate from the University of Ghana Business School. She also holds a Bachelor of Arts degree in Information Studies from University of Ghana. Her research interests include Social Media marketing, fashion marketing and Knowledge Management.

Jens Myrup Pedersen is Associate Professor at Aalborg University, Department of Electronic Systems. His research interests include network planning, traffic monitoring, and network security. He is author/co-author of more than 70 publications in international conferences and journals, and has participated in Danish, Nordic and European funded research projects. In addition to technical research he is involved in testing and developing new teaching methods in both national and international context. He is currently project coordinator of the Erasmus+ Strategic Partnership Colibri. He is also board member of a number of companies within technology and innovation.

Mirjana Radović-Marković, PhD, was born in Belgrade. She gained complete expert education from the Faculty of Economics in Belgrade, where she got her PhD in 1987. After her dissertation completing, she continued her advanced studies in the Netherlands, USA and Russia, where she specialized in 1988 at Lomonosow on the multidisciplinary studies department. Since she was twenty-five she is a scientist. Her scientific career started at the Economics Institute in Belgrade and continued later at the Institute of Economic Sciences, also in Belgrade. Meanwhile, she was fulltime and part-time engaged as a lecturer and professor for entrepreneurship and management at the Faculty for Management BK in Belgrade, at the Faculty Farleigh Dickinson University in the USA, Akamai University US, Lacrosse University USA, Pebble Hills University International, EU, CalCampus, US .She is an author of programs as follow: "Women's Entrepreneurship", "Human Resource Management", "Small Business Management", "Entrepreneurship for Genealogists", "Organizational Behaviour", "E-Business" and, "Principles of Management". Since 2004, prof. Dr. Mirjana Radovic-Markovic has employed full time at the Institute of Economic Sciences. She is Chairman of Scientific Board, Head of Center for Economic Researches and member of the Managing Board of the Institute of Economic Sciences. Also, she is Editor-in-Chief of peer Journals: Economic Analysis and Women's Entrepreneurship and Education and the editor of five international peer journals, of which one is on the Thomson Reuters list. She was elected to the position of full professor in a number of universities- She teaches "Entrepreneurship" at the University of Kragujevac, as well as the " Applied Business Economics and Entrepreneurship "at the Irish University Business School, London, "Management and Entrepreneurship "at the Pebble Hills University International, EU," Female entrepreneurship "at Akamai University and" Entrepreneurship and female entrepreneurship" at the International College of Management and Technology (ICMT) - Center for Women and Gender Studies. In addition, she has taught worldwide classes as "Women as Entrepreneurs", "Global Challenge" (GVF) at the Faculty Farleigh Dickinson University, New Jersey, US. By invitation, she has given a number of lectures abroad. Recently, she had presentation during the meeting of OECD experts (March, 2010) and gave a lecture at Said Business School (June, 2010), Oxford University, UK. Professor Radović-Marković has written twenty books and over one hundred peer articles. Professor `s new book is WOMEN IN BUSINESS: Theory, Practice and Flexible Approaches, published by Adonis & Abbey Publishers Ltd, June 2010. London, UK.

Aidin Salamzadeh, PhD Researcher at the Faculty of Entrepreneurship, University of Tehran. He has several publications in international journals and participated in several conferences in some countries. His main areas of interest are: startups, social entrepreneurship, entrepreneurial universities, and entrepreneurship policy making. He serves as the Editor-in-Chief of the Journal of Entrepreneurship, Business and Economics (Canada), and as a member of the editorial board in some journals such as JWE, and IE (Serbia), JEIM (Turkey), IJMP (Brazil), etc. He is also a member of the European SPES Forum, and the Asian Academy of Management.

Julia E. von Schuckmann is a PhD Researcher in Management Sciences at Esade Business School-URL. Her research is focused on cultural marketing, price communications techniques, in-group/out-group behaviors and ethics.

Ezer Yeboah-Boateng is a professional ICT Specialist and Telecoms Engineer with a strong background in cyber-security, digital forensics, business development, change management, knowledge management, strategic IT-enabled business value creation and capabilities to develop market-oriented strategies aimed at promoting growth and market share. An Executive with 25 years of domestic and global experience conceptualizing ideas, seizing opportunities, building operations, leading highly successful new business development initiatives and ventures. A Consultant with emphasis on Cyber-security, digital forensics, telecommunications, Internet, and network integration technologies, with additional experience related to dealing with refurbished and overstock equipment, and manufacturing. Strong presentation, negotiation, and team building skills.

Index

K

L

M

N

O

P

S

T

V

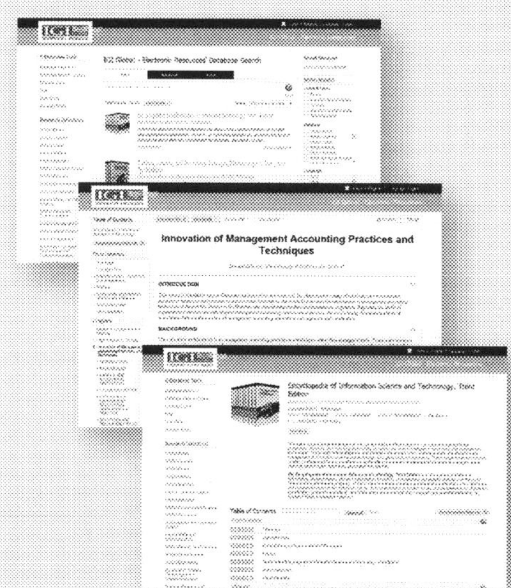

Printed in the United States
By Bookmasters